CAMBRIDGE GREEK AND LATIN CLASSICS

GENERAL EDITORS

E. J. KENNEY
Emeritus Kennedy Professor of Latin, University of Cambridge

AND

P. E. EASTERLING
Regius Professor of Greek, University of Cambridge

VIRGIL

GEORGICS

VOLUME 1: BOOKS I–II

EDITED BY

RICHARD F. THOMAS

Professor of Greek and Latin,
Harvard University

CAMBRIDGE
UNIVERSITY PRESS

Published by the Press Syndicate of the University of Cambridge
The Pitt Building, Trumpington Street, Cambridge CB2 1RP
40 West 20th Street, New York, NY 10011-4211, USA
10 Stamford Road, Oakleigh, Melbourne 3166, Australia

First published 1998
Reprinted 1990, 1994, 1998

British Library cataloguing in publication data

Virgil
Georgics. –
(Cambridge Greek and Latin classics).
Vol. 1: Books 1–2
I. Title II. Thomas, Richard F. III. Series
871'.01   PA6804

Library of Congress cataloguing in publication data

Virgil.
Georgics. Vol. 1: Books 1–2
(Cambridge Greek and Latin classics)
Text in Latin; commentary in English.
I. Thomas, Richard F. II. Title. III. Series.
PA6804.A6 1988 873'.01   87-23834

ISBN 0 521 27850 3 paperback

Transferred to digital printing 2002

For Joan

CONTENTS

Fled are those times when in harmonious strains
The rustic poet praised his native plains.
No shepherds now in smooth alternate verse
Their country's beauty or their nymphs' rehearse.

Ye gentle souls, who dream of rural ease,
Whom the smooth stream and smoother sonnet please;
Go! if the peaceful cot your praises share,
Go, look within, and ask if peace be there.

George Crabbe, *The Village*

PREFACE

In keeping with the aim of the series, I have tried to 'provide the student with the guidance that he needs for the interpretation and understanding of the [poem] as a work of literature'. In the case of this poem, and this poet, that is not an easy task. The *Georgics* has been read, and still is read, in diverse ways, and though my understanding of it may not please all, it does, I think, reflect the relatively recently acknowledged view that this poem is infinitely more complex and subtle than it was once thought to be.

Much of the commentary, particularly those parts dealing with Virgil's use of his inherited tradition, is intended as much for scholars as for students, but the latter will not be baffled. There was a time when Hellenistic poetry was regarded in the classroom as something of a closed book, too difficult even to approach and hardly worth the effort. In my experience neither of these judgements is legitimate, and I have assumed throughout that such literature is accessible to most students; the assumption has been a necessary one, since the *Georgics* is a poem which cannot be fully appreciated without an appreciation of the literature to which it constantly refers.

Space has been at a premium, and much has been compressed in order to make production possible. One vital *caveat*: where I have referred the reader to a passage within or outside the poem, I assume, even where a full citation has not been given, that the thorough reader will consult the reference. Virgil is the most referential and self-referential Latin poet, and he expects much of his reader. Longer Greek citations have been given only in English, and longer lemmata have often been compressed. References without book notation (e.g. 'cf. 468n.') are to lines within the same book; if otherwise, the book number is given (e.g. 'cf. 2.468n.').

The introduction is found only in the first volume. It could have been printed in each, after the manner of T. E. Page's and R. D. Williams's commentaries on the *Aeneid*, but such a procedure seemed inelegant. And, more importantly, I have not wished to encourage the teaching of only one half of the poem, since the *Georgics* has suffered greatly from being excerpted.

To the Department of Classics at the University of Cincinnati I am

grateful for the *otium* provided by two generous summer grants, as I am
to Mrs Linda Noe Laine for a grant which permitted the purchase of a
machine which greatly expedited the completion of this work. Susan P.
Moore was most helpful in subediting the work for the Press. I wish to
thank those graduate students and colleagues from Harvard University
and the University of Cincinnati who participated in seminars on the
Georgics in 1983 and 1984 respectively. Mr David Ball has my thanks
for performing the tedious chore of checking references. It is a plea-
sure to record my gratitude for the suggestions and advice generously
given by several friends and colleagues, in particular Professors A. J.
Christopherson, W. V. Clausen, P. E. Knox, J. S. Rusten, R. S. Scodel,
D. R. Shackleton Bailey, R. J. Tarrant and D. Wiebe. To the General
Editors, Professor E. J. Kenney and Professor P. E. Easterling, I am
indebted for the opportunity to undertake this work, for the criticisms,
suggestions and encouragement without which the commentary would
have been infinitely the poorer, and for the decision to allow more space
than is usually permitted in the series. Professor Kenney's characteristi-
cally keen eye and perceptive judgement have been invaluable, and the
commentary has been greatly improved by his generous and substantial
contributions. Finally, to Professor D. O. Ross, with whom I first began
to work on the *Georgics*, and who read and commented on the entire
typescript with his usual acumen and vigilance, I am deeply grateful.

Cincinnati, Ohio   R.F.T.
July 1986

INTRODUCTION

1. THE HISTORICAL BACKGROUND

Though the date of composition is still somewhat in dispute, from external and internal evidence it is likely that the *Georgics* occupied Virgil for seven years and was completed in 29 B.C., in August of which year it was read to Octavian by Virgil and Maecenas.[1] In other words the poem was begun, and much of it was written, in a time of the utmost political uncertainty, when 'it was more easy to witness and affirm the passing of the old order than to discern the manner and fashion of the new'.[2] This uncertainty, a fact of life for Virgil since childhood, pervades the poem. Even with the support and patronage of Maecenas,[3] and therefore ultimately of Octavian, his hopes for the relative security which the next decade was to provide can have been no more than that; the prayer towards the end of Book 1 (500–1 *hunc saltem euerso iuuenem succurrere saeclo | ne prohibete*) is soon succeeded by a simile revealing the realities of national existence (513–14 *frustra retinacula tendens | fertur equis auriga neque audit currus habenas*). Times changed after Actium, and the closing lines of the poem (4.559–62) reflect that fact (though see 4.560–1n.), but those lines have little to do with the central themes and concerns of the *Georgics* or with the dark visions of Virgil, which were not dispersed by political settlements, and which continued to find expression throughout his poetry (see below sect. 7).

2. THE *GEORGICS* AND VIRGIL'S POETIC CAREER

The *Georgics* is a middle poem in spirit as well as in time. As Virgil's poetic career developed, at least by the time the *Georgics* was nearing completion, and as the *Aeneid* began to take shape in his mind, the poet came to see and to present this poem as one of transition. At the beginning of the second half of the *Eclogues* his adherence to the poetics of Callimachus had been stated without qualification, as is clear from

---

[1] So *Vita Donati* 25, 27; *Vita Servii* 25; and there is no good reason to suspect the details.

[2] Syme (1939) 255.

[3] Cf. 3.41n. on the question of Maecenas' involvement in the poem.

1

the virtual translation of *Aet.* 1, fr. 1.21–4:[4]

> cum canerem reges et proelia, Cynthius aurem
> uellit et admonuit: 'pastorem, Tityre, pinguis
> pascere oportet ouis, deductum dicere carmen.'
> nunc ego (namque super tibi erunt qui dicere laudes,
> Vare, tuas cupiant et tristia condere bella)
> agrestem tenui meditabor harundine Musam:
> non iniussa cano. (*E.* 6.3–9)

And in the same relative position of the *Aeneid*, in the delayed proem of Book 7, with what looks like a recantation, Virgil refers to his earlier stance:

> dicam horrida bella,
> dicam acies actosque animis in funera reges,
> Tyrrhenamque manum totamque sub arma coactam
> Hesperiam. maior rerum mihi nascitur ordo,
> maius opus moueo. (*A.* 7.41–5)

Between the refusal and the commitment, at the beginning of the second half of the *Georgics*,[5] Virgil occupies middle ground:

> interea Dryadum siluas saltusque sequamur
> intactos, tua, Maecenas, haud mollia iussa.
>
> mox tamen ardentis accingar dicere pugnas
> Caesaris ... (3.40–1, 46–7)

Were it not for the existence of the *Aeneid* this last statement might be seen merely as a variation on the *recusatio*, carrying no implication of a commitment to a future large-scale poetic enterprise.[6] But the fact is that in every programmatic utterance of the poem Virgil characterizes his position as transitional: at 2.39–46 he invokes the support of Maecenas in such a way as to suggest a poem of epic proportions (41 *pelagoque uolans da uela patenti*), only to recover his Callimachean position (44 *ades*

---

[4] On this see Clausen (1982) 21–3.

[5] In a passage which was clearly composed not long before the completion of the poem; cf. 3.1–48n.

[6] *mox*, which can mean 'in due course', 'when the time comes', contributes to the ambiguity.

et primi lege litoris oram; see 41−5n.); at 3.290−4 he speaks of the need to treat in high style (*magno nunc ore sonandum*) themes of a lowly nature (*angustis . . . rebus*), an antithesis which will be varied at the beginning of the fourth book (4−6 *duces . . . et proelia dicam. | in tenui labor*; see 4.6n.); and throughout the proem of the third book, the most extensive poetic manifesto in the corpus, he justifies the departure from his earlier attenuated mode (3.1−48n.).[7]

In manner and composition the *Georgics* is deeply indebted to Callimachus. The four books find their closest analogy in the four books of the *Aetia*, and Virgil indicates the structural dependence at various points (e.g. 1.32; 3.19−20; 4.559−66 and nn.); and if one word best describes Virgil's manner of reference to his literary tradition that word is 'Callimachean' (see below sect. 4). But as the preceding passages show, this affiliation was tempered by a sense that the literary climate, and Virgil's own genius, had developed to a point where such poetics were no longer the main issue: 3.3−9 *cetera, quae uacuas tenuissent carmine mentes, | omnia iam uulgata . . . temptanda uia est, qua me quoque possim | tollere humo uictorque uirum uolitare per ora.*

3. GENERIC AFFILIATIONS

Vergilius in operibus suis diuersos secutus est poetas: . . . Hesiodum in his libris, quem penitus reliquit (Serv. *ad G.* 1 *prooem.*). The mind of the critic, ancient or modern, tends to strive for neatness, encouraged by the need to systematize. Servius is not alone in regarding the *Georgics* as a didactic poem, in the mould of Hesiod's *Works and Days* or Lucretius' *De Rerum Natura*;[8] and Virgil himself invites the characterization (2.176 *Ascraeumque cano Romana per oppida carmen*), just as Horace seemed to restrict his claims for the *Odes* to his formal achievement: 3.30.10−14 *dicar . . . | princeps Aeolium carmen ad Italos | deduxisse modos*. But it is one of the marks of Roman poetry that generic appearance need not imply the same generic intent. The real concerns of Horace in the *Odes* are directed more

---

[7] For a more detailed study of this subject cf. Thomas (1985).

[8] In the most recent general study of Roman literature, Wilkinson (1982) 25, who is by no means unrepresentative, says of Virgil and the poem 'He next aspired to be the Roman Hesiod [having established himself as the Roman Theocritus] . . . Lucretius would show him how a didactic poem could be moving by its descriptive power and its moral-philosophic fervour.'

towards Hellenistic poetry than archaic lyric,[9] and Hesiod is far from being the most important influence on Virgil in the *Georgics* – certainly outside the first book (see sect. 4).

As for Lucretius, his linguistic influence upon the *Georgics* is pervasive, but it is chiefly so in a particular way: Virgil draws from him to create a didactic appearance for his poem. So he is at his most Lucretian on a very small scale, for instance with transitional or other phrases whose function is to provide a flavour (e.g. 1.56 *nonne uides*; 1.187 *contemplator item, cum*; 2.177 *nunc locus*; 2.346; 4.51 *quod superest*; 4.149–50 *nunc age ... expediam*; see nn.). With one notable exception,[10] the debt of Virgil to Lucretius in the *Georgics* is predominantly formal, consisting of the borrowing of phrases, or occasionally the rearranging of an appealing image (cf. 2.279–83n.);[11] see also 2.475–94n.

Furthermore, a poem which is to be truly didactic in content as well as form (such as the *De Rerum Natura*) implies the existence of an audience which is to be instructed, and in spite of the long-held view that the function of the *Georgics* was to restore an interest in Italian agriculture, the fact is that no Roman farmer would have read the poem for practical instruction when Varro's *Res Rusticae* was available; had he done so, moreover, his success would have been limited, for Virgil is extremely selective with his precepts.[12]

4. THE MODELS FOR THE *GEORGICS*

There is no single model, surviving or lost, for the *Georgics*. The title, but little else, was taken from a work of Nicander (probably second century B.C.), now largely lost, the technical details are taken predominantly from Theophrastus (*c.* 370–288/5 B.C.) and Varro (116–27 B.C.), but they are transformed to suit their new setting, and for the rest Virgil

---

[9] Cf. the observation of L. P. Wilkinson (1946) 118, n. 2: 'it is noteworthy that 140 pages of Pasquali [*Orazio Lirico* (Florence 1920)] suffice for Aeolic influence and 68 for Roman, while no fewer than 500 are required for Hellenistic'.

[10] The description of the plague – which is without any didactic rationale (3.478–566n.).

[11] This fact emerges clearly from the compendium of parallels gathered by Merrill (1916).

[12] Ovid, as elsewhere, was to expose the generic fiction with the *Ars Amatoria*, which had little intention, but all the formal appearances, of teaching its audience.

drew from the whole range of Greek and Roman literature. Few Latin poems draw so extensively, or so creatively, from their inherited tradition. Virgil's models in the *Georgics* extend in time from Homer to the *Eclogues*, in their disparate nature from Aristotle to Catullus. His manner of reference to the tradition is also extremely complex, ranging from casual reminiscence, to correction, apparent reference, self-reference and, the most complex and typically Virgilian type, conflation or multiple reference.[13] Some distinction may be made between the more literary and the technical models, though it needs to be said that Virgil is often equally allusive and constructive with both; and it is often neither easy nor desirable completely to separate the two.[14]

a. Poetic models

In genre the *Georgics* may look chiefly to Hesiod, but *Homer* was the poet with whom Virgil was most familiar, in this poem as in the *Aeneid*. His method of reference to Homer, as to other predecessors, varies. The manner may be intended simply to give a flash of Homeric colour, as at 1.383, where overall adaptation of Aratus is interrupted by reference to a Homeric context (see n.). Homeric reference may be combined with reference to another author, for instance Callimachus, as at 1.138 (see n.). Virgil corrects Homeric detail, as when he reverses the order in which the Giants piled up Olympus, Pelion and Ossa in their attack on Jupiter (cf. 1.281–2n.). In one instance a Homeric simile is converted into Virgilian reality (in the description of the irrigator at 1.104–10); in this case Virgil expects the reader to recall both the original simile and its outer context which silently informs the adaptation (see n.).[15] At

---

[13] For a typology of reference in the poem, see Thomas (1986b). By 'model' is meant the demonstrable use of a predecessor, seldom casual, generally employed with the intention that the reader bring the context of the model to the new setting.

[14] Wilkinson (1969) 56–68 offers a useful study of some of Virgil's literary predecessors.

[15] Virgil treats his own earlier poetry in a similar way in the *Aeneid*, when for instance, at *A*. 8.449–53, in describing the work of the Cyclopes, he repeats with minimal changes the simile of *G*. 4.170–5 (where the Cyclopes represent the toil of the bees). He also reverses the process when, for instance, the snake to which Neoptolemus is compared at *A*. 2.471–5 is described in terms almost identical to those used of the real snake at *G*. 3.437–9.

4.334–48, in the middle of an intensely Homeric context, Virgil pro-
duces a catalogue of nymphs apparently reminiscent of the catalogue at
Il. 18.39–49, which on closer examination is thoroughly non-Homeric
(see n.). And finally Homer provides an extensive continuous model for
the poem: *Od.* 4.351–570 is closely adapted, with the characters and
details altered but clearly recognizable, at 4.387–452 (387–414n.).

In spite of Virgil's designation of the poem as an *Ascraeum carmen* (cf.
2.176 and n.), explicit reference to *Hesiod* is limited, much more so than
reference to Theocritus in the *Eclogues*, or to Homer in the *Aeneid*. For
Virgil as for Callimachus (who also knew Homer better than he knew
Hesiod) Hesiod is more of a notional model, important for Virgil
because of his importance to the Alexandrians.[16] Hesiodic reference is to
be found in the poem, for instance in the notorious prescription at 1.299
nudus ara, sere nudus, or in the description of the drones at 4.244 (see nn.),
but it is in general limited to such minor reminiscence, to the structural
appearance of the first book (which treats first 'works' then 'days'),[17] to
the lines on the plough (1.160–75; but see n.) and to a single extended
reference (1.276–86) which, though Hesiodic in appearance, is non-
Hesiodic in content and contains a central panel which is a close
imitation and correction of Homer, rather than of Hesiod (see n.); to this
extent the lines are another instance of apparent, rather than real,
reference. On the view of the *Georgics* as a poem celebrating the Hesiodic
notion of the moral value of toil, see sect. 7.

The chief areas of Greek influence on Virgil, and not just in the
Georgics, are either archaic or Hellenistic;[18] he seems to have found
little active use for the literature of the classical period. [19] In this poem,
at least in thematic terms, he is particularly indebted to *Aratus*
(*c.* 315–240/39 B.C.). Indeed most of the second half of the first book
(351–463), at times with great exactitude, looks to that poet's treatment

---

[16] Cf. Hardie (1971) 8 'Hesiod is seen through the eyes of Callimachus.'

[17] There are indications that Virgil at the outset of the poem viewed Hesiod as
the primary model, but came to see the poem as having other concerns as it
progressed.

[18] There are references in the *Georgics* to Apollonius of Rhodes and Theocritus,
but they are not extensive; the latter had already dominated the *Eclogues*, as the
former was to serve as one of the prime models for the *Aeneid*.

[19] Though the situation changes somewhat in the *Aeneid*, where the speeches
have a natural affinity with those of tragedy. And in *A.* 4 there is a more profound
debt to tragedy.

of weather-signs (*Phaen.* 733–1154). The highly technical nature of Aratus' poem often seems unpalatable to the modern reader, but it is in many ways the quintessentially Alexandrian production, and holds obvious appeal to the scholar-poet; Callimachus admired it (*Epigr.* 27 Pf.), it was translated by Cicero and Varro of Atax before Virgil, by Germanicus and Avienus after him, and 27 commentaries are known. Virgil the poet, however, was careful in his use of the work; he compresses, conflates references to it with those to Homer, Varro of Atax and others, and varies the technical material with poetic colour (e.g. 1.404–9 and n.). His use of Aratus is also in part structural: the first book shows the influence of archaic Greek (Hesiod) in the first part, Hellenistic (Aratus) in the later portions. Though the influence of Aratus' poem is elsewhere visible in the *Georgics* (e.g. 2.473–4, 537), it is chiefly influential only in the first book.

The influence of *Callimachus* (*c.* 300–240 B.C.) is of a special type. Virgil refers to him directly at certain points in the poem (e.g. 1.138, 509; 3.1–2, 19–20, 36; 4.341–2; see nn.), and there is little doubt that such references would be seen to be more numerous if more of Callimachus had survived (cf. 4.333–86n.). But the importance of Callimachus lies in two less obvious features of the *Georgics*. Virgil's decision to structure his poem in four books (for which there is no known agronomical model) is in part an acknowledgement of the appearance of Callimachus' best-known work, the four books of the *Aetia*. It is now clear that Virgilian references to the *Victoria Berenices* (Callim. *Aet.* 3, *SH* frr. 254–68) are precisely where they belong, in the same relative position in the *Georgics* (3.1–48n.); and the excesses of the prayer to Octavian at 1.24–42 may owe something to the attitude of Callimachus to Berenice (see n.). The second mark of Callimachus' influence, though more nebulous, is at the very basis of the poem; the fact that it is an agricultural poem, didactic in appearance but without the intention of teaching its apparent subject, the learning and interest in recondite matters of scholarly concern which it shows throughout, and the polemical attitudes which it demonstrates towards the entire tradition which informs it – these are the hallmarks of Callimacheanism.

At 1.231–58 Virgil's discussion of the terrestrial and celestial zones is based fairly exactly on some lines from the *Hermes* of Eratosthenes (*c.* 275–194 B.C.), but this poet does not otherwise seem to have served as a model for the *Georgics* – though Virgil may well have been familiar with his geographical and ethnographical works. And finally, from *Nicander* Virgil took first his title and secondly the Alexandrian notion that the traditional or classical restrictions on what is or is not 'poetical' are not necessarily valid. Otherwise the influence of this poet is chiefly limited to an – admittedly careful and close – adaptation from the *Theriaca* (3.414–39n.).[20]

It is difficult fully to appreciate the degree to which Virgil drew from the Latin tradition. The influence of *Lucretius* (?94–51 B.C.), both in details and as a generic model, has already been noted.[21] But there is perhaps an equal debt to neoteric poetry, and to the poetry, almost completely lost, of the two decades between the death of Catullus and the mid-thirties. Virgil drew from *Catullus* himself (?84–54 B.C.) in a fairly restricted manner, for the most part adapting phrasing and stylistic features (e.g. 1.206; 2.352–3 and nn.); and sometimes the context of Catullus informs the Virgilian setting (e.g. 1.50 and n.). It is, however, when he is at his most elevated that he is most affected by his neoteric predecessor; as has been demonstrated,[22] the song of Proteus (4.453–527), which tells the story of Orpheus and Eurydice, and which may justly be seen as an attempt to incorporate the epyllion into a larger context, is indebted in style and diction to Cat. 64 (4.466, 490–1, 504–5, 507, 515nn.). The theme, that of an ill-starred or unrequited love, is common to both poets and is a hallmark of the genre. It is also common to the epyllia of Catullus' friends and fellow neoterics, *Cinna* (the *Zmyrna*) and *Calvus* (the *Io*), and the influence of these two is doubtless greater than can now be ascertained. A fragment of the former may be visible at 4.465–6 (see n.), and it is almost certain that Virgil elsewhere drew from Calvus, in his treatment of the gadfly (3.152–3n.).

Varro of Atax (82 B.C.–?) exerted a special influence on the poem. Servius preserves seven lines of his (?) *Epimenis*, a work which draws from Aratus' *Phaenomena*, and to which Virgil referred more explicitly (while generally adapting Aratus himself) than he did to any other extant Latin poetry, anywhere in his corpus (1.374–87n.); there is a briefer

---

[20] Little of Nicander's *Georgica* survives, so that it is impossible to be sure; however, it was in two books (Athen. 3.126b5–7), none of the surviving fragments has any sure connection with Virgil's poem, and a sentence in Quintilian (10.1.56 *Nicandrum frustra secuti Macer atque Vergilius?*) proves nothing specific.

[21] See above, pp. 3–4.

[22] Cf. Crabbe (1977).

reference to the work at 1.397 (see n.). In light of the precision with which Virgil adapted Varro, and given that Servius' preservation of the lines is doubtless for the most part a fortunate accident, it is safe to assume that the influence of the *Epimenis*, at least on the first book of the *Georgics*, was reasonably extensive. Virgil treated Varro's *Chorographia* in the same fashion, conflating references to it with his overall adaptation of his, and Varro's, ultimate source, the *Hermes* of Eratosthenes (1.237–8n.). Virgil was also acquainted with Varro's *Argonautica*, a Latin version of Apollonius' poem (1.14–15; 2.404nn.).[23]

The works of three friends, *Cornelius Gallus*, *Varius Rufus* and *Horace*, are referred to in brief but significant ways. Gallus poses a special problem, and will be treated below (sect. 6). The influence of the *De Morte* of Varius is apparent at 2.506–7, 3.116–17 and 253–4 (see nn.) – these have ensured the survival of three of the five extant fragments of this poet.[24] The question of the direction of influence between Virgil and Horace is in general not an easy one, but there is no doubt that at 3.537–8 Virgil, while suggesting that the effects of the plague constitute a grim return to the golden age, refers to Horace's golden-age setting in the Sixteenth Epode, a poem which Virgil must have read well before the publication of the book of *Epodes*. Other possible references (e.g. 4.289n.) are of a more casual nature.

Finally there are the *Eclogues*, to which Virgil refers precisely as he does to other works in his tradition. The theme of *amor*, prominent in the pastoral collection, continues into the *Georgics*, its destructive powers no longer merely private and personal (as in *E.* 2 and 10 – though the figure of Orpheus owes much to that of Gallus), but now developed on a larger scale in the first half of *Georgics* 3. And the dictum *omnia uincit Amor* (*E.* 10.69) is replaced by the overriding theme of the new poem – *labor omnia uicit* (1.145). In more detailed ways Virgil also uses the *Eclogues* to inform and impart meaning to the *Georgics* (e.g. 2.32–4, 155–7nn.; above, sect. 2).

---

[23] Only three fragments (two of them preserved for purely grammatical reasons) survive from the third book, and given Varro's status as an amatory poet (Prop. 2.34.85–6) the loss is considerable. It is difficult to imagine that Virgil's extensive references to Ap. Rhod. *Arg.* 3 in *Aeneid* 1 and 4 were not tempered by reference to the intervening Roman version.

[24] See 3.253–4n. for the view of Richter that Varius is in fact referring to the *Georgics*, a view which is difficult to support.

b. Prose models

There is a qualitative distinction between Virgil's use of poetic and of prose models. While his use of the poetic tradition has various functions ranging from poetic embellishment to correction to conflation, his primary interest in prose authors is in the technical material they provide. While it is doubtless true that Virgil had a familiarity with, and a deep attachment to, the Italian countryside, he was no agronomist, and he depended throughout on the works of the agricultural writers, Greek and Roman. This dependence created, moreover, a special problem for the poet; he had to compress and enliven a body of literature which in his own day as now can (with some exceptions) scarcely have been regarded as having any great literary merit. The success with which he responded to this challenge is testimony to his genius. In the process of compressing and transforming this material, he often produces a version which is of little practical use to the farmer (particularly when compared with the thoroughness of the model) – further evidence that instructional motives did not greatly concern him (see above, sect. 3).

At *R.R.* 1.1.1–11 Varro refers to the more than 50 agricultural prose treatises in Greek, and he names 47 of the authors. He names no Latin authors, but we have fragments of more than a dozen who wrote before his own time.[25] Virgil was highly selective, drawing for the most part from Theophrastus among the Greeks, and from Varro himself in the Roman tradition.[26]

The details of Virgil's debt to *Theophrastus* have long been recognized.[27] The second book of the poem is replete with references chiefly to the *Historia Plantarum*, and to a lesser extent to the *De Causis Plantarum*. Virgil's division of trees according to the manner of their propagation (natural vs. cultivated), together with his subdivisions within these

---

[25] Most conveniently collected in the edition of Speranza (1974). Figures like Licinius Stolo and Tremelius Scrofa, interlocutors in Varro's treatise, may well have had some influence.

[26] Aristotle exerted some influence, but with one exception (cf. 3.280–3 and n.) was of rather superficial interest to Virgil. Much, however, of the information on bees in the fourth book is Aristotelian.

[27] Cf. Jahn (1903); Mitsdörffer (1938).

areas (from seed, from the root, etc.) is taken directly from Theophrastus (cf. 2.9–34n.); his treatment of the variety of the earth's trees (2.109–35), together with the ethnographical colour which enlivens those lines, is an adaptation of a much fuller account by Theophrastus,[28] and his instructions on manuring and protection of young trees (2.346–53) show a debt to *C.P.* 3.4.3 and 3.6.1–2. Virgil, then, used Theophrastus' works ostensibly as a technical model, drawing from them as convenient sources of information, compressing and varying, developing colourful digressions, and occasionally misunderstanding (2.350–2n.); this information he then diverted to accommodate his own poetic purposes.

The attitude towards *Varro* is comparable, though here Virgil's debt is greater; indeed, it is fair to say that the *Georgics* would have looked very different had Varro not published his treatise shortly before Virgil began work on his poem.[29] Virgil used it as a source of information on a number of subjects: in the treatment of soil types, on livestock, and particularly on the bees. And the prayer which opens the poem, parallel to, although very different from, Varro's own opening prayer, partly functions as an acknowledgement of Virgil's debt (1.1–42n.). None of this is to suggest that the *Georgics* is in any way an imitation of Varro's work. When Varro referred to the bees' society *haec ut hominum civitates* (*R.R.* 3.16.6; the observation is not original with him), Virgil doubtless noticed, but the vision of the bees' world that he presents in the fourth book is his own. Nor was Virgil a slavish imitator, even on technical details; he pointedly disagrees with Varro not only on matters of vital importance to the poem (4.92n.), but even on such apparently tangential details as the size of the ideal cow's hoof – in doing so he has good agrarian authority outside Varro (cf. 3.54–5). Such polemic is the mark of the scholar-poet intellectually rooted in Alexandria.

[28] Virgil even preserves, in translation, a false MS variant from the *H.P.*, otherwise found only in Athenaeus (2.131n.).

[29] The date of publication is not absolutely fixed, but it seems that Varro's work was available to Virgil while he was still writing the *Eclogues*; see Ross (1980). It should be noted, however, that the influence of the *Res Rusticae* is not much in evidence in *Georgics* 1 (the opening prayer is a major exception, but that was probably not composed early), which may suggest that the poem was actually under way before Virgil began to make use of it.

5. STRUCTURE

The structural complexities of the *Georgics* are great, and the student of the poem has a daunting array of schemes from which to choose. Following the sense and restraint of Wilkinson[30] ('tabular schemes are useful but unreadable'), and with a further, more practical, motive (*spatiis exclusus iniquis*), this writer has avoided postulating a section-by-section diagram of the poem's structure, preferring to note correspondences in the body of the commentary, and briefly to treat such details in discussing the poem in general (see below, sect. 7).[31]

Some general observations will suffice here: Virgil is attuned, on every level, to the potential of structural arrangement for the imparting of meaning.[32] So the recurrence of the same word in a parallel line of a different book may be intentional and meaningful (1.509n.), or the parallel placement of entire sections may be similarly intended (as occurs, for instance, in the placement of 1.125–49 and 4.125–48; see nn.). Often structural relationships are merely a mark of artistic virtuosity. The pattern of the four appearances of Maecenas' name (1.2; 2.41; 3.41; 4.2), while structurally appealing, has little to do with meaning. Or, on a larger level, the opening pattern of *Georgics* 2 (8 + 26 + 12 + 26 + 10 + 26 + 26) seems to show a pattern beyond the bounds of coincidence, but perhaps does little more than suggest Virgil's concern for structural symmetry.[33]

As between individual sections so among the four books various connections have been suggested. The result is often confusing and of limited help: 'Books III and IV agree in their essential plan of arrangement (*vis-à-vis* I and II) ... There is also a designed correspondence

---

[30] Wilkinson (1969) 75.

[31] The issue is in any case a subjective one, which necessarily involves the forcing of details to fit the desired scheme; for instance, although the schemes of Richter – which occupies 36 pages – and Otis (1963) are in many respects similar, and are both in essence acceptable, there are sufficient divergences (for instance one sees the second book as falling into three sections, the other, four) to create the impression that there is indeed no single, necessary structure to the poem.

[32] Recent work on numerical patterns in Augustan poetry, particularly that of O. Skutsch, has created a climate of acceptance for such ordering, so alien to the romanticist view of poetry. Critical subjectivity, however, is always a danger, as is clear from the several numerological schemes proposed for the *Eclogues*, for instance; where the will exists, numbers can be made to work out.

[33] Though cf. 2.9–34n.

between I and III and II and IV ... there are four main *contrasts* in the poem: that between I and II; that between III and IV; that between I–III and II–IV; and that between I–II and III–IV.'[34] It will be useful to state a general correspondence, on which all critics are agreed: the strongest links, in tone as in structure, appear between *Georgics* 1 and 3 on the one hand, and 2 and 4 on the other. The first book is marked by two failures, the storm which destroys the crops (1.311–34) and the civil war which comes in spite of the *signa* which precede it (1.464–514); in the third book there is a parallel movement between the account of the disastrous effects of uncontrollable *amor* on livestock (3.242–83) and that of the catastrophe of plague (3.440–566). Books 2 and 4, on the other hand, treat the relationship between man and nature in different ways; they are distinct from 1 and 3 in structure and tone, and are tied to each other in the greater complexity with which they present man and his works (see sect. 7).

6. THE *LAVDES GALLI*

hic [Gallus] primo in amicitiis Augusti Caesaris fuit: postea cum uenisset in suspicionem, quod contra eum coniuraret, occisus est. fuit autem amicus Vergilii adeo, ut quartus georgicorum a medio usque ad finem eius laudes teneret: quas postea iubente Augusto in Aristaei fabulam commutauit. (Servius *ad E.* 10.1)

sane sciendum, ut supra diximus, ultimam partem huius libri esse mutatam: nam laudes Galli habuit locus ille, qui nunc Orphei continet fabulam, quae inserta est postquam irato Augusto Gallus occisus est. (Servius *ad G.* 4.1)

There is much of value in the Servian commentaries, many observations without which our understanding of Virgil would be severely impaired. There is also much in the way of jejune interpretation, poor philology, extrapolation for the purpose of creating biographical details, and downright nonsense – much that we could well have done without. Included in this second category are the above passages which, more than any other detail, have diverted the energies of Virgilian critics.

---

[34] Otis (1963) 151–2; the overall impression from all this, a correct one, is that no book is unconnected from any other.

Servius invites us to believe that the entire second half of the fourth book (*a medio usque ad finem*) contained the praises of Cornelius Gallus, the elegiac poet and prefect of Egypt who was compelled to commit suicide in 27, or possibly 26, B.C.; further, that Virgil under orders from Augustus removed the *laudes* and replaced them with the epyllion which is now found in their place;[35] and finally that no trace of the original lines, written by Rome's greatest poet and in publication for at least two years, survived from the first edition. That a steady stream of critics has actually believed this is testimony to the complexity of the poem, particularly of the second half of the fourth book – in a sense Servius' claim permits the reader to avoid the issue of interpretation altogether.

This is not the place for a full-scale elaboration of the arguments against the details of the Servian passages,[36] but two questions need to be addressed: why are the details untenable, [37] and what gave rise to them?[38] The most serious objection (i) has to do with unity and the shape and movement of the poem: it is quite simply inconceivable to imagine the possibility that the second half of *Georgics* 4 was occupied by praises of any contemporary figure; such a sequence could have no reference to the poem as a whole.[39] Related to this is the fact (ii) that Virgil shows great restraint in the degree to which he admits encomium of contemporaries. The prayer to Octavian has a special literary func-

[35] The *Georgics* was written at an average rate of one line per day; but those who believe Servius' statements must assume that Virgil produced 250 of his most careful and allusive lines in a very short time.

[36] They are easily accessible, as are the arguments in favour, in a number of studies. For bibliography see the most recent (Jacobson (1984)), a piece which in effect proposes to redate (to 27) and rewrite the poem; it originally ended happily, with a successful Orpheus retrieving Eurydice, but 'Gallus' death changed all that. It impressed on Vergil, as probably nothing else could have, the folly of believing that death was avoidable or revocable' (p. 292). Such a view does no justice to Virgil, and suggests an unawareness of the darkness of vision behind such lines as 3.66–8.

[37] Cf. Griffin (1979) 75–6 for a good summary of the objections.

[38] This second does not in fact require an answer, for the answer may simply lie beyond our reach, in the mind of Servius or his source.

[39] No argument satisfactorily resolves this issue. Indeed those who support the validity of Servius' comments do not confront the poem as a whole; notably Jacobson (1984) makes no mention of any line of the poem before 4.287. Nor is it plausible to claim that these *laudes* need not have been extensive; *a medio usque ad finem* can only mean what it says, and *ultimam partem* in the second Servian passage means the same thing, since Servius refers the reader to the first notice (*ut supra diximus*).

tion (1.24–42n.), as does the proem of the third book (3.1–48n.), and otherwise such references are strictly limited: Octavian is placed in the *sphragis* at 4.559–62, and in a passing reference, integrated into its context, in the *laudes Italiae* (2.170–2), while Maecenas is mentioned once in each book; his appearance has no impact on the progression of the poem. And would Virgil conceivably have included extensive praises of Gallus side by side with abbreviated references to Octavian and Maecenas? (iii) Some fragment of the first version, or at the very least some reference to it other than the comments in Servius, would certainly have survived. (iv) That Augustus 'ordered' Virgil to write or delete anything is in any case highly improbable, and is not supported by phrases such as *tua . . . haud mollia iussa* (3.41), which are merely part of the dramatization of the patron-poet relationship (see n.). If Hor. *Epist.* 2.1.1–4 is really in part a response to a playful complaint from Augustus that the poet has not mentioned his ruler's name sufficiently often (see Suet. *Vit. Horat.*), then it is quite clear that nothing in the way of real pressure was ever brought to bear on the favoured Augustan poets. (v) Finally, if Octavian could have expunged the name of Gallus from the *Georgics* after their publication, why not from the *Eclogues* as well? *E.* 10.72–4, in particular, could have been easily removed.

As for an explanation for the basis of Servius' misunderstanding, either of two possibilities, both entirely plausible, may be adduced. The first is that Servius or his source confused a notice that the praises of Gallus are to be found at the end of the *Eclogues*, where Gallus indeed does occupy centre stage (*E.* 10). Once *georgicorum* had supplanted *bucolicorum* an explanation for the absence of Gallus from the end of the *Georgics* had to be constructed.[40] Another possible, and attractive, explanation is that Gallus was always to be found, and still is, at the end of the *Georgics*; specifically that the song of Proteus may to a large extent be viewed as Virgil's acknowledgement of the style and content of the poetry of Gallus. The theme of Orpheus' tragic and unsuccessful love for Eurydice is precisely the type of mythological *exemplum* which must have concerned Gallus in his *Amores*,[41] while the style and manner of the story is that of epyllion, and, as far as we can tell, of the elegy of Gallus

---

[40] So Anderson (1933); he has been followed in this view by several influential scholars, including Norden in the following year. The objections of Jacobson (1984) 275–6 do no damage to the theory.

[41] Cf. the *exempla* of Parthenius' *Erotica Pathemata*, purportedly intended as raw material for the poetry of Gallus.

(4.453–527n.). A subsequent reader, with the information that Virgil acknowledged Gallus at the end of the *Georgics*, but with no awareness of the lines of poetic influence between Gallus and Virgil, invented the rest.[42]

7. THE POEM

The *Georgics* is perhaps the most difficult, certainly the most controversial, poem in Roman literature, and any attempt to explain it *as a single, unified poem* must begin with the discarding of central assumptions and generalizations which have filled the handbooks, commentaries and critical works in general since antiquity. Some recent scholars, at least in practice more free of preconceptions, and perhaps more attuned to the complexities of the Virgilian outlook, provide a more rational basis for judging the intent of the poem.

In the nineteenth century in particular the *Georgics* was seen as having a single, overriding theme: 'a strong sense of the necessity and dignity of labour breathes throughout the poem from beginning to end'.[43] And the view persists: 'In the shameful darkness of contemporary Rome and Italy it shines a ray of hope and pride.'[44] That man's pursuit of toil, *labor*, is the chief theme of the poem is clear; an evaluation of the poem necessarily involves examining the nature of such toil, and the results of man's relationship with it.

The *Georgics* is a remarkably realistic poem, particularly when set beside the works of Virgil's contemporaries. While Horace, after the public poetry of some of the *Epodes*, largely retreated to the more private worlds of *convivia*, the idealized harmony of his Sabine farm, and the generalities of ethical philosophy, and while the elegists explored themes which for the most part by definition excluded the problems of nation and civilization, Virgil in the *Georgics* squarely confronted the issues of real existence. By the mid-thirties, the fantastic solutions of the fourth

---

[42] This is a modification of the view of Coleman (1962), who believes that the ending as we have it is a second edition, but that it refers in a number of ways to Gallus. This seems to complicate things even further, and the first of his assumptions is unnecessary. If Virgil is referring to the *poetry*, not the life or exploits, of Gallus, there is no need to assume the poet was himself dead at the time.

[43] The view of Page (xxix) is representative of the critical attitude.

[44] Wilkinson (1982) 27.

Eclogue, with its promise of a tranquil golden age, were exposed as such;
the premise of the *Georgics* is that the spontaneity of that age no longer
exists, as Virgil states early in the poem:

> pater ipse colendi
> haud facilem esse uiam uoluit, primusque per artem
> mouit agros, curis acuens mortalia corda
> nec torpere graui passus sua regna ueterno.
>
> labor omnia uicit
> improbus et duris urgens in rebus egestas. (1.121–4, 145–6)

In between come the well-known details of the transition from the age of
Saturn to that of Jupiter: spontaneous growth and productivity end, the
wolf begins to prowl, the snake is given venom, navigation is invented.
The passage places the cultural setting of the *Georgics* after the Fall, and
it is a passage which Virgil intends the reader to apply throughout the
poem; where the language of the golden age is found, it either creates a
conflict with the realities of the poem (2.136–76, 458–540nn.), or it is
applied with irony (3.537–45n.). The agents of Jupiter are toil and
want, toil which is insatiable and pervasive, and want which presses
when times are hard.[45] How does Virgil judge the relationship between
man and these forces? That is, what effect does man have on them, and
they on him? These are the issues around which the poem moves.

a. Books 1 and 3

The first book, reflecting Virgil's early attention to the Hesiodic model,
treats the farmer's operations (43–203) and then his calendar (204–
463) – what to do and when to do it.[46] In the first part he treats the
actual work, ploughing, treatment of the soil (rotation, fallowing,
stubble-burning, etc.), irrigation and drainage (43–117), then, after the
interruption of 118–46, proceeds to describe the manner of man's work:
the need for constant toil, and account of the agricultural *arma*, the need
for vigilance against deterioration: *pestes* endanger the threshing-floor,

---

[45] Cf. 1.145–6n. on the lines which all critics see as crucial to the poem, and
whose sense most, until Altevogt (1952), tried to mitigate.

[46] This second part may be seen as falling into two sections (204–350 and
351–514), so that the book as a whole really consists of three parts.

and seeds, without careful selection, fall naturally into degeneration (147–203). The second part of the book treats the best time for sowing (204–30), tasks for the winter and holy days (259–75), and for night-time (287–310). And finally Virgil treats signs of bad and fair weather (350–423), and signs provided by the moon and the sun (424–63).

Within this technical scheme Virgil inserts three progressive crescendos, expressing his judgement of the success which may be expected. The first is ominous in a general way; degeneration is a natural law:

> sic omnia fatis
> in peius ruere ac retro sublapsa referri,
> non aliter quam qui aduerso uix flumine lembum
> remigiis subigit, si bracchia forte remisit,
> atque illum in praeceps prono rapit alueus amni. (199–203)

This generalization finds specific expression first at 311–34, where the storms of autumn and spring descend with complete destruction on the very crops whose preparation Virgil has so carefully prescribed.[47] Natural violence finds its responsion in civic violence at the end of the book (463–514), where Virgil gives a compelling picture of the strife which followed the death of Julius Caesar, strife which was attended by celestial *signa* (the theme of the preceding technical sections), but which, again, came in spite of those *signa* and man's knowledge of them. The closing simile, likening the world out of control to a charioteer who has lost control of his team (512–14), resumes and extends the simile of 199–203.

The application of *labor* is no more successful in Book 3, where the resurgence of nature follows a parallel movement. Didactic material on the selection, care and training of cattle and horses (49–208) is followed by an overriding injunction: the prime concern must be to combat a different manifestation of nature's resurgence, the threat posed by sexual passion (209–10 *sed non ulla magis uiris industria firmat | quam Venerem et caeci stimulos auertere amoris*). The injunction has a place in the agronomical rule-book, but that does not justify the focus it here receives; as the simply didactic mode retreats, the primary issue of the poem, *labor omnia uicit*, is reinforced by the theme of the *Eclogues: omnia uincit amor*. And at 242–83 the threat becomes reality, as all the creatures of

---

[47] Some see in the words *in primis uenerare deos* (338) mitigation of, or at least possible salvation from, the effects of the storm, but there is nothing to suggest that such actions in any way divert the violence of nature (1.335–50n.).

the earth, including man – and the toil he has expended – are swept away by a different storm (244 *in furias ignemque ruunt*).

The second half of the book mirrors the first; the destruction is merely presented at a starker level. The ostensible subject is the care of smaller animals: 288 *lanigeros agitare greges hirtasque capellas*. Among other concerns is fumigation of the steading, a process which drives out the snake; the *pestes* which threatened the threshing-floor at 1.181 have been replaced by the more ominous scourge (419 *pestis acerba boum*), which itself is merely a harbinger of the real *pestis*, the plague which increases in strength, again in spite of the *signa* (440) which precede it, in spite of the medical and religious remedies to which man resorts (440–73). The last hundred lines of the book follow the nightmarish progress of the disease and its unrelieved destruction of man's toil; the final four bring the disease to man himself.

b. Book 2

The second book has traditionally been seen as an antidote to 1 and 3, as depicting 'man's happy co-operation with ... nature'.[48] From what follows, and from the commentary, it will be clear that such views represent a misreading of the book.[49]

The book has two large technical movements, describing first the variety in arboriculture, of species of trees, and of soil (9–258), then treating the planting and care of vines, olives and other trees (259–457). Three sets of *laudes*, of Italy (136–76), of spring (315–45) and of the happy rustic (458–540), are intertwined with the technical material.

In contrast to Books 1 and 3, where the forces of nature destroy the works of man, *labor* is successfully applied in this book, but it is the nature or quality of that success which Virgil calls into question, as well as the desirability of the products of the *labor*. The tone is set early on (61–2):

> scilicet omnibus est labor impendendus, et omnes
> cogendae in sulcum ac multa mercede domandae.

The two verbs of forcing, *cogere* and *domare*, and the tricolon of

[48] Otis (1963) 153; also Wilkinson (1969) 85: 'To turn from the end of Book 1 to the beginning of Book 2 is like waking up from a nightmare on a fine morning.'

[49] More recent criticism has come to question the purely positive assessment of this difficult book; see Thomas (1982a); Ross (1987).

gerundives – a pattern reserved for this book – [50] set the tone: the personified plants are to be compelled to follow man's will.[51] This emerges particularly in the focus given to grafting and inoculation, processes which of necessity imply the diverting of nature, a theme underscored by Virgil's language (80–2; see n.):

> nec longum tempus, et ingens
> exiit ad caelum ramis felicibus arbos
> miratastque nouas frondes et non sua poma.

Grafting provides a virtual metaphor for the ways in which man succeeds in this book; he succeeds by transforming the natural order, by exercising a quasi-military force over the plants (368–70):

> tum stringe comas, tum bracchia tonde
> (ante reformidant ferrum), tum denique dura
> exerce imperia et ramos compesce fluentis.

Virgil concludes the technical part of Book 2 with a striking passage, an attack on the vine, whose product is responsible for war and strife (454–7; see n.). Thus the very plant which has been the object of man's 'successful' application of *labor* is vitiated. In this attack Virgil states that those trees which grow with little or no culture, but produce in their natural state, have the greater claim to our praise.[52]

The so-called digressions of the book[53] reinforce Virgil's subtle denigration of the vine, and of the process of arboriculture. Many of the details of the *laudes Italiae*, when scrutinized against the ethnographical tradition of which they are a part, suggest that the Italian landscape has been moulded and changed from its natural state by man's force.[54] This

---

[50] See 2.61–2n.

[51] Of these lines Otis (1963) notes 'The accent is ... on the assistance of a happily co-operating nature', Wilkinson (1969) 'The tempo is brisk and enthusiasm predominates.' This is representative of the critical violence which has been done to Virgil's language in Book 2: *cogere* and *domare* do not convey co-operation, and 62 is completely spondaic except for the fifth foot.

[52] Otis (1963) 168 calls this a 'splendid conclusion', while Wilkinson (1969) 184 at least finds it 'an odd and unsatisfactory conclusion to Book 2 before the finale'.

[53] It is assumed throughout the commentary that passages of a higher, non-technical nature merely reflect and further the themes of the technical sections; the very word 'digression', implying as it does a suspension of the central theme, should probably not even be used.

[54] See Thomas (1982a) 38–50; also Putnam (1975); Ross (1987) 115–19.

passage, and the two other sets of *laudes*, also contain deliberate false-hoods, whose effects can only serve to qualify the apparent success of man's activities throughout the book (136–76, 323–45, 458–540nn.). Book 2 cannot, then, be viewed merely as a demonstration of the successful application of *labor*; rather it presents, on a suggestive level, and in a complex manner, the notion that man's activities in the age of Jupiter do not simply succeed or fail: success itself may cost a price.

c. Book 4

Though the book is to be seen as a unity, and as a part of the unity of the poem, it will be useful to consider its two halves separately.[55]

(i) **1–282.** The two themes of the poem, that of failure before the resurgent forces of the natural world, and of success which is tainted by a spiritual failure, come together in the fourth book. If little else is agreed upon by critics, it is generally felt that the bees represent a human society.[56] This fact is a part of the progression of the poem: in Book 2 Virgil presented a plant world which was animated, which was assigned familial relationships and moved by sentient impulses,[57] while in the third the boundary between man and animal is constantly crossed.[58] In the fourth Virgil treats bees (and in doing so gives them a totally disproportionate prominence from the technical standpoint), but it is clear from the outset that his theme is man.[59] The question which follows is the determination of the nature of this society, and the answer must presumably be in terms relevant to the rest of the poem.

[55] The critical issue of this book, and of the entire poem, is the relationship of the two parts. It is a question which has not been, and doubtless never will be, resolved to full satisfaction. Cf. Griffin (1979) for a convenient summary of the major theories.

[56] Few would hold with the conservatism of Williams (1956) 170 'It is about bees before it is about anything else.'

[57] E.g. 2.23 *hic plantas tenero abscindens de corpore matrum* ...

[58] For instance in the alternating application of the word *iuuenis*, now to animals, now to human beings; see 3.258n.

[59] Dahlmann (1954) demonstrated beyond doubt that the whole account is modelled on the tradition of ethnographical writing, a tradition reserved for description of human societies. Though his article was at first received without enthusiasm, it now seems to have assumed the prominence it deserves; cf. Leach (1977) 15; Thomas (1982a) 70–2; Ross (1987) 248 ('Dahlmann's standard [work]').

The bees both succeed and fail. As products of the age of Jupiter (149–50 *naturas apibus quas Iuppiter ipse | addidit expediam*), they are committed to the ethos of *labor*, which they pursue to the exclusion of all else, for the sake of community over individual, and at the expense of the individual life: 205 *tantus amor florum et generandi gloria mellis*. Theirs is an existence without art and without love, the two aspects of human existence which more than any others inform Virgil's world, for better or for worse. To that extent their work, and their success, may be seen as related to the work and the success of the grower in the second book; as there, so here, there seems to be a missing spiritual ingredient, hard to objectify, except by reference to Virgilian thought, as it is transmitted both in the *Georgics* and elsewhere in the corpus.[60]

But the bees, and the society they represent, are more complex, for they share the fragility of existence as depicted in Books 1 and 3. Toil alone does not defend them from the imbalances of nature. In spite of the view that their life is immortal (219–227), in the last analysis they are susceptible to the same conditions that affect all societies: 251–2 *si uero, quoniam casus apibus quoque nostros | uita tulit, tristi languebunt corpora morbo*... As in Book 3, so here, *morbus* leads to death, and to the death of the race: 281 *sed si quem proles subito defecerit omnis*...

(ii) **283–558.** Redemption and optimism are detected in the *bugonia*, the means of generating bees from the carcass of an ox. The phenomenon frames the second half of the book (283–314, 528–58), with the epyllion occupying the centre, and falling into four parts: Aristaeus comes complaining of his loss to his mother Cyrene (315–32), she receives him and reveals that the sea-god Proteus will tell him the cause of his troubles (333–414), and he then secures Proteus (415–52), who sings the song of Orpheus and Eurydice, for whose deaths Aristaeus is ultimately responsible (453–527).

First *bugonia*, the event which has encouraged some critics to find a burst of optimism and cheer at the end of the book, and, more importantly, at the end of the poem.[61] Two observations may be made. (1) the phenomenon is an obvious fiction, an eastern θαῦμα ('marvel'), designated as such by Virgil himself (cf. 287–94n.); it has nothing to do with

---

[60] See the perceptive article of Griffin (1979).

[61] E.g. Otis (1964) 188–9. It needs to be said that a poem of the complexity of the *Georgics* can hardly be judged, in any case, merely from the tenor of its closing lines; Virgil intends that we read in more than one direction.

the realities of the agricultural struggle as depicted throughout the poem. Nor does it ensure immortality, for in logical terms, *morbus* can, and in the world of Jupiter will, strike again. (2) The point has been made best by Griffin: 'For my part I cannot feel that the restoration of the bees outweighs the suffering and death of Orpheus and Eurydice, especially in view of the way Virgil has handled the story. An exquisite ambivalence surely remains.'[62]

Which leads to the great question of the poem: 'What of Aristaeus, what of the song of Proteus depicting Orpheus' failure and loss?' The words *cui non dictus Orpheus?* present themselves, and with them the impulse to pass over the question, so difficult is it, so varied the judgements of so many scholars, and so apparently subjective and personal any answer.[63] But the question must be addressed, not only for the intrinsic importance it holds for any unified appreciation of the poem, but also because it is precisely critical despair over the meaning of these lines which leads to the view that Virgil inserted them, under constraint, as an extraneous 'filler', once the '*laudes Galli*' had been removed.[64]

The terms of the epyllion are on a different plane, the poetic mode is distinct, but it surely continues the major issues of the *Georgics* – success and failure. For all his artistic perfection and ability to control the natural world through song, Orpheus fails, and his failure comes from *amor*, the same destructive natural force which impeded success in Book 3. Eurydice and all his efforts, his toil, are lost (*omnis | effusus labor*, 491–2), like those of the farmer in Books 1 and 3, like those of the plague-stricken ox itself (*quid labor aut benefacta iuuant?*, 3.525). Aristaeus, on the other hand, succeeds, unjustly as it has seemed to some, and at the expense of the blameless Orpheus and Eurydice; his hive is restored to him. Nor is he merely a beekeeper, for at 4.329–30 he is active in the three areas of agriculture, the areas which are the theme of *Georgics* 1–3; his success is that of the *agricola* in general. But what of the cost? At 4.512–13 Orpheus is compared to a nightingale, driven by the plough-man from its nest, its young lost – *quos durus arator | obseruans nido implumis detraxit*. If Aristaeus ultimately represents the ploughman, we have met him before, in the 'successful' second book, where he turns 'idle' wood-

---

[62] Griffin (1979) 71.

[63] Again see Griffin (1979) for summary and synthesis of the secondary literature.

[64] See above, sect. 6.

land into gleaming ploughland, at a cost whose implications are unstated:

> aut unde iratus siluam deuexit arator
> et nemora euertit multos ignaua per annos,
> antiquasque domos auium cum stirpibus imis
> eruit. (2.207–10)

One simile resumes the theme of another reality, relationships are suggested, never spelled out; here, as throughout, the complexity, ambivalence and ultimate darkness of the Virgilian world shine through.

8. STYLE AND LANGUAGE

Perhaps the greatest challenge facing Virgil as he began the *Georgics* was a stylistic one: how, while transmitting the subject-matter of Theophrastus, Varro and the like, to produce a poetry which was not arid and merely bookish. It is Virgil's successful response to this challenge which separates the poem in its entirety from other Greek and Roman poetry whose basis, formal or real, is technical and didactic in nature. For all its learning the *Phaenomena* of Aratus, or the poetry of Nicander, could never be called great, and the shortcomings are ultimately shortcomings of style and language as much as of content. Lucretius too saw the problem, and confronted it mainly by variation of stylistic levels; 'purple passages', often not wholly intrinsic to the philosophical argument, and of a more elevated style, alternate with purely scientific or technical sections.[65]

Virgil to some extent followed suit. The style of the 'digressions' is often distinct from that of the technical passages, and these digressions are so situated in the poem as to function as stylistic (as well as thematic) crescendos. But Virgil's method is ultimately distinct from that of Lucretius; it is not really legitimate to speak of the 'two styles' of the *Georgics*. In that Virgil's poem is didactic only in appearance, he was freer to condense, omit, expand upon, or otherwise alter his technical sources, and this he did consistently. So for instance Aratus' treatment of weather-signs (*Phaen.* 733–1154) is reduced by Virgil to a quarter of its original size (1.351–463) – the theme could be sustained no longer with-

[65] See Kenney (1971) 14–29.

out becoming tedious and unpoetical. Or again, pigs and asses and mules, of greater importance to the Roman farmer than horses, have no part in the didactic scheme of the poem; the nobility of the horse, and its military associations, not its use around the farm, were what concerned Virgil.

The technical material which is included is constantly invigorated by what can only be called the Virgilian genius. One example may stand for many: at 3.322–38 Virgil treats the summer pasturing of sheep and goats:

> at uero Zephyris cum laeta uocantibus aestas
> in saltus utrumque gregem atque in pascua mittet,
> Luciferi primo cum sidere frigida rura
> carpamus, dum mane nouum, dum gramina canent,   325
> et ros in tenera pecori gratissimus herba.
> inde ubi quarta sitim caeli collegerit hora
> et cantu querelae rumpent arbusta cicadae,
> ad puteos aut alta greges ad stagna iubebo
> currentem ilignis potare canalibus undam;   330
> aestibus at mediis umbrosam exquirere uallem,
> sicubi magna Iouis antiquo robore quercus
> ingentis tendat ramos, aut sicubi nigrum
> ilicibus crebris sacra nemus accubet umbra;
> tum tenuis dare rursus aquas et pascere rursus   335
> solis ad occasum, cum frigidus aera Vesper
> temperat, et saltus reficit iam roscida luna,
> litoraque alcyonen resonant, acalanthida dumi.

The instructions are technically sound, and clearly derived from Varro, *R.R.* 2.2.10–11:

(10) eaeque [i.e. oues] ibi, ubi pascuntur in eadem regione, tamen temporibus distinguuntur, aestate quod cum prima luce exeunt pastum, propterea quod tunc herba roscida meridianam, quae est aridior, iucunditate praestat. sole exorto potum propellunt, ut redintegrantes rursus ad pastum alacriores faciant. (11) circiter meridianos aestus, dum deferuescant, sub umbriferas rupes et arbores patulas subigunt, quaad refrigeratur. aere uespertino rursus pascunt ad solis occasum. ita pascere pecus

oportet, ut auerso sole agat; caput enim maxime ouis molle est. ab
occasu paruo interuallo interposito ad bibendum appellunt et
rursus pascunt, quaad contenebrauit; iterum enim tum iucun-
ditas in herba redintegrabit.

A world of difference. Virgil, whose diction coincides with that of his
model only in one instance, the common phrase *solis ad occasum* (for
Varro's *ad solis occasum*), has faithfully transmitted the specific details;[66]
indeed his version is even more didactic in appearance than that of
Varro, by whom the information is put as a statement of fact.[67] But he
has reworked a mundane, functional passage into some of the most
exquisite poetry of the *Georgics*. After a line specifying the season (322)
the four periods of the day are presented in four lines each, with the
structure of the shepherd's day reflected in the neatness of the verse.
Varro's *sole exorto* has become an evocative couplet (324–5), high in style
and marked by the elegantly varied anaphora of *dum*. For *tunc herba
roscida meridianam ... iucunditate praestat* Virgil borrows a line from the
Eclogues (326 = *E.* 8.15), appropriately evoking in an instant the world
of his own pastoral.[68] Varro's *circiter meridianos aestus, dum deferuescant, sub
umbriferas rupes et arbores patulas subigunt*, becomes 331 *aestibus at mediis
umbrosam exquirere uallem*, with *umbrosam* elaborated over three artful lines
(332–4) consisting of two balancing clauses defined by anaphora of
sicubi. The whole passage ends on a sonorous note, as evening falls: 338
litoraque alcyonen resonant, acalanthida dumi.

Virgil uses other means to break down the distinction between the
technical and the more poetic parts of the poem. One is simile; so at
2.279–83, having described the *quincunx*, the ideal layout for planting
trees, he compares the arrangement to that of a legion, ready to do
battle. Nor is the effect mere embellishment, for the context of the simile
reinforces Virgil's suggestion throughout the book that arboriculture is
a form of warfare (see n.). Or a horse in training is compared to a storm
sweeping down on sea and land (3.196–201), an image which evokes a
Homeric simile and also serves to connect larger themes of the poem
(see n.).

Another stylistic feature, serving to invigorate and expand upon

[66] He omits the second evening pasturing, doubtless for the sake of neatness.
[67] Cf. in Virgil 325 *carpamus*, 329 *iubebo*.
[68] As he does throughout the passage; cf. 328, 331–4, 338nn.; also 322–38n. for
the important implications of the evocation to Book 3.

technical passages, is the vignette, or homely detail, usually coming as clausula and creating a vivid image. So at 1.390–2 the final weather-sign is that given by a sputtering lamp; but the real focus of the lines is on the young woman (the only human figure in the passage) who uses the lamp as she spins through the winter night. Similar is the detail at 1.273–5, where a section on the types of work permitted on sacred days closes with a compelling picture of the donkey-driver going into town to sell his produce.

Mythology serves throughout the poem both to embellish and, more importantly, to suggest connections between the immediate world of the farmer and higher levels of meaning.[69] This is a feature which reaches its most crucial point in the figures of Aristaeus, Proteus and Orpheus in the second half of the fourth book, but in shorter sequences mythology also has a central function. The Giants (1.278–83), Scylla and Nisus (1.404–9), the Centaurs and Lapiths (2.455–7), Io and the gadfly (3.146–56), Hero and Leander (3.258–63), Glaucus and the mares of Potniae (3.267–8), the Cyclopes at their smithies (4.170–5) – these and others have a function which is both stylistic and thematic (see nn.).

In short, while there are ostensible distinctions in subject matter in the *Georgics* (the technical and the lyrical), Virgil constantly breaks down those distinctions: the existence of the farmer is a metaphor for existence in general. Style and theme are inextricably related, and the final impression of the style of the poem is of a unity, with all parts contributing to the poetry. Nothing could be more lyrical, or more evocative, than Virgil's description of the best areas for grazing (around Tarentum in the south, Mantua in the north):

> saltus et saturi petito longinqua Tarenti,
> et qualem infelix amisit Mantua campum
> pascentem niueos herboso flumine cycnos. (2.197–9)

In language and technique, the poem is representative of Virgil's general practice. The effect of the neoterics, and of Virgil's own audacity in the *Eclogues* is evident, but the restraint that leads to classicism is

[69] The standard view of mythology in the *Georgics*, that it functions in a purely ornamental way, is no longer widely held; see Frentz (1967) passim against the general judgement of Wilkinson (1969) 185: 'By and large mythology plays no great part in the *Georgics*, outside the Aristaeus epyllion, and such contribution as it does make may generally be classed as "ornament".'

already apparent. Golden lines, and lines of equally intricate order
(1.117; 2.531nn.), are employed throughout, but in a much more
sparing fashion than occurs in Catullus, or subsequently in Ovid.[70]
Greek lines, normally redolent with reference to the poetic tradition,
occur consistently, but not to excess (e.g. 1.138, 332; 4.336). The same
may be said of poetic coinages, modelled on the practice of the neoterics,
and often with reference to them (1.207; 2.352nn.). And in general the
use of technical diction, of the actual language of the farm, is restricted.
While Virgil is prepared to employ such diction to a limited degree, a
glance, for instance, at any corresponding passage from Varro demon-
strates that his aim throughout, as far as choice of diction is concerned,
is for poetic integrity rather than technical exactitude.

The song of Proteus (4.453–527), heavily indebted as it is to neoteric
epyllion, shows some distinctive stylistic features, chiefly those designed
to create emotional effect: 465–6 an apostrophe with carefully balanced
cola built around anaphora of *te* (which occurs at the beginning of the
verse and after the main caesura in each line); the emotional exclama-
tions *heu* (491, 498) and *a* (526); 504–5 a series of (indirect) delibera-
tive questions pathetic in their effect and familiar from Catullus 64;
525–6 the echoing anaphora of *Eurydicen*, which forms the climax of the
song. In other ways, however, though there are specific reminiscences of
Catullus and perhaps Gallus (4.453–527n.), the lines are not stylisti-
cally separable from the rest of the poem.

9. METRE

That the Virgilian hexameter is the supreme metrical system of Latin
literature is generally agreed. Why that is so, and what the dynamics of
the metre are, are another matter. The issue is simply put, if not simply
resolved: 'Is the normal stress of the individual Latin word, determined
by the penultimate rule, the guiding accentual feature of the line, or
does the quantitative system generate its own accentual rhythm,
overriding the accent of individual words?'[71] That is, is the first line of

---

[70] And usually such lines function as clausulae; see 1.117n.

[71] For a survey of views on the matter see Allen (1973) 335–59. The problem
is further complicated by special idiosyncrasies, for instance those imposed by the
French, who as a rule refuse to see in the Latin language what does not exist in
their own, namely a regulated system of word accents ('la prétendue influence
de l'accent', Nougaret (1946) 261).

the *Georgics* to be read (respecting word stress alone)[72]

   quíd fáciat laétas ségetes, quó sídere térram

or (treating the quantitative system as generating the stress)

   quíd faciát laetás segetés, quo sídere térram?

Though the second method, that of reading by 'scansion', has existed since antiquity, it is true to say that the current practice, at least among English-speaking readers, is to respect the word-accents.[73] A purely quantitative reading would imply that the adoption of an alien (Greek) metrical system actually transformed the essence of Latin pronunciation – an unlikely linguistic scenario. If, moreover, quantity were supreme, the metre would lapse into a tediously repetitive pattern, which does not occur in Greek, where a melodic word pitch complements quantity. This Greek precedent has led some to speculate that the Latin word accent became a pitch accent (under the influence of learned Greeks in Rome), and that the metre then functioned like its Greek counterpart.[74] But the use of a social explanation for a linguistic phenomenon is largely (and rightly) rejected. Moreover, such a system would result in the doubling of stress: *quíd fáciát laetás ségetés* . . . – hardly likely.[75]

 Just as acceptance of quantitative dynamism creates the problem of how to treat the individual stress accents, so the reverse, seeing the system as essentially determined by the natural stress of the constituent words, leads to the question 'How, particularly in a heavily spondaic line, does the dactylic rhythm of the verse convey itself?' The most satisfactory answer to this difficult question is that the ictus of the verse establishes a rhythmic pattern. Ictus for the purposes of this commen-

---

[72] The question of the stressing of monosyllables is here ignored, although it is perhaps reasonable to assume that *quid* and *quo*, as pronoun and adjective, would be stressed.

[73] A system which can be shown to have existed at least since the fifth century A.D.; a papyrus of that date (*PGL* 1 (1912) 47) contains parts of *Aen.* 4.66–8, 99–102 in which word accents alone are marked (presumably as an aid in reading). And Horace's borrowings from Terence's senarii (where scansion and word accent coincide) would hardly be perceived as borrowings unless stressed the same way (*Sat.* 2.3.264 *exclúsit*; *réuocat*; *rédeam?*, *Epist.* 1.19.41 *hinc íllae lácrimae*); in their hexameter setting this accentuation no longer coincides with the scansion. See Wilkinson (1963) 95.

[74] Kent (1920).

[75] Cf. Allen (1973) 341–2.

tary means the first, strong measure of each foot, and does not imply
stress or loudness – 'Ictus naturally implies stress only to those who start
with the assumption that it *is* stress.'[76] The rhythm established by ictus is
based on temporal, not accentual, patterns, much like the rhythm of
musical time; one reads the Latin verse, as Wilkinson has well described
it, 'as though it were natural speech (as one reads English verse),
[letting] the now familiar metre make itself felt as an undercurrent'.[77]

To those who assert that in a heavily spondaic line the reading would
be identical to that of prose, and would therefore not constitute poetry,
the response is first a subjective one, that even with such a line the
essentially dactylic nature of the verse is maintained; in such lines our
expectations of a dactylic rhythm are not entirely frustrated, but rather
put in suspension. We know that we are reading a poem in dactylic
hexameter, and that, at least descriptively, in spondaic feet a long
syllable is merely substituted for two short ones – that will hardly destroy
expectations of the dactylic rhythm. And, less subjectively, those expec-
tations are also fulfilled by the consistent coming together of temporal
(quantitative) and accentual rhythm at the end of the line. The Latin
hexameter behaved entirely unlike its Greek model in maintaining to a
very high degree the dactylic integrity of the fifth foot,[78] and in drasti-
cally restricting word-end after the first element of the fifth foot;[79] the
combined effect of these restrictions is quite clear: provided the word
which begins the fifth foot does not extend to a final monosyllable,[80] the
word accent will coincide with the verse ictus in the fifth foot. If at the

[76] Bennett (1898) 382.

[77] Wilkinson (1963) 94.

[78] There are only five spondaic lines in the *Georgics*: 1.221; 2.5; 3.276; 4.270,
463; the large number of such lines in Cat. 64 is to be seen as a stylistic affectation,
in imitation of Alexandrian poetry.

[79] Of the 37 instances of such word-end in the *Georgics* the vast majority consist
of breaks between word-groups (e.g. *et bona, me quoque, non sua*), often with elision
(*atque haec*), and cannot really be regarded as constituting strong word-ends.
Some are Greek formations (e.g. 1.436; 4.183, 251). It is worth noting that
applying same broad criteria for determining word-end, the figure 37 has been
reached in the *Iliad* before 150 lines have passed – strong proof of the different
dynamics of the two hexameters.

[80] As for instance happens at 1.181 *exiguus mus*, 313 *imbriferum uer*; 3.255 *exacuit
sus*; these are the only such instances of this pattern in the poem, and they are
intended, at least in the two latter cases, to suggest rapidity (see nn.).

same time the line does not end with a monosyllable,[81] coincidence is
assured in the sixth foot as well. The coming together of accentual word
stress and subtle rhythmic verse ictus at the end of the line guarantees its
metrical, or quantitative integrity.

The special quality of the Virgilian hexameter lies in the fact that this
coincidence was, as far as was possible, not only virtually mandatory for
the fifth and sixth feet, but was to a large extent avoided in the fourth
foot.[82] The result is a line which shows clash and conflict in the middle,
but harmony and order at the end, a line which is clearly dactylic
through the greater stringency at the end, but which escapes the possi-
bility of rhythmic monotony through the first four feet.

If coincidence and clash of accent and ictus are what concern the poet
in the Latin hexameter, then the phenomenon of 'caesura' (word-break
in the middle of the foot) is merely a necessary consequence.[83] This is
best demonstrated through observation of the third foot. In *Georgics* 1 all
but two lines (350, 482) have a caesura, word-end, in the third foot.[84]
Almost 90% have a strong, or masculine, caesura, and the reason seems
clear: provided the word ending at that point is not a stressed monosyl-
lable, such a caesura *guarantees* conflict of accent and ictus in the third
foot. Moreover, it also creates a strong likelihood of conflict in the fourth
foot.[85] Perhaps more telling are the phenomena accompanying a third-
foot feminine, or weak, caesura (of which there are 49, fewer than 10%,

[81] Of which there are only five examples in the poem, other than those cited in
the preceding note: 1.247, 314, 370; 2.321, 3.358. One (1.247) is an Ennian
imitation, one (2.321) has a special effect, and the other three hardly qualify as
monosyllables (*et*/*nec cum*).

[82] See the table of Knight (1939), which shows the *Eclogues*, *Georgics* and *Aeneid*
with 37.27%, 33.45% and 35.95% coincidence in the fourth foot; this compared
with 51.49% and 61.25% in Lucretius and Catullus 64 respectively. He also
shows that in the *Aeneid* 74 of these instances could have been avoided by
transposition (for instance the transposing of *Troiae qui* in *A.* 1.1, which would
also give a more 'normal' word-order), while only 5 could so be avoided in
Lucretius: the lower ratio of coincidence in the fourth foot in Virgil is clearly a
consciously intended effect.

[83] In the commentary the word 'caesura' is merely used to describe position in
the line; such positions are important only from an artistic point of view; see
4.465-6.

[84] Since relatively few are sense pauses, the notion that the reader needed to
pause for breath in the middle of the line is obvious nonsense.

[85] Such conflict will occur if an anapaest or spondee follows the caesura.

in Book 1). Now this caesura guarantees (undesirable) coincidence of accent and ictus in the third foot, but, provided it is followed by an iambic word, (desirable) conflict in the fourth foot is also guaranteed. In 47 of those 49 instances an iambic word follows; in the other two cases (357, 514), the regularity of rhythm contributes to the sense. Patterns of caesura, then, are to be seen as a result of the striving for effects of conflict and coincidence.[86]

10. THE TEXT

There is no apparatus criticus. As Shackleton Bailey has pointed out, 'when E. R. Dodds pronounced that our texts are good enough to live with, he cannot have been thinking of G. Lehnert's edition of the longer declamations falsely ascribed to Quintilian';[87] but he was perhaps thinking of the text of Virgil. As will be seen from the conspectus below, the present text departs from both Mynors's OCT and Geymonat's Paravia edition in only 16 instances,[88] and in all but a few of those it has support from other editions.[89] Considerations of space have therefore led to the omission, mitigated by discussion of *cruces* in the body of the commentary. In such discussions there is an assumption of familiarity with the titles of the major fourth- and fifth-century MSS, on which the reader may consult the prefaces of Mynors or Geymonat.

In the matter of orthography and punctuation divergences have generally not been reported, unless the differences have affected meaning (as e.g. at 2.65, 347). The orthography is by and large familiar rather than necessarily 'correct'.[90] In such matters the present text agrees with Mynors against Geymonat some 325 times, with Geymonat

---

[86] This is surely a more satisfactory way of viewing such patterns than that proposed by those who believe that caesura has some sort of independent dynamic pattern; the rule 'a third-foot weak caesura must be accompanied by a fourth-foot strong caesura' is on its own virtually without meaning.

[87] Shackleton Bailey (1976) 73.

[88] No new conjecture has been admitted to the text, but a few are suggested in the commentary (cf. 2.409; 3.413; 4.382nn.; also 3.44n.).

[89] Mynors is followed against Geymonat in 11 instances, Geymonat against Mynors also in 11.

[90] So *equum* is preferred to *equom*, *inuertant* to *inuortant*, *difficile est* to *difficilest* etc. – though, as Kenney (1986) shows, Virgil may well have written *difficilest*. The orthography of the Gallus papyrus demonstrates that the choice often has as much to do with modern as with ancient taste.

against Mynors about 60; the vast majority are in minor points of punctuation, and the imbalance may reflect as much as anything else the conventions of English punctuation.

Occasional differences in the marking of section boundaries are not recorded here, but are discussed in the commentary.

Differences in the text

locus	Thomas	Mynors	Geymonat
1.152	silua,	silua	silua,
1.157	umbras	umbras	umbram
1.180	fatiscat.	fatiscat,	fatiscat,
1.181	inludunt	inludant	inludant
1.208	die	die	dies
1.218	aduerso	auerso	auerso
1.277	Orcus	Orcus	Horcus
1.360	a curuis	a curuis	curuis
2.52	uoces	uoles	uoles
2.65	coryli nascuntur	coryli. nascuntur	coryli. nascuntur
2.71	castaneas fagus	castaneae fagos	castaneae fagos
2.106	discere	dicere	discere
2.136	siluae, ... terra,	siluae ... terra	siluae, ... terra,
2.157	subterlabentia	subter labentia	subter labentia
2.222	olcae	oleo	oleo
2.296	tendens	tendens	pandens
2.347	terra.	terra,	terra
2.379	admorso	admorsu	admorso
2.433	(*bracketed*)	(*accepted*)	(*accepted*)
2.469	et	at	et
2.514	hinc ... hinc	hic ... hinc	hic ... hinc
3.33	gentes	gentis	gentes
3.77	minacis	minacis	minantis
3.202	hic	hinc	hinc
3.384	silua,	silua	silua,
3.385	tribolique,	tribolique	tribolique,
3.435	ne	ne	nec
4.78	concurritur, ... alto	concurritur, ... alto	concurritur ... alto,
4.112	pinosque	tinosque	tinosque

4.141	pinus	tinus	pinus
4.202	refingunt	refingunt	refigunt
4.228	angustam	augustam	augustam
4.291	*post* 293	*post* 293	*post* 292
4.297	addunt	addunt	addunt,
4.338	(*bracketed*)	(*omitted*)	(*bracketed*)
4.505	qua	quae	quae
4.509	astris	antris	astris

THE GEORGICS
BOOKS I–II

P. VERGILI MARONIS GEORGICON I–II

GEORGICON I

Quid faciat laetas segetes, quo sidere terram
uertere, Maecenas, ulmisque adiungere uitis
conueniat, quae cura boum, qui cultus habendo
sit pecori, apibus quanta experientia parcis,
hinc canere incipiam. uos, o clarissima mundi   5
lumina, labentem caelo quae ducitis annum;
Liber et alma Ceres, uestro si munere tellus
Chaoniam pingui glandem mutauit arista,
poculaque inuentis Acheloia miscuit uuis;
et uos, agrestum praesentia numina, Fauni,   10
ferte simul Faunique pedem Dryadesque puellae:
munera uestra cano; tuque o, cui prima frementem
fudit equum magno tellus percussa tridenti,
Neptune; et cultor nemorum, cui pinguia Ceae
ter centum niuei tondent dumeta iuuenci;   15
ipse nemus linquens patrium saltusque Lycaei,
Pan, ouium custos, tua si tibi Maenala curae,
adsis, o Tegeaee, fauens, oleaeque Minerua
inuentrix, uncique puer monstrator aratri,
et teneram ab radice ferens, Siluane, cupressum;   20
dique deaeque omnes, studium quibus arua tueri,
quique nouas alitis non ullo semine fruges
quique satis largum caelo demittitis imbrem.
tuque adeo, quem mox quae sint habitura deorum
concilia incertum est, urbisne inuisere, Caesar,   25
terrarumque uelis curam, et te maximus orbis
auctorem frugum tempestatumque potentem
accipiat cingens materna tempora myrto;
an deus immensi uenias maris ac tua nautae
numina sola colant, tibi seruiat ultima Thyle,   30

teque sibi generum Tethys emat omnibus undis;
anne nouum tardis sidus te mensibus addas,
qua locus Erigonen inter Chelasque sequentis
panditur (ipse tibi iam bracchia contrahit ardens
Scorpius et caeli iusta plus parte reliquit);   35
quidquid eris (nam te nec sperant Tartara regem,
nec tibi regnandi ueniat tam dira cupido,
quamuis Elysios miretur Graecia campos
nec repetita sequi curet Proserpina matrem),
da facilem cursum atque audacibus adnue coeptis,   40
ignarosque uiae mecum miseratus agrestis
ingredere et uotis iam nunc adsuesce uocari.
    Vere nouo, gelidus canis cum montibus umor
liquitur et Zephyro putris se glaeba resoluit,
depresso incipiat iam tum mihi taurus aratro   45
ingemere et sulco attritus splendescere uomer.
illa seges demum uotis respondet auari
agricolae, bis quae solem, bis frigora sensit;
illius immensae ruperunt horrea messes.
ac prius ignotum ferro quam scindimus aequor,   50
uentos et uarium caeli praediscere morem
cura sit ac patrios cultusque habitusque locorum,
et quid quaeque ferat regio et quid quaeque recuset.
hic segetes, illic ueniunt felicius uuae,
arborei fetus alibi atque iniussa uirescunt   55
gramina. nonne uides, croceos ut Tmolus odores,
India mittit ebur, molles sua tura Sabaei,
at Chalybes nudi ferrum uirosaque Pontus
castorea, Eliadum palmas Epiros equarum?
continuo has leges aeternaque foedera certis   60
imposuit natura locis, quo tempore primum
Deucalion uacuum lapides iactauit in orbem,
unde homines nati, durum genus. ergo age, terrae
pingue solum primis extemplo a mensibus anni
fortes inuertant tauri, glaebasque iacentis   65

puluerulenta coquat maturis solibus aestas;
at si non fuerit tellus fecunda, sub ipsum
Arcturum tenui sat erit suspendere sulco:
illic, officiant laetis ne frugibus herbae,
hic, sterilem exiguus ne deserat umor harenam.   70
   Alternis idem tonsas cessare noualis
et segnem patiere situ durescere campum;
aut ibi flaua seres mutato sidere farra,
unde prius laetum siliqua quassante legumen
aut tenuis fetus uiciae tristisque lupini   75
sustuleris fragilis calamos siluamque sonantem.
urit enim lini campum seges, urit auenae,
urunt Lethaeo perfusa papauera somno;
sed tamen alternis facilis labor, arida tantum
ne saturare fimo pingui pudeat sola neue   80
effetos cinerem immundum iactare per agros.
sic quoque mutatis requiescunt fetibus arua,
nec nulla interea est inaratae gratia terrae.
saepe etiam sterilis incendere profuit agros
atque leuem stipulam crepitantibus urere flammis: 85
siue inde occultas uiris et pabula terrae
pinguia concipiunt, siue illis omne per ignem
excoquitur uitium atque exsudat inutilis umor,
seu pluris calor ille uias et caeca relaxat
spiramenta, nouas ueniat qua sucus in herbas,   90
seu durat magis et uenas astringit hiantis,
ne tenues pluuiae rapidiue potentia solis
acrior aut Boreae penetrabile frigus adurat.
multum adeo, rastris glaebas qui frangit inertis
uimineasque trahit cratis, iuuat arua, neque illum   95
flaua Ceres alto nequiquam spectat Olympo;
et qui, proscisso quae suscitat aequore terga,
rursus in obliquum uerso perrumpit aratro
exercetque frequens tellurem atque imperat aruis.
   Vmida solstitia atque hiemes orate serenas,   100

agricolae; hiberno laetissima puluere farra,
laetus ager. nullo tantum se Mysia cultu
iactat et ipsa suas mirantur Gargara messis.
quid dicam, iacto qui semine comminus arua
insequitur cumulosque ruit male pinguis harenae,   105
deinde satis fluuium inducit riuosque sequentis,
et, cum exustus ager morientibus aestuat herbis,
ecce supercilio cliuosi tramitis undam
elicit? illa cadens raucum per leuia murmur
saxa ciet, scatebrisque arentia temperat arua.   110
quid qui, ne grauidis procumbat culmus aristis,
luxuriem segetum tenera depascit in herba,
cum primum sulcos aequant sata, quique paludis
collectum umorem bibula deducit harena?
praesertim incertis si mensibus amnis abundans   115
exit et obducto late tenet omnia limo,
unde cauae tepido sudant umore lacunae.
   Nec tamen, haec cum sint hominumque boumque labores
uersando terram experti, nihil improbus anser
Strymoniaeque grues et amaris intiba fibris   120
officiunt aut umbra nocet. pater ipse colendi
haud facilem esse uiam uoluit, primusque per artem
mouit agros, curis acuens mortalia corda
nec torpere graui passus sua regna ueterno.
ante Iouem nulli subigebant arua coloni;   125
ne signare quidem aut partiri limite campum
fas erat; in medium quaerebant, ipsaque tellus
omnia liberius nullo poscente ferebat.
ille malum uirus serpentibus addidit atris
praedarique lupos iussit pontumque moueri   130
mellaque decussit foliis ignemque remouit
et passim riuis currentia uina repressit,
ut uarias usus meditando extunderet artis
paulatim et sulcis frumenti quaereret herbam,
ut silicis uenis abstrusum excuderet ignem.   135

tunc alnos primum fluuii sensere cauatas;
nauita tum stellis numeros et nomina fecit
Pleiadas, Hyadas, claramque Lycaonis Arcton;
tum laqueis captare feras et fallere uisco
inuentum et magnos canibus circumdare saltus;   140
atque alius latum funda iam uerberat amnem
alta petens, pelagoque alius trahit umida lina;
tum ferri rigor atque argutae lammina serrae
(nam primi cuneis scindebant fissile lignum),
tum uariae uenere artes. labor omnia uicit   145
improbus et duris urgens in rebus egestas.
    Prima Ceres ferro mortalis uertere terram
instituit, cum iam glandes atque arbuta sacrae
deficerent siluae et uictum Dodona negaret.
mox et frumentis labor additus, ut mala culmos   150
esset robigo segnisque horreret in aruis
carduus; intereunt segetes, subit aspera silua,
lappaeque tribolique, interque nitentia culta
infelix lolium et steriles dominantur auenae.
quod nisi et adsiduis herbam insectabere rastris   155
et sonitu terrebis auis et ruris opaci
falce premes umbras uotisque uocaueris imbrem,
heu magnum alterius frustra spectabis aceruum
concussaque famem in siluis solabere quercu.
    Dicendum et quae sint duris agrestibus arma,   160
quis sine nec potuere seri nec surgere messes:
uomis et inflexi primum graue robur aratri,
tardaque Eleusinae matris uoluentia plaustra,
tribulaque traheaeque et iniquo pondere rastri;
uirgea praeterea Celei uilisque supellex,   165
arbuteae crates et mystica uannus Iacchi;
omnia quae multo ante memor prouisa repones,
si te digna manet diuini gloria ruris.
continuo in siluis magna ui flexa domatur
in burim et curui formam accipit ulmus aratri.   170

huic a stirpe pedes temo protentus in octo,
binae aures, duplici aptantur dentalia dorso.
caeditur et tilia ante iugo leuis altaque fagus
stiuaque, quae currus a tergo torqueat imos,
et suspensa focis explorat robora fumus.   175
  Possum multa tibi ueterum praecepta referre,
ni refugis tenuisque piget cognoscere curas.
area cum primis ingenti aequanda cylindro
et uertenda manu et creta solidanda tenaci,
ne subeant herbae neu puluere uicta fatiscat.   180
tum uariae inludunt pestes: saepe exiguus mus
sub terris posuitque domos atque horrea fecit,
aut oculis capti fodere cubilia talpae,
inuentusque cauis bufo et quae plurima terrae
monstra ferunt, populatque ingentem farris aceruum   185
curculio atque inopi metuens formica senectae.
contemplator item, cum se nux plurima siluis
induet in florem et ramos curuabit olentis:
si superant fetus, pariter frumenta sequentur
magnaque cum magno ueniet tritura calore;   190
at si luxuria foliorum exuberat umbra,
nequiquam pinguis palea teret area culmos.
semina uidi equidem multos medicare serentis
et nitro prius et nigra perfundere amurca,
grandior ut fetus siliquis fallacibus esset   195
et quamuis igni exiguo properata maderent.
uidi lecta diu et multo spectata labore
degenerare tamen, ni uis humana quotannis
maxima quaeque manu legeret. sic omnia fatis
in peius ruere ac retro sublapsa referri,   200
non aliter quam qui aduerso uix flumine lembum
remigiis subigit, si bracchia forte remisit,
atque illum in praeceps prono rapit alueus amni.
  Praeterea tam sunt Arcturi sidera nobis
Haedorumque dies seruandi et lucidus Anguis,   205

quam quibus in patriam uentosa per aequora uectis
Pontus et ostriferi fauces temptantur Abydi.
Libra die somnique pares ubi fecerit horas
et medium luci atque umbris iam diuidit orbem,
exercete, uiri, tauros, serite hordea campis   210
usque sub extremum brumae intractabilis imbrem;
nec non et lini segetem et Cereale papauer
tempus humo tegere et iamdudum incumbere aratris,
dum sicca tellure licet, dum nubila pendent.
uere fabis satio; tum te quoque, Medica, putres   215
accipiunt sulci et milio uenit annua cura,
candidus auratis aperit cum cornibus annum
Taurus et aduerso cedens Canis occidit astro.
at si triticeam in messem robustaque farra
exercebis humum solisque instabis aristis,   220
ante tibi Eoae Atlantides abscondantur
Cnosiaque ardentis decedat stella Coronae,
debita quam sulcis committas semina quamque
inuitae properes anni spem credere terrae.
multi ante occasum Maiae coepere; sed illos   225
exspectata seges uanis elusit auenis.
si uero uiciamque seres uilemque phaselum
nec Pelusiacae curam aspernabere lentis,
haud obscura cadens mittet tibi signa Bootes:
incipe et ad medias sementem extende pruinas.   230
   Idcirco certis dimensum partibus orbem
per duodena regit mundi sol aureus astra.
quinque tenent caelum zonae: quarum una corusco
semper sole rubens et torrida semper ab igni;
quam circum extremae dextra laeuaque trahuntur   235
caeruleae, glacie concretae atque imbribus atris;
has inter mediamque duae mortalibus aegris
munere concessae diuum, et uia secta per ambas,
obliquus qua se signorum uerteret ordo.
mundus, ut ad Scythiam Riphaeasque arduus arces   240

consurgit, premitur Libyae deuexus in Austros.
hic uertex nobis semper sublimis; at illum
sub pedibus Styx atra uidet Manesque profundi.
maximus hic flexu sinuoso elabitur Anguis
circum perque duas in morem fluminis Arctos,   245
Arctos Oceani metuentis aequore tingi.
illic, ut perhibent, aut intempesta silet nox
semper et obtenta densentur nocte tenebrae;
aut redit a nobis Aurora diemque reducit,
nosque ubi primus equis Oriens adflauit anhelis   250
illic sera rubens accendit lumina Vesper.
hinc tempestates dubio praediscere caelo
possumus, hinc messisque diem tempusque serendi,
et quando infidum remis impellere marmor
conueniat, quando armatas deducere classis,   255
aut tempestiuam siluis euertere pinum.
  Nec frustra signorum obitus speculamur et ortus
temporibusque parem diuersis quattuor annum.
frigidus agricolam si quando continet imber,
multa, forent quae mox caelo properanda sereno,   260
maturare datur: durum procudit arator
uomeris obtunsi dentem, cauat arbore lintres,
aut pecori signum aut numeros impressit aceruis.
exacuunt alii uallos furcasque bicornis
atque Amerina parant lentae retinacula uiti.   265
nunc facilis rubea texatur fiscina uirga,
nunc torrete igni fruges, nunc frangite saxo.
quippe etiam festis quaedam exercere diebus
fas et iura sinunt: riuos deducere nulla
religio uetuit, segeti praetendere saepem,   270
insidias auibus moliri, incendere uepres
balantumque gregem fluuio mersare salubri.
saepe oleo tardi costas agitator aselli
uilibus aut onerat pomis, lapidemque reuertens
incusum aut atrae massam picis urbe reportat.   275

  Ipsa dies alios alio dedit ordine luna
felicis operum. quintam fuge: pallidus Orcus
Eumenidesque satae; tum partu Terra nefando
Coeumque Iapetumque creat saeuumque Typhoea
et coniuratos caelum rescindere fratres.   280
ter sunt conati imponere Pelio Ossam
scilicet atque Ossae frondosum inuoluere Olympum;
ter pater exstructos disiecit fulmine montis.
septima post decimam felix et ponere uitem
et prensos domitare boues et licia telae   285
addere. nona fugae melior, contraria furtis.
  Multa adeo gelida melius se nocte dedere
aut cum sole nouo terras inrorat Eous.
nocte leues melius stipulae, nocte arida prata
tondentur, noctes lentus non deficit umor.   290
et quidam seros hiberni ad luminis ignis
peruigilat ferroque faces inspicat acuto.
interea longum cantu solata laborem
arguto coniunx percurrit pectine telas,
aut dulcis musti Volcano decoquit umorem   295
et foliis undam trepidi despumat aëni.
at rubicunda Ceres medio succiditur aestu
et medio tostas aestu terit area fruges.
nudus ara, sere nudus; hiems ignaua colono:
frigoribus parto agricolae plerumque fruuntur   300
mutuaque inter se laeti conuiuia curant.
inuitat genialis hiems curasque resoluit,
ceu pressae cum iam portum tetigere carinae,
puppibus et laeti nautae imposuere coronas.
sed tamen et quernas glandes tum stringere tempus   305
et lauri bacas oleamque cruentaque myrta,
tum gruibus pedicas et retia ponere ceruis
auritosque sequi lepores, tum figere dammas
stuppea torquentem Balearis uerbera fundae,
cum nix alta iacet, glaciem cum flumina trudunt.   310

Quid tempestates autumni et sidera dicam,
atque, ubi iam breuiorque dies et mollior aestas,
quae uigilanda uiris? uel cum ruit imbriferum uer,
spicea iam campis cum messis inhorruit et cum
frumenta in uiridi stipula lactentia turgent?   315
saepe ego, cum flauis messorem induceret aruis
agricola et fragili iam stringeret hordea culmo,
omnia uentorum concurrere proelia uidi,
quae grauidam late segetem ab radicibus imis
sublimem expulsam eruerent: ita turbine nigro   320
ferret hiems culmumque leuem stipulasque uolantis.
saepe etiam immensum caelo uenit agmen aquarum,
et foedam glomerant tempestatem imbribus atris
collectae ex alto nubes; ruit arduus aether
et pluuia ingenti sata laeta boumque labores   325
diluit; implentur fossae et caua flumina crescunt
cum sonitu feruetque fretis spirantibus aequor.
ipse pater media nimborum in nocte corusca
fulmina molitur dextra, quo maxima motu
terra tremit, fugere ferae et mortalia corda   330
per gentis humilis strauit pauor; ille flagranti
aut Atho aut Rhodopen aut alta Ceraunia telo
deicit; ingeminant Austri et densissimus imber;
nunc nemora ingenti uento, nunc litora plangunt.
hoc metuens caeli mensis et sidera serua,   335
frigida Saturni sese quo stella receptet,
quos ignis caelo Cyllenius erret in orbis.
in primis uenerare deos, atque annua magnae
sacra refer Cereri laetis operatus in herbis
extremae sub casum hiemis, iam uere sereno.   340
tum pingues agni et tum mollissima uina,
tum somni dulces densaeque in montibus umbrae.
cuncta tibi Cererem pubes agrestis adoret:
cui tu lacte fauos et miti dilue Baccho,
terque nouas circum felix eat hostia fruges,   345

omnis quam chorus et socii comitentur ouantes
et Cererem clamore uocent in tecta; neque ante
falcem maturis quisquam supponat aristis
quam Cereri torta redimitus tempora quercu
det motus incompositos et carmina dicat.   350
  Atque haec ut certis possemus discere signis,
aestusque pluuiasque et agentis frigora uentos,
ipse pater statuit quid menstrua luna moneret,
quo signo caderent Austri, quid saepe uidentes
agricolae propius stabulis armenta tenerent.   355
continuo uentis surgentibus aut freta ponti
incipiunt agitata tumescere et aridus altis
montibus audiri fragor, aut resonantia longe
litora misceri et nemorum increbrescere murmur.
iam sibi tum a curuis male temperat unda carinis,   360
cum medio celeres reuolant ex aequore mergi
clamoremque ferunt ad litora, cumque marinae
in sicco ludunt fulicae, notasque paludes
deserit atque altam supra uolat ardea nubem.
saepe etiam stellas uento impendente uidebis   365
praecipitis caelo labi, noctisque per umbram
flammarum longos a tergo albescere tractus,
saepe leuem paleam et frondes uolitare caducas
aut summa nantis in aqua conludere plumas.
at Boreae de parte trucis cum fulminat et cum   370
Eurique Zephyrique tonat domus, omnia plenis
rura natant fossis atque omnis nauita ponto
umida uela legit. numquam imprudentibus imber
obfuit: aut illum surgentem uallibus imis
aëriae fugere grues, aut bucula caelum   375
suspiciens patulis captauit naribus auras,
aut arguta lacus circumuolitauit hirundo
et ueterem in limo ranae cecinere querelam;
saepius et tectis penetralibus extulit oua
angustum formica terens iter, et bibit ingens   380

arcus, et e pastu decedens agmine magno
coruorum increpuit densis exercitus alis.
iam uariae pelagi uolucres et quae Asia circum
dulcibus in stagnis rimantur prata Caystri,
certatim largos umeris infundere rores,   385
nunc caput obiectare fretis, nunc currere in undas
et studio incassum uideas gestire lauandi.
tum cornix plena pluuiam uocat improba uoce
et sola in sicca secum spatiatur harena.
ne nocturna quidem carpentes pensa puellae   390
nesciuere hiemem, testa cum ardente uiderent
scintillare oleum et putris concrescere fungos.
     Nec minus ex imbri soles et aperta serena
prospicere et certis poteris cognoscere signis:
nam neque tum stellis acies obtunsa uidetur,   395
nec fratris radiis obnoxia surgere Luna,
tenuia nec lanae per caelum uellera ferri;
non tepidum ad solem pennas in litore pandunt
dilectae Thetidi alcyones, non ore solutos
immundi meminere sues iactare maniplos.   400
at nebulae magis ima petunt campoque recumbunt,
solis et occasum seruans de culmine summo
nequiquam seros exercet noctua cantus.
apparet liquido sublimis in aëre Nisus,
et pro purpureo poenas dat Scylla capillo: 405
quacumque illa leuem fugiens secat aethera pennis,
ecce inimicus atrox magno stridore per auras
insequitur Nisus; qua se fert Nisus ad auras,
illa leuem fugiens raptim secat aethera pennis.
tum liquidas corui presso ter gutture uoces   410
aut quater ingeminant, et saepe cubilibus altis
nescio qua praeter solitum dulcedine laeti
inter se in foliis strepitant; iuuat imbribus actis
progeniem paruam dulcisque reuisere nidos.
haud equidem credo, quia sit diuinitus illis   415

ingenium aut rerum fato prudentia maior;
uerum ubi tempestas et caeli mobilis umor
mutauere uias et Iuppiter uuidus Austris
denset erant quae rara modo, et quae densa relaxat,
uertuntur species animorum, et pectora motus   420
nunc alios, alios dum nubila uentus agebat,
concipiunt: hinc ille auium concentus in agris
et laetae pecudes et ouantes gutture corui.

   Si uero solem ad rapidum lunasque sequentis
ordine respicies, numquam te crastina fallet   425
hora, neque insidiis noctis capiere serenae.
luna reuertentis cum primum colligit ignis,
si nigrum obscuro comprenderit aëra cornu,
maximus agricolis pelagoque parabitur imber;
at si uirgineum suffuderit ore ruborem,   430
uentus erit: uento semper rubet aurea Phoebe;
sin ortu quarto (namque is certissimus auctor)
pura neque obtunsis per caelum cornibus ibit,
totus et ille dies et qui nascentur ab illo
exactum ad mensem pluuia uentisque carebunt,   435
uotaque seruati soluent in litore nautae
Glauco et Panopeae et Inoo Melicertae.

   Sol quoque et exoriens et cum se condet in undas
signa dabit; solem certissima signa sequentur,
et quae mane refert et quae surgentibus astris.   440
ille ubi nascentem maculis uariauerit ortum
conditus in nubem medioque refugerit orbe,
suspecti tibi sint imbres: namque urget ab alto
arboribusque satisque Notus pecorique sinister;
aut ubi sub lucem densa inter nubila sese   445
diuersi rumpent radii, aut ubi pallida surget
Tithoni croceum linquens Aurora cubile,
heu, male tum mitis defendet pampinus uuas:
tam multa in tectis crepitans salit horrida grando.
hoc etiam, emenso cum iam decedit Olympo,   450

profuerit meminisse magis; nam saepe uidemus
ipsius in uultu uarios errare colores:
caeruleus pluuiam denuntiat, igneus Euros;
sin maculae incipiunt rutilo immiscerier igni,
omnia tum pariter uento nimbisque uidebis   455
feruere: non illa quisquam me nocte per altum
ire neque a terra moneat conuellere funem.
at si, cum referetque diem condetque relatum,
lucidus orbis erit, frustra terrebere nimbis
et claro siluas cernes Aquilone moueri.   460
denique, quid Vesper serus uehat, unde serenas
uentus agat nubes, quid cogitet umidus Auster,
sol tibi signa dabit. solem quis dicere falsum
audeat? ille etiam caecos instare tumultus
saepe monet fraudemque et operta tumescere bella;   465
ille etiam exstincto miseratus Caesare Romam,
cum caput obscura nitidum ferrugine texit
impiaque aeternam timuerunt saecula noctem.
tempore quamquam illo tellus quoque et aequora ponti,
obscenaeque canes importunaeque uolucres   470
signa dabant. quotiens Cyclopum efferuere in agros
uidimus undantem ruptis fornacibus Aetnam,
flammarumque globos liquefactaque uoluere saxa!
armorum sonitum toto Germania caelo
audiit, insolitis tremuerunt motibus Alpes.   475
uox quoque per lucos uulgo exaudita silentis
ingens, et simulacra modis pallentia miris
uisa sub obscurum noctis, pecudesque locutae
(infandum!); sistunt amnes terraeque dehiscunt,
et maestum inlacrimat templis ebur aeraque sudant.   480
proluit insano contorquens uertice siluas
fluuiorum rex Eridanus camposque per omnis
cum stabulis armenta tulit. nec tempore eodem
tristibus aut extis fibrae apparere minaces
aut puteis manare cruor cessauit, et altae   485

per noctem resonare lupis ululantibus urbes.
non alias caelo ceciderunt plura sereno
fulgura nec diri totiens arsere cometae.
ergo inter sese paribus concurrere telis
Romanas acies iterum uidere Philippi;   490
nec fuit indignum superis bis sanguine nostro
Emathiam et latos Haemi pinguescere campos.
scilicet et tempus ueniet, cum finibus illis
agricola incuruo terram molitus aratro
exesa inueniet scabra robigine pila,   495
aut grauibus rastris galeas pulsabit inanis
grandiaque effossis mirabitur ossa sepulcris.
di patrii Indigetes et Romule Vestaque mater,
quae Tuscum Tiberim et Romana Palatia seruas,
hunc saltem euerso iuuenem succurrere saeclo   500
ne prohibete! satis iam pridem sanguine nostro
Laomedonteae luimus periuria Troiae;
iam pridem nobis caeli te regia, Caesar,
inuidet atque hominum queritur curare triumphos,
quippe ubi fas uersum atque nefas: tot bella per orbem,   505
tam multae scelerum facies, non ullus aratro
dignus honos, squalent abductis arua colonis,
et curuae rigidum falces conflantur in ensem.
hinc mouet Euphrates, illinc Germania bellum;
uicinae ruptis inter se legibus urbes   510
arma ferunt; saeuit toto Mars impius orbe,
ut cum carceribus sese effudere quadrigae,
addunt in spatia, et frustra retinacula tendens
fertur equis auriga neque audit currus habenas.

GEORGICON II

Hactenus aruorum cultus et sidera caeli;
nunc te, Bacche, canam, nec non siluestria tecum
uirgulta et prolem tarde crescentis oliuae.

huc, pater o Lenaee: tuis hic omnia plena
muneribus, tibi pampineo grauidus autumno   5
floret ager, spumat plenis uindemia labris;
huc, pater o Lenaee, ueni, nudataque musto
tinge nouo mecum dereptis crura coturnis.
　　Principio arboribus uaria est natura creandis.
namque aliae nullis hominum cogentibus ipsae   10
sponte sua ueniunt camposque et flumina late
curua tenent, ut molle siler lentaeque genistae,
populus et glauca canentia fronde salicta;
pars autem posito surgunt de semine, ut altae
castaneae, nemorumque Ioui quae maxima frondet   15
aesculus, atque habitae Grais oracula quercus.
pullulat ab radice aliis densissima silua,
ut cerasis ulmisque; etiam Parnasia laurus
parua sub ingenti matris se subicit umbra.
hos natura modos primum dedit, his genus omne   20
siluarum fruticumque uiret nemorumque sacrorum.
sunt alii, quos ipse uia sibi repperit usus:
hic plantas tenero abscindens de corpore matrum
deposuit sulcis, hic stirpes obruit aruo,
quadrifidasque sudes et acuto robore uallos.   25
siluarumque aliae pressos propaginis arcus
exspectant et uiua sua plantaria terra;
nil radicis egent aliae, summumque putator
haud dubitat terrae referens mandare cacumen.
quin et caudicibus sectis (mirabile dictu)   30
truditur e sicco radix oleagina ligno;
et saepe alterius ramos impune uidemus
uertere in alterius, mutatamque insita mala
ferre pirum, et prunis lapidosa rubescere corna.
　　Quare agite o proprios generatim discite cultus,   35
agricolae, fructusque feros mollite colendo,
neu segnes iaceant terrae. iuuat Ismara Baccho
conserere atque olea magnum uestire Taburnum.

tuque ades inceptumque una decurre laborem,
o decus, o famae merito pars maxima nostrae,   40
Maecenas, pelagoque uolans da uela patenti.
non ego cuncta meis amplecti uersibus opto,
non mihi si linguae centum sint oraque centum,
ferrea uox. ades et primi lege litoris oram;
in manibus terrae. non hic te carmine ficto   45
atque per ambages et longa exorsa tenebo.
    Sponte sua quae se tollunt in luminis oras,
infecunda quidem, sed laeta et fortia surgunt;
quippe solo natura subest. tamen haec quoque, si quis
inserat aut scrobibus mandet mutata subactis,   50
exuerint siluestrem animum, cultuque frequenti
in quascumque uoces artis haud tarda sequentur.
nec non et, sterilis quae stirpibus exit ab imis,
hoc faciat, uacuos si sit digesta per agros;
nunc altae frondes et rami matris opacant   55
crescentique adimunt fetus uruntque ferentem.
iam quae seminibus iactis se sustulit arbos,
tarda uenit seris factura nepotibus umbram,
pomaque degenerant sucos oblita priores,
et turpis auibus praedam fert uua racemos.   60
scilicet omnibus est labor impendendus, et omnes
cogendae in sulcum ac multa mercede domandae.
sed truncis oleae melius, propagine uites
respondent, solido Paphiae de robore myrtus,
plantis edurae coryli nascuntur et ingens   65
fraxinus Herculeaeque arbos umbrosa coronae
Chaoniique patris glandes; etiam ardua palma
nascitur et casus abies uisura marinos.
inseritur uero et fetu nucis arbutus horrida,
et steriles platani malos gessere ualentis,   70
castaneas fagus; ornusque incanuit albo
flore piri, glandemque sues fregere sub ulmis.
    Nec modus inserere atque oculos imponere simplex.

nam qua se medio trudunt de cortice gemmae
et tenuis rumpunt tunicas, angustus in ipso   75
fit nodo sinus; huc aliena ex arbore germen
includunt udoque docent inolescere libro.
aut rursum enodes trunci resecantur, et alte
finditur in solidum cuneis uia, deinde feraces
plantae immittuntur; nec longum tempus, et ingens   80
exiit ad caelum ramis felicibus arbos,
miratastque nouas frondes et non sua poma.
   Praeterea genus haud unum nec fortibus ulmis
nec salici lotoque neque Idaeis cyparissis,
nec pingues unam in faciem nascuntur oliuae,   85
orchades et radii et amara pausia baca,
pomaque et Alcinoi siluae, nec surculus idem
Crustumiis Syriisque piris grauibusque uolemis.
non eadem arboribus pendet uindemia nostris
quam Methymnaeo carpit de palmite Lesbos;   90
sunt Thasiae uites, sunt et Mareotides albae,
pinguibus hae terris habiles, leuioribus illae,
et passo psithia utilior tenuisque lageos
temptatura pedes olim uincturaque linguam,
purpureae preciaeque et, quo te carmine dicam,   95
Rhaetica? nec cellis ideo contende Falernis.
sunt et Aminneae uites, firmissima uina,
Tmolius adsurgit quibus et rex ipse Phanaeus,
argitisque minor, cui non certauerit ulla
aut tantum fluere aut totidem durare per annos.   100
non ego te, dis et mensis accepta secundis,
transierim, Rhodia, et tumidis, bumaste, racemis.
sed neque quam multae species nec nomina quae sint
est numerus, neque enim numero comprendere refert;
quem qui scire uelit, Libyci uelit aequoris idem   105
discere quam multae Zephyro turbentur harenae
aut, ubi nauigiis uiolentior incidit Eurus,
nosse quot Ionii ueniant ad litora fluctus.

    Nec uero terrae ferre omnes omnia possunt.
fluminibus salices crassisque paludibus alni   110
nascuntur, steriles saxosis montibus orni;
litora myrtetis laetissima; denique apertos
Bacchus amat collis, Aquilonem et frigora taxi.
aspice et extremis domitum cultoribus orbem
Eoasque domos Arabum pictosque Gelonos: 115
diuisae arboribus patriae. sola India nigrum
fert hebenum, solis est turea uirga Sabaeis.
quid tibi odorato referam sudantia ligno
balsamaque et bacas semper frondentis acanthi?
quid nemora Aethiopum molli canentia lana,   120
uelleraque ut foliis depectant tenuia Seres?
aut quos Oceano propior gerit India lucos,
extremi sinus orbis, ubi aëra uincere summum
arboris haud ullae iactu potuere sagittae? –
et gens illa quidem sumptis non tarda pharetris.   125
Media fert tristis sucos tardumque saporem
felicis mali, quo non praesentius ullum,
pocula si quando saeuae infecere nouercae,
[miscueruntque herbas et non innoxia uerba,]
auxilium uenit ac membris agit atra uenena.   130
ipsa ingens arbos faciemque simillima lauro,
et, si non alium late iactaret odorem,
laurus erat: folia haud ullis labentia uentis,
flos ad prima tenax; animas et olentia Medi
ora fouent illo et senibus medicantur anhelis.   135
    Sed neque Medorum siluae, ditissima terra,
nec pulcher Ganges atque auro turbidus Hermus
laudibus Italiae certent, non Bactra neque Indi
totaque turiferis Panchaia pinguis harenis.
haec loca non tauri spirantes naribus ignem   140
inuertere satis immanis dentibus hydri,
nec galeis densisque uirum seges horruit hastis;
sed grauidae fruges et Bacchi Massicus umor

impleuere; tenent oleae armentaque laeta.
hinc bellator equus campo sese arduus infert,   145
hinc albi, Clitumne, greges et maxima taurus
uictima, saepe tuo perfusi flumine sacro,
Romanos ad templa deum duxere triumphos.
hic uer adsiduum atque alienis mensibus aestas:
bis grauidae pecudes, bis pomis utilis arbos.   150
at rabidae tigres absunt et saeua leonum
semina, nec miseros fallunt aconita legentis,
nec rapit immensos orbis per humum neque tanto
squameus in spiram tractu se colligit anguis.
adde tot egregias urbes operumque laborem,   155
tot congesta manu praeruptis oppida saxis
fluminaque antiquos subterlabentia muros.
an mare quod supra memorem, quodque adluit infra?
anne lacus tantos? te, Lari maxime, teque,
fluctibus et fremitu adsurgens Benace marino?   160
an memorem portus Lucrinoque addita claustra
atque indignatum magnis stridoribus aequor,
Iulia qua ponto longe sonat unda refuso
Tyrrhenusque fretis immittitur aestus Auernis?
haec eadem argenti riuos aerisque metalla   165
ostendit uenis atque auro plurima fluxit.
haec genus acre uirum, Marsos pubemque Sabellam
adsuetumque malo Ligurem Volscosque uerutos,
extulit, haec Decios Marios magnosque Camillos,
Scipiadas duros bello et te, maxime Caesar,   170
qui nunc extremis Asiae iam uictor in oris
imbellem auertis Romanis arcibus Indum.
salue, magna parens frugum, Saturnia tellus,
magna uirum: tibi res antiquae laudis et artem
ingredior sanctos ausus recludere fontis,   175
Ascraeumque cano Romana per oppida carmen.

    Nunc locus aruorum ingeniis, quae robora cuique,
quis color et quae sit rebus natura ferendis.

difficiles primum terrae collesque maligni,
tenuis ubi argilla et dumosis calculus aruis,   180
Palladia gaudent silua uiuacis oliuae:
indicio est tractu surgens oleaster eodem
plurimus et strati bacis siluestribus agri.
at quae pinguis humus dulcique uligine laeta,
quique frequens herbis et fertilis ubere campus,   185
qualem saepe caua montis conualle solemus
despicere (huc summis liquuntur rupibus amnes
felicemque trahunt limum), quique editus Austro
et filicem curuis inuisam pascit aratris:
hic tibi praeualidas olim multoque fluentis   190
sufficiet Baccho uitis, hic fertilis uuae,
hic laticis, qualem pateris libamus et auro,
inflauit cum pinguis ebur Tyrrhenus ad aras,
lancibus et pandis fumantia reddimus exta.
sin armenta magis studium uitulosque tueri   195
aut ouium fetum aut urentis culta capellas,
saltus et saturi petito longinqua Tarenti,
et qualem infelix amisit Mantua campum
pascentem niueos herboso flumine cycnos:
non liquidi gregibus fontes, non gramina deerunt,   200
et quantum longis carpent armenta diebus
exigua tantum gelidus ros nocte reponet.
nigra fere et presso pinguis sub uomere terra
et cui putre solum (namque hoc imitamur arando)
optima frumentis: non ullo ex aequore cernes   205
plura domum tardis decedere plaustra iuuencis;
aut unde iratus siluam deuexit arator
et nemora euertit multos ignaua per annos,
antiquasque domos auium cum stirpibus imis
eruit; illae altum nidis petiere relictis,   210
at rudis enituit impulso uomere campus.
nam ieiuna quidem cliuosi glarea ruris
uix humilis apibus casias roremque ministrat,

et tofus scaber et nigris exesa chelydris
creta negant alios aeque serpentibus agros   215
dulcem ferre cibum et curuas praebere latebras.
quae tenuem exhalat nebulam fumosque uolucris,
et bibit umorem et, cum uult, ex se ipsa remittit,
quaeque suo semper uiridi se gramine uestit
nec scabie et salsa laedit robigine ferrum,   220
illa tibi laetis intexet uitibus ulmos,
illa ferax oleae est, illam experiere colendo
et facilem pecori et patientem uomeris unci.
talem diues arat Capua et uicina Vesaeuo
ora iugo et uacuis Clanius non aequus Acerris.   225
    Nunc quo quamque modo possis cognoscere dicam.
rara sit an supra morem si densa requires
(altera frumentis quoniam fauet, altera Baccho,
densa magis Cereri, rarissima quaeque Lyaeo),
ante locum capies oculis, alteque iubebis   230
in solido puteum demitti, omnemque repones
rursus humum, et pedibus summas aequabis harenas.
si deerunt, rarum pecorique et uitibus almis
aptius uber erit; sin in sua posse negabunt
ire loca et scrobibus superabit terra repletis,   235
spissus ager: glaebas cunctantis crassaque terga
exspecta et ualidis terram proscinde iuuencis.
salsa autem tellus et quae perhibetur amara
(frugibus infelix ea, nec mansuescit arando
nec Baccho genus aut pomis sua nomina seruat)   240
tale dabit specimen. tu spisso uimine qualos
colaque prelorum fumosis deripe tectis;
huc ager ille malus dulcesque a fontibus undae
ad plenum calcentur: aqua eluctabitur omnis
scilicet et grandes ibunt per uimina guttae;   245
at sapor indicium faciet manifestus et ora
tristia temptantum sensu torquebit amaro.
pinguis item quae sit tellus, hoc denique pacto

discimus: haud umquam manibus iactata fatiscit,
sed picis in morem ad digitos lentescit habendo.   250
umida maiores herbas alit, ipsaque iusto
laetior. a, nimium ne sit mihi fertilis illa,
nec se praeualidam primis ostendat aristis!
quae grauis est ipso tacitam se pondere prodit,
quaeque leuis. promptum est oculis praediscere nigram,   255
et quis cui color. at sceleratum exquirere frigus
difficile est; piceae tantum taxique nocentes
interdum aut hederae pandunt uestigia nigrae.
  His animaduersis terram multo ante memento
excoquere et magnos scrobibus concidere montis,   260
ante supinatas Aquiloni ostendere glaebas
quam laetum infodias uitis genus. optima putri
arua solo: id uenti curant gelidaeque pruinae
et labefacta mouens robustus iugera fossor.
at si quos haud ulla uiros uigilantia fugit,   265
ante locum similem exquirunt, ubi prima paretur
arboribus seges et quo mox digesta feratur,
mutatam ignorent subito ne semina matrem.
quin etiam caeli regionem in cortice signant,
ut, quo quaeque modo steterit, qua parte calores   270
austrinos tulerit, quae terga obuerterit axi,
restituant: adeo in teneris consuescere multum est.
collibus an plano melius sit ponere uitem,
quaere prius. si pinguis agros metabere campi,
densa sere: in denso non segnior ubere Bacchus;   275
sin tumulis accliue solum collisque supinos,
indulge ordinibus; nec setius omnis in unguem
arboribus positis secto uia limite quadret:
ut saepe ingenti bello cum longa cohortis
explicuit legio et campo stetit agmen aperto,   280
derectaeque acies ac late fluctuat omnis
aere renidenti tellus, necdum horrida miscent
proelia, sed dubius mediis Mars errat in armis.

omnia sint paribus numeris dimensa uiarum,
non animum modo uti pascat prospectus inanem,   285
sed quia non aliter uiris dabit omnibus aequas
terra, neque in uacuum poterunt se extendere rami.
    Forsitan et scrobibus quae sint fastigia quaeras.
ausim uel tenui uitem committere sulco;
altior ac penitus terrae defigitur arbos,   290
aesculus in primis, quae quantum uertice ad auras
aetherias, tantum radice in Tartara tendit.
ergo non hiemes illam, non flabra neque imbres
conuellunt; immota manet multosque nepotes,
multa uirum uoluens durando saecula uincit,   295
tum fortis late ramos et bracchia tendens
huc illuc media ipsa ingentem sustinet umbram.
    Neue tibi ad solem uergant uineta cadentem,
neue inter uitis corylum sere, neue flagella
summa pete aut summa defringe ex arbore plantas   300
(tantus amor terrae), neu ferro laede retunso
semina, neue oleae siluestris insere truncos.
nam saepe incautis pastoribus excidit ignis,
qui furtim pingui primum sub cortice tectus
robora comprendit, frondesque elapsus in altas   305
ingentem caelo sonitum dedit; inde secutus
per ramos uictor perque alta cacumina regnat,
et totum inuoluit flammis nemus et ruit atram
ad caelum picea crassus caligine nubem,
praesertim si tempestas a uertice siluis   310
incubuit, glomeratque ferens incendia uentus.
hoc ubi, non a stirpe ualent caesaeque reuerti
possunt atque ima similes reuirescere terra;
infelix superat foliis oleaster amaris.
    Nec tibi tam prudens quisquam persuadeat auctor   315
tellurem Borea rigidam spirante mouere.
rura gelu tum claudit hiems, nec semine iacto
concretam patitur radicem adfigere terrae.

optima uinetis satio, cum uere rubenti
candida uenit auis longis inuisa colubris,   320
prima uel autumni sub frigora, cum rapidus Sol
nondum hiemem contingit equis, iam praeterit aestas.
uer adeo frondi nemorum, uer utile siluis,
uere tument terrae et genitalia semina poscunt.
tum pater omnipotens fecundis imbribus Aether   325
coniugis in gremium laetae descendit, et omnis
magnus alit magno commixtus corpore fetus.
auia tum resonant auibus uirgulta canoris,
et Venerem certis repetunt armenta diebus;
parturit almus ager Zephyrique tepentibus auris   330
laxant arua sinus; superat tener omnibus umor,
inque nouos soles audent se gramina tuto
credere, nec metuit surgentis pampinus Austros
aut actum caelo magnis Aquilonibus imbrem,
sed trudit gemmas et frondes explicat omnis.   335
non alios prima crescentis origine mundi
inluxisse dies aliumue habuisse tenorem
crediderim: uer illud erat, uer magnus agebat
orbis et hibernis parcebant flatibus Euri,
cum primae lucem pecudes hausere, uirumque   340
terrea progenies duris caput extulit aruis,
immissaeque ferae siluis et sidera caelo.
nec res hunc tenerae possent perferre laborem,
si non tanta quies iret frigusque caloremque
inter, et exciperet caeli indulgentia terras.   345
　　Quod superest, quaecumque premes uirgulta per agros
sparge fimo pingui et multa memor occule terra.
aut lapidem bibulum aut squalentis infode conchas;
inter enim labentur aquae, tenuisque subibit
halitus, atque animos tollent sata. iamque reperti   350
qui saxo super atque ingentis pondere testae
urgerent: hoc effusos munimen ad imbris,
hoc, ubi hiulca siti findit Canis aestifer arua.

Seminibus positis superest diducere terram
saepius ad capita et duros iactare bidentis,   355
aut presso exercere solum sub uomere et ipsa
flectere luctantis inter uineta iuuencos;
tum leuis calamos et rasae hastilia uirgae
fraxineasque aptare sudes furcasque ualentis,
uiribus eniti quarum et contemnere uentos   360
adsuescant summasque sequi tabulata per ulmos.
Ac dum prima nouis adolescit frondibus aetas,
parcendum teneris, et dum se laetus ad auras
palmes agit laxis per purum immissus habenis,
ipsa acie nondum falcis temptanda, sed uncis   365
carpendae manibus frondes interque legendae.
inde ubi iam ualidis amplexae stirpibus ulmos
exierint, tum stringe comas, tum bracchia tonde
(ante reformidant ferrum), tum denique dura
exerce imperia et ramos compesce fluentis.   370
Texendae saepes etiam et pecus omne tenendum,
praecipue dum frons tenera imprudensque laborum;
cui super indignas hiemes solemque potentem
siluestres uri adsidue capreaeque sequaces
inludunt, pascuntur oues auidaeque iuuencae;   375
frigora nec tantum cana concreta pruina
aut grauis incumbens scopulis arentibus aestas,
quantum illi nocuere greges durique uenenum
dentis et admorso signata in stirpe cicatrix.
non aliam ob culpam Baccho caper omnibus aris   380
caeditur, et ueteres ineunt proscaenia ludi,
praemiaque ingeniis pagos et compita circum
Thesidae posuere, atque inter pocula laeti
mollibus in pratis unctos saluere per utres.
nec non Ausonii, Troia gens missa, coloni   385
uersibus incomptis ludunt risuque soluto,
oraque corticibus sumunt horrenda cauatis,
et te, Bacche, uocant per carmina laeta, tibique

oscilla ex alta suspendunt mollia pinu.
hinc omnis largo pubescit uinea fetu,   390
complentur uallesque cauae saltusque profundi
et quocumque deus circum caput egit honestum.
ergo rite suum Baccho dicemus honorem
carminibus patriis, lancesque et liba feremus,
et ductus cornu stabit sacer hircus ad aram,   395
pinguiaque in ueribus torrebimus exta colurnis.
    Est etiam ille labor curandis uitibus alter,
cui numquam exhausti satis est: namque omne quotannis
terque quaterque solum scindendum glaebaque uersis
aeternum frangenda bidentibus, omne leuandum   400
fronde nemus. redit agricolis labor actus in orbem,
atque in se sua per uestigia uoluitur annus.
ac iam olim, seras posuit cum uinea frondes
frigidus et siluis Aquilo decussit honorem,
iam tum acer curas uenientem extendit in annum   405
rusticus, et curuo Saturni dente relictam
persequitur uitem attondens fingitque putando.
primus humum fodito, primus deuecta cremato
sarmenta, et uallos primus sub tecta referto;
postremus metito. bis uitibus ingruit umbra,   410
bis segetem densis obducunt sentibus herbae;
durus uterque labor: laudato ingentia rura,
exiguum colito. nec non etiam aspera rusti
uimina per siluam et ripis fluuialis harundo
caeditur, incultique exercet cura salicti.   415
iam uinctae uites, iam falcem arbusta reponunt,
iam canit effectos extremus uinitor antes;
sollicitanda tamen tellus puluisque mouendus
et iam maturis metuendus Iuppiter uuis.
    Contra non ulla est oleis cultura, neque illae   420
procuruam exspectant falcem rastrosque tenacis,
cum semel haeserunt aruis aurasque tulerunt;
ipsa satis tellus, cum dente recluditur unco,

sufficit umorem et grauidas, cum uomere, fruges.
hoc pinguem et placitam Paci nutritor oliuam.   425
    Poma quoque, ut primum truncos sensere ualentis
et uiris habuere suas, ad sidera raptim
ui propria nituntur opisque haud indiga nostrae.
nec minus interea fetu nemus omne grauescit,
sanguineisque inculta rubent auiaria bacis;   430
tondentur cytisi, taedas silua alta ministrat,
pascunturque ignes nocturni et lumina fundunt.
[et dubitant homines serere atque impendere curam?]
quid maiora sequar? salices humilesque genistae,
aut illae pecori frondem aut pastoribus umbram   435
sufficiunt saepemque satis et pabula melli.
et iuuat undantem buxo spectare Cytorum
Naryciaeque picis lucos, iuuat arua uidere
non rastris, hominum non ulli obnoxia curae.
ipsae Caucasio steriles in uertice siluae,   440
quas animosi Euri adsidue franguntque feruntque,
dant alios aliae fetus, dant utile lignum
nauigiis pinus, domibus cedrumque cupressosque;
hinc radios triuere rotis, hinc tympana plaustris
agricolae, et pandas ratibus posuere carinas.   445
uiminibus salices fecundae, frondibus ulmi;
at myrtus ualidis hastilibus et bona bello
cornus; Ituraeos taxi torquentur in arcus.
nec tiliae leues aut torno rasile buxum
non formam accipiunt ferroque cauantur acuto,   450
nec non et torrentem undam leuis innatat alnus
missa Pado, nec non et apes examina condunt
corticibusque cauis uitiosaeque ilicis aluo.
quid memorandum aeque Baccheia dona tulerunt?
Bacchus et ad culpam causas dedit: ille furentis   455
Centauros leto domuit, Rhoecumque Pholumque
et magno Hylaeum Lapithis cratere minantem.
    O fortunatos nimium, sua si bona norint,

agricolas! quibus ipsa procul discordibus armis
fundit humo facilem uictum iustissima tellus.   460
si non ingentem foribus domus alta superbis
mane salutantum totis uomit aedibus undam,
nec uarios inhiant pulchra testudine postis
inlusasque auro uestis Ephyreiaque aera,
alba neque Assyrio fucatur lana ueneno,   465
nec casia liquidi corrumpitur usus oliui;
at secura quies et nescia fallere uita,
diues opum uariarum, at latis otia fundis,
speluncae uiuique lacus et frigida tempe
mugitusque boum mollesque sub arbore somni   470
non absunt; illic saltus ac lustra ferarum
et patiens operum exiguoque adsueta iuuentus,
sacra deum sanctique patres; extrema per illos
Iustitia excedens terris uestigia fecit.
    Me uero primum dulces ante omnia Musae,   475
quarum sacra fero ingenti percussus amore,
accipiant caelique uias et sidera monstrent,
defectus solis uarios lunaeque labores;
unde tremor terris, qua ui maria alta tumescant
obicibus ruptis rursusque in se ipsa residant,   480
quid tantum Oceano properent se tingere soles
hiberni, uel quae tardis mora noctibus obstet.
sin has ne possim naturae accedere partis
frigidus obstiterit circum praecordia sanguis,
rura mihi et rigui placeant in uallibus amnes,   485
flumina amem siluasque inglorius. o ubi campi
Spercheosque et uirginibus bacchata Lacaenis
Taygeta! o qui me gelidis conuallibus Haemi
sistat, et ingenti ramorum protegat umbra!
felix qui potuit rerum cognoscere causas   490
atque metus omnis et inexorabile fatum
subiecit pedibus strepitumque Acherontis auari.
fortunatus et ille deos qui nouit agrestis

Panaque Siluanumque senem Nymphasque sorores.
illum non populi fasces, non purpura regum   495
flexit et infidos agitans discordia fratres,
aut coniurato descendens Dacus ab Histro,
non res Romanae perituraque regna; neque ille
aut doluit miserans inopem aut inuidit habenti.
quos rami fructus, quos ipsa uolentia rura   500
sponte tulere sua, carpsit, nec ferrea iura
insanumque forum aut populi tabularia uidit.
sollicitant alii remis freta caeca, ruuntque
in ferrum, penetrant aulas et limina regum;
hic petit excidiis urbem miserosque penatis,   505
ut gemma bibat et Sarrano dormiat ostro;
condit opes alius defossoque incubat auro;
hic stupet attonitus rostris, hunc plausus hiantem
per cuneos geminatus enim plebisque patrumque
corripuit; gaudent perfusi sanguine fratrum,   510
exsilioque domos et dulcia limina mutant
atque alio patriam quaerunt sub sole iacentem.
agricola incuruo terram dimouit aratro:
hinc anni labor, hinc patriam paruosque nepotes
sustinet, hinc armenta boum meritosque iuuencos.   515
nec requies, quin aut pomis exuberet annus
aut fetu pecorum aut Cerealis mergite culmi,
prouentuque oneret sulcos atque horrea uincat.
uenit hiems: teritur Sicyonia baca trapetis,
glande sues laeti redeunt, dant arbuta siluae;   520
et uarios ponit fetus autumnus, et alte
mitis in apricis coquitur uindemia saxis.
interea dulces pendent circum oscula nati,
casta pudicitiam seruat domus, ubera uaccae
lactea demittunt, pinguesque in gramine laeto   525
inter se aduersis luctantur cornibus haedi.
ipse dies agitat festos fususque per herbam,
ignis ubi in medio et socii cratera coronant,

te libans, Lenaee, uocat pecorisque magistris
uelocis iaculi certamina ponit in ulmo,   530
corporaque agresti nudant praedura palaestra.
hanc olim ueteres uitam coluere Sabini,
hanc Remus et frater; sic fortis Etruria creuit
scilicet et rerum facta est pulcherrima Roma,
septemque una sibi muro circumdedit arces.   535
ante etiam sceptrum Dictaei regis et ante
impia quam caesis gens est epulata iuuencis,
aureus hanc uitam in terris Saturnus agebat;
necdum etiam audierant inflari classica, necdum
impositos duris crepitare incudibus ensis.   540
   Sed nos immensum spatiis confecimus aequor,
et iam tempus equum fumantia soluere colla.

COMMENTARY

Georgics 1

1–42 Encapsulation and opening prayer

A summary of the four books is followed by a prayer for the poem's success, addressed first to the appropriate deities, then to Octavian. The carefully constructed prayer is a vast edifice of vocatives and their modifying clauses, with the main verbs coming only at the end in four imperatives (*da ... adnue ... ingredere ... adsuesce*, 40–2) – and strictly speaking their subject is Octavian alone (*tuque*, 24). The whole is carefully balanced, with 19 lines devoted to the agricultural deities, 19 to Octavian. V.'s source is Varro, *R. R.* 1.1.4–6, instructive chiefly for its *dissimilarities*: Varro's gods are in part conventional (Jupiter, Tellus, Ceres, Liber, etc.), in part odd and archaic figures who can scarcely even be called 'deities' (Robigo, Lympha, Bonus Eventus); these are the real forces of the farmer's world, whose favour or opposition are crucial to survival. V.'s list naturally includes more conventional figures – the absence of Jupiter is somewhat troubling, for he does appear in the poem, in his role of rain-god (cf. 418–19); at times he seems to have been supplanted by Octavian: 24–42; 4.560–1n. And, of course, Jupiter's cultural position in the poem is somewhat ambiguous, for it is he who will end the natural spontaneity of things, and impose *labor* on man (121–46). Some of Virgil's deities are almost purely literary, important to the *Georgics*, but hardly the natural objects of a farmer's prayer (e.g. Aristaeus, Triptolemus). That these figures are not even named, but must be identified from the functions or provenances with which their names are glossed (and the clues are by no means obvious), is an immediate indication of the non-technical nature of the poem. Finally, in V.'s prayer (as against Varro's) there is a sense of the 'modern' or 'sophisticated', what perhaps provides the best definition of the term 'Augustan'.

1–4 The four books are summarized in four lines, conveying a strong didactic tone, with which programmatic statements are not permitted to interfere (these are delayed until the openings of the remaining books). At the same time, V. avoids the impression of a list by enjambing each line, a concentration paralleled only (and only partially) in passages of high emotional content (e.g. *A.* 2.282–6; 3.707–11). The varied manner of the indirect questions has the same effect.

1 laetas: here, and often in the poem, = 'fertile', 'teeming' (its primary, though somewhat less common, meaning).

quo sidere: i.e. 'at what time of the year'; *sidera* in the same position at 2.1 clearly refers to this instance; cf. 73.

2 Maecenas: V.'s patron and the addressee of the poem appears here, at 4.2 and at line 41 of each of the other two books. He seems otherwise to have little to do with the poem (cf. 3.41n.).

ulmisque adiungere uitis: the 'yoking' or 'wedding' of vines to their supporting trees is a common figure; cf. Cat. 62.54 *ulmo coniuncta marito*; Hor. *Epd.* 2.10 *maritat*; *Odes* 4.5.30 *ducit.* The elm was most commonly used for the *uitis arbustiua*; cf. 2.221, 361; 4.144.

3 conueniat: with the same force, and in the same position, at 255; otherwise the impersonal verb occurs in V. only at *A.* 12.184, in the technical setting of a treaty agreement.

cura boum: *cura*, of all animals, will be a key notion in Book 3 (cf. 3.124n.).

3–4 qui ... pecori 'what care is needed in keeping a herd'; cf. 3.159 *pecori ... habendo.*

4 The final syllable of *pecori* is also in hiatus at 3.155.

apibus ... parcis: sc. *sit habendis*, and cf. 3–4n. The important term *experientia* defines the skill which comes to the bees' society through experience or practice (cf. Servius, *usu nata doctrina*), and which sets them apart from the other societies of the poem. It is a feature of the world after the Fall (cf. 133–4n.). Cf Lucr. 5.1452 *usus et impigrae simul experientia mentis.* Notably the word is otherwise used by V. only of man's discovery of the *bugonia* (4.316), though cf. 118–19 *labores | ... experti*; 4.156–7 *laborem experiuntur* (also of the bees).

parcis: in this quality too the bees are unique (*solae ... uenturaeque hiemis memores ... in medium quaesita reponunt*, 4.153–7) – somewhat inconsistently (cf. 186).

5 hinc canere incipiam: *cano* is used at the outset of Books 2 (*nunc ...canam*, 2) and 3 (*canemus*, 1), but is replaced by *dicam* in 4 (cf. 4.4–5n.). It appears in a contrary-to-fact subjunctive at 4.120, at the beginning of a section which Conington aptly called 'the plan of what might have been a fifth Georgic'. The subject-matter of Varro's second book is so introduced: *incipiam hinc, R. R. 2, Praef.* 6.

5–6 I.e. the Sun and Moon, Varro's second pair, who play an important part in this book (351–468); not Liber and Ceres (Servius). This gives a tally of twelve gods, as in Varro.

7–9 Liber et alma Ceres: the chief deities of the second and first books respectively, with their contributions presented in reverse order, and with old (*glandem … Acheloia*) and new (*arista … uuis*) occupying parallel positions. The two are paired at 2.227–9 (see n.), and less artfully at Lucr. 5.14–15.

7 Liber: the Italic name is used only here in the poem (after Varro?); throughout Book 2 he is Bacchus, Lyaeus or Lenaeus.

alma: as Servius noticed, the epithet is not ornamental (*ab alendo*).

8 The transition from the age of Saturn (125–49) is foreshadowed; cf. 147–9 *prima Ceres … instituit, cum iam glandes … deficerent.*

Chaoniam … glandem: the food of pre-agricultural man, associated here, as at 149 and 2.67, with Dodona in Epirus, and with its ancient oracle of Zeus.

pingui: an important adjective, appearing over 20 times in the poem, always with the sense 'plump', 'rich', 'full to the brim'; used of soil (64, 105; 2.92, 139, 184, 203, 248, 274; 4.118), plants or trees (14, 192 (but see n.); 2.304, 425; 4.183), animals (341; 2.525), manure and the earth's nutrients (80, 87; 2.347), and of the full bee-hive (4.14) – so applied to each of the four subjects of the poem. Also used with grim irony of the blood-rich plains of Pharsalus (*pinguescere*, 492 and n.); and cf. 2.193n.

9 pocula … Acheloia: an apt periphrasis for water, Achelous being the oldest river, and therefore appropriate to the Saturnian age (cf. *Chaoniam*, 8).

10–12 Fauns and Dryads seem a little out of place in a georgic poem, but they are associated with shepherding through Pan (though here separated from him; cf. 16–17), and cf. 3.40 *interea Dryadum siluas saltusque sequamur*, referring to the subject of the third book.

12–19 The literary nature of the prayer is heightened, as V. selects deities, and stresses attributes, which were subject to debate in the tradition preceding him. This, together with the manner of reference (cf. 14–15n.), is a sign of the Alexandrian nature of the *Georgics*.

12–14 Absent from the prayer of Varro (who includes only those figures associated with agriculture proper), Neptune appears as the god of horses, of which race he later figures as the ultimate ancestor (3.122). The feat here described occurred variously in Attica or Thessaly, and in some versions he produces a spring – Servius claims that several MSS have *aquam* for *equum*! See 12–19n.

prima: cf. 3.113n.

fudit: the verb can apply either to water or plants (cf. 2.460), and the stress is here on abundance.

14–15 I.e. Aristaeus, son of Apollo and the nymph Cyrene, here presented as a *pastor*; he loses then regains his bees in Book 4. The manner of reference is Alexandrian; Aristaeus' name is suppressed, and the reader must deduce it from the fact that he farmed on the island of Ceos, or Cea. Such information is not readily accessible, and is found in Hellenistic aetiology, at Ap. Rhod. *Arg.* 2.500–27 (which treats Aristaeus' migration from Phthia to Ceos, which he saved from affliction by Sirius), and Callim. *Aet.* 3, fr. 75 Pf., on the same topic, where there is also a periphrasis for the name of Acontius (ὁ Κεῖος γαμβρός, 'the Cean bridegroom', 32–3). In short, V.'s lines amount to a reference to these two passages. Aristaeus is also unnamed when he appears in Book 4 (*Arcadii...magistri*, 283), the provenance being in that case somewhat of a mystery. Servius claims Pindar has him moving from Ceos to Arcadia, which looks a little like scholiastic extrapolation (Pind. *P.* 9 treats Cyrene and mentions Aristaeus). Perhaps V. found the detail in Varro of Atax, whom he imitates closely at 373–89, and who, according to Probus (on 14), told of Aristaeus.

It is noteworthy that Aristaeus here has nothing to do with bees (4.329–31n.).

ter centum ... iuuenci: as three represents a small number, 300 stands generally for a large number; cf. Hor. *Sat.* 1.5.12–13 *trecentos inseris: ohe, iam satis est*; Plaut. *Trin.* 963–4; and perhaps Ov. *Fast.* 2.663–4.

16–18 linquens ... adsis: the Greek god is exhorted to leave his native setting (invoked also in the proem of Book 3: 3.1–2n.) and bring his protection to Italy, a theme of great importance to V.'s view of his poetry and to the part played in it by Italian landscapes (3.10–15n.). Horace had a similar attitude towards his Sabine farm; cf. *Odes* 1.17.1–3 (where Pan is given his Italic title, producing a very typical hybrid of Greek and Latin): *uelox amoenum saepe Lucretilem | mutat Lycaeo Faunus et igneam | defendit capellis....* See Thomas (1982a) 25.

adsis: V. uses the subjunctive *adsis* only here in the poem and four times in the *Aeneid* (4.578; 8.78; 10.255, 464), always to invoke deities;

the indicative *ades* with imperative force at 2.39, 44 and four times in the *Eclogues* (2.45; 7.9; 9.39, 43; *A.* 11.380 is a true indicative), to invoke human beings and inhabitants of the pastoral world.

tua si tibi Maenala curae 'as your own Maenalus is dear to you'; the masc. sing., Maenalus, is the more common form of the word, which otherwise V. uses only in the *Eclogues*.

Tegeaee: like Lycaeus and Maenalus, stressing Pan's Arcadian setting.

fauens: a gloss in the learned manner (14–15n.) on the name Faunus (the Italic Pan), to which *faueo* is related.

18–19 oleaeque Minerua | inuentrix: the inventor of the olive gets three words; her product fares little better (2.420–5n.).

19 uncique puer monstrator aratri: again no name, and though V. no doubt intended Triptolemus (cf. Callim. *H.* 6.21 ἁνίκα Τριπτόλεμος ἀγαθὰν ἐδιδάσκετο τέχναν, 'what time Triptolemus was taught the worthy art [of ploughing]'), he was surely aware that Osiris was also a candidate (*primus aratra manu sollerti fecit Osiris*, Tib. 1.7.29). He may have in mind the conflated figure Osiris–Triptolemus, on whom see Koenen (1976) 143–4.

20 ab radice ferens: sc. *ereptam* i.e. 'uprooted'; cf. Cat. 64.288–9 *tulit radicitus ... | fagos.*

Siluane: he appears in the poem, with Pan, but in a passage which very much looks to the *Eclogues* (2.493–4n.), of which he is a more natural inhabitant (cf. *E.* 10.24). According to Servius he is connected with the cypress through his love for Cyparissus.

21–3 dique deaeque omnes: a good instance of the Roman sacral practice of 'covering oneself' by an all-inclusive invocation. Varro does not do this, but Cato, whose treatise is more reflective of the religious and superstitious side of agricultural activity, does: e.g. *Agr.* 139 *si deus, si dea es, quoium illud sacrum est ...*

non ullo semine fruges ... satis: their responsibilities fall into two categories: care of spontaneous and of cultivated plants. This distinction, crucial throughout the *Georgics*, finds expression on two levels, the one mythical, the other real and agricultural. On the first, we have the transition from the spontaneity of the golden age (*tellus | omnia liberius nullo poscente ferebat*, 127–8) to the realities of the agricultural world following Jupiter's termination of that age. At the same time, particularly in arboriculture, spontaneity and cultivation exist side by side

and as realities (cf. 2.9–34n.). At times the two categories, the mythical
and the real, seem to become merged, and it is particularly at such
moments (e.g. 2.459–60; see n.) that the poem becomes both profound
and difficult.

24–42 The second set of 19 lines, ostensibly the culmination of the
prayer (*tuque adeo*, 24), but in truth a separate address to Octavian. It is a
curious piece, presumably composed shortly before publication, in
which the *princeps*, his future deification already guaranteed, is assigned,
according to his option, to rule over one of the four domains: earth, sea,
heavens, or Underworld (the last possibility is dismissed). Octavian has
virtually replaced the absent Jupiter (see 1–42n.); the implied omni-
potence seems somewhat out of place for Rome in 29 B.C. None of the
possible reasons advanced for the apparent excess is totally reassuring:
poetic embellishment or exaggeration, the frequency with which heroes
receive deification (normally, however, mythical or quasi-mythical
figures such as Hercules or Romulus), the fact that Octavian's elimina-
tion of his opposition brought with it a very real relief. The motivation
may be in part literary, from Hellenistic encomium, specifically from
the attitude of Callimachus to his queen Berenice, elsewhere a demon-
strable influence on V. (cf. 32; 3.17–22nn.).

Octavian also occupies the end of the poem, where as a mortal he
brings peace through war to the globe (4.559–62).

24–35 The syntax is rather awkward: from 25 a series of alternative
indirect questions (with vivid present, rather than the more cumber-
some future, subjunctives), dependent on *incertum est*, and in apposition
to *quae sint habitura deorum | concilia*: 'and you, Caesar, whose forthcoming
position on the gods' council is not yet fixed, whether you wish ... '

24 adeo: marks a crescendo, and gives prominence to the word it
follows: 'yes, and you too ... ' Cf. 94; 2.323; 3.242.

mox: Servius explains as *postea*, releasing Virgil from the charge,
which he suggests had been made, of wishing Octavian a speedy depar-
ture. Cf. 503–4, where the gods are presented as eager to have the ruler
among them.

25 urbisne: provides a good instance of the lengths to which
ancient grammarians went to support their readings; Gellius (13.21.4)
reports that Probus claimed to have seen this form of the *i*-stem acc. pl.
in a text '*manu ipsius* [i.e. *Vergili*] *correctum*'. Cf. 4.141n.

27 See 470n. for four-word lines in the poem.

auctorem frugum: a curious coincidence (but probably no more), in that *auctor* and Augustus (the title was not conferred until early in 27 B.C.) are both from *augeo*.

28   cingens materna tempora myrto: aptly, Aeneas will do the same (*uelat* for *cingens*) at *A.* 5.72, and cf. *E.* 7.62 *gratissima ... formosae myrtus Veneri.* The association with Venus may come from the myrtle's liking for the coast (2.112, 4.124), the locale of most cults of Aphrodite (e.g. Paphos, 2.64). Aeneas and Octavian are both, of course, descended from Venus.

29   immensi ... maris: cf. 3.541 and Pind. *I.* 1.53 ἐξ ἀμετρήτας ἁλός. The epithet is used at 2.541 with *aequor*, which however there = 'plain'. See too 50n.

uenias: colourless, for *sis.*

30   Thyle: perhaps Iceland, and proverbial for the northernmost point of Ocean.

31   Tethys: as in what follows, V. is influenced by Catullus: *tene suam Tethys concessit ducere neptem,* | *Oceanusque,* 64.29–30. Oceanus, husband of Tethys, and the better-known of the two, is here omitted, perhaps under influence of Callim. *H.* 3.44, a passage known to V. (cf. 4.341–2n.).

emat: as for Catullus, the metaphor is of dowering, this verb rather bluntly conveying the true nature of the institution.

32–5   The catasterism of Octavian (should he choose to rule over the heavens). His constellation will occupy the position held by Libra, appropriately, given his birth-date of 23 September (Suet. *Aug.* 5); see 35n. Octavian's sign is to be between Virgo and Scorpio; on the other side of Virgo, between her and Leo, is the constellation Coma Berenices, discovered and named by Conon, friend and contemporary of Callimachus – whose playful but encomiastic account of the lock's catasterism provides the final episode of the *Aetia* (fr. 110 Pf.). Virgil's reminiscence of this context, through reference to Catullus 66, the translation of Callimachus (cf. 32n.), constitutes a literary, as much as a political, acknowledgement.

32   nouum ... sidus: so Berenice's lock became a new star among the old: *me | sidus in antiquis diua nouum posuit,* Cat. 66.63–4; ἄστρον [ἔθηκε νέον, Callim. *Aet.* 4, fr. 110.64 Pf.

tardis 'lingering', because the days of the summer months are longer.

33   Erigonen inter Chelasque sequentis: cf. Cat. 66.65 (the

position of the Coma Berenices) *Virginis et ... Leonis.* Erigone is the
standard Greek name for Virgo (though cf. 2.473–4n.); she was placed
in the heavens after hanging herself on the death of her father, Icarius.
The claws of Scorpio (*Chelae*) occupy the position of Libra, which did
not exist as a sign before the first century B.C.; it is the standard des-
ignation for Libra in Aratus.

35 caeli iusta plus parte reliquit 'has left more than a due share
of heaven'. With its claws Scorpio took up more than the 30 degrees to
which the single sign is entitled; this changes when it makes way for
Libra.

36–7 Tartarus would not expect Octavian to rule it, nor would he
want to; the language of 37, however, is ambiguous: 'nor would such a
terrible desire as to be a *rex* come over you'. *regni/regnandi cupido* is a
political phrase of the utmost opprobrium: Livy 1.6.4, 17.1; 21.10.4; cf.
Brutus to Cicero, *ad Brut.* 24.3 *ista uero imbecillitas et desperatio ... Caesarem
in cupiditatem regni impulit.* And V.'s *ueniat* can also be jussive. The words
dira cupido occur in an Underworld context at *A.* 6.721.

38 quamuis Elysios miretur Graecia campos: the first re-
ference to Greek poetic tradition, gently polemical, as at 2.16; cf.
3.19–20, 90, 147–8nn.

39 nec ... sequi curet Proserpina: a foreshadowing of
Eurydice's return: *pone sequens (namque hanc dederat Proserpina legem),*
4.487.

40 audacibus ... coeptis: contemplating the task ahead; cf. 4.565
audaxque iuuenta, referring to the poet of the *Eclogues.*
   adnue: appropriate to a deity; cf. *numen.*

41 ignarosque uiae mecum miseratus agrestis: a line as re-
sponsible as any for creating the view that the poem's intent was to
revitalize Roman agriculture. Within the didactic pose it is traditional,
and seems indebted to two passages of Lucretius: 1.112 (*ignoratur enim
quae sit natura animai*) and 2.7–14 (*alios ... uidere | errare atque uiam palantis
quaerere uitae,* 9–10; *o miseras hominum mentis!,* 14).
   mecum: with *miseratus,* not, as Servius and Miles (1980) 70 have
held, with *ignaros.* Cf. 45 *mihi,* and n.

42 uocari: the standard hymnic verb, 'to invoke', here in essence
meaning 'to invoke successfully'; cf. 347; 2.388, 529; 4.7; Hor. *Odes*
1.2.25.
   iam nunc: i.e. 'even before your deification'.

43–70   On seasonable ploughing

With a rich soil in early spring, with a poorer one in the autumn. For the most part didactic in their information, the lines are nevertheless carefully composed, establishing from the outset the aesthetics behind even the more 'mundane' sections of the poem (cf. 2.1–135n.): *umor* appears in the first and last line, with the repetition of *glaeba* (44, 65) supporting the ring-composition; see 2.179n.

43   Vere nouo ...: the poem proper, like the farmer's year, begins as spring arrives. There is a sense of joy and promise, as when spring brings out the new plants (*Zephyrique tepentibus auris*, 2.330), the flock ventures out into its summer pasture (*Zephyris ... uocantibus*, 3.322), or the bees leave their hive at winter's close (*ubi pulsam hiemem sol aureus egit*, 4.51).

44   putris ... glaeba 'the crumbling clod'; the best type of soil (cf. 65). See 2.177–287 for the treatment of soil types, and cf. 2.262–3 *optima putri | arua solo*. For the thought of the line cf. 2.330–1.

45   mihi: dat. of interest ('I would have the bull ...'), the first and slightest of many intrusions by the didactic narrator. Cf. 456–7; 2.252–3; 3.56, 435–6nn. for more extensive interjections, and 3.8–9n. for a slightly different type.

47   seges 'soil', as at 4.129.

48   bis ... bis: it seems best to take this, with Servius, and against Pliny (*N.H.* 18.181), as meaning two ploughings, rather than four: best is that which has twice felt the heat (of day) and the cold (of night). For the anaphora see 2.150n.

49   ruperunt: the perfect indicates that the action has followed immediately; cf. 4.212–13 *rege ... amisso rupere fidem.*

50   ac prius ignotum ferro quam scindimus aequor: a line which, with one change (e.g. *pinu* for *ferro*), would refer not to ploughing, but to seafaring; cf. Cat. 64.12, *quae simul ac rostro uentosum proscidit aequor.* The near ambiguity (for which see 2.503, 541nn.) is deliberate, for V., particularly in the first book, closely links farming and navigation (204–7, 253–4, 303–4, 371–3, 429, 436, 456–7), and the two share the same cultural status – they are the prime activities of post-Saturnian man, who will soon provide the focus of the poem (118–46), and whose plight is V.'s chief concern. The choice in 'Red sky at night shepherd's/sailor's delight' presumably depends largely on geographical location; and V. links the two activities precisely in this detail:

correct interpretation of, and obedience to, *signa*; cf. 51, 252–6, 351nn.

scindimus: cf. 2.237n.

51–3 praediscere ... cura sit: the weather of the region and the disposition of its land must be discerned before the choice of crop or tree.

51 praediscere: not a common word, and used three times by V. in the same context: 252 (of the weather); 2.255 (of soil).

52 patrios cultusque: cf. 2.35 *proprios ... cultus*. Each place has its own traditional methods of cultivation; see also 2.116n.

53 Another important theme: the world's variety and regional peculiarities. This is developed at 2.109–35, and is a mark of post-Saturnian existence: before Jupiter everything grew everywhere (*omnis feret omnia tellus*, *E.* 4.39), not so after (*nec uero terrae ferre omnes omnia possunt*, 2.109; see n.). Varro treats the same theme, without the cultural discussion (*R.R.* 1.7.5–8).

54–6 The agricultural and arboricultural options: crops, vines, fruit-trees and spontaneous grasses; again the contrast between cultivation (*segetes*) and spontaneity (*iniussa*); cf. 21–3n. and 128 (*nullo poscente*); also Hor. *Epd.* 16.49 *illic iniussae ueniunt ad mulctra capellae.*

55 arborei: adjectives in -*eus* proliferate in poetry, partly as being more poetic than a modifying genitive, partly, as here, because the genitive (*arborum*) will not go into the hexameter; so, for instance, Virgil uses *femina* and *femineus* an equal number of times (10 vs. 11), the former, of course, only in the nom. sing. *arbusta* stands in for *arbores* at 3.328, *nemus* at 2.429.

56 nonne uides: a didactic device, occurring 15 times in Lucretius, and chiefly used, as here, to introduce a following *exemplum*; cf. 3.103, 250. Cf. Prop. 1.2.9 *aspice quos summittat humus formosa colores* (cf. V.'s *mittit*, with the same sense).

56–9 The place-names provide the first indication of V.'s ethnographical interest (2.136–76n.), as he exemplifies the theme of variety with a list of exotic regions and their particular products. The same topic, with some of the same places (India, Sabaea), recurs at 2.109–35.

57 mittit: the subjunctive might be expected (cf. Prop. 1.2.9; 56n.), and some MSS in fact have *mittat*.

molles ... Sabaei: Arabians, like most easterners, are traditionally depicted as soft or effeminate; there may be a contrast with the Chalybes who follow, or at least with their product (*ferrum*), and also with the earth's first inhabitants (*durum genus*, 63).

58 Chalybes nudi ferrum: their reputation as iron-workers (οἱ σιδηροτέκτονες Χάλυβες, Aesch. *Prom.* 714–15; also Ap. Rhod. *Arg.* 2.1002–8) became proverbial: Berenice's lock (Callim. fr. 110.48–50 Pf.; Cat. 66.48–50) is made to curse their race for the invention of iron (whence scissors). Possibly a reference to the iron age is intended (cf. 60–3n.), for this connection is already implicit in Callimachus (Χαλύβων ὡς ἀπόλοιτο γένος ... οἵ ... πρῶτοι ..., fr. 110.48–50 Pf., 'A curse on the race of the Chalybes, who first found and worked iron'). As the *first* iron-workers (a designation apparently due to Callimachus), they are clearly representative of that age. The cursing of the πρῶτος εὑρετής ('inventor') of an evil art or substance is a topos of Greek and Latin literature (cf. Barrett on Eur. *Hipp.* 407–9).

58–9 uirosaque Pontus | castorea: *uirosa* refers to the unpleasant smell, but in that castor-oil was taken from the testicles of the beaver V. perhaps glosses the stuff (*uirosa*); see Ross (1987) 42–3.

59 Eliadum palmas Epiros equarum 'Epirus gives us the Olympian victories of her mares'. The syntax is varied to offset the 'list' effect: *Eliadum* is a transferred epithet, and the produce, of course, is the mares, not the victories; for Epirus and its horses cf. 3.121.

60–3 Variety and restriction come to the world after the Flood and Deucalion's creation (for a detailed treatment of the story, see Ov. *M.* 1.313–415), an act which for V. is the cultural equivalent of the transition from the Saturnian to the iron age (see 53, 58, 118–46nn.)

60 continuo: temporal and thus also logical: 'thereupon', almost 'automatically'; here, as at 169, 356, 3.271, placed first for emphasis, with the subordinate but prior action following (*quo tempore*, 61).

has leges aeternaque [sc. haec] foedera: here specific laws of nature (*quid quaeque queant per foedera naturai*, Lucr. 1.586), though V. surely intends a more general reference: *leges* come only with the rest of the arts of civilization: *A.* 8.322; Ov. *M.* 1.90; Sen. *Ep.* 90.6.

certis 'separate', 'allotted'.

61 quo tempore primum: picks up *continuo*: 'the very instant Deucalion threw ... thereupon ...'

63 homines ... durum genus: i.e. born from stones (62), but also with specific reference to Lucretius' hardy cave-men (*at genus hum-anum multo fuit illud in aruis | durius, ut decuit, tellus quod dura creasset,* 5.925–6). Cf. 2.341n. Moral as well as physical hardiness is implied: so Numanus Remulus of the primitive Latins (*durum a stirpe genus, A.* 9.603), compared to the soft Trojans (*desidiae cordi,* 615).

63–70 A return to the theme in hand: when to plough rich, and poor, soil.

63 ergo age 'up, then, . . .', since nature has imposed restrictions and laws on man.

64 pingue solum: the best soil should be ploughed in early spring, partly to control weeds (69), partly because it needs and can tolerate exposure to extremes in the weather, unlike a sandy soil (70). See 8n. on *pinguis*.

65 fortes: such soil should be ploughed as deeply as possible, in contrast to the weaker type (68).

inuertant: in V. only of ploughing: 2.141; 3.161, 526; *A.* 11.202.

66 puluerulenta coquat maturis solibus aestas: five words brilliantly convey the sun's potency as it warms (*coquat*) the new soil with its increasing strength (*maturis* – which may also actively describe the sun's effects), so breaking up the clods (*puluerulenta*).

puluerulenta: adjectives in -*lentus* are in essence archaic and vulgar, and this is the only one used by V. Lucretius had given him a precedent (*puluerulenta Ceres*, 5.742), as had Varro (*R.R.* 3.16.20), whose instance, however, V. suppressed (4.96–8n.).

67–8 sub ipsum | Arcturum: i.e. in early September.

68 tenui ... suspendere sulco: the soil is lifted with a light furrow, and left 'hanging'; an odd term, perhaps suggested by Hes. *W.D.* 463 ἔτι κουφίζουσαν ἄρουραν, 'when the soil is still light'.

69–70 illic ... hic: referring alternately to rich (64 *pingue*) and poor (67 *non ... fecunda*) soils.

69 The first hint of the toil to come: weeds (*herbae*), along with shade and blight, pose the greatest threat to crops (120–1, 151–9).

officiant: used by V. only here and at 121, where the subject is the same.

70 ne deserat umor harenam: see 84–93n. for the importance of correct balance of the elements.

71–99 Care of the soil

Leaving fallow, rotation, manuring, stubble-burning, harrowing, cross-ploughing. All are agriculturally important, with the possible exception of stubble-burning, which occupies the central position, is treated at the greatest length, and is vital to the poem (84–93n.).

71, 79 alternis: adverbial: 'with alternation', here 'every other year'; cf. *E*. 3.59 *alternis dicetis*.

71–2   idem ... patiere 'likewise [lit. 'as the same person'] allow ...'; for the future (also 73 *seres*), cf. 2.230–2; 3.155nn.

tonsas 'when you have cropped them'.

noualis 'fallow' land which after having a crop on it is then renewed (*nouatur*) by a second ploughing (Varro, *R.R.* 1.29.1). So Pliny: *nouale est quod alternis annis seritur*, *N.H.* 18.176.

73–9 By trial and error the ancients must have hit upon what we now know as nitrogen-fixation, the effect of rotating regular crops such as wheat or spelt (*farra*, 73) with nitrogen-restoring leguminous plants (74–6).

73   flaua: also used, with this association, of Ceres (96).

mutato sidere: i.e. in a different season; cf. 1n.

74–5   legumen | ... uiciae: *uicia* is vetch, a member of the Pea Family, while *legumen* is some sort of pulse; it often (as at Varro, *R.R.* 1.23.2) refers generally to edible leguminous plants.

75   tristisque lupini: the epithet no doubt describes the bitterness of the seed (cf. 2.126, 247), but V. may also intend a (false) etymological gloss (λύπη, 'sadness', 'grief'); the difference of quantity does not vitiate such word-plays.

77–8   urit ... urit ... urunt: flax, oats and poppies exhaust (*uro*) the soil (and therefore should not be rotated with wheat: this is the implication of *enim*). The tricolon (in this case abundans), with the key word repeated in each of the cola, is used often for emphasis; cf. 266–7, 289–90; 2.190–3, 221–2, 323–4, 416–17. This verb also looks forward to the treatment of stubble-burning (84–93n.), which, with almost contrasting meanings, it frames (*urere*, 85; *adurat*, 93).

papauera: grown for its seeds as well as for the opium (*Lethaeo perfusa ... somno*); cf. 1.212; 4.545.

79   facilis labor: almost an oxymoron, given the place of *labor* in the poem; see 145–6n.

79–81 Manuring and fertilization are presented as adjuncts to rotation (*alternis*, 79), but the advice is doubtless more universally intended. The agricultural writers are all emphatic about this vital practice, and Cicero, or rather, his Cato, is almost rhapsodic: *quid de utilitate loquar stercorandi?*, *Sen*. 53; cf. 2.347.

80   ne ... pudeat 'don't be embarrassed to ...'; the Virgilian sensibility intrudes (see 2.130n.), with some humorous intent and, as Page noted, the homely rhythm (an extremely rare clash of accent and ictus in the fifth foot) supports the effect.

fimo pingui: as at 2.347.

82   sic quoque: referring to rotation (73–8), which brings the same benefits as leaving fallow (71–2), but is preferable as more productive.

83   nec nulla ... gratia: litotes; cf. 3.306 *nec minor usus erit*.

84–93 A section of great importance to the poem, but of less, it would seem, to the farmer: stubble-burning, unlike the other activities of these lines, is advised nowhere before this passage, and otherwise appears only in two rustic calendars of imperial date (*stupulae incenduntⁿur⟩, CIL* vi.2305, 2306), and in Pliny, apparently in deference to Virgil (*sunt qui accendant in aruo et stipulas, magno Vergilii praeconio, N.H.* 18.300). It allows V. to introduce a theme which will concern him throughout: the interplay of hot, cold, wet and dry. He gives no clear reason for the practice, just possibilities: (*a*) the soil thereby derives hidden strength and nutrients; (*b*) the defects and useless moisture are thereby 'sweated out'; (*c*) the heat opens up passages for moisture to enter; (*d*) (the opposite of (*c*)) the heat closes off the earth so that excessive rain and cold cannot enter. Apart from (*a*), which is probably the right reason (the creation of wood-ash, and therefore of potassium), each of these involves redressing or preventing an imbalance in the elements. The theme is emphasized by an unparalleled concentration of the appropriate vocabulary: *incendere, urere, flammis, ignem, excoquitur, exsudat, umor, calor, sucus, pluuiae, solis, frigus, adurat*.

When things go wrong in the *Georgics* (e.g. the storm in Book 1, the plague in Book 3, the death of the bees in Book 4), the disaster is accompanied or motivated by an imbalance of the elements; Thomas (1982a) 83–4. Cf. 4.425–8, 517–19nn. on the extremes of heat and cold which characterize the settings of Proteus and Orpheus respectively.

84   profuit 'it has proved useful'; the same form, with the same didactic tone, at 3.459, 509; also 451 *profuerit*; 4.267 *proderit*.

85 The completely dactylic rhythm, and the sound of the two central words, strongly links sound and sense.

urere flammis: balanced by *frigus adurat* (93): 77–8n.

86–91   siue ... siue ... seu ... seu: the style is Lucretian.

87   pinguia: cf. 8n.

88   uitium: for V. a chilling word which implies a profound defect, here in the soil, elsewhere (the only other instances) in the atmosphere (*E.* 7.57 *uitio . . . aeris* = plague), or in the body (3.454; where it leads to plague).

exsudat: the first intransitive use of the word ('is sweated out'); cf. Colum. 2.18.3 (*umor . . . exsudet atque excoquatur*); Stat. *Theb.* 6.208.

90   spiramenta: also used of the vents or crevices of the beehive (4.39).

92–3 Something of a zeugma, as *adurat* has as its subjects *pluuiae*, *potentia solis* and *frigus*.

92   tenues pluuiae 'thin', and therefore 'penetrating' rains, not 'slight' (i.e. 'insufficient').

92–3   rapidiue potentia solis | acrior: cf. Hes. *W.D.* 414 μένος ὀξέος ἠελίοιο, 'the piercing force of the sun'; cf. also 2.321 *rapidus Sol*, 373 *solemque potentem*.

penetrabile frigus: from Lucr. 1.494, *penetraleque frigus*. Adjectives in -*bilis* are by derivation passive, but in poetry often have an active force; so here 'penetrating', as at *A.* 10.481 *penetrabile telum*.

adurat: with *frigus* almost creating a paradox. V. in these lines plays on the forces of -*uro*: here 'blast', 'wither' (with cold), at 77–8 'exhaust' (the soil), at 85 'burn' (with fire).

94–9 Harrowing and cross-ploughing close the section, both activities sharing the same main clause: *multum . . . iuuat arua qui . . . , et qui . . .*

94   adeo: 24n.

94–5   rastris . . . cratis: two processes are envisioned, as is clear from Colum. 2.17.4: the clods remaining after ploughing are broken up with hoes (*rastra*), then the soil is reduced to tilth with harrows, or hurdles (*crates*); cf. White (1967) 146–8.

rastris glaebas qui frangit inertis: the vine-dresser is given the same advice: *glaebaque uersis | aeternum frangenda bidentibus*, 2.399–400.

95–96   neque ... Olympo: conflation of archaic and Hellenistic models; the primary source is Hes. *W.D.* 300–1 φιλέῃ δέ σ' εὐστέφανος Δημήτηρ | αἰδοίη, βιότου δὲ τεὴν πιμπλῇσι καλιήν, '[work,] that Demeter may love you and fill your barn with food'; V. has imposed on this a reference to Callim. *H.* 3.129 οἷς δέ κεν εὐμειδής τε καὶ ἵλαος αὐγάσσηαι [cf. *spectat*], | κείνοις εὖ μὲν ἄρουρα φέρει στάχυν, 'the field bears a plentiful crop for those on whom you look smiling and with your grace'.

nequiquam: the first in a series of suggestions that without intense work man's efforts will end in failure (155–9, 191–2); in each the thought and diction is parallel, with the key word *nequiquam* as here and at 192, or *frustra* at 158. These all culminate in the splendid simile of 201–3.

97 proscisso: cf. 2.237n.

98 rursus ... perrumpit: cross-ploughing, done at right angles (*in obliquum*) to the first furrow; V. avoids the more 'correct' adverb, *iterum* ('for a second time'), perhaps because it is precisely what we expect, the technical term for cross-ploughing being *iterare*: *si proscideris, offringi oportet, id est iterare, ut frangantur glaebae*, Varro, *R.R.* 1.32.1; cf. also 1.29.2; Cic. *De Orat.* 2.131. Horace's famous line, *cras ingens iterabimus aequor* (*Odes* 1.7.32), a good instance of the merging of navigational and agricultural diction, is metaphorical in precisely this sense (cf. Nisbet – Hubbard *ad loc*).

99 exercetque ... tellurem: cf. Hor. *Epd.* 2.3 *paterna rura ... exercet*.

imperat aruis: the first use of military language (*exercetque* begins the metaphor) to define the relationship between agrarian man and his task; cf. 104–5, 125, 155 and 160–75nn. The farmer and the soldier are brought into contact at 496 (see n.), and such language plays a particularly crucial part in Book 2 (2.23n.). The line is reshaped at 2.369–70 *dura | exerce imperia*.

100–17   Irrigation, grazing down and drainage

The balance of wet and dry, a condition vital for success. The activities of these lines are presented through a neat syntactical progression (*quid dicam ... qui | quid qui | quique*), with seven lines for irrigation (104–10), seven for grazing down and drainage (111–17). Homeric adaptation (104–10n.) balances Hesiodic (111–17, 111nn.).

100 solstitia: i.e. summers (as at *E.* 7.47); moist summers and dry winters are best.

101 agricolae: addressed as a group only here and at 2.36; cf., however, 3.288 *coloni*.

hiberno laetissima puluere farra: Macrobius records a rustic song, allegedly from the first book composed in Latin: *hiberno puluere, uerno luto, grandia farra, camille, metes, Sat.* 5.20.18. V.'s alteration (*laetissima* for *grandia*) is slight, but significant (1.1n.).

102–3 nullo ... messis 'under no [other] tillage does Mysia so parade itself, and at such a time [sc. *hoc cultu*] Gargara itself marvels at its own harvests'. The fertility of Asia is proverbial, and when the conditions are right it becomes almost miraculous (so *mirantur*, on which see 2.82n.). Mysia and Gargara (3.269–70n.) specify the region of the Troad, and may well be chosen to provide a transition to the Homeric adaptation which follows; so Ross (1987) 48–51.

104–10 A *tour de force*, as V., commending a necessary but essentially mundane practice, irrigation, embarks on the first of many extended literary adaptations in the poem; the simile from the *Iliad* (21.257–62), which exemplifies Achilles' struggle with the river Scamander, needs to be quoted:

> ὡς δ' ὅτ' ἀνὴρ ὀχετηγὸς ἀπὸ κρήνης μελανύδρου
> ἂμ φυτὰ καὶ κήπους ὕδατι ῥόον ἡγεμονεύηι
> χερσὶ μάκελλαν ἔχων, ἀμάρης ἐξ ἔχματα βάλλων·
> τοῦ μέν τε προρέοντος ὑπὸ ψηφῖδες ἅπασαι   260
> ὀχλεῦνται· τὸ δέ τ' ὦκα κατειβόμενον κελαρύζει
> χώρωι ἔνι προαλεῖ, φθάνει δέ τε καὶ τὸν ἄγοντα.

'As a man conducting a channel from a spring of dark water guides the stream among his plants and his gardens, a mattock in hand as he knocks down the blockages in the conduit. And as it flows on all the pebbles are swept away, as the dripping water suddenly spurts out on a steep place, and outstrips the man who is guiding it.'

First, a general observation: the Homeric simile, which, as often, comes from the poet's everyday world and therefore contrasts with the epic society which it exemplifies, has become V.'s reality. Indeed, V. elsewhere reverses the process entirely, using an epic or military simile to depict his georgic reality (2.279–83n.); and in the *Aeneid* reverts to the Homeric method, with agricultural simile elucidating heroic action (e.g. 12.715–22) – the simile in that case having once served as the reality of the *Georgics* (3.217–18 and n.); cf. also 4.162–9, 170–5nn.

V.'s imitation is here fairly straightforward (cf. the complexity of 1.231–58, for instance), but two original features are introduced: (*a*) military language (104–5; cf. 99, 160nn.) – for the reader who recalls the Homeric narrative context (which is not mentioned: the Alexandrian poet at work again?), the impression of this act as one of virtual warfare will be even stronger; moreover, the Virgilian battle is to be fought against nature, just as Achilles struggled against a natural force, the river; (*b*) the other theme which here concerns him, the necessity for balance of the elements (107, 110).

104   iacto ... semine: cf. 2.14n.

104–5   comminus ... insequitur, ... ruit: on the military language see 99, 104–10, 160nn.

105   cumulosque ruit male pinguis harenae: here the farmer first lays low mounds of sand; in Homer he cleared away blockages (ἔχματα) *after* commencing irrigation. V. has suppressed the Homeric mattock (χερσὶ μάκελλαν ἔχων), reducing the sense of a purely agricultural act.

106   fluuium ... riuosque sequentis: hendiadys, with *sequentis* ἀπὸ κοινοῦ: 'the following streams of the river'.

inducit: irrigation brings water in, drainage removes it (*deducit*, 114); cf. 269n.

**107   Severe drought (*exustus, morientibus, aestuat*) is the motivation; Homer does not mention heat, a central concern of V. (84–93, 104–10nn.).

108   ecce: a highly dramatic interjection, used sparingly in the *Georgics* (otherwise at 1.407 and 3.515) to interrupt a current action or state of affairs with a new, arresting development: 'the fields are burning with drought when, look! over the slope comes a channel of water'. Cf. *A.* 2.203, where Laocoon is occupied with sacrifices to Neptune: *ecce autem gemini a Tenedo ...*

supercilio cliuosi tramitis undam | elicit: a good instance of V.'s ability to invigorate his model: cf. *Il.* 21.262 χώρωι ἔνι προαλεῖ, 'in a sloping place'. This is the first occurrence of *cliuosus* (also at 2.212).

109   elicit: a favoured emphatic device: a dactylic verb at the beginning of the line, followed by a strong break (diaeresis); cf. 326, 333; 2.210; 3.389, 422, 516 (515 also begins with *ecce*), 543; 4.107.

110   scatebrisque: the rare noun, = a 'jet', or 'gush' of water (it appears before V. only at Acc. *trag.* fr. 505 R.), imitates in rarity, metrical shape (virtually) and meaning Homer's κελαρύζει.

arentia temperat arua: as at 84–93 (see n.), the aim is for balance, the root and active meaning of *tempero* (cf. 237–8n.).

111–17   Two activities are covered: grazing down the young crops, and drainage. Why allow the former to intrude between the natural opposites, irrigation and drainage? Elsewhere (2.251–2) excessive moisture generates excessive growth, so the two are connected, but the real answer is perhaps literary: the transitional topic allows an imitation of Hesiod (111n.), balancing the Homeric imitation of the preceding lines.

111   ne grauidis procumbat culmus aristis: a reminiscence of Hes. *W.D.* 473 (ἀδροσύνηι στάχυες νεύοιεν ἔραζε, 'your ears of corn will bow to the ground with fullness'), seen by that poet as a positive sign of plenty. Taken literally it would render harvesting impossible, and V. perhaps intends a correction (cf. 2.412–13n. for similar reversal of the model, also Hesiod). Excessive fertility (cf. *luxuriem*, 112, with its ethical overtones, and recalling Hesiodic ὕβρις?) is no more desirable than scanty production (cf. 191; 2.252–3; 3.135nn.).

114   'draws off the gathered moisture with thirsty sand' rather than 'from the spongy soil' (a difficult sense for *harena* and unlikely, given 105); *harena* is abl. of means (Page), though it is tempting to connect it to the pre-verb *de-* (see 480n. for a similar phenomenon). *deducit* picks up *inducit* (106n.).

bibula: cf. 2.348n.

115   praesertim: cf. 2.310n.

incertis ... mensibus: the first hint of the threat posed by the uncertainty of spring and autumn, a threat which will be realized in the storm which sweeps away man's works at 311–34 (*tempestates autumni ... imbriferum uer*).

117   A 'golden' line. The term is used indiscriminately of chiastic (as here: A–a–V–n–N) and non-chiastic order (as, e.g., at 190: A–a–V–N–n). At 2.387 (but only there in this poem) the nouns precede the verb and the adjectives follow. Smaller, uninflected, words (such as *unde* in this line) hardly disturb the pattern. V. is more sparing in his use of such patterns than Catullus and the poets of the *Ciris* and *Moretum* (see Kenney (1984) xliv–xlv), and particularly favours them, as here, as clausulae: cf. 190, 251, 266, 468, 497; 2.198, 362, 387, 390, 465, 522, 540; 3.25, 178, 330, 399, 448, 469, 487; 4.302, 366, 417, 506. Cf. 2.531n. for the equally ordered arrangement, N–a–V–A–n – a 'silver' (though in fact not less artful) line?

sudant umore: cf. 88 *exsudat ... umor*.

118–46   The transition of the ages and advent of labor

Mention of other threats to man's success leads into the first 'digression' of the poem, the so-called theodicy, relating Jupiter's curtailing of the golden age of Saturn, and his imposition of *labor* on man. The spontaneously beneficent world of the Fourth Eclogue has gone, replaced by the reality of toil and by the possibility of failure, and it is that reality which concerns Virgil throughout the *Georgics*, one which he unequivocally establishes early in the poem. When elements of the golden age return (2.136–7, 458–542; 3.537–45) they must be considered in the light of the cultural system defined here and operative throughout.

The details in the description of the two ages are traditional (cf. Hes. *W.D.* 109–200; Arat. *Phaen.* 96–136; *E.* 4.18–45; Hor. *Epd.* 16.41–66; and the most accessible straightforward account, Ov. *M.* 1.89–150), but V.'s treatment is initially distinct in two ways: there is no overt mention of a metallic age, and the latter age, the time of Jupiter, is characterized almost solely by its commitment to *labor* (cf. 145–6n.) – moral judgement, the focus of all other versions, is restricted to the most difficult, and perhaps the most important, word of the poem: *improbus* (145–6 and n.). The lines may also be indebted to Calvus (*Schol. Bern. ad* 1.125 = p. 87 Morel): *dicunt Iouem commutasse omnia, cum bonus a malo non discerneretur, terra omnia liberius ferente, quod Caluus canit*; cf. the wording of 128.

118–21 Though knowledge of ploughing, irrigation, etc. may be gained, still harm can come from geese, cranes, chicory or shade; that has been the way of things since Jupiter brought the Saturnian age to a close (121–46). The litotes *nec ... nihil* emphasizes the threat.

118   tamen: cf. 2.418n.

hominumque boumque labores: cf. Hom. *Od.* 10.98 οὔτε βοῶν οὔτ' ἀνδρῶν φαίνετο ἔργα, 'the workings of oxen and of men were not seen', though V. may intend a conflation of Homeric ἔργα ἀνθρώπων and Hesiodic ἔργα βοῶν (*W.D.* 46).

118–19   labores ... improbus: picked up at the end of the passage (145–6n.).

119   experti: cf. 4n.

improbus: most see a playfulness in this application of the adjective, but the damage caused by birds is real and serious, and the word is always essentially pejorative (145–6n.); the closest parallel is at 3.431, in a passage where humour plays no part.

120   Strymoniaeque grues: the adjective is perhaps ornamental (cf. *A.* 10.265; 11.580), though it was used by Callimachus (*H.* 4.26, the first occurrence where it does not refer to the Strymonians themselves), and the Strymon is the setting for Orpheus' grief (4.508).

intiba: chicory or endive, whose roots are also said to be troublesome (*amaris . . . fibris*) by Theophrastus (*H.P.* 7.11.3). It stands for weeds in general, which V. here as elsewhere presents as a fellow-pest of shade (151–9), and is otherwise used only in the same line (120) of Book 4, just prior to the 'digression' on the old man of Tarentum – a passage linked in relative position as in importance with the ensuing theodicy here in Book 1.

121   officiunt: cf. 69n.

umbra nocet: also destructive of crops at 156–7, of the vine at 2.410, of crops (*nocent et frugibus umbrae*) and much more at *E.* 10.75–6.

pater ipse: so of Jupiter at 328 and 353 (*ipse pater*).

122   haud facilem: the new agricultural age, unlike that of Saturn (*nullo poscente*, 128), has no part in ease, a fact stressed throughout the poem, and to be kept in mind when we meet the 'contented farmer' of Book 2 (*fundit humo facilem uictum iustissima tellus*, 460). Cf. 118–46n.

primusque: both Jupiter and his assistant Ceres (147) are desig-nated as πρῶτοι εὑρεταί (58; 3.113nn.), as was Neptune (12).

per artem: ars (τέχνη) thoroughly characterizes the post-Saturnian world, and the word recurs in the following lines (133, 145). Much like *experientia* (4n.), it too is a quality of the bees (4.56).

123   mouit agros 'caused the fields to be cultivated'. Cf. 130 *iussit pontumque moueri*, a more natural use of the verb; here the very common political sense may be hinted at: the relationship between man and nature is to be one of strife (cf. 99n.).

124   The line has had enormous ethical appeal, and has greatly influenced interpretation of the *Georgics*, particularly in the last century; that the poem in fact plays out the triumph of activity over sloth cannot, however, be simply assumed: that is merely Jove's motivation for the change.

125–46   The description proper of the transition of ages, with 11 lines on the changes actually effected by Jupiter (125–35), and 11 on the resulting activities of man (136–46).

125 subigebant: cf. 99n.

coloni: the word is elsewhere used as a variant for *agricola* (1.299, 3.288), but the sense of 'settled inhabitant' (2.385) may give special force to the line: 'before Jupiter no soldier/farmer [the most familiar type of *colonus* to Virgil; *E.* 1.70, 9.4] subjugated the land – or anything else'. There is otherwise no mention here of the introduction of warfare (but see 143–4n.), the most important detail in the tradition, as for V. himself (2.539–40; *E.* 4.32–3; *A.* 8.325–7).

127 in medium quaerebant: acquisitiveness was for the community. This trait is shared by the bees (*in medium quaesita reponunt*, 4.157) – for them an oddly unique golden-age attribute which is vitiated by the preceding words: *laborem | experiuntur* (4.156–7). See too 4.177n.

127–8 ipsaque tellus | omnia liberius nullo poscente ferebat: a closely imitated detail from Hesiod's golden age: καρπὸν δ' ἔφερε ζείδωρος ἄρουρα | αὐτομάτη πολλόν τε καὶ ἄφθονον, 'of her own will the plentiful earth bore in abundance and unstintingly', *W.D.* 117–18. V.'s verb is the same, his subject in the same position. Cf. too *E.* 4.39 *omnis feret omnia tellus*, and 2.109n. See 118–46n. for the possible influence of Calvus.

ipsaque ... liberius nullo poscente: the emphasis goes far beyond Hesiod's αὐτομάτη, establishing early in the poem the range of words expressing spontaneity which resonate throughout: 2.10, 440, 459, 500; 3.316 (*ipsa*); 2.10 (*nullis hominum cogentibus*). Only the common and obvious *sponte sua* (used at 2.11, 47, 501; *E.* 4.45) is here omitted. Similarly Ovid on his golden age: *uindice nullo*, *M.* 1.89; *sponte sua*, 90; *ipsa ... per se dabat omnia tellus*, 101–2; *nullo cogente*, 103. See 21–3; 2.459–6onn. for the two levels on which V. treats the theme of spontaneity.

ferebat: that world is past; where we meet spontaneity in the present, in the age of *labor*, we must closely examine V.'s motives (2.459–60 n.).

129–32 Two lines for noxious additions (*addidit*); two for regrettable suppressions (*decussit ... remouit ... repressit*). In all, two tricola, decrescens followed by abundans, with a mirror effect at the ends of the central lines: *pontumque moueri – ignemque remouit*.

129 Snakes, or at least their venomous nature, came with Jupiter; cf. *E.* 4.24; Hor. *Epd.* 16.52. V. excludes snakes from his idealized Italy at 2.153–4; see n. and 3.544–5n.

addidit: this form of the verb appears once elsewhere in the *Georgics*, at 4.150, where Jupiter is also the subject, the indirect object being, significantly, the bees, at the outset of a passage which presents them as creatures of *labor*. Cf. in the same line of Book 1 (150), and in the same context, *frumentis labor additus*.

atris 'dark', and therefore 'deadly'; of poison at 2.130, diseased blood at 3.507, the snake's maw at 3.430–1, the tigress at 4.407.

130   praedarique lupos iussit: cf. 3.537–8 and n.

131–2   A negation of the golden age as it is described at *E.* 4.29–30 *incultisque rubens pendebit sentibus uua | et durae quercus sudabunt roscida mella.*

131   mellaque decussit foliis: cf. 4.1n.

ignemque remouit: a detail from the story of Prometheus, and a close adaptation of Hes. *W.D.* 50 κρύψε δὲ πῦρ ('and he hid fire'). V. represents the Hesiodic recovery by Prometheus as one of the *artes* forced on man (135), with *abstrusum* recalling Hesiod's κρύψε.

133–4   Jupiter's purpose: 'that experience might by meditation gradually hammer out the various arts'. *usus* is here the equivalent of *experientia*, on which see 4n. and cf. Lucr. 5.1452–3.

extunderet: apart from *A.* 8.665, V. used the verb only here and of Aristaeus, once as inventor of the *bugonia* (4.315), once as representative of agricultural man (4.326–32) – roles inseparable from the present context (see nn.).

paulatim: of the 11 instances of the word in V., three occur in each of his three major accounts of cultural change: here, at *E.* 4.28 (the gradual return to the golden age), and at *A.* 8.326 (the passing of the golden age). Also at Lucr. 5.1453 (see above).

134   sulcis: abl. of means: 'with furrows', i.e. 'by ploughing'.

135   In shape, sound and sense an almost exact copy of 133: both begin with *ut*, the first three words of each are of the same shape, both have elision at the fourth-foot caesura, *excuderet* echoes *extunderet*, and *ignem* is one of the *artes*.

136–46   The non-agricultural *artes* of the modern age are enumerated: sailing and navigation, trapping and hunting, fishing, and the use of metal tools. The sequential style (*tunc ... tum ... tum ... et ... atque ... -que ... tum ... tum*) helps to suggest that we have here the details of a topos (cf. 2.495–9n.).

136   tunc ... primum fluuii sensere: the same personification occurs when Aeneas brings the first ship up the Tiber: *mirantur et undae, | miratur nemus insuetum fulgentia longe | scuta uirum fluuio pictasque innare* *carinas*, *A.* 8.91–3. Both look to the description of the maiden voyage of the Argo at the beginning of Cat. 64. Cf. *sentire* of the soil at 48, of fruit-trees at 2.426.

138 Pleiadas, Hyadas, claramque Lycaonis Arcton: the three constellations, particularly the first two, were those most commonly used in navigation, marking by their spring risings and autumn settings the limits of the sailing season. V. may have known a (now lost) line, Πληιάδας θ' Ύάδας τε, κλυτήν τε Λυκάονος Ἄρκτον (so Forbiger). That indeed is the impression he may have desired, but wholly 'Greek' lines should put us on our guard, for often there was no model at all (cf. 279) or, as here, conflation rather than mere transliteration: the first half is Homeric (Πληιάδας θ' Ύάδας τε, *Il.* 18.486), the second half is odd, for it combines a reference to the constellation Arctos (the Bear) with the patronymic *Lycaonis*, Lycaon being father of Callisto before her metamorphosis and catasterism. Such allusiveness points to Alexandria, and V. in fact used for the end of his line Callim. *H.* 1.41 Λυκαονίης Ἄρκτοιο, so conflating, as often, archaic and Hellenistic models. Callimachus also had the more 'normal' combination 'Callisto daughter of Lycaon' in the *Coma Berenices* (fr. 110.66 Pf.), though the line is lost and must be recovered from Cat. 66.66. On V.'s method, cf. 1.332, 437nn.

Pleiadas: the last syllable, as a Greek acc. pl. normally short, is treated as long in ictus; so (in each case the final syllable) at 2.5 *grauidus*, 71 *fagus*, 211 *enituit*; 3.76 *ingreditur*, 118 *labor*, 189 *inualidus*, 332 *Iouis*; 4.92 *melior*, 137 *tondebat*, 453 *nullius*.

139–40 captare ... fallere ... circumdare: generally taken as dependent on the impersonal verb *inuentum* (sc. *est*): 'men discovered how to ...' Though the sense is not much affected, it is perhaps better to consider them subjects of the verb ('trapping, etc. were discovered'), as at Lucr. 5.1250–1 *nam fouea atque igni prius est uenarier ortum | quam saepire plagis saltum canibusque ciere.* Cf. 307–10 (in winter the farmer can set traps and hunt); 3.404–13 (on *cura canum*).

141–2 Two types of fishing are envisioned: with the hand-net in rivers, and with drag-nets at sea.

alta petens 'seeking the bottom [of the river]'; elsewhere in V. it means the opposite, 'seeking the heavens' (*A.* 5.508; 9.564), or has the generally more normal sense, 'heading for the open sea' (*A.* 7.362, 8.691).

143–4 The last *ars* provides the climax. Ostensibly V. refers to iron tools, specifically the saw (*lammina serrae*), but by frustrating our expectations of metallic terminology (118–46n.) he invests the opening words of 143 (*tum ferri rigor*) with the meaning for which we have been waiting: 'then came the hardness of [the age of] iron'. As we read on, we adjust the translation, but the impression remains, and is intended. Page sees a reference to warfare ('the sword's pitiless nature'); if so (and this would complement rather than preclude a reference to the iron age), the passage begins (125n.) and ends with allusions to warfare. Cf. 2.501–2n.

145 tum uariae uenere artes: the remaining arts (including those which are to be the subject of the poem) are mentioned as a group. On the heels of the art of agriculture will come its assailants, and V. soon connects the two: *tum uariae inludunt pestes*, 181 and n.; also 3.549n.

145–6 labor omnia uicit | improbus et duris urgens in rebus egestas: these most crucial lines of the poem have been made to say what they do not, so that the poem may say what it does not.

Altevogt (1952) established that for V. the adjective *improbus* always retains its base sense, 'not *probus*'. There may be a quantitative range from 'rascally' (*cornix ... improba*, 1.388) to 'unconscionably cruel' (*improbe Amor*, *A*. 4.412) to 'insatiably savage' (the bloody jaws of a lion in a simile describing Mezentius, *A*. 10.727), but to make it mean 'unflinching', thus allowing the first clause to have a very optimistic sense, is to disregard Virgilian, and Latin, usage.

Alternatively, some translate: 'Grim toil overcame all difficulties ... ' Two objections prevent this: (*a*) in this poem (as in life) toil does *not* overcome all difficulties: the farmer's crops are destroyed by sudden, unseasonable storms (311–34), the oxen succumb to plague *in spite of* their toil (*quid labor aut benefacta iuuant?*, 3.525), as do the bees, those instruments of *labor* (4.184), and, finally, Orpheus suffers the same fate (*omnis | effusus labor*, 4.491–2). In these key sections of the poem *labor* does not of itself guarantee success, and it would be strange if a poet such as Virgil here claimed that it did; (*b*) the realities of *labor* and its susceptibility to failure provide the major theme of the poem, just as, in *Eclogue* 10, and throughout much of that collection, it is *amor*, and man's inability to free himself from love's power, that concern V. (themes which still matter in the *Georgics*). He carefully notes the parallelism: *labor omnia uicit* answers *E*. 10.69 *omnia uincit amor*. So at 3.244 love affects all creatures (*amor omnibus idem*), while at 4.184 rest and toil are the same for all the bees (*labor omnibus unus*). *E*. 10.69, and the parallel importance of its theme, make it impossible to translate the present passage 'Grim toil overcame all difficulties.'

The meaning is 'Insatiable toil occupied all areas of existence' – not a comfortable notion, but one consonant with the Latin, and with the poem, which proceeds to explore man's confrontation of this reality.

duris urgens in rebus egestas: need or want (*egestas*) prevails when *labor* does not succeed (*duris ... in rebus*); in *urgens* there is perhaps a note of hope: man is pressed on towards progress. The sentiment has a history going back to the fifth century, and was for V. most accessibly expressed by Theocritus: ἁ πενία, Διόφαντε, μόνα τὰς τέχνας ἐγείρει, 'It is poverty alone, Diophantus, that awakes the arts', 21.1 (see Gow ad loc.). On *egestas* cf. 3.319n.

147–59   Ceres introduces agriculture. The necessity for constant vigilance against the enemies of the crops

There is a break after the climactic lines 145–6, so it seems best to follow Geymonat in treating these lines as a separate section (cf. too 148–9n.).

147–8   prima Ceres ... instituit: from Lucr. 5.14–15 *namque Ceres fertur ... instituisse.* The verb, appearing in the *Georgics* only here, is also used of the contributions of culture-heroes in the *Eclogues*: 2.33 (Pan); 5.30 (Daphnis). On *prima* cf. 122n.

**148–9   ** The beginning of cultivation is motivated by the failure of the acorn and the arbute (the fruit of the so-called strawberry-tree), spontaneous foods of the golden age, and here associated with Dodona and its oracular oak-trees (cf. 8n.). Acorn-eating frames the passage, placed here before the age of agriculture, and at 159, the consequence of the failure of *labor*.

glandes atque arbuta: the unappetizing pair recurs at 2.520, also with golden-age overtones (see n. and Thomas (1982a) 13); the botanical name of the strawberry-tree (*Arbutus unedo*) provides an amusing example of the state of linguistics in ancient Rome: if you try it, you will eat only one (*unum edo*, Plin. *N.H.* 15.99)!

siluae: variously taken as nom. pl. ('the forest failed the acorns'), gen. ('acorns of the forest failed'), or dat. ('acorns failed the forest') – we would expect *siluam*, for normally *deficere* + dat. = 'be wanting in one's duty towards' (Liv. 1.24.7). The first seems the wrong way around, but not impossible in poetry; Conington notes that *sufficio* provides an analogy, and the resulting parallel of 2.520 (see above) is compelling: *dant arbuta siluae* – the reverse sense of the present passage, if *siluae* is taken as nom. pl.

150 mox et frumentis labor additus: the struggle begins immediately. *labor* here = 'distress', 'trouble', although given the proximity to 145 the conventional sense is also felt: 'distress and the toil which must follow' (cf. 155–7). On *additus* see 129n.

150–1 ut mala culmos | esset robigo: mildew affects crops as the real plague will beasts and men (3.566 *edebat*); hence Varro's concern to propitiate Robigus in his prayer (*R.R.* 1.1.6).

152 carduus: the thistle, as baneful as mildew, in V. only here and at *E.* 5.39, where it springs up as part of the agricultural reversion following the death of Daphnis (and cf. 154n.).

intereunt segetes: so die the animals in the Scythian wasteland: 3.368 *intereunt pecudes*; the verb, which suggests total extinction, otherwise in V. only at 3.544, where the plague carries off even the snake, itself a metaphor for plague (3.419n.).

subit: a verb with sinister suggestions, used in the *Georgics* of the unseen forces of destruction: 180 *ne subeant herbae*; 3.67 *subeunt morbi tristisque senectus.*

152–3 aspera silua, | lappaeque tribolique: V. further diminishes the barrier between plant and animal life when he uses the same words to warn of the threat of these things to wool production (3.384–5).

-que of *lappaeque* is treated as long (following Homeric treatment of τε) in ictus, before two consonants or mute + liquid (so at 164, 352, 371; 3.385; 4.222, 336).

154 Repeated, with a change of verb, from *E.* 5.37 (cf. 152n.). *infelix* and *sterilis*, antonyms of *felix, fecundus, laetus*, etc. imply the complete failure of agricultural endeavour (see 2.303–14, 440nn.).

155–9 The precarious position of the farmer is again the focus (cf. 95–6, 191–203nn.), with *frustra* (158) linked to *nequiquam* in 96 and 192.

155–7 herbam ... auis ... umbras: these threats are recapitulated from 119–21.

155 insectabere: the process is one of warfare (cf. 99, 160–75nn., and 105 *insequitur*), and it is unending (*adsiduis ... rastris*).

157 falce premes: cf. Hor. *Odes* 1.31.9–10 *premant Calenam falce quibus dedit | fortuna uitem.*

uotisque uocaueris imbrem: the first real suggestion (beyond the conventional opening prayer) that religious activity plays a part in securing agricultural success. This important issue will be discussed at 1.335–50; 3.455–6nn.

158 Developed from Hes. *W.D.* 394–5, which states that seasonable sowing, ploughing and reaping must be carried out, μή πως τὰ μέταζε χατίζων | πτώσσηις ἀλλοτρίους οἴκους καὶ μηδὲν ἀνύσσεις, 'lest later being in need you go begging at the houses of others, and yet get nothing'. V.'s adaptation is obvious, but only one word, *alterius*, is actually a 'translation', and he has put it in the same metrical position as its source, ἀλλοτρίους; and both are of the same metrical shape (cf. 110n.). The adaptation also recalls Lucretius, with a characteristic alteration of sense: *suaue ... | e terra magnum alterius spectare laborem*, 2.1–2.

frustra spectabis: recalls the opposite, and favourable, outcome of 96 [*neque ... Ceres*] ... *nequiquam spectat*.

159 The closing frame: reversion to the pre-agricultural way of life (not a happy fate in the age of Jupiter); cf. 148–9n.

160–75   The farmer's weapons

After a brief summary of farm implements (plough, wagon, sledge, drag, hoe and wicker items), V. focuses on the plough (169–75). These lines have received enormous attention, partly because they provide the only extant description of a Roman plough, and few are the commentaries that do not attempt a reconstruction of the device, often including a diagram (see, e.g., Page, who in fact has three such diagrams). Those interested in real ploughs should consult Aitken (1956); White (1967). The plough is described for two reasons, both literary rather than agricultural: first, Hesiod, without the technical detail, provides a model (*W.D.* 427–36), and secondly, V. is thereby able to give us the equivalent of the Homeric 'arming scene': it is the plough (*duris agrestibus arma*; cf. 160n.) that is the chief instrument in man's struggle with the soil. The use of *dicendum* reinforces this suggestion (see 160n.).

160   Dicendum ... quae sint ... arma: the simple use of *arma* for *instrumenta* occurs here for the first time, and, given the trend towards military diction so far (99, 105nn.), is surely intended to suggest all it seems to (at *A.* 1.177 *Cerealiaque arma* the adjective removes the metaphorical impact (cf. e.g. Hor. *A.P.* 379 *campestribus armis*), as does the fact that the usage is no longer a neologism). In *dicendum* . . . *arma* there may even be an anticipation of the opening of the *Aeneid* (*arma* . . . *cano*); cf. 174n.

162–6   The items are all in the nominative, in apposition to *quae sint* . . . *arma*.

162   inflexi ... aratri: cf. 169 *flexa*, where the reference is to the stock; here *inflexi* describes the overall appearance.

163   tardaque ... uoluentia: for the adj. with adverbial force and qualifying a participle cf. 2.377; 3.149, 350; 4.122, 270, 425.

Eleusinae matris: i.e. Ceres (Demeter); so wicker ware is assigned to Celeus (165), the winnowing fan to Iacchus (166), both of whom are connected with Eleusis and Demeter.

164   tribulaque traheaeque 'threshing sledge and drags'; both were used in threshing, being dragged over the harvested stalks to separate the ears of grain from the straw (prior to tossing, which separated the grain from the chaff); see White (1967) 152–6. Cf. 152–3n. on the metre of -*que*.

iniquo pondere: from the user's point of view (cf. *graue robur*, 162; also *iniusto sub fasce*, 3.347, of the Roman soldier).

165–6   uirgea ... arbuteae: cf. 55n. on adjectives in -*eus*.

Celei: Celeus, king of Eleusis, entertained Ceres during her search for Proserpina, and, according to Servius (*ad* 163), was in return taught the art of agriculture; normally, however, this honour is given to his son Triptolemus (cf. 19; Callim. *H.* 6.21; Apollod. 1.5.2).

mystica uannus Iacchi: Iacchus, perhaps in origin an independent Eleusinian figure, is merged with Dionysus or Bacchus from the middle of the fifth century (Soph. *Ant.* 1146–54), and doubtless earlier. V.'s wording recalls the song sung in honour of Dionysus, ὁ μυστικὸς Ἴακχος (Herod. 8.65.1).

167   'Remember to provide and set aside all of these well in advance'; a close translation of Hes. *W.D.* 457 τῶν πρόσθεν μελέτην ἐχέμεν οἰκήια θέσθαι, 'take care to store these up at home in advance'. For the future (*repones*) as imperative cf. 71–2n.

memor ... repones: forethought, vital for the inhabitant of the world of *labor*, is likewise a quality of the bees: *uenturaeque hiemis <u>memores</u> aestate laborem | experiuntur et in medium quaesita <u>reponunt</u>*, 4.156–7.

168   'if the glory provided by the divine country is in store for you in full measure'; a key line in the poem: success depends on right action at every step.

diuini: the sacred associations of the countryside are developed at 338–50.

169–75 V.'s description of the plough is adapted from Hes. *W.D.* 427–36; however, he has radically trimmed the Hesiodic account, giving the necessary details, but removing all asides and poetic embellishments, almost as if his concern was to complete the description as soon as possible.

169–70   magna … ulmus: a living elm is trained to take on the curved shape of the stock or beam (*buris*), a shape which is attributed to the whole plough (*curui formam accipit … aratri*), since the stock creates the overall impression. *domare* is a strong word, also used of man's exerting his will over trees at 2.62 (see 2.61–2n.), over colts (twice) at 3.206.

170   formam accipit: cf. 2.450 *formam accipiunt*.

171–4 To the top of the stock is attached an eight-foot long pole (*temo*), to connect with the yoke at its base, and on either side two ears (*aures*) are attached (these will ensure good sloping of the furrow), and in between these are secured the *dentalia*, the 'share-beams' (from *dens*, 'share'), to the front of which the share itself (*uomer*) will be fastened; this last component is not mentioned by V., since the wooden part of the plough has still to be seasoned (175). Linden (lime-wood) is used for the yoke, beech for the handle (*stiua*), which will join the stock at its base.

172 A remarkably awkward line, with two elisions, and no caesura in the third foot; the lack of break is perhaps reflected by the verb, *aptantur*.

173–4   tilia … leuis: here the linden is to be light (*lĕuis*), at 2.449 it is described as smooth (*lēuis*).

altaque fagus | stiuaque 'and a tall beech for the handle'; not exactly a hendiadys, as Page notes, but rather *stiuaque* is explanatory of *fagus*.

174   currus: the plough is described as a chariot, and, given the striking use of *arma* in 160 (see n.), this suggests that ploughing is a military activity. Catullus' use of *currus* for the Argo (64.9) is also audacious, but is explained and justified by his emphasis on the ship's speed (*uolitantem*).

175   et suspensa focis explorat robora fumus: the model seems to be Hesiodic, but not from the section on the plough; when sailing is over for the year, the rudder should be seasoned: πηδάλιον δ' εὐεργὲς ὑπὲρ καπνοῦ κρεμάσασθαι, 'and hang your well-made rudder over the smoke',

W.D. 629. Wicker and other wooden implements are stored in the same way: *fumosis deripe tectis*, 2.242.

176–203   Nature's assaults on man's efforts

The ways in which *labor* may be frustrated by natural forces. V.'s subjects are the threshing-floor, the walnut-tree as an indicator of the harvest, seed-selection and general degeneration. The whole passage, and particularly the simile at 201–3, provides the first crescendo of the book.

176–7   Possibly a reminiscence of Lucr. 1.400 *multaque praeterea tibi possum commemorando* ... and 410 *quod si pigraris paulumue recesseris ab re*.

ueterum praecepta: one of the very few specific references to traditional precepts (cf. 3.177 *more patrum*, where, however, the *mos* is rejected), perhaps motivated by V.'s close attention to Cato and Varro at 178–86 (see n.).

tenuisque ... curas: V. elsewhere refers to the apparent mundaneness of his subject: *nec sum animi dubius uerbis ea uincere magnum | quam sit et angustis hunc addere rebus honorem*, 3.289–90; also 4.6 *in tenui labor*. Of course, given the poetic associations of *tenuis* and *angustus*, these are scarcely apologetic references.

178–86   The threshing-floor must be packed down to prevent weeds, rodents and other pests from making it their home. The advice is given by Cato (*Agr.* 91, 129) and Varro (*R.R.* 1.51), and comparison is instructive: both give detailed instructions on the preparation of the floor, including the treating of it with oil-lees, and V. was familiar with their accounts (see 194n. and Richter on 178ff.); they then briefly give their reasons: Cato mentions weeds, ants and water, Varro, water, mice, ants and weeds. V. proceeds with reverse emphasis: a couplet giving didactic advice, then seven lines enumerating the *pestes* which threaten the floor; he does not mention water, in reality the most disastrous threat. As elsewhere, he is concerned not with instruction, but with suggesting the fragility of existence in the world of *labor*, a fragility which will be realized in the climax of this passage (197–203). There is little here or in Book 4 of the mock-heroic (cf. 181; 4.3nn.).

178–9   aequanda ... uertenda ... solidanda: cf. 2.61–2n. on the special force of the gerundive in a tricolon, apart from this instance a usage reserved for Book 2.

aequanda cylindro: cf. Cato, *Agr.* 129 *cylindro ... coaequato*.

solidanda: the verb reflects the technical subject-matter; it perhaps occurs for the first time here, is next found in Vitruvius, and is very rare in literary Latin.

180   subeant: cf. 152n.

puluere uicta 'overcome by dust'; i.e. 'crumbling to dust'.

181   inludunt: so Servius, the correctors of M and P and the ninth-century Codex Bernensis 184 (the Augusteus has *ludunt*); this reading, with a strong break at the end of 180, seems superior to *inludant*. 181 starts a new development, with its catalogue of *pestes*: 'Pack the floor well, lest weeds spring up or it gape open crumbling with dust. That is when a multitude of plagues mock you: the mouse . . . ' Cf. 145 *tum uariae uenere artes*, which V. surely intends as parallel (see n.) and perhaps 4.406 *tum uariae eludent species*; also 2.375 *inludunt*, of the animals which similarly destroy the young plants. This reading is also now favoured by Ross (1987) 76.

pestes: not a light-hearted word ('instrument of destruction'); it otherwise appears in the *Georgics* only in Book 3, at 153 of the gadfly which afflicts Io, at 419 of the snake which endangers livestock (*pestis acerba boum*), and at 471 of the plague which will carry them off. In effect the threat implied here, though directed against the inanimate threshing-floor, is as disastrous (see too 184–5n.). Cf. 4.242–7, where a similar list of intruders threatens the hive.

exiguus mus: would commentators be so amused, if we did not have the subsequent and famous line of Horace, *parturient montes, nascetur ridiculus mus, A.P.* 139? While it is true that a final monosyllable may suggest majesty and size, it need not always do so, and the alternative is not necessarily a mock-heroic effect: mice may be amusing to genera-tions which experience them as cartoon figures, but if it is allowed that they pose a grave threat to the precarious world which is V.'s subject, then the seriousness of this reference will also be allowed. V. clearly saw the danger of using the world of nature, and particularly its smaller inhabitants, for the expression of higher and more profound ideas (3.289–90n.), and when animals or even insects take on human charac-teristics (182–6n.), motives other than humour should be suspected (cf. 4.3n.).

182–6   The attribution of human institutions and motives (*domos, horrea, cubilia, populat, metuens . . . senectae*) magnifies the importance, and ultimately the threat, of these creatures (see 185–6n.).

182   sub terris posuitque domos: not unlike the bees at 4.43 *sub terra fouere larem.* The initially subterranean nature of that other *pestis,* the snake, is particularly chilling: 3.416–20, and *A.* 2.472 *frigida sub terra* (cf. 184–5n.).

183   oculis capti 'robbed of sight', 'blind'; so Livy of Hannibal: *altero oculo capitur* (22.2.11). *talpae* are elsewhere fem. (cf. *timidi dammae,* 3.539).

184   bufo: a toad, according to Servius of unusually large size (though it is hard to see what danger a toad could pose). To all intents and purposes a hapax legomenon, the word seems to be Italic, and may come from the countryside of V.'s youth.

184–5   quae plurima terrae | monstra ferunt 'all the monstrous creatures which the earth breeds'. *monstra* does not merely mean 'pests', and V. here suggests an equation (not mock-heroic) with those other earth-born monsters, the Giants, whom he will soon treat (*tum partu Terra nefando ... creat,* 278–9), and who assail Jupiter's kingdom on the mythical level, just as these *monstra* attack the works of Jupiter's age; cf. Hor. *Odes* 3.4.73 *iniecta monstris Terra dolet suis.*

185–6   populatque ... senectae: cf. 182–6n. The verb *populare* (more commonly deponent) seems to be used of animals for the first time here. At *A.* 4.402–3 V. conflates these lines with 4.156 (see n.) in a simile for *human* activity: *ac uelut ingentem formicae farris aceruum | cum populant hiemis memores tectoque reponunt. senecta/senectus* is used of livestock at 3.67, 96, where the world of man is also suggested. The ant's usual role of frugality and industry is here reversed.

187   contemplator item, cum: the archaic imperative of the deponent recurs at 4.61 (cf. also 2.425 *nutritor*), and is strongly didactic; V. has clearly borrowed directly from Lucretius (*contemplator enim, cum ...* , 2.114; 6.189).

plurima: the repetition from 184 is not significant, and the sense here is virtually adverbial: 'when the walnut-tree richly clothes itself...' For *plurima* with this meaning cf. 2.166, 183. Servius took *nux plurima* to mean 'long nut', indicating the almond; *nux,* however, refers to the tree, and seems always to be modified (*Nux graeca* or *amygdalina*) when = 'almond'.

189–92   If the tree's fruit prevails (over its foliage), a bumper harvest is indicated; if the reverse, your threshing will produce only chaff. The information is first attested here, but appears in the later Greek authors Philo and Theophylactus.

190   A golden line (cf. 117n.), and an unusual one in that forms of the same adj. modify the two nouns.

magno ... calore: suffered by the thresher, owing to the huge harvest; cf. 298.

191   luxuria foliorum: excessive growth is always ominous in the *Georgics* (cf. 111; 2.252–3; 3.135nn.).

192   nequiquam: the third of the potential and related failures of the last hundred lines: *nequiquam*, 96; *frustra*, 158; they all build up to the closing vignette at 197–203.

pinguis palea ... culmos: a bitter irony, like 159; *pinguis palea*, 'rich [only] in chaff' is a deliberate contradiction in terms, *pinguis* in the *Georgics* regularly expressing positive abundance of production, as at 8 *pingui arista* (see n.).

teret area: so at 298 *terit area*.

193   semina: of beans (cf. 195).

uidi: with 197 (resumptive) and 318 the only instance of this form of the verb in the poem (though 4.125–7 *memini me ... uidisse* comes to the same thing); this is not autobiographical, but didactic, emphatically asserting the veracity of the detail which follows. See 316–18n. for related expressions.

194   nigra perfundere amurca: a curious displacement has occurred. *amurca*, the *faex* or dregs left over after the olive is pressed, is not found outside the agricultural writers, and it seems to have been regarded as the farmer's cure-all: Cato (*Agr.* 91–103; also 69, 128–30) has what amounts to a *laus amurcae* (useful for plastering, treating sterile olive-trees, as a grease for axles, belts and shoes, etc.). He also recommends it for treating scab in sheep, and V. follows him in this (3.448). The only use to which it is not put is the present one; V.'s admirers, Pliny (*N.H.* 18.157) and Columella (2.10.11; 3.10.18), both mention the practice, but only through quotation of the poet (Columella defensively adds as a source *prisci rustici*, whoever they may be). Now the main use for the stuff seems to have been as a sealant for the threshing-floor, and it is so mentioned by Cato (twice) and Varro, the latter stating *amurca solent perfundere* – the very words of V., who may have transferred the phrase in order to indicate the communality of all these *praecepta*, perhaps archly adding to Cato's already exhaustive list (and see 178–86n.). Theophrastus (*H.P.* 2.4.2) – clearly V.'s source at this point (cf. 195–6n.) – advises soaking the seeds in nitre (Virgil's *nitro*), but no more.

195–6   Soaking the seeds makes chick-peas bigger (Theophr. ὥστε μεγάλους = *grandior ut* ...) and pulses in general easier to cook (μὴ γίνεσθαι ἀτεράμονα = *et quamuis igni exiguo properata maderent*).

fallacibus: large pods may be deceptive, concealing the smallness of their contents.

197–9   uidi ... legeret: the sentence is a brilliantly constructed ring-composition, with the key words *degenerare tamen* (cf. 2.59 *degenerant*) ominously occupying the centre: *lecta* is answered by *legeret*, *diu* by *quotannis*, *multo ... labore* by *uis humana*. The structure negates the slight optimism of the protasis: 'I have seen long-selected and laboriously watched seeds degenerate nevertheless, should man's attention not carefully select the largest every year' (but he has seen degeneration occur in spite of this attention – the slight difference between *diu* and *quotannis* does little to reassure); the logical lapse is deliberate, leaving us only with *degenerare*, and the *sententia* and simile which expand on it (199–203). The diction shows a debt to Lucretius (*ni uis humana resistat*, 5.207; *magno quaesita labore*, 5.213).

uidi: cf. 193n.

199–203   'A characteristic instance of Virgil's "pessimism", and also of the art by which he embellishes his subject with philosophical reflections' (Page); 'This statement of the inevitable degeneration of Nature unless man intervenes stresses once again *labor*, the main theme of the *Georgics*' (Williams) – in other words, a brief lapse into pessimism which will be replaced by the successful application of *labor*. But *labor* has just shown itself *unequal* to the task, and explicitly so: *multo spectata labore | degenerare tamen.* And where is the *uis humana* which can throughout life and without respite row against an opposing current? And finally, where in the poem is *labor* applied with explicit success (cf. 145–6n.)? This is not a passing touch of pessimism, nor is it embellishment, it is the very heart of the poem.

200   ruere ac ... referri: historic infinitives; the alliteration of *r, re* in this line and of *pr, r, a* in 203 forms a frame to the lines.

201–3   The metaphor is matched and paralleled by that at the end of the book, where (also in three lines) the strife-torn world of Rome is compared to a chariot and charioteer out of control (511–13); see too 273–5n.

203   atque illum in praeceps prono: the reminiscence of Cat. 65.23 (*atque illud prono praeceps*) although conscious, is apparently no more than artful. Curiously some MSS of V. omit *in* (P, followed by Ribbeck) or read *prono in praeceps* (corrector of R), in either case, and particularly in the latter, bringing V. even closer to Catullus.

atque: although the usage is found only in Plautus, it is perhaps better to take this = *statim* (as it was understood by Servius, Gellius and Nonius): 'just as when a man is rowing his boat against the current, should he slacken his arms, at once the current carries him off downstream'. Alternatively *atque* connects *remisit* and *rapit*, *refertur* being understood after *quam* in 201, but to make the final line part of the protasis seems to weaken it intolerably.

illum ... alueus: the (channel of the) river carries it (the boat) off; this is better than taking *alueus* as the boat, *illum* as the rower.

204–30   When to plough and sow

Varro, *R.R.* 1.29–37 treats the same subject, and V. has also been influenced by Hes. *W.D.* 618–94, dealing with the sailing season – as elsewhere navigation and agriculture are equated (cf. 50n.). This section, and even more the one to follow (231–58), is peppered with reminiscence and conflation of archaic Greek, Hellenistic and Roman models. It is also given structure by five couplets (204–5, 208–9, 217–18, 221–2, 229–30), highly literary in nature, which prescribe agricultural acts through astronomical detail.

204–7 Observation of the constellations is as crucial for the farmer (*nobis*) as for the sailor.

204   Praeterea: also begins a section at 2.83; 4.210.

204–5   sidera ... [et] dies seruandi: *seruandi* refers to both nouns, but agrees with the closer, *dies*. Cf. 335 *caeli mensis et sidera serua*. The last part of the book (351–463) will be devoted to observation of the heavens. The constellations of these lines (Bootes [in which lies the star Arcturus], the Kids and Draco) are particularly useful ones: the first two have their risings in the spring and settings in October and late September respectively – unsettled times of the year (cf. 311–15); Draco does not set (cf. 244–6), and its proximity to the North Pole recommends it particularly as a navigational constellation.

206   quam quibus: i.e. *quam eis quibus*, *eis* being dat. of agent with *seruandi* (parallel to *nobis*), *quibus* dat. of agent with *temptantur*.

in patriam uentosa per aequora uectis: the use of the perf. part.

(*uectis*) for the present = ('voyaging,' with aorist aspect) is well attested
particularly with deponents (cf. 293, 339). It occurs here chiefly because
V. is adapting a favourite passage from Catullus, the opening of the
epitaph for his brother, *multas per gentes et multa per aequora uectus | aduenio*
(101.1–2), where *uectus* is perfect in aspect, 'having voyaged.' In *A.* 6 the
words are reworked, once referring to 206 (*uentosa per aequora vectos*, 335),
once looking more directly to Catullus, and recalling his context: the
shade of Anchises addresses his son, *quas ego te terras et quanta per aequora
uectum | accipio!* (692–3).

207   Catullus remains in V.'s mind (206n.), though he now has
company. In his poem on gastronomic delicacies (*Hedyphagetica* [?])
Ennius referred to the oysters for which Abydos was apparently famous:
sunt ... asperaque ostrea plurima Abydi, 2 – a translation of his overall
source, Archestratus of Gela (ἔχει ... ὄστρεια δ' Ἄβυδος, *ap.* Athen.
92d). Catullus fr. 1, four lines of a Priapeum, ends with the line *Helles-
pontia, ceteris ostriosior oris*, a line which derives much of its effect from the
creation of a new adjective in *-osus*. V. knew his Ennius, for the name
Abydos is absent from Catullus, and so he has referred to both his
predecessors, in the process coining a *-fer* adjective, *ostriferi*, which not
only matches Catullus' *ostriosior* (which will not fit the hexameter), but
in fact corrects it: this type of adjective in *-osus* means 'full of — ', 'with
lots of — '; but oysters are a product, and V. insists on the compound
meaning 'producing lots of — '. His form is taken over at Luc. 9.959;
Val. Flacc. 1.456, while *Cyzicos ostriosus* at *Priap.* 75.13 perhaps reflects
generic and metrical affiliation to Catullus.

208–9   An elegant periphrasis for the autumnal equinox, the time to
begin sowing barley (*hordea*, 210).

die: between them the MSS and grammarians record every possi-
bility for the fifth declension genitive: *diei, dies, die, dii*. The MS evidence
supports *die*, which is printed by Mynors, while Geymonat and Williams
prefer *dies*, supported by Gellius (9.14.7), whose argumentation, how-
ever, proves little: ... *ut facile his credam qui scripserunt idiographum librum
Vergilii se inspexisse, in quo ita scriptum est* ... (cf. 25n.). The sound of *die͜
somnique* is less elegant.

210   **uiri:** this vocative is unique in the exhortations of the *Georgics*,
and, like *usque*, doubtless stresses the effort (almost 'if you be men');
normally the didactic addressee is not specified, but cf. *agricolae* at 101
and 2.36.

211 'Right up to the border of the winter rain which puts an end to work', not 'to the final end of intractable winter's rain', for that would involve a contradiction, and when the rain begins, ploughing and sowing cannot go on (214); the sense is the same at *A.* 4.52–3, where sailing, the equivalent of farming (204–30n.), stops for the winter: *dum pelago desaeuit hiems ... dum non tractabile caelum*; cf. 2.321n.

212 lini segetem et Cereale papauer: at 77–8 flax and poppies, together with oats, were not to be rotated with wheat crops, since they exhaust the soil; planting them at the same time as barley and wheat (219–24) could prevent this.

Cereale: Ceres used the poppy to soften her grief at the loss of Proserpina. Since the seed is in fact a grain, the epithet also defines the poppy's practical, as much as its recreational, status; cf. 4.131n.

213 tempus ... tegere et ... incumbere: metrically useful infinitives for cumbersome gerunds = *tempus est tegendi et incumbendi*, as at 2.73 *modus inserere* = *modus inserendi*.

215 uere fabis satio: as Pliny notes (*N.H.* 18.120), V. is thinking of his native Po valley; in the warmer southern regions the bean can survive through the winter, and is planted in the autumn.

Medica: lucerne (for whose praises see Colum. 2.10.25), which is a perennial, as can be inferred from the reference to millet, which is not: *milio uenit annua cura*. V.'s apostrophe, as well as his personification, are features which become more frequent in Books 2 and 3.

217–18 An elegant periphrasis for April, with *aperit* functioning as a gloss on the unstated month (*nam quia uer aperit tunc omnia ... Aprilem memorant ab aperto tempore dictum*, Ov. *Fast.* 4.87–9); cf. 3.303–4n. It is in the middle of the month that the sun enters Taurus, as Sirius (*Canis*) is setting. V. presents the phenomena as a complex of advance and retreat: 'the Dog-star sets, giving way to the opposite constellation [i.e. Taurus]'. *aduerso* (in M and known to Servius) makes better astronomical sense than *auerso* ('Sirius with its star turned away'), even though copyists regularly replace *au-* with *adu-*. A 'star', unlike a constellation, cannot 'turn away', and on the astronomy see Getty (1948) 24–45.

219–20 Wheat (*triticum*) and its inferior relative spelt (*far*, whence Eng. 'barley') were sown in the autumn, beginning in early to mid-November (221–2); spring sowings occurred with very rich soils, or when the autumn crop failed.

exercebis humum: cf. 99 *exercetque ... tellurem*, and n.

solisque instabis aristis 'and strive only after corn' (lit. 'ears of corn').

221–2   V. intends a reference to mid-November, which is conveyed by 221 (the setting of the Pleiades occurs on November 11), but not very exactly by 222, since the Crown does not set in Rome until the middle of December. Its setting in Alexandria is in late November, and the inconsistency may result from imitation of a Hellenistic source (Richter); while this is possible, the imitation would have to be extensive (the equivalent of 219–24), and such specific imitation seems unlikely here. The astronomical inexactitude may be the result of literary motives (cf. 222n.).

221   The line has a strong Greek flavour, with hiatus in the third foot, and ending in a *spondeiazon* – the first of only three in the poem: see 4.270 and 463, in which the Greek element is also strongly felt.

Eoae Atlantides: the Pleiades, this being the first occurrence of the plural form in Greek or Latin. Hesiod has the sing. Ἀτλαντίς at *Theog.* 938 (as does Ap. Rhod. at *Arg.* 1.196; 4.475), but for the group prefers Πληιάδων Ἀτλαγενέων (*W.D.* 383). Although the plural does not survive, V. may have found it in Hesiod's *Catalogue of Women*, where Merkelbach and West certainly entitle the section *Atlantides* (fr. 169–204); if so, it is worth noting V.'s rather curious way of referring to the Pleiades' morning setting (*Eoae*), for that, at least visually, is the alternative title for Hesiod's catalogue (HOIAI). A Hellenistic source for *Atlantides* is possible, although its absence from Aratus discourages such a view, and V.'s use of it may be original. Cf. 288n. for the quantity of *Eous*.

222   Cnosiaque ardentis decedat stella Coronae: one of the few golden lines of the poem not serving as a sentence clausula (cf. 117n.), with strong references to the greatest adherent of such lines: Cat. 64.172 *Cnosia Cecropiae tetigissent litora puppes* is a golden line whose opening epithet *Cnosia* seems to have appeared first in Latin in Catullus, second here in the *Georgics*, and whose speaker is Ariadne, soon to become V.'s constellation Corona. V. returned to the line, modifying it for Dido, literary descendant of Ariadne: . . . *si litora tantum | numquam Dardaniae* [cf. *Cecropiae*] *tetigissent nostra carinae, A.* 6.657–8.

223   debita: the seeds are intended for the furrows, from the latter's point of view 'due' to them.

224   anni spem: with one exception (3.105), *spes* is used at critical moments in the poem with pathetic reference to the future of crops (as here), animals (3.73, 473) and the hive (4.162).

225   Maiae: one of the Pleiades and here representing all seven, although V. may have in mind Aratus' list at *Phaen.* 261–3, where Maia is mentioned last.

225–6   sed illos | exspectata seges uanis elusit auenis: *exspectata seges* looks to *anni spem* (224), the hope here frustrated through wrong action. The sentiment is very close to that at 155–9 and 191–2, where the result is also nature's mockery of man. Cf. too 181 *tum uariae inludunt pestes*.

uanis ... auenis: at 154 *steriles ... auenae* were included with weeds; that epithet like *uanis* specifies the undesirable wild oat (*Auena fatua*), a degeneration from the cultivated variety.

227–30   The leguminous vetch, eye bean and lentil are to be sown after the end of October, when Bootes has its evening setting; they are harvested in the spring, and also enrich the soil by nitrogen-fixation during the winter.

uilemque ... aspernabere: 'Virgil's epithet is perhaps unduly derogatory to a useful vegetable' (Sargeaunt); vetch and lentils were used for fodder, and the phrasing is applied to the whole group.

231–56   The zones and man's operations within them

The lines are based, at times very exactly, on a passage from the *Hermes* of Eratosthenes (fr. 16 Powell), the Alexandrian critic, astronomer and geographer. Page notes the difficulty involved in precisely accounting for V.'s system (did he really conceive of a southern temperate zone, and how is his description of the Underworld (242–3) accommodated by a spherical world, if indeed he intended us to think of one?). The answer is a literary one: although the passage makes general sense, V.'s primary concern is to recall precisely a number of authors – seven, from Homer to Varro of Atax, are treated below – and thereby to indicate the range of his models and his ability to conflate and subsume them. See Thomas (1986b) 195–7.

231–2   'To that end the golden sun directs its path, measured off by fixed divisions, through the world's twelve constellations [the Zodiac].'

Idcirco: looks to the previous passage: that man may know when to sow.

233   quinque tenent caelum zonae: as Eratosthenes began with πέντε (3), so does V. with *quinque*. The zones are here represented as celestial, their effects being imposed on the corresponding terrestrial zones beneath. This is not in the Greek source, and it is likely that V. alludes to Varro of Atax: *at quinque aethereis zonis accingitur orbis*, p. 96 Morel (see 237–8n.).

233–4 V. begins with the torrid equatorial zone, excluding a rather intrusive couplet from Eratosthenes (4–5) which encapsulates the hot and cold zones prior to describing them, and generally reorganizing his model.

semper ... semper: in Eratosthenes it was the cold of the polar belts that was thus unremitting: αἰεί ... αἰεί; V. applies the adverbs to the opposite climate, perhaps supporting what he elsewhere suggests, that extremes of hot and cold present parallel and similar problems (cf. 84–93n.).

rubens ... ab igni: reversing, with precise renditions, Eratosthenes' ἐκ πυρὸς ... ἐρυθρή (5).

235–6 'around this, at the ends [poles], stretch two to the right and the left ...' Again V. orders and compresses his source, which had five lines on the frigid zones (4, 9–12).

circum ... trahuntur: a virtual tmesis, given περιπεπτηυῖαι (Erat. 9).

dextra laeuaque: a necessary periphrasis for ἑκάτερθε (Erat. 9).

caeruleae: in sense matching γλαυκοῖο κελαινότεραι κυάνοιο, 'darker than the greenish-blue sea' (Erat. 4), in rhythm matching κρυμαλέαι, 'icy' (10), and perhaps recalling Hom. *Il.* 4.282 κυάνεαι (Nettleship), which it matches in sense, shape and position in the line.

glacie concretae atque imbribus atris: an exact translation: αἰεί κρυμαλέαι, αἰεί δ' ὕδατι νοτέουσαι (Erat. 10).

237–8 has ... diuum: 'between these outer ones and the middle one ...': the most important areas come last, the two temperate zones; and with them comes an intensification of literary reference. Eratosthenes is less visible (*mortalibus ... concessae* recalls rather vaguely ἐν δέ μιν ἄνδρες | ἀντίποδες ναίουσι (18–19)) and is replaced by a reference to Lucretius (*mortalibus aegris*, 6.1 – the reference could also be to Ennius, who uses *mortales* as an epicism for *homines*) and a clear reminiscence of Varro of Atax (*sic terrae extremas inter mediamque coluntur*, p. 97 Morel) – *has* in 237 referring of course to *extremae* in 235.

The treatment is curious. For Eratosthenes as for V. it is the temperate zone that matters most: that is where agricultural, and all civilized, activity is conducted, and yet V.'s description is perfunctory, making no reference to climate, and specifically lacking a translation of the crucial term ἐύκρητοι. This is precisely our 'temperate' (from κεράννυμι = *tempero*, 'to mix'), and in Greek and Roman treatments of climate is always the standard by which lands are judged. Servius Auctus noted the omission (*sicut dictum est, temperatae ex calido medio et frigidis extremis circulis*), as did Ovid, at the close of his own treatment of zones: *totidem inter utramque locauit | temperiemque dedit mixta cum frigore flamma, M.* 1.50–1 – with *mixta* functioning as a gloss on the central term. Now while *temperies* will go into the hexameter (it is first found in Hor. *Epist.* 1.16.8), the two terms attested before the *Georgics* (*temperatio*, Cic. *Verr.* 4.98; *temperatura*, Varro *ap.* Non. 179.12) will not do so, and possibly this accounts for the omission. If so, it is noteworthy that in the lines which follow there are five words with a root in *temp-*, 247–58. When what is expected is omitted, the result may be emphasis rather than omission; our surprise accentuates what is not there. What engages V. in this poem is not balance of the elements, but rather *imbalance*, and the workings of a world where harmony is elusive (cf. 84–93; 2.149; 3.336–7nn.). See Thomas (1982a) 11–12, passim.

238–9 et uia ... qua ... ordo 'and a path [the ecliptic] was cut through both [between the tropics], along which the slanting array of the constellations [the Zodiac] might revolve'.

240–1 The earth is seen as rising up towards Scythia in the north, and sloping down to Libya in the south. The opposition is developed at 3.339–83, in the 'excursus' on Libya and Scythia; cf. too *E.* 10.65–8.

Riphaeasque ... arces: the noun (Ῥῖπαι) does not occur in Latin, and the adjective seems to be in essence Hellenistic: Ῥιπαίοις ἐν ὄρεσσιν, Ap. Rhod. *Arg.* 4.287; Ῥιπαίου ... ἀπ' οὔρεος, Callim. *Aet.* fr. 186.9 Pf. V. refers to these Scythian mountains only in the *Georgics*, where the emphasis is on extreme cold: *Riphaeo ... Euro,* 3.382 (see n.); *Riphaeis ... pruinis,* 4.518.

242–3 V.'s view of the poles is extremely odd; the north pole is naturally above us, but the south is represented as being in the same relative position for the inhabitants of the Underworld. This sits rather uneasily with what seems to be a discussion of the southern hemisphere at 247–51, and suggests that V.'s concerns are literary rather than purely scientific in this passage.

sub pedibus 'beneath *our* feet'; V. is perhaps thinking of Lucr. 3.27, which is related and begins with the same phrase.

244–6   These lines, treating Draco and the Bears, the northern constellations which never set, are at first sight superfluous, for they are hardly parallel in thought (although they are so presented) to 247–51, which pose the natural and relevant question, 'Does the sun appear in the southern regions?' The passage is a close adaptation of Aratus (*Phaen.* 45–8), who is V.'s primary model throughout the second half of the book:

> τὰς δὲ δι' ἀμφοτέρας οἵη ποταμοῖο ἀπορρὼξ
> εἰλεῖται μέγα θαῦμα, δράκων, περί τ' ἀμφί τ' ἐαγὼς
> μυρίος· αἱ δ' ἄρα οἱ σπείρης ἑκάτερθε φέρονται
> Ἄρκτοι, κυανέου πεφυλαγμέναι ὠκεανοῖο.

'Between both circles the Dragon, a great marvel, as it were the branch of a river, winding endlessly around and about; and the Bears, which shun the blue sea, are borne along on either side of his coil.'

The imitation is clear and careful: *circum perque* responds to περί τ' ἀμφί τ', as does *in morem fluminis* to οἵη ποταμοῖο ἀπορρὼξ and *Arctos* (in the same position) to Ἄρκτοι (Hesiod (ποταμῶι ῥείοντι ἐοικώς, fr. 293 Merk. and West) did not influence V. (so Servius), but Aratus may have had him in mind; cf. Callim. *Epigr.* 27). But V.'s allusion is complex, for he has effected an exquisite conflation, referring back both to Aratus' Homeric source and to Cicero's translation of the *Phaenomena*: line 246 says much the same as *Phaen.* 48, but it says it in the manner of *Il.* 18.487–9 Ἄρκτον ... οἵη ἄμμορός ἐστι λοετρῶν Ὠκεανοῖο, 'she alone does not share in the baths [cf. V.'s *tingi*] of Ocean' (cf. 138n. for conflation of these same Homeric lines with Callim. *H.* 1.41); and in *flexu sinuoso* (244) there must be a reference to and 'correction' of Cic. *Arat.* fr. 8 *sinus ... flexos* (the Greek has only εἰλεῖται): V. has inverted Cicero's adjective with his noun, perhaps in the process coining an adjective in *-osus* (this is the first attested instance).

Arctos, | Arctos: this anaphora is not common in V.; cf. *E.* 9.47–8, *astrum, | astrum.*

247–51   The southern regions are either in eternal darkness, or dawn and evening come to them when they leave the north. It is difficult to see how V. could have been thinking of a spherical world.

247   illic: looks back to *hic* at 242, and forward to *illic* at 251, the repetition forming a frame.

ut perhibent: cf. Norden on *A.* 6.14 for the various levels of intent in such phrases (*ut traditur, ut fama est, ferunt*, etc.), which really constitute the poetic 'footnote'; also Stinton (1976). They often refer to traditional views, specifically poetic ones, and are sometimes to be seen as allusive references to precise sources; alternatively they may express *diffidentia*, a means of separating the poet from the reported information (Servius' reading of the present instance: *suam denegat fidem*). There may be a reference to Lucr. 5.650–5, which deals with the same topic.

intempesta silet nox: *nox intempesta* is an Ennian formula (*Ann.* 33, 160 Skutsch), which V. has artfully arranged so as to produce an Ennian cadence unique in the *Georgics* (an iambic word bridging the fifth and sixth feet with, of course, a monosyllabic close) – there are 24 such endings in the *Annals*, a rate of over 4%. The phrase is normally taken = 'the dead of night', though the precise meaning of *intempesta* is not settled; the best explanation is 'unseasonable' (i.e. not a time for work).

250 equis ... anhelis: repeated by the shade of Anchises, which must leave Aeneas as dawn approaches: *et me saeuus equis Oriens adflauit anhelis, A.* 5.739.

251 A golden line closes the description (cf. 117n.).

252 hinc 'hence', referring to the whole discussion of zones and constellations. *hinc ... hinc* is not parallel to *illic ... illic*, 247–51 (247n.).

tempestates ... praediscere 'forecast the weather'; see 51n.

253–6 Agriculture and navigation, here as elsewhere (cf. 50, 351nn.), are linked, specifically in their dependence on correct interpretation of *signa*.

254–6 In discussing navigation, V. seems to have the elements in reverse order: 'when to row the ships, when to launch them, and when to fell the pine [to make them]'. This surely refers to the famous illogicality of order at the opening of Euripides' *Medea*: 'Would that the Argo had not sailed, nor the pine for it been felled, and set men's hands to rowing.' V.'s version is more truly hysteron-proteron. See Thomas (1982c) 154–5.

254 infidum remis impellere marmor: the construction follows Ennius (*caeruleum spumat sale* [nom.] *conferta rate pulsum, Ann.* 378 Skutsch; *marmore* occurs in the preceding line), but is in fact closer to Hom. *Il.* 7.5–6 ἐλάτῃσι | πόντον ἐλαύνοντες, 'driving the sea with their oars'. There may also be a debt to Cat. 64.7 (*caerula uerrentes abiegnis aequora palmis*) which itself looks to Ennius. Elsewhere V. inverts the construction, making the oars the object of *impello*: [sc. *mari*] *impellite* *remos! A.* 4.594; similarly 2.211, *impulso uomere*; for a similar inversion, cf. 430n.

255 conueniat: cf. 3n.

armatas: though *armare* can = merely 'fit out', 'rig', military overtones are heard, and warships are certainly suggested by *classis*; cf. 160n.

256 tempestiuam ... pinum: the tree was used for houses as well as ships (cf. 2.442-3), but given 254-5 V. has the latter chiefly in mind. Cato (*Agr.* 31) used *tempestiuus*, 'ready [for cutting]' in the same sense: *tum erit [arbor] tempestiua, cum ...*

euertere: cf. 2.208 *nemora euertit*, where the violence implied by the verb is strongly felt (see n.).

257-310   Work to be done in bad weather, on holy days, at night and in winter

A brief adaptation of the Hesiodic *Days* (276-86) provides an interlude. Hesiod (*W.D.* 493-503) and Cato (*Agr.* 2.3, 37, 39) give advice on winter work, and the strongly didactic tone in these lines shows V.'s debt to them. Traditionally 257-8 are included in the preceding section, but they provide a feeble closing (Ribbeck therefore placed them before 252). They go as well with the present section (introducing winter work), and are similar in tone to the opening at 351.

257 Nec frustra: the same litotes at 95-6 *neque ... nequiquam*; there is also the implication that failure to follow prescripts *will* result in frustration (cf. 158 *frustra*; 192 *nequiquam*); cf. too 4.353 *non frustra*.

258 parem diuersis: an appealing oxymoron: the year achieves balance through the rhythm of seasonal contrasts.

**259 A clear reminiscence of Hes. *W.D.* 494-5 ὥρηι χειμερίηι, ὁπότε κρύος ἀνέρα ἔργων | ἰσχάνει, 'when the cold keeps a man from his work'.

frigidus ... imber: the combination suggests winter, as well as rainy weather; this is often the force of *imber* (1.211, 236; 2.293; 3.441); cf. Cato, *Agr.* 39 *per imbrem*.

260-1 properanda ... maturare: in the winter the opportunity is given to do in good time (*maturare*) what would have to be hurried (*properare*) if left until the weather improved. Gellius discusses the distinction between the two verbs, citing these lines (10.11.6); elsewhere (16.14.2) he cites Cato (*de suis uirtutibus* 131 Malcovati), who has a rather contradictory view, on the difference between *properare* and *festinare*: *qui unum quid mature transigit, is properat, qui multa simul incipit neque perficit, is festinat.*

maturare datur: parallel in shape and sense to *fas et iura sinunt* (269).

261–2   The ploughman hammers out the blunted share, the only part of the plough not treated at 169–75 (see 171–4n.).

262   cauat arbore lintres: though this recalls 136 (*tunc alnos primum fluuii sensere cauatas*), and though the farmer is a boat-maker at 2.445, V. is more likely to be referring to wine-vats (Cato, *Agr.* 11.5; Tib. 1.5.23).

263   Branding and labelling; the former recurs in a rather similar line at 3.158. *impressit* creates a zeugma, going more properly with *signum* than *numeros*.

264   uallos furcasque: to be put to use in the next book; cf. 2.25, 359, 409.

265   Amerina ... retinacula 'ties from Ameria'; the place was obviously noted for its willows, the adjective referring to wicker in general: *corbulas Amerinas*, Cato, *Agr.* 11.5.

266–7   nunc ... nunc ... nunc 'in wet weather'; paralleled by 289–90 (*nocte ... nocte ... noctes*), treating the chores to be done at night, and by 305–8 (*tum ... tum ... tum*), which deal with winter work (see 77–8n. for V.'s repetition of a key word in the tricolon).

266   Like 222, that rarity in the *Georgics*, a golden line which does not end a sentence (see 117n.). The singer of *E.* 10 is similarly engaged: *dum sedet et gracili fiscellam texit hibisco* (71).

267   Rephrased at *A.* 1.179, with the same verbs in the same position: [*fruges*] *... et torrere parant flammis et frangere saxo*. Cf. Lucr. 1.881–2 *fruges ..., minaci | robore cum saxi franguntur.*

268–75   In fact (*quippe*), even on holy days, some tasks are permitted by divine and human law. At *Agr.* 2.4 Cato allowed substantial work to be done on these days (most having to do with cleaning: *munditias fieri* (cf. 271–2)). Clearly there was no abatement of *labor* at such times, in spite of the picture of the 'happy' rustic, who spends his festal days picnicking: *ipse dies agitat festos fususque per herbam, ...* (2.527 and n.).

269   riuos deducere 'bringing down water [for irrigation]'; this seems better than referring to draining, the force of *deducere* at 114. At 106 *inducere* = 'irrigate', but the difference is merely a matter of perspective. Macrobius (*Sat.* 3.3.10) asserts that the digging of irrigation channels was forbidden on holy days.

270   religio: the first syllable is perforce treated as long in poetry (cf. Lucr. 1.101, 109, passim). The word, which appears only here in the poem, was falsely perceived as deriving from *religare*, that which 'holds one back' from wrong action; it probably has the more positive sense 'have regard for', the root being the *-leg-* in *diligo, neglego*.

saepem: cf. 2.436n.

271   insidias auibus moliri: at 307–10 preparations for hunting and trapping (which came with the age of Jupiter; 139–40) are tasks for the winter.

271–2   incendere ... salubri: the activities are separate, but strangely *uepres* occur in the poem only here and at 3.444 (where they cut and allow infection into the hides of the sheep), while *mersare* is otherwise used by V. only at 3.447 (to which the present instance looks), where dipping is advised to combat that infection. Sheep are *balantes* only here and at 3.457 (cf. 3.457–8n.), where attempts to stave off the plague have failed; *salubris* is used here and at 3.530, later on in the account of the plague.

273–5   As later (390–2), V. closes the section with a very graphic vignette, here of the farmer taking his produce to town to trade it for supplies. Both descriptions occupy three lines, as do the equally visual closing similes at 201–3 and 512–14; the inner passages are marked by tranquillity and order, while the similes exemplify a world out of control.

273–4   tardi costas ... aselli ... onerat: perhaps a wry allusion to the exquisite comment of Cato: *mulis, equis, asinis feriae nullae, Agr.* 138.

aselli: ἀπὸ κοινοῦ with *costas* and *agitator*.

274–5   lapidemque ... | incusum: a rough-dressed stone used as a hand-mill; cf. Colum. 7.1.3.

275   urbe: the city does not elsewhere intrude into the 'technical' portions of the poem; the hive is twice called *urbs* (4.154, 193), but that is hardly to be compared; on *oppidum* cf. 3.402n.

276–86   Days

These lines are ostentatiously Hesiodic, recalling the *Days* (*W.D.* 765–828), from which at first sight V. appears to give a straightforward translation, apparently excerpting 802–13, treating the fifth, seventeenth, and nin(eteen)th. However, the Hesiodic material is changed, the Grecisms in language and metrics are Virgilian contributions rather than symptoms of transliteration (cf. 138n.), and the most specific verbal influence is Homeric rather than Hesiodic. Cf. 4.333–86n.

276–7   dies … operum: the title of Hesiod's poem, *Works and Days* (Ἔργα καὶ Ἡμέραι) is not attested until Lucian (67.6), but as West notes 'it is hard to imagine that it was called anything [else] … in Callimachus' *Pinakes*' (Comm. p. 136). The standard translation into Latin is *Opera et Dies*, and given the nature of V.'s lines an allusion to the title seems probable – the first attested reference.

dedit … luna: as regulator of the month the moon is held to fix the character of the days; the detail is not Hesiodic.

felicis operum: gen. of respect, 'favourable for work'; cf. 3.498 *infelix studiorum*, 'unhappy in his pursuits'. Such genitives vary in their origins, but this one is probably to be seen as an extension of the objective genitive: 'favouring work'.

277–8   quintam fuge: pallidus Orcus | Eumenidesque satae: bad also for Hesiod: πέμπτας δ' ἐξαλέασθαι, ἐπεὶ χαλεπαί τε καὶ αἰναί, *W.D.* 802, 'avoid the fifth days, for they are troublesome and terrible'. Hesiod goes on to explain that on the fifth Eris (Strife) gave birth to Horcus (Oath), with the Furies (Erinyes) in attendance. V. has made three alterations: he has civilized the Erinyes, giving them their cult name, Eumenides; he has their birth on this day; and Horcus has become Orcus, god of the Underworld. This is an appropriation of the original, but on the last detail Page should be quoted: 'To suppose that Virgil *mistranslated* the word Ὅρκον in Hesiod is absurd.' V. clearly felt that the Latin Orcus was a more fitting companion for the Furies (hence their birth occurs along with his), and so he exploited the orthographical similarities. In addition he comments on the alteration: the following lines contain material not in Hesiod, the concurrent birth of the Titans and similar monsters, who took an oath (*coniuratos*, cf. ὅρκος) to bring down Jupiter.

278–83   The central panel of the passage (six lines, with three before and three following) has nothing to do with Hesiod's *Days*, and demonstrates V.'s almost purely literary concerns; through his enumeration of Jupiter's enemies he conflates disparate passages of archaic Greek: the Titans Coeus and Iapetus are born of Earth at Hes. *Theog.* 134, while she produces Typhoeus *after* the defeat of the Titans at *Theog.* 821. The brothers (*fratres*), on the other hand, are Otus and Ephialtes, who do

not appear in Hesiod at all, but rather in the *Odyssey* (11.305–20), in a
passage which V. reworked with great care (see 281–2n.). And their
mother was not Earth, but Iphimedia, which V. well knew, since she is
the virtual speaker of the Homeric passage. Just as all these mythical
figures are conflated, so are the poems in which they appear: V. appro-
priates his archaic models.

278–9   partu Terra ... creat: cf. γηγενής, 'born of Earth [Gaia]',
i.e. 'Giants' (Γίγαντες); the association is old: γηγενέων ἀνδρῶν μιμού-
μενοι ἔργα Γιγάντων, 'rivalling the exploits of those earth-born men, the
Giants', [Hom.] *Batr.* 7. Cf. 184–5n.

279   The line looks like a transliteration from Greek, but it is V.'s
own, although in a sense he has conflated Hes. *Theog.* 134 [τέκε] Κοῖόν τε
... Ἰαπετόν τε and 821 τέκε ... Τυφωέα πελώρη.

Typhoéa: Greek acc.; in Hesiod four syllables (as at Ov. *M.* 5.347),
here three, with the final two vowels undergoing synizesis (cf. *E.* 6.30
Orphéa).

280   coniuratos: cf. 277–8n.

281–3   In the middle of the Hesiodic section, V. places an adapta-
tion of Hom. *Od.* 11.315–16 Ὄσσαν ἐπ' Οὐλύμπωι μέμασαν θέμεν, αὐτὰρ
ἐπ' Ὄσσηι | Πήλιον εἰνοσίφυλλον, 'eager they were to pile Ossa on
Olympus, and on Ossa Pelion with its quivering leaves'. The Homeric
pile (from the ground up) is thus: Olympus–Ossa–Pelion; V. (noticing
that at *Od.* 11.313 Olympus is the goal) reverses the order: Pelion–Ossa–
Olympus. At the same time his word-order is more artful than
Homer's, visually reflecting the new arrangement: *Pelio Ossam ... Ossae
... Olympum*; and the foliage is now appropriately on Olympus (*fron-
dosum*), rather than on the crushed Pelion. Horace (*Odes* 3.4.52) and
Propertius (2.1.19–20) rejected V.'s audacity (their wording suggests
they have him in mind), adhering to the Homeric pattern. V. has also
added a Homeric feature not in the model, epic shortening (correption)
of the final syllable of *Pelio*.

The hiatus at the main caesura of 281, the three elisions in 282, and
the predominance of spondees in both lines mirror the exertion involved
in the assault on heaven.

ter conati ... ter ... disiecit: another skilful touch: a triple effort
met by triple frustration is Homeric, but it occurs in *Od.* 11 not with the
assault on Zeus, but 100 lines earlier, when Odysseus relates his at-
tempts to embrace his mother in Hades: τρὶς μὲν ἀφορμήθην ... τρὶς δέ ...

ἕπτατ', *Od.* 11.206–8. V. recreated that scene, with this same formula, and now in the Homeric context, in relating Aeneas' attempts to embrace the shades of Creusa (*A.* 2.792–4) and Anchises (*A.* 6.700–2).

284   septima post decimam: the seventeenth follows the fifth, as in Hesiod (μέσσηι δ' ἑβδομάτηι, *W.D.* 805), but there the similarities end; Hesiod recommended this period (that of the waning moon) for beginning threshing and for woodcutting, and the Roman technical tradition agrees with him (Varro, *R.R.* 1.37.1; Plin. *N.H.* 18.322). V., however, assigns to this day three activities scattered throughout the Hesiodic passage: planting the vine, breaking in oxen and setting up the loom. It may be no accident that these tasks, though not presented sequentially in Hesiod, are placed on the twelfth, thirteenth and fourteenth of the month.

284–6   ponere ... domitare ... addere: epexegetical infinitives, dependent on *felix*: 'lucky for planting, etc.' The device occurs several times in the Hesiodic model.

285–6   licia telae | addere 'for putting loops on the warp' (preparatory to weaving); Tib. 1.6.78 is similar: *adnectit licia telis*. See Wild (1970) 61–78 for details of the ancient loom.

286   nona fugae melior, contraria furtis: the simplest explanation of this rather whimsical line seems the best. Hesiod noted that the ninth was good for the works of men (772–3), and later (811) that it was quite harmless for men. V., knowing that on this day the moon was approaching its full state, interprets: that so, if a man was a runaway, it would indeed be a good time, and by the same reasoning burglary would be discouraged, making it a harmless time for the rest of us. This also provides a clever transition to the section that immediately follows – work to be done at night.

287–310   Night work, winter work

V. devotes 12 lines to each, with the transition presented through a series of opposites at 297–300 *aestu ... aestu ... hiems ... frigoribus*.

287 'Yes, and many tasks present themselves better in the cool of the night.' *melius* mirrors *melior*, assisting the transition (286n.); *dedere* is a gnomic perfect.

288   inrorat Eous: the slight personification of the morning-star may owe something to a line from Cinna's *Zmyrna*: *te matutinus flentem*

conspexit Eous, p. 88 Morel (see 4.465-6n.). The first syllable of *Eous* is
here short (as in Cinna's line), long elsewhere in the poem (221; 2.115).

289-90   nocte ... nocte ... noctes: anaphora of a key word in each
of the units of a tricolon occurs a number of times in the poem (see 77-8,
266-7; 2.323-4, 368-70, 408-10, 514nn.; also 3.409n.). Mowing is
best done by night because the dew makes the job easier.

leues ... stipulae: cf. 85 *leuem stipulam.*

noctes: object of *deficit* 'night is not deserted by the softening
moisture'.

291-6   A very homely picture of an evening's activity in the cottage.
Page notes on *et quidam*: 'used when the writer has some definite person
in mind, but thinks it needless to give his name'. We might modify this
slightly: 'when the writer wishes to give the *impression* that he has ... '
The same may be said of V.'s mode of introducing the old man of
Tarentum: *memini me ... uidisse* (4.125-48n.).

291   Night has become the night of winter, since the work of that
season has been the main subject since 259; presumably in the active
seasons the farmer would be early to bed.

292   inspicat: in effect a hapax legomenon, meaning 'to split the
end in such a way that it resembles a *spica* [ear of corn]'.

293-4   The wife solaces her *labor* by singing at the loom. A couplet
with some tantalizing resonances: Circe is involved in the same actions
at *A.* 7.11-14, where 14 = 294 here, with the necessary alteration of
coniunx to *tenuis*, making Circe's weaving sound very much like a meta-
phor for poetic composition (Thomas (1985)). The deserted Cynthia so
consoled herself (*nam modo purpureo fallebam stamine somnum,* | *rursus et
Orpheae carmine, fessa, lyrae,* Prop. 1.3.41-2), and Ovid may have V. in
mind when exemplifying the purpose of his exile poetry (to ease his
pains): *cantantis pariter data pensa trahentis,* | *fallitur ancillae decipiturque labor,*
Trist. 4.1.13-14. Ovid also gives as an example the case of Orpheus (*bis
amissa coniuge,* 18; cf. *G.* 4.504 *rapta bis coniuge*). Indeed in 293 there may
be a reference to the doomed motives of Virgil's Orpheus (*ipse caua solans
aegrum testudine amorem,* 4.464) – *coniunx* appears in 4.465, in the same
position as in 1.294, these being the only two instances of the nom. in the
Georgics; cf. 145-6n. on the parallelism of *amor* and *labor* for Virgil.

arguto: of the shrill sound made by the shuttle.

295-6   The boiling down of must was a means of bypassing fermen-
tation. There is a similar stove scene at Ov. *M.* 8.641-50, where Jupiter

and Mercury are entertained by the impoverished Baucis and Phile-
mon. Ovid also refers to the cooking-water as *unda* (an epicism), and
since he is almost certainly adapting from Callimachus' *Hecale*, it is
possible that the 'epic homeliness' of V.'s lines may also owe something
to the famous epyllion.

Volcano: the metonymy for fire is an epicism, and in this context
again creates the inconcinnity between style and theme that is a mark of
Hellenistic epyllion. Cf. Horace's description of the kitchen fire (wit-
nessed by V.) encountered on the mock-epic journey to Brundisium:
*nam uaga per ueterem dilapso flamma culinam | Volcano summum properabat
lambere tectum, Sat,* 1.5.73–4.

umorem: hypermetric, like 2.69, 344, 443; 3.242, 377, 449 (all but
two of which result from words ending in -*que*); perhaps here suggesting
the boiling over of the must.

despumat 'removes the foam from'; first attested here, and other-
wise not found before silver Latin. Servius refers to 112, which treats the
'grazing down' of excessive lushness (*luxuriem*); perhaps V. coined *de-
spumat* by analogy with *depascit* in that line.

297–8 Reaping and threshing are both to be done through the heat
of midday; Theocritus (10.48–52) advised the same for threshing, but
recommended a siesta from reaping; V., whose climate was cooler, may
intend a 'correction' of Theocritus. Cf. 190n.

medio ... aestu | ... medio ... aestu: an elegant epanalepsis, with
the second *aestu* occupying the same position as the first *medio*. Cf. 3.331
aestibus ... mediis.

tostas ... fruges: dried by the sun, not by fire as at 267 *nunc torrete
igni fruges.*

299 nudus ara, sere nudus: i.e. plough and sow in the warm
seasons; the oddity of expression reflects the archaism of V.'s source
(γυμνὸν σπείρειν, γυμνὸν δὲ βοωτεῖν, Hes. *W.D.* 381), but that did not
save him from the waggish pen of an anonymous parodist: '*nudus ara, sere
nudus': habebis frigore febrem* (*ap.* Serv., p. 105 Morel). For the style cf.
3.420 and n.

300–4 See 50n. for V.'s approximation of farming to sailing. Repe-
tition and chiasmus bring them into close contact: *agricolae ... laeti ...
laeti ... nautae*; cf. similarly 371–3n.

300 frigoribus 'in the cold seasons'; abl. of time when.

parto ... fruuntur 'enjoy their produce'; cf. *A.* 8.316–17, of the aboriginal Italians, in their pre-agricultural state: *nec ... norant ... parcere parto.*

301   laeti conuiuia curant: a glimpse of the more extensive relaxation which comes at 2.523–40 (see n.); here, however, in the world of reality, there is still work to be done: *sed tamen ...* (305).

303   portum tetigere carinae: cf. *A.* 4.657–8 *litora ... tetigissent ... carinae*, which also looks to Cat. 64.172 *tetigissent litora puppes.*

305–9   tum ... tum ... tum: the winter's activities are presented in a tricolon, with the items in the units decreasing in number, but with an increase in syntactical complexity; see 266–7n.

305–6   Acorns were used as winter fodder for pigs and cattle; laurel and myrtle, also paired at *E.* 2.54, were valued for their aroma, the latter in particular being used in wine-making.

307–8   ceruis | ... lepores ... dammas: hunting of these is also treated at 3.410–13, under *cura canum.*

308   auritosque: Macrobius (*Sat.* 6.5) quotes Afranius, fr. 404 Ribb. *nam ... uulgo me praedicant | aurito me* [sc. *Priapum*] *parente natum*, meaning an ass. For this description Callim. *Aet.* 1, fr. 1.31 Pf., a passage well-known to V., seems to offer the first parallel in Greek: θηρὶ μὲν οὐατόεντι, 'the long-eared beast'. In applying the adjective to the hare V. may have recalled Meleager's epitaph for Phanion's pet hare: οὐατόεντα λαγών (*Anth. Pal.* 7.207.2) = *auritum leporem.*

309   'whirling the hempen thongs of the Balearic sling'; the inhabitants of the Balearic Islands (Maiorca, Minorca, etc.) had a proverbial skill with slings.

310   A fine close to the passage, well capturing the grip of winter. This line, and those preceding it, seem to look to the description of winter hunting in Scythia at 3.371–5, the point there too being that snow facilitates the activity. The first half of the line recalls the beginning of Horace's Soracte Ode: *uides ut alta stet niue ...* (1.9.1); the second half means 'when rivers push the ice up into frazil', not 'when they roll the ice down to the sea'. Cf. 334n.

311–50   The Great Storm

The passage serves as a climax to the second movement of the book (see Introduction, p. 18), standing at the transitional point between the farmer's calendar and the investigation of signs. The storm comes without warning, and is as devastating as its political counterpart at the end of the book – the civil strife which tears Rome apart. It is difficult to avoid the conclusion that this sequence negates all the advice that has preceded it: in spite of all, the unseasonable and unpredictable storm may bring destruction to the works of the farmer. The only hope against this is piety, and within the workings of the *Georgics* that is no hope at all (cf. 335–50n.).

311–15 autumni ... uer: autumn and spring storms each receive two and a half lines. The equinox is the time of seasonal uncertainty and imbalance, when the year is in flux and sure forecasting is not possible. The storm which occupies the body of the passage also occurs in the spring, during the cutting of 'winter wheat'.

313 ruit imbriferum uer 'spring comes down in showers'; cf. 324n. A final monosyllable also appears with *ruit* at 3.255 and *A.* 2.250, where as here abruptness of metre reinforces the meaning.

314 spicea iam campis cum messis inhorruit: given the impending battle (*uentorum ... proelia*, 318) and the fact that *spiculum* ('javelin') is related to *spicum* ('ear of corn'), it seems certain that V. intends a military image: the crops stand waiting for the onslaught of the storm. There is a reminiscence of Ennius' powerfully artless line: *sparsis hastis longis campus splendet et horret* (*Varia* 14 V.). V. accommodates the two images at 2.142, when referring to the harvest of warriors in Colchis (*nec galeis densisque uirum seges horruit hastis*), and at *A.* 12.663 the agricultural metaphor stands behind the surface meaning, which is military: *stant densae strictisque seges mucronibus horret | ferrea*; also at *A.* 3.46 *telorum seges*; 7.526 *horrescit strictis seges ensibus.* Cf. 316–34n.

315–21 A careful pattern: *stipula ... culmo ... culmum ... stipulas.*

315 turgent: otherwise in V. only at *E.* 7.48, also of the effects of summer's heat, *iam lento turgent in palmite gemmae.* The image of 315 supplies the transition from spring to summer.

316–34 In the actual description of the storm V. has three models: Hom. *Il.* 16.384–92; Hes. *W.D.* 507–16; Lucr. 1.271–6; 6.253–61. As usual, one model predominates; here Homer. The storm from the *Iliad* is in a simile, exemplifying the onslaught of Patroclus and the horses of Achilles. Precisely as at 104–10 (see n.), V. makes the simile his reality, but he expects the reader to recall the original context of the simile (warfare), and he reinforces that context by using military language to depict the struggle between the farmer and his works and the forces of nature (314, 316–17, 318, 322nn.). These lines are recalled by the destructive fire-storm of 2.303–14, and by the restoration of storm-simile to describe the parallel and equally destructive plague at 3.470–1 (see nn.). At *A.* 2.416–19 V. uses a storm in the Homeric context (with Lucretian overtones), as a simile for the Greek attack against Troy.

316–18   saepe ego ... uidi: cf. 193n. on the use of this verb to impart *fides*, an impression strengthened by *saepe*, repeated at 322. Cf. too 365 *saepe ... uidebis* (*saepe* repeated at 368), 451 *saepe uidemus*, 471–2 *quotiens ... | uidimus*; 2.32 *saepe ... uidemus*, 186–7 *saepe ... solemus | despicere*. With 2.101, this is the only use of *ego* in the didactic parts of the poem.

316–17   cum flauis messorem induceret aruis | agricola: continuing the military imagery (316–34n.); *inducere* is often used (cf. *A.* 11.620) of generals leading their troops onto the field.

318   omnia: effectively a transferred epithet: all the *winds* are doing battle.

uentorum concurrere proelia: the military language reaches its climax. For the clash of the winds as a simile for battle, with reminiscence of these lines, cf. *A.* 2.416–19; also Hor. *Odes* 1.9.10–11 *uentos ... deproeliantis*.

319–20   quae ... eruerent: better seen as a relative clause of result ('so as to tear up') than of purpose, although the meaning is not much affected.

grauidam: often used in the poem of ripe or ready crops or fruits (e.g. 2.5, 143, 424); but here (as at 111) with the secondary meaning 'heavy', and therefore emphasizing the power of the storm. Cf. 321 *leuem*.

ab radicibus imis: the phrase is Lucretian (1.352).

320   sublimem: predicative.

ita: a transitional particle connecting *ferret* with *eruerent*: 'in such wise ...'

turbine: otherwise in the *Georgics* only at 3.470 (see 316–34n.), where *hiemem*, like *hiems* here, also means 'storm'; cf. 323, 324nn.

321   culmumque ... stipulasque: cf. 315n.

322   agmen: used often enough of the course of rivers and other moving objects, but after *proelia* the more common military sense suggests itself; cf. 316–34n.

323 glomerant: also used of the wind's effects on the fire at 2.311 (cf. 320n.).

imbribus atris: cf. 236.

324 ruit arduus aether: cf. 313 *ruit imbriferum uer*, and (transitive) of the fire at 2.308 *ruit*, the storm at 3.470 *ruit aequore turbo*; cf. 316–34n. At *A.* 1.129, a storm at sea is called *caeli ruina*.

325–6 sata laeta boumque labores | diluit: the phrasing recurs in the storm simile of *A.* 2.306, the thought at the end of this book, as one of the omens accompanying the death of Caesar and the storm of civil war: *fluuiorum rex Eridanus ... | cum stabulis armenta tulit*, 482–3 (cf. 311–50n.). As at 118, *boumque labores* is ultimately Hesiodic (ἔργα βοῶν, *W.D.* 46), but V. recalls the effects of a storm at Ap. Rhod. *Arg.* 4.1282–3 (ἠέ τιν' ὄμβρον | ἄσπετον, ὅτε βοῶν κατὰ μυρία ἔκλυσεν ἔργα, 'or some mighty storm, which deluges the countless works of oxen'), a passage which also influenced him at the end of the book (464–88n.). On the emphatic position of *diluit* see 109n. and cf. *proluit*, 481.

326–7 An artful couplet, with carefully arranged sound-patterns at the beginnings of words (*f, c, f, c | s, f, f, s*), and with the arrangement of detail reflecting the journey of the rains from ditch (*fossae*) to river (*flumina*) to inlet (*fretis*) to sea (*aequor*).

328 ipse pater: Jupiter, so named also at 121 (*pater ipse*) and 353, joins the battle, apparently against the very arts which his age brought in; *ipse* emphasizes his personal involvement. See 1–42n. on his ambivalence in the poem.

329–30 More elaborate sound-patterns, with juxtaposition and accumulation of words beginning with *m, f* and *t*.

332 aut Atho aut Rhodopen aut alta Ceraunia: a line of some complexity. The first half is taken from Theocritus (ἢ Ἄθω ἢ Ῥοδόπαν, 7.77), but the second half (*aut alta Ceraunia*) has no relation to Theocritus' continuation ἢ Καύκασον ἐσχατόωντα, to which however V. does refer at *E.* 8.44 *aut Tmaros aut Rhodope aut extremi* [= ἐσχατόωντα] *Garamantes*. This is the first suggestion in Greek or Latin of the name Acroceraunia (*alta* glosses ἄκρος in its other sense); until now the promontory is known merely as Ceraunia. The first actual instance of the full Greek name is at Hor. *Odes* 1.3.20 (*mare turbidum et | infamis scopulos Acroceraunia*) – in the propempticon to V. Nisbet–Hubbard (*ad loc.*), who are not concerned with the *Georgics*, argue plausibly that many of the items in Horace's propempticon are borrowed from Cinna's propempticon to Pollio, and since Cinna mentioned Corcyra (p. 88 Morel), it is very likely that Acroceraunia, which is just north of that island, also figured in his poem. If so, then 332, like 138 (see n.), constitutes a conflation of two poets, in this instance Hellenistic and neoteric. This scheme is perhaps confirmed by the context of the Theocritean line; it comes from the song of Lycidas – from a propempticon. V. would thus have conflated not only two favoured poets, but the propemptica of two favoured poets. Cf. also 437n.

Atho: the MSS, along with Val. Flacc. 1.664 (which looks to V.), have *Athon* (as if from ῎Αθος); but Theocr. 7.77, shows decisively that V., who did not shrink from producing epic shortening even when it was *not* in his Greek model (281–3n.), wrote *Atho*.

333   deicit: cf. 109n.

ingeminant: the same form, in the opposite context, at 411 (see n.).

334   The description of the storm closes, as did the preceding passage (310), with anaphora and asyndeton; see 335n.

335–50   In three lines V. enjoins careful observation of the seasons, and in a further three veneration of the gods. The remainder of the passage depicts a rustic festival to Ceres (the Cerealia, held in mid-April) – though the temporal setting varies, since 341–7 suit the Ambarvalia (late May), while 347–50 look to the beginning of the harvest. Appealing as the lines are, they offer no palliative to the destruction of the storm that has immediately preceded: observation of the calendar and the signs is of no avail against storms, and there is no suggestion in the *Georgics* that piety is of any use in the struggle between man and his environment – indeed, the final vignette of the storm was of an unprovoked Jupiter directing the deluge (328–33); cf. 2.393n. Cf. man's inability to prevent the civil storm at the end of the book, or the plague at the end of Book 3, where religion fails spectacularly: 3.455–6, 486–93 (see 466; 3.513nn.).

335   Parallel in structure to 311, as is 334 (see n.) to 310.

metuens: *metus* and its verb are used frequently in the poem (186; 2.333, 419; 4.37, 239) of the fear or dread which results from inability to control the natural world, and it is the man who can conquer this dread through the intellect, not the pious man, who is V.'s ideal: *felix qui . . . | . . . metus omnis . . . | subiecit pedibus*, 2.490–2.

sidera serua: cf. 311 *quid ... sidera dicam*, and especially 204–5 *Arcturi sidera ... Haedorumque dies seruandi.*

336–7 frigida ... ignis: Saturn is the coldest of the planets known to V., Mercury the hottest.

337 ignis ... Cyllenius: i.e. the planet Mercury, from Mt Cyllene, birthplace of the god, of whom the adjective is used as early as the Homeric *Hymn to Hermes* 318.

erret: Servius saw the gloss (*bene 'erret'; nam planetae uocantur ἀπὸ τῆς πλάνης* ['from "wandering"'], *id est ab errore*), though it is not noted by most modern commentators.

338 in primis uenerare deos: so Cyrene to Aristaeus at 4.535: *facilis uenerare Napaeas.* There, at some cost (4.538–58n.), the advice works, but Aristaeus' propitiation is in response to a specific transgression (his ultimate responsibility for the deaths of Eurydice and Orpheus), and it is difficult to relate that situation to this more general reference (see 335–50n.).

339 laetis ... in herbis: the picnic at the end of Book 2 occurs *in gramine laeto* (525), and, on a more chilling note, that is where the calves die as religion fails before the onslaught of plague: *hinc laetis uituli uulgo moriuntur in herbis,* 3.494 (see 335–50n.).

340 extremae ... hiemis 'right at the setting of the winter's end'; cf. 211 *usque sub extremum brumae intractabilis imbrem,* where the reference, however, is to a point *within* winter, when the rains make work impossible.

341–2 A tranquil tricolon describes the spring setting. On anaphora (here of *tum*) within a tricolon see 266–7n. The model is Hes. *W.D.* 585 τῆμος πιόταταί τ' αἶγες καὶ οἶνος ἄριστος, 'then are the goats plumpest, and the wine best'. Virgilian restraint suppresses the next detail (μαχλόταται δὲ γυναῖκες, 'then women most lustful'), which is replaced by sweet sleep. There is perhaps a conflation with Theocr. *Id.* 11, the poem which V. adapted in *E.* 2: Theocritus' Polyphemus addresses a number of rustic compliments to Galatea (19–21), among them ἁπαλωτέρα ἀρνός ('softer than a lamb' – Hesiod's goats have become *agni* in 341) and φιαρωτέρα ὄμφακος ὠμᾶς ('sleeker [?] than an unripe grape'). He proceeds with an image whose elegance and pathos appealed to Horace (*Odes* 4.1.37–40): 'When sweet sleep (γλυκὺς ὕπνος) holds me, you approach, when it leaves, you are gone in flight.' V.

otherwise modifies *somnus* with *dulcis* only at *A.* 4.185 (where the context is erotic, as it was for Theocritus).

In 341 the unusual hiatus at the main caesura slows down the line and reinforces the sense of tranquillity.

343 tibi: dat. of interest: 'See that all the youth worship ...'

344 lacte fauos et miti dilue Baccho: milk, honey and wine are rather strange as a libation for Ceres. Along with water they are offered to the dead at Hom. *Od.* 11.27, and the three are miraculously produced by the thyrsus of Dionysus at Eur. *Bacch.* 704–11 (cf. Dodds, *ad loc.*), which perhaps led to the impossible interpretation mentioned by Servius, connecting *cui* and *Baccho*. Ceres and Bacchus are, however, natural partners (as at 7–9), and the festival of Ceres here is matched by the sacrifice of a goat to Bacchus at 2.380–96 (see 345, 350nn.).

345 circum ... eat hostia fruges: so the *suouetaurilia* (the offering of a pig, sheep and calf) was first led around the land whose purification and productivity its sacrifice was to ensure: *quoius rei ergo agrum terram fundumque meum suouetaurilia circumagi iussi*, Cato, *Agr.* 141.2.

felix 'propitious', 'auspicious'.

346 chorus et socii: 'band of companions'; hendiadys, or 'the use of two words or phrases simply put side by side, instead of a single complex phrase in which the words qualify each other' (Page). Cf. 2.192; 3.56; 4.39, 99.

347 et Cererem clamore uocent in tecta: the picture is similar to that at the end of Book 2 (cf. 2.528 *socii*, 529 *uocat*); both there and here the image of rustic celebration is idealized and somehow distinct from the practical, everyday life of the farmer (see too 350n.).

349 torta redimitus tempora quercu: cf. *A.* 3.81 where Anius, a priest of Apollo, is appropriately wreathed: *sacra redimitus tempora lauro*.

350 The rare and clumsy rhythm (no third-foot caesura) emphasizes the uncouth nature (*incompositos*) of the rustic dance. The same phenomenon occurs at 3.226 where, however, there seems less reason for it. Though these *carmina* are presumably hymns to Ceres, in juxtaposition with *motus incompositos* they look to the archaic, even specifically Saturnian, verses of 2.386 (*uersibus incomptis ludunt*); V. perhaps refers to Horace on Lucilius: *nempe incomposito dixi pede currere uersus | Lucili, Sat.* 1.10.1–2. As at 347, the archaic flavour of the line distinguishes it, and the account of rustic piety which it closes, from the more modern

realities of the bulk of the poem. The activity described in these lines
belongs to the age of Saturn, not Jupiter (2.538).

det motus: relevant also is Livy's discussion of the beginnings of
drama: *haud indecoros motus more Tusco dabant*, 7.2.4; and later in the same
passage: *qui non, sicut ante, Fescinnino uersu similem incompositum ...* (7.2.7).

351–463   Weather-signs

In the last portion of the book V. is concerned with weather-signs. The
influence of Hesiod gives way to that of Aratus, specifically the Aratus of
Phaenomena 733–1154, lines once held to constitute a separate poem, the
Διοσημίαι (*Weather-signs*), but now generally considered but a part of
the whole poem. Roughly speaking, V. has reversed the order of his
model, as lines 351–423 depend on *Phaen.* 909–1043 (indications of bad
and good weather), while lines 424–63 look to *Phaen.* 733–891 (the
moon and sun). The reversal allows the sun, placed last in the poem, to
serve as a transition (through its eclipse at the death of Julius Caesar) to
the final sequence (463–514). V.'s adaptation is at times extremely
close, but is not limited to mere 'translation'. He has completely re-
shaped Aratus' material, abbreviating, expanding for his own special
purposes (e.g. 390–2 and n.), and incorporating reference to Aratus'
two Roman translators, Cicero (e.g. 378n.) and Varro of Atax
(373–92n.); nor are his models limited to these. The result is an ex-
quisite and thoroughly Virgilian passage, looking back to the tradition,
but poetically superior to it, and with a purpose of its own – to lead up to
the depiction of civil war which forms the climactic finale of the book. As
V.'s reshaping of the Hesiodic *Works and Days* culminated in the storm of
311–34, so his adaptation of Aratus culminates in the storm which
overwhelms Rome. See Jermyn (1951).

351–92   Forecasting bad weather

351   certis ... signis: throughout the poem, wherever change or
disaster occurs, *signa* come first. *signis* looks immediately to the first
word of Aratus' treatment of the same topic (cf. 351–463n.), σῆμα
(*Phaen.* 909), but for V. its importance transcends that reminiscence. Cf.
354 (*quo signo caderent Austri*) and 394 (*certis ... signis*), and the stress laid

on the word in the treatments of the sun and of civil war: *sol ... | signa dabit; solem certissima signa sequentur*, 438–9; *sol tibi signa dabit*, 463; *signa dabant*, 471. The plague of Book 3 is preceded by signs (*morborum quoque te causas et signa docebo*, 440; *haec ante exitium primis dant signa diebus*, 503), as is its counterpart of Book 4, the death of the hive (*quod iam non dubiis poteris cognoscere signis*, 253). Man, then, can learn (*discere, cognoscere*) of impending disaster, but still that disaster always occurs, and occurs completely, *in spite of* the signs that tell of its coming.

352 aestusque: see 152–3n. on the 'lengthening' of *-que*, here before mute + liquid.

353 ipse pater: cf. 328n.

353–5 moneret, | ... caderent ... tenerent: subjunctives in indirect deliberative questions (formally indistinguishable from normal indirect questions): 'what warning the moon was to give ...'

355 propius stabulis armenta tenerent: in Scythia a continuous state: *illic clausa tenent stabulis armenta*, 3.352; and cf. 3.214. The flood which is soon to accompany civil disorder will render the present caution useless (*cum stabulis armenta tulit*, 483); and the plague will bring the same outcome at 3.556–7 (see n.).

356–9 A careful adaptation of Arat. *Phaen.* 909–12, where there are four signs of a coming gale: the swelling of the sea, breakers on the beach, echoing headlands and the wind moaning in the mountain-tops. V. too has four *signa*, but they are alternated between land and sea: the sea swells and the mountains sound, or the shore resounds and the woods murmur. The syntax (*aut ... aut*, with each alternative containing a doublet connected by *et*) underlines the artful arrangement. The sound of the lines is highly descriptive.

356 uentis surgentibus: not one of the *signa*, as some suppose, but rather what is signalled: 'as the winds come up, either the seas begin to swell, etc.' V. follows Arat. *Phaen.* 909 σῆμα δέ τοι ἀνέμοιο, 'a sign of wind'.

357 tumescere: as the sea swells at the coming of the storm, so do hidden wars later in the book: *operta tumescere bella*, 465 (464–5n.). V. otherwise used the verb only at 2.479 (again of the sea).

358 resonantia: a translation of Aratus' ἠχήεσσαι (*Phaen.* 911), reflecting the sounds not only of the shore, but of the lines describing those sounds (cf. 2.328n.).

359   The sound-pattern is chiastic: *increbrescere* reflects *misceri*, as *murmur* does *nemorum*.

360   iam ... carinis 'then too the wave does not spare the curved keels'. The detail is not in Aratus, and it presents a textual difficulty. The weight of MSS and grammarians supports *iam sibi tum curuis*, in which case *curuis carinis* may be dative (*sibi temperat = parcit*; if so, the extension of usage is a bold one), or ablative of separation (though there is no support for such a use of *temperare* without a preposition). The preposition is included here, although the elision is rather harsh – no more so, however, than that at 2.405 *iam tum acer*.

361–4   Wilkinson (1969), with acknowledgements to Jermyn (1951), provides the best account of V.'s literary, rather than meteorological, motivation: 'Aratus (agreeing with Theophrastus) gives at 913ff. as signs of a gale blowing up at sea the landward flight of heron, petrel, duck and gull. Cicero (fr. 4) substitutes for the heron "cana fulix", the coot, presumably referring to its white forehead. He may have known that the heron is a bird of marsh and estuary, not sea; but unfortunately the coot is not a sea-bird either, nor does it make a noise. Virgil (360–4) restores Aratus' heron, rightly however picturing it not as flying in from the sea, but leaving its usual marsh-haunt to soar above the clouds. But he also (no doubt in deference to Cicero) includes the *fulix* (as *fulica*) with the epithet *marina* to explain how its disporting itself on dry land can be a prognostic of bad weather at sea; yet a sea-coot is a non-bird' (p. 235). This is a good instance of Virgilian conflation and correction (see e.g. 244–6n.) which in this case involves the introduction of ornithological error as well.

365–9   The next groups of storm-signs are shooting stars on the one hand, and on the other chaff or leaves flying in the wind or feathers playing on the surface of water. V. has adapted them from Aratus, *Phaen.* 921–32, but in reverse order. Cf. too Aratus' source, Theophr. *Weather-signs* 13, 37, though there is no suggestion, as there is elsewhere (see 410–23n.), that V. refers to him.

saepe ... uidebis | ... saepe: parallel to the coming of the storm at 316–23 *saepe ... | ... uidi | ... saepe.*

365–7   This sign may foreshadow one of the portents attending civil war at 487–8: *non alias caelo ceciderunt plura sereno | fulgura nec diri totiens arsere cometae*; see 355, 357nn.

366–7   noctisque ... tractus: V. begins from Arat. *Phaen.* 926–7 καὶ διὰ νύκτα μέλαιναν ὅτ᾽ ἀστέρες ἀίσσωσιν | ταρφέα, τοὶ δ᾽ ὄπιθεν ῥυμοὶ ὑπολευκαίνωνται, 'and when through the black night shooting stars thickly fly, and behind their trails are white'. With *umbram* and *albescere* he has retained the vivid contrast of Aratus, but has grafted the image on to Lucretian language (treating the same subject), which becomes invigorated in the process: *nocturnasque faces caeli sublime uolantis* | *nonne uides longos flammarum ducere tractus*, Lucr. 2.206–7.

368   paleam: V. has chaff, leaves and feathers where Aratus had thistle-down *(Phaen.* 921); the first seems particularly novel. Possibly he had in mind the passage from which Aratus took the verb ὑπολευκαίνομαι (V.'s *albescere*, 367). That is the only other occurrence of the word down to the Hellenistic period, namely in the simile at Hom. *Il.* 5.499–502 for the Greeks' turning white from the dust raised by the horses: ὡς ... | αἱ δ᾽ ὑπολευκαίνονται ἀχυρμιαί, 'as the chaff-heaps turn white'.

369   conludere: a colourful and animating touch, rendering Aratus' ἐπιπλώωσι, 'they float' *(Phaen.* 923).

**370–3   Adapted from Arat. *Phaen.* 933–7, which tell of the sailor's fear when lightning comes from the east and south, from the west, and the north. V.'s omission of the south may be due to geographical differences. Aratus proceeds to warn against the appearance of fleece-like clouds, whose treatment V. postpones to 397 (see n.).

370   fulminat: impersonal, 'lightning strikes'; otherwise in the poem only at 4.561, in a transferred sense, where Octavian strikes like lightning (4.560–1n.).

371   Eurique: the final syllable is treated as long before double consonant (ζ); see 152–3n.

371–3   omnia ... legit: Aratus referred only to the danger of sailing at such times, but as elsewhere V. has brought the worlds of agriculture and navigation together (cf. 50n.). Here the subjects are alternately the countryside *(rura)* and the sailor *(nauita)*, with *omnia/omnis* enforcing the parallelism; at 429, on the same subject, animate and inanimate are reversed, as V. refers to the farmer and the sea *(agricolis pelagoque).*

372   omnis: *omni* (which would balance *omnia*) has been suggested and merits consideration.

**373–92   A new movement begins within the general theme, as V. treats the signs given by animals and insects (the one exception, at

380–1, has a point; see n.); the climax comes with the close at 390–2, as the human world intrudes into that of the animals, a transition used to great effect at the end of Book 3 (3.563–6n.).

The manner of reference becomes more complex, parallel in many ways to that of 231–58, as V.'s rearrangement and compression of Aratus (*Phaen*. 942–87) is accompanied by clear reference to Homer, as well as to Aratus' two Roman translators, Cicero and Varro of Atax.

373–4 numquam imprudentibus imber | obfuit 'rain has never caused problems to men without their being warned'. At first sight this seems to say what it cannot, and in M this motivated the change to *prudentibus*. V. does not say that rain or its effects can be avoided, merely predicted – this is the extent of the value of forecasting, and it will be of little comfort, for instance, at 463–514.

374–87 It is worth quoting the version of Varro of Atax, fortunately preserved by Servius (*ad* 375), which V. had before him:

> tum liceat pelagi uolucres tardaeque paludis
> cernere inexpletas studio certare lauandi
> et uelut insolitum pennis infundere rorem;
> aut arguta lacus circumuolitauit hirundo,
> et bos suspiciens caelum – mirabile uisu –
> naribus aërium patulis decerpsit odorem,
> nec tenuis formica cauis non euehit oua. (p. 99 Morel)

Büchner suggests a lacuna of nine lines after line 4 of the fragment (*FPL* ad loc.), to account for material in Aratus but missing from Servius' citation. But V., who demonstrably drew from *both* Aratus and Varro, as well as from Cicero (378 n.), similarly abbreviates, though, just as Varro reordered Aratus, he executes his own rearrangement, now closer to one model, now to the other. It is impossible to judge the extent of Varro's treatment of 'animal-signs' but it may well have been limited to what Servius quotes. On Varro cf. 2.404n.

375 grues: cranes appear in Aratus, but not in the same relative position, and foretell calm, not rain (*Phaen*. 1010–12); here V. contradicts both Aratus and his source, Theophr. *Weather-signs* 52. Aratus and Varro both began with sea-birds, which V. postpones until 383–7.

375–6 aut bucula caelum | suspiciens patulis captauit naribus auras: very close to 5–6 of Varro's version (374–87n.). The diminutive *bucula* replaces *bos*, a form V. seems not to have favoured (it occurs only twice, in the *Aeneid*), *captauit* expresses repetition better than *decerpsit*, and *auras* is a visual improvement on *odorem* (besides being a better representation of Aratus' αἰθέρος, 'air', *Phaen.* 955). Varro's *mirabile uisu*, which looks like filler, is dispensed with.

377   aut arguta lacus circumuolitauit hirundo: exact repetition of Varro (4), as far as can be known an extreme rarity for V. (2.404n.). Did he merely intend a compliment? In part, but this may not be the entire picture. The reader is to notice the precision of the imitation, and when proceeding to V.'s next line, to observe that it is not represented in Varro's version; for that he must go back to Varro's source, Aratus, and to his other translator, Cicero. The precision therefore functions as a means of setting up multiple reference (see 378n.).

378   et ueterem in limo ranae cecinere querelam: not in Varro, but looking back to Arat. *Phaen.* 946–7 where frogs also immediately follow the swallows (χελιδόνες): ἢ μᾶλλον δειλαὶ γενεαί, ὕδροισιν ὄνειαρ, | αὐτόθεν ἐξ ὕδατος πατέρες βοόωσι γυρίνων, 'or more wretched tribes, a boon for water-snakes, the fathers of the tadpoles croak from the very water'. Cf. Jermyn (1951) who, however, does not treat the relationship between V. and Varro: 'In Cicero's very free paraphrase "the fathers of the tadpoles" becomes *aquai dulcis alumnae* [*Arat.* fr. 4]. Now this phrase not only is an almost literal translation of the λιμναῖα κρηνῶν τέκνα of Aristophanes [*Frogs* 211], but contains in *alumnae* a sound-echo of λιμναῖα. Virgil took the hint and improved on it. In his line ... the word *ueterem* is an obvious pointer to antiquity [indeed, *uetus comoedia* is the standard term for Old Comedy]; *in limo*, both in sound and meaning, echoes λιμναῖα, and *cecinere querelam* reproduces three of the k- sounds of βρεκεκεκέξ [the refrain of Aristophanes' frogs]' (p. 36). In short, V. has referred to Aratus, to Cicero, through Cicero to Aristophanes, and by omission to Varro (377n.). For a similar accommodation of sound to sense, cf. 3.328.

379–80   tectis penetralibus extulit oua | angustum formica terens iter: V. again improves: *tectis penetralibus* is more vivid than Aratus' κοίλης ... ὀχῆς, 'hollow nest', *Phaen.* 956 (rendered more exactly by Varro, *cauis*, 7); *extulit* (for Varro's *euehit*) is a more precise rendition of Aratus' ἐξ ... ἀνηνέγκαντο, and Varro's simple designation of size (*tenuis formica*) is transformed into the colourful phrase *angustum ... terens iter*.

380–1   et bibit ingens | arcus: a brilliant παρὰ προσδοκίαν, 'and there drinks a huge – rainbow'. In Aratus and Varro the ox and the ant were set side by side. V. removed the ox to an earlier point (375–6), and from *Phaen.* 940 took the rainbow, the only inanimate item of his passage, designated it huge (*ingens*), set it beside the tiny world (*angustum*) of the ant, gave it animation (*bibit*), and through enjambment produced surprise. The verb also reflects the notion that the rainbow takes up water, which is then released as rain; cf. Plaut. *Curc.* 131a *ecce autem bibit arcus, pluet credo hercle hodie.*

381–2 V. inverts Aratus' order of signs given by raven (*coruus*) and crow (*cornix*, 388) although he generally follows his model in the activities assigned to each (but cf. 388–9n.).

agmine … exercitus: the language perhaps prepares us for the Homeric adaptation of the next two lines; Homer's simile (383–4n.) describes the massing of the Achaean forces.

densis … alis: V. has been accused of mistranslating Arat. *Phaen.* 969 πτερὰ πυκνά, 'frequent flapping'; *crebris* would have been more exact than *densis*. Perhaps he was looking to the Homeric simile, where the stress is on numbers: ὀρνίθων πετεηνῶν ἔθνεα πολλά, 'the multitudinous races of winged birds', *Il.* 2.459.

383–7 Anacoluthon: V. begins with nominative subjects (*uariae … uolucres …*), but with *infundere … obiectare … currere … uideas gestire* implies accusatives.

383 pelagi uolucres: V. borrows the wording from the first line of Varro. Both look to Arat. *Phaen.* 942 εἰνάλιαι ὄρνιθες.

383–4 The adaptation of Aratus and his translators is interrupted by Homeric reference, as at 104–10, in its original context a simile but for V. the reality; the proper names specify the borrowing: Ἀσίωι ἐν λειμῶνι, Καϋστρίου ἀμφὶ ῥέεθρα, 'in the Asian meadow, around the waters of Cayster', *Il.* 2.461. The reference is motivated by Aratus' simple epithet, λιμναῖα, *Phaen.* 942 (= *tardaeque paludis* of Varro).

385 umeris infundere rores: the divergence from Varro (*pennis infundere rorem*) humanizes these birds, though V. may be looking back to Aratus' crow: ποταμοῖο ἐβάψατο μέχρι παρ' ἄκρους | ὤμους ἐκ κεφαλῆς, 'dips from head to *shoulder* in the river', *Phaen.* 951–2.

387 studio incassum uideas gestire lauandi: again very close to Varro ([*liceat*] *cernere inexpletas studio certare lauandi*), whose verb *certare* is made by V. to govern all the activities through the adverb *certatim* (385).

388–9: cf. 381–2n. In Aratus (*Phaen.* 950–3) the crow (κορώνη) walks on the shore, bathes and caws, in Cicero (*Arat.* fr. 4.8–9) the crow (*cornix*) only walks and bathes, and here it walks and caws, since bathing has been transferred to the sea- and marsh-birds (385n.).

sola ... secum: from elsewhere in Aratus (*Phaen.* 1003), where ravens (not crows) caw individually, καὶ κόρακες μοῦνοι μὲν ἐρημαῖοι βοόωντες | δισσάκις, 'and ravens when single and alone they let out two cries' (see 410n.). V.'s image of the crow's solitary walk is a very human one, preparing us for the purely human image which immediately follows (390–2). The wording is in fact close to that used of the grieving Orpheus: *te solo in litore secum,* | ... *canebat,* 4.465–6.

390–2 The suggestion comes from Aratus (*Phaen.* 976–81), who warns of snuff gathering on the lamp, of its giving off sparks, or quivering rays (cf. too 1033–6, and Theophr. *Weather-signs* 14). V. focuses attention on the human observer of these phenomena: we no longer have the mere description of the lamp's behaviour, but see it through the eyes of girls who sit spinning at night. V. was perhaps influenced by the homely vision from Callimachus' *Hecale:* ὁππότε λύχνου | δαιομένου πυρόεντες ἄδην ἐγένοντο μύκητες, 'when as the lamp was burning lots of snuffs of the wick were formed', fr. 269 Pf.

ne nocturna quidem: *ne ... quidem* normally emphasizes the material it surrounds, and the contrast is generally explained as that between day and night: 'even at night, girls, as they spin, have not failed to notice ...' It is possible, given what leads up to this passage, that the contrast is also between the animal and the human world: 'even night-spinning girls ...' The assimilation of *ne ... quidem* to *nec,* evident in Silver Latin, has perhaps already begun.

uiderent: resumes *uidebis* (365); *uideas* (387).

393–423   Forecasting fair weather

Aratus is still the primary source, though cf. 404–9n.

394   certis poteris cognoscere signis: recapitulates the opening of the previous section: see 351n.

395 From Arat. *Phaen.* 1091 οἱ δ' εἶεν καθύπερθεν ἐοικότες ἀστέρες αἰεί, 'may the stars shine duly above you'.

acies obtunsa: the image is of sharp steel (the root sense of *acies*) not being blunted (*obtunsa*), on which cf. 433n. *acies* comes to mean 'something sharply defined' as here, 'something with a sharp edge' (battle-line), etc.

396 'nor does the Moon seem to rise indebted to her brother's [the Sun's] rays'; i.e. she is so bright that her light seems to be her own. This mention of moon and sun looks forward to the next section (424–63).

397 V. refers to the *absence* of a phenomenon whose *presence* was for Aratus an indication of the opposite weather: νέφεα ... | οἷα μάλιστα πόκοισιν ἐοικότα ἰνδάλλονται, '[before a storm] fleece-like clouds appear', *Phaen.* 938–9. Another fragment of Varro of Atax (*nubes* [*sic*] *ut uellera lanae* | *constabunt*, p. 98 Morel) seems to have given V. his wording, although like Aratus, Varro seems to have presented such clouds as a *positive* sign, presumably of storm. Lucr. 6.504 (*ueluti pendentia uellera lanae*) may stand behind the two Latin poets; it is noteworthy that while Aratus, Lucretius and Varro deal in simile (ἐοικότα, *ueluti*, *ut*), V. refers to the clouds merely as *lanae ... uellera*.

tenuia: scanned as a dactyl, with the *u* treated as a consonant, and therefore 'making position'.

398–9 The mythical halcyon (identified with the kingfisher, which figures at 3.338) was thought to choose fourteen consecutive calm days in winter to make its nest and produce its young at sea (*non ... in litore*); see Ov. *M.* 11.745–8. This detail is not in Aratus, and as at 383–4 (see n.), V. has interrupted his reference to the primary model, here with reminiscence of Theocr. 7, a poem already referred to (332n.): χάλ-κυόνες στορεσεῦντι τὰ κύματα τάν τε θάλασσαν | ... | ἀλκυόνες, γλαυκαῖς Νηρηίσι ταί τε μάλιστα | ὀρνίχων ἐφίληθεν 'the halcyons shall lay the waves and the sea to rest ... halcyons, of birds most dear to the green Nereids' (57–60). Theocritus' Nereids have been particularized to Thetis, but the reminiscence is unmistakable.

399–400 'nor do dirty swine have a mind to toss to pieces with their snouts bales of straw'. *solutos* is proleptic. Did V. read σύες ('pigs') instead of μύες ('mice') at Arat. *Phaen.* 1140, καὶ μύες ἡμέριοι ποσσὶ στιβάδα στρωφῶντες | κοίτης ἱμείρονται, 'and in the daytime mice toss straw and desire to build a nest'? If so, his text was superior to ours. Pliny also has foul pigs (*turpes porci*) tossing straw, or rather hay, at *N.H.* 18.364. See Thomas (1986a).

401 Also from Aratus (*Phaen.* 988–90).

403 noctua: Aratus (*Phaen.* 999–1000) merely has the owl's hooting as a sign of fair weather, but V. gives the bird a personality: in such conditions the owl (which is ill-omened) vainly (*nequiquam*) calls for *bad* weather. V. is sparing and restrictive in his references to owls: *noctua* occurs only here, *ulula* only at *E.* 8.55, and *bubo* at *A.* 4.462–3, where also it bodes no good.

404–9   Nisus, changed into a sea-hawk, chases his daughter Scylla (also changed to the mythical bird, the *ciris*) as he seeks revenge for her cutting off his magic lock, and for the resultant fall of his city to Minos. The story survives extensively in the pseudo-Virgilian *Ciris* and at Ovid, *M.* 8.1–151. V.'s six lines are not represented in Aratus, and though they may be purely of his own devising, it is very likely that we have a superimposed reference to another predecessor, as at 383–4 (see n.). Callimachus and Parthenius, the late Hellenistic poet who was perhaps involved in the transference of Alexandrian poetic ideals to Rome, both seem to have treated the myth (Lyne (1978) 6–14), and their involvement makes it likely that V. had *some* model in mind. Lines 406–9 are produced with great attention to visual effect (see n.), almost artificially so. The closest parallel for such artistry can be found at Cat. 64.4–7. Such concinnity and striving for visual effect is a mark of neoteric, rather than Virgilian, poetry. Lyne has noted that '*some* influential ... version of Scylla and Nisus seems to have been current by Augustan times' (14), and it may be that we have in these lines a close reference to Cornelius Gallus – the style seems suitable, as does the involvement of Parthenius (who wrote his Ἐρωτικὰ Παθήματα for Gallus), and the theme of love gone wrong will have been one that appealed to the elegist. If so, the lines may be seen as balancing 374–87, which adapt Gallus' poetic contemporary Varro of Atax. Lines 406–9 are repeated verbatim at the close of the *Ciris* (538–41).

404–5   Fairly closely adapted at [Virg.] *Cir.* 49–52, but both passages may look to a common model (404–9n.).

404   apparet: the placement at the beginning of the line and sentence conveys the bird's sudden appearance; V. so uses the same verb, with the same effect, at *A.* 2.483–4 (in anaphora) and 622.

405   purpureo ... capillo: so *Cir.* 52, and Callim. fr. 288.2 Pf. πορφυρέην ... κρέκα.

406–9   The structure is extremely artful (404–9n.): the word-groups *illa leuem fugiens* and *secat aethera pennis* (the former varied in position) frame the passage, the line endings give a mirror effect (*pennis |... auras|... auras|... pennis*), and the actions of the two characters alternate from subordinate to main clause (*quacumque illa ... secat, ... insequitur Nisus; qua se fert Nisus ... illa secat*).

secat ... secat: V. glosses the (omitted) name of the bird: the *ciris*, which once cut (κείρω) her father's lock, now 'cuts' the air with her wings; cf. Ov. *M.* 8.150–1 *plumis in auem mutata uocatur | Ciris et a tonso est hoc nomen adepta capillo.*

410–23 This section is based on Arat. *Phaen.* 1003–8; in both passages the behaviour of the birds has a human quality. V. perhaps refers to Theophr. *Weather-signs* 52–3 (410–11n.).

410 corui ... gutture: the two words are repeated at the end of the passage (*gutture corui*, 423) to provide a frame.

410–11 ter ... | aut quater: Aratus' ravens caw twice (δισσάκις, *Phaen.* 1004) individually, and then cry out *en masse* (ἀθρόα). Theophrastus (*Weather-signs* 52–3) has ravens calling three times, then repeating indefinitely, and crows cawing three times. V.'s wording may be intended as a reference to this 'dispute' over numbers; if so, this is one of the few indications that he knew of Theophrastus' treatise.

411 ingeminant: here of the ravens' heralding of fair weather, at 333 in the same position of the sound of the storm.

cubilibus: as at 3.230, 4.45 and 4.243 the word brings the animal world closer to that of man.

412 'joyous with some unaccustomed delight'. V. has developed Arat. *Phaen.* 1006 χαίρειν κέ τις οἴσσαιτο, 'you would think they were glad ...' The springtime activity of the bees is described in the same way: *hinc nescio qua dulcedine laetae | progeniem nidosque fouent*, 4.55–6 (cf. 414n.).

414 progeniem paruam dulcisque reuisere nidos: as in the preceding note, there seems to be a connection with the bees of 4.56 (*progeniem nidosque fouent*).

415–16 V. rejects divine or supernatural explanations for the ravens' behaviour (Aratus had not brought up the question), preferring (417–22) more rational, barometric reasoning; this is in keeping with his attitude throughout the poem. The issue recurs when V. treats the bees in Book 4 (creatures associated with the crows; cf. 414n.), and though he is less emphatic, it seems clear that there too he is at least sceptical of theories which see divinity active in the animal world (4.219–27n.).

diuinitus: only here in V. (although cf. 4.219–21 *quidam ... | esse* *apibus partem diuinae mentis* ... | ... *dixere*). The word is here parallel to *fato*: they are not given a higher intelligence by heaven, nor assigned superior foresight by fate.

prudentia: a technical and predominantly prose word, otherwise used by V. only at *A*. 3.433 of the prophetic ability of the seer Helenus.

418 Iuppiter uuidus Austris: i.e. Jupiter Pluuius, here amounting to little more than 'rain'.

419 'condenses what was recently thin, and thins out what was recently dense'; i.e. changes the weather from fine to rainy, and vice versa. V., preoccupied by the topic of what motivates the birds' actions, is now thinking of the whole range of weather-signs; he may have in mind, although the wording is vague, some sort of humoral theory.

420–2 et ... concipiunt 'and their breasts take on impulses, now of one sort, now of a sort different from that assumed while the wind was chasing the clouds away'. The compression is extreme, but V. continues from 419 to think of both types of weather; only at 422–3 does he return to the original subject, signs of fair weather exclusively.

pectora: the breast as the seat of sentient or intellectual activity. The word is so used in the *Georgics* only here and, again, of the bees (4.83).

422 hinc: resumes the topic of fair-weather signs, broadening from those provided by ravens to birds in general (*auium concentus*), as well as the herds (*laetae pecudes*), but for the sake of ring-composition ending with the cry of the ravens: *ouantes gutture corui* (410n.).

423 laetae: here 'glad', somewhat unusually for this poem (1n.), picking up *laeti* at 412. Used of animals it more often means 'fertile': *armentaque laeta*, 2.144.

424–63   Signs given by the moon

This section is based on Arat. *Phaen*. 733–818 (see 351–463n. on V.'s inversion of the original order). Varro (*R.R.* 1.27–37) treated the subject in some detail, but V. seems not to have used him.

424–6 Through repeated second persons (*respicies, te, capiere*) and through explanation of the uses to which observation of the sun and moon may be put, V. conveys a strong didactic impression, not represented in Aratus, who after a brief opening (οὐχ ὁράαις, *Phaen*. 733) merely proceeded with his signs.

lunasque sequentis | ordine 'the phases of the moon which follow in succession'.

427-37 V. has condensed *Phaen.* 778–818, but in one respect has adapted very carefully. At *Phaen.* 783–7 Aratus introduced an acrostic, the first line beginning with the word λεπτή ('slender'), and the first letters of the subsequent four lines combining to give the same word. Callimachus, for whom the word was important in characterizing the correct poetic style ('attenuated'), surely noticed the acrostic: χαίρετε λεπταί | ῥήσιες, Ἀρήτου σύμβολον ἀγρυπνίης, 'hail slender sayings, stamp of Aratus' midnight-oil', *Epigr.* 27.3–4. Given the importance of the word, and of its Latin equivalent *tenuis*, for V. (cf. *E.* 6.8), and given his close reworking of Aratus, it seems most unlikely that he did not notice the acrostic – indeed he has deliberately suppressed the important term, λεπτός (433n.). Thus it is difficult to resist the claim of Brown (1963) that at lines 429, 431 and 433 (that is, in alternate lines) V. created his own modified acrostic to match that of Aratus, precisely at the point of translating the pertinent lines; they begin, with the order reversed, with the first two letters of the poet's full name: *pu-, ue-, ma-.* Line 429, like the first line of Aratus' acrostic, is the sixth line of the section. If, as Servius (*ad A. praef.*) and the Suetonian life (11) tell us, his nickname really was Parthenias ('Maidish'), then *uirgineum* (430) is an exact translation of that nickname.

427 I.e. when the new moon is waxing.

colligit: refers to her light being borrowed.

429 agricolis pelagoque: farmers and sailors are again linked (50n.), and the present pattern alternates with 371–2 where animate (*nauita*; here the other occupation, *agricolis*) was coupled with inanimate (*rura*; here the other environment, *pelago*).

430 at si uirgineum suffuderit ore ruborem: an exquisite touch to describe the soft glow of the moon (the goddess Diana, virgin and therefore prone to blushing). The line, suggested by Aratus' bare participle, ἐρευθομένηι, 'blushing', 803, is evocative of Apollonius' description of the afflicted Medea (θερμὸν δὲ παρηίδας εἶλεν ἔρευθος, 'a warm blush came over her cheeks', *Arg.* 3.963; also 3.298, 681). Dido does not so behave (not a *uirgo?*), but Lavinia, who meets the requirements, does: *flagrantis perfusa genas, cui plurimus ignem | subiecit rubor, A.* 12.65–6.

V. seems to have inverted the more normal construction, *os rubore suffundere*; cf. 254n.

432 (namque is certissimus auctor): V., in taking a clear moon on the fourth day as a sign of fair weather *throughout* the month, departs radically from Aratus, who has more complex divisions of the month, and allows forecasting to be reliable only within them; again V. abbreviates the technical material, and in the process distorts it. The statement *is certissimus auctor* refers of course to the fourth rising (*ortus*), but given V.'s preoccupation with his literary source, might we not see in it also a complimentary aside to Aratus himself? Brown (cf. 427–37n.) detects a reference to V. himself – a sort of *sphragis*.

433   pura neque obtunsis ... cornibus: V. condenses two separate appearances of the moon from Aratus (*Phaen.* 783–7), choosing one adjective from each. For Aratus if the moon is slender (λεπτή) and pure (καθαρή = *pura*), the weather will be fine, if rather thick (παχίων) and with blunted horns (ἀμβλείηισι κεραίαις = *obtunsis ... cornibus*), wind and rain are in store. Given the acrostic on λεπτή (427–37n.), as well as the literary importance of the opposing adjectives, λεπτός and παχύς (not to mention καθαρός), the alert reader who is following the Aratean original will note the omission of the equally well-established Latin equivalents *tenuis* and *pinguis*. Perhaps V. felt that, at least as a pair, they should be reserved for discussion of poetics (as at *E.* 6.4–8). Alternatively suppression of the expected may serve as a means of emphasis (237–8n.).

434   et qui nascentur ab illo: the words recur at *A.* 3.98 (*et qui nascentur ab illis*), in a very different sense, however, referring to the descendants of Aeneas.

436–7   The image of sailors making offerings on their safe return is traditional, but is not taken from Aratus. Again V. deals with the world of navigation (50n.), here even to the exclusion of agriculture.

437   Glauco et Panopeae et Inoo Melicertae: a line, like 138 and 332 (see nn.), which at first sight seems ornamental but on investigation appears to have important literary affiliations. Gellius tells us (13.27.1–2) that V. imitated a line of the poet Parthenius (on whom cf. 404–9): Γλαύκωι καὶ Νηρεῖ καὶ εἰναλίωι Μελικέρτηι, 'to Glaucus and Nereus and the sea-god Melicertes'. As at 281 there is a Greek correption (between *Glauco* and *et*), not present in the Greek model. V. makes two changes, tasteful (*uenuste*) in the view of Gellius, replacing Nereus with one of his daughters, the nymph Panopea, and giving Melicertes the matronymic, 'son of Ino'. He may again be conflating his models. Macrobius (*Sat.* 5.18) has altered the ending of Parthenius' line, making it a transliteration of V.'s (Ἰνώωι Μελικέρτηι), and an epigram of Lucian

(*A.P.* 6.164) has the same change (both of these have Nereus, rather than the Virgilian Panopea). Assuming, as most do, that Gellius correctly records the line of Parthenius, we ask, 'Whence Panopea, and whence "son of Ino"?' In both cases it seems plausible to suggest a Callimachean source. V.'s *Panopea* is a transliteration of Πανόπεια, a form occurring in no other Latin author except Hyginus (the normal Greek form, since Homer, is Πανόπη), and its presence in Nonnus (the first in Greek) makes it likely that both he and V. got it from Callimachus. More telling is Melicertes' matronymic *Inoo*, for Callim. *Aet.* 4, frr. 91–2 Pf. dealt with Melicertes, with, it seems, particular focus on Ino's hurling herself and her son into the sea. These figures are fairly obscure, and it is not unreasonable to suggest that they figured in Callimachus' treatise, *On Nymphs* (4.333–86n.).

At *A.* 5.823–5 Glaucus, Panopea and Melicertes (with the name he assumed in divinity, Palaemon) are all mentioned.

438–63   The sun

The section is adapted from Arat. *Phaen.* 819–91, the chief difference lying again in V.'s compression of technical material, in his mythological colouring (446–7), and in the very individual purpose to which he put sun-signs: through the phenomenon of eclipse (not in Aratus) the sun provides a transition to the closing crescendo of the book – on civil war (463–514).

438–40   Risings and settings both give signs; from the opening line of Aratus' treatment: ἠελίοιο δέ τοι μελέτω ἑκάτερθεν ἰόντος, 'be concerned with the sun when it moves in the east and the west', *Phaen.* 819.

Sol ... | signa dabit; solem ... : the anaphora of *sol*, and the specific wording, are repeated at the end of the section: *sol tibi signa dabit. solem* ..., 463. This is perhaps the best reason for following Geymonat (against most editors) in seeing a new paragraph at 438. Aratus' section is likewise framed by the words σήματα (820) and σήμασι | σημαίνεται (890–1), 'signs', 'gives signs'; on *signa* see 351n., and cf. 471 *signa dabant*.

certissima: in the poem only here and at 432 (on which see n.); otherwise in V. only at *A.* 6.322.

441–2   uariauerit ... | conditus in nubem ... refugerit: the personification of the sun continues, reaching its most extreme at 467, when in pity for Rome he hides his head in eclipse.

441 maculis 'with blotches', rendering Aratus' ποικίλλοιτο ('is variegated', *Phaen.* 822). The word is repeated at 454, and later provides a *signum* for the judging of cows (3.56), sheep (3.389) and bees (4.91).

443 suspecti tibi sint imbres: cf. 429 *parabitur imber*.
urgent: for *urgeo* used intransitively cf. 3.199–200n.

444 arboribusque satisque ... pecorique: the subjects of Books 2, 1 and 3 respectively; for such lines, and for the deliberate exclusion of Book 4 which they imply, see 2.143–4; 4.559–60nn.

445–6 sese | diuersi rumpent: from Arat. *Phaen.* 830 σχιζόμεναι βάλλωσι, '[the beams] part and are thrown out'.

446–7 I.e. when sunrise comes pale. Aratus does not use mythological language in this section, and as often in the Aratean section (383–4, 404–9, 437) V. has overlaid the primary model with reference to another source, here Homer: Ἠὼς δ' ἐκ λεχέων παρ' ἀγαυοῦ Τιθωνοῖο | ὄρνυθ' 'and Dawn rose from her bed and from the side of noble Tithonus', *Il.* 11.1–2 = *Od.* 5.1–2. This heightens the literary level and the element of personification (441–2n.). The figure is repeated in the *Aeneid*, partially at 4.129, completely at 9.460. Aurora secured eternal life, but not youth, for her husband Tithonus, son of Laomedon.

448 heu, male tum ...: the authorial interjection is not in Aratus, and becomes more intense at 456–7 (see n.); with this instance cf. particularly 3.249 *heu, male tum ...*, 435 *ne mihi tum ...*; also 2.252–3n.
male ... mitis defendet pampinus uuas: the vine-leaf (*pampinus*) is personified in its inability to protect its grapes (*uuas*).
male: i.e. *non, uix*.

449 Especially in the middle of the line sound and sense are well accommodated. The verb *crepitare* lends itself readily to such effects; cf. *A.* 5.458–9 *quam multa grandine nimbi | culminibus crepitant ...* The effect of *horrida* is both visual and auditory.

450 hoc: best taken with what follows. The preceding lines have dealt with the signs given by the rising sun; V. now proceeds with those of the setting sun (*emenso ... decedit Olympo*); the first of them introduced by explanatory *nam* (= Greek γάρ).

451 profuerit: see 84n. on V.'s use of this 'didactic' verb.
magis: from Aratus, whose treatment concluded with an emphasis on the signs given by the sun at its setting: ἑσπερίοις καὶ μᾶλλον ἐπίτρεπε σήμασι τούτοις, 'rely even more on those signs in the west', *Phaen.* 890.

saepe uidemus: see 316–18n; the formula is Lucretian: 2.768; 4.61, 598; 5.460.

453 An elegant line, restating, abbreviating and improving upon Arat. *Phaen.* 836–7 καί τοι τὰ μὲν [sc. εἰ μελανεῖ] ὕδατος ἔστω | σήματα μέλλοντος, τὰ δ' ἐρεύθεα πάντ' ἀνέμοιο, 'and let dark stains be signs for you of coming rain, and every blush a sign of wind'.

454 maculae: cf. 441 and n.

immiscerier: the archaic form of the passive infinitive occurs only here in the *Georgics*; there are five instances in the *Aeneid*, all hapax legomena for V.: *accingier*, 4.493; *admittier*, 9.231; *defendier*, 8.493; *dominarier*, 7.70; *farier*, 11.242.

455–6 omnia ... feruere: pointedly parallel to the beginning of the storm (316–34): *omnia uentorum concurrere proelia uidi*, 318; this is the first hint (see 461–2n.) that another storm, this one civil, is imminent (463–514).

feruĕre: the less common third-conjugation form, *feruo*, is both old and poetic. V. uses it exclusively in the infinitive, perhaps for metrical convenience: *A.* 4.409, 567; 8.677; 9.693; cf. also 471 *(ef)feruĕre*. For other inflections he prefers the second conjugation, *ferueo*: 1.327; 4.169; *A.* 1.436; 4.407. The presence of both forms in such close proximity at *A.* 4.407–9 is doubtless artful, a sign of *uariatio*. Cf. 4.262n. on *strido/strideo*.

456–7 V.'s intrusion *(me)* resumes the aside of 448; so specific an authorial comment is paralleled only by 3.435–9, V.'s horror at the thought of lying outdoors in the spring, when the snake emerges from his winter hibernation.

As at 436–7, the world of seafaring stands in for that of agriculture.

non ... moneat: a prohibition; *non* for *ne* (a rareish usage in poetry before Ovid; but cf. *E.* 10.5 *non intermisceat*) perhaps because it is *illa*, rather than the clause as a whole, that is being stressed: 'not on a night such as *that* may anyone advise me ...' (Conington well compares *A.* 12.78).

conuellere: the infinitive with *moneo* is a poeticism (also in Tacitus), and a natural one given the cumbersome nature of the jussive noun clause; cf. 4.186–7 *decedere ... | admonuit*. Very similar is 2.315–16: *nec ... quisquam persuadeat auctor | ... mouere*. Such infinitives are indeed metrically useful.

458 cum referetque diem condetque relatum: an elegant way of referring to sunrise and sunset, with *diem* appropriately positioned between the two verbs, and with *relatum* picking up *referet*.

459   frustra terrebere 'you will have no cause to fear'.

460   claro: emphatic: 'and it will be a *clear* north wind that you will see stirring the woods'.

461–2   A couplet containing a tricolon with equal members, the second element being enjambed, is rather unusual for V. More commonly two units occupy the first line, one the second; occasionally this pattern is inverted (e.g. 2.221–2).

quid Vesper serus uehat: an extreme oddity, the effect of which verges on the humorous: Gellius twice reports (1.22.4; 13.11.1) that one of Varro's Menippean Satires was entitled *Nescis quid uesper serus uehat*, and that it dealt with the correct number of guests, dress and etiquette for dinner parties. It seems unlikely that V. was unaware of these implications, and though it is hard to see any reason for humour here, the reference at least gives a parallel for that notorious and even stranger reminiscence at *A.* 6.460, where Aeneas, encountering the shade of Dido, is made to refer to the mock-elevated apology of Berenice's lock (Cat. 66.39).

cogitet: the verb, which occurs in V. only here (it belongs to comedy and prose) can imply 'plotting', and in that sense looks forward to the *fraus* and the assassination of Julius Caesar which follow immediately (see 455–6n.).

463   sol tibi signa dabit. solem ...: see 438–40n.

463–514   *Portents and civil war*

The famous close of the first book, with its enumeration of portents attending the assassination of Caesar and leading to civil war, with the expression of hope that Octavian will deliver the world from its ills, and with the final simile of the charioteer out of control and careering to his destruction, stands in the same relationship to the preceding technical material as the storm scene of 311–50 (see n.). As that storm came unseasonably and in spite of man's precautions, so comes the storm of civil discord; the sun may tell of its coming (though it does so *after* the fact, *exstincto*, 466 and n.), but that is of little comfort or aid. By the end of *Georgics* 1 the *artes* of the world of *labor* have brought man no great advancement.

The passage clearly made its mark as a set piece (Ovid's imitation at
M. 15.783–831 is but the most interesting), but it is wrong and anach-
ronistic to view these lines as 'rhetorical', for that term applies not to V.
but to his adaptors. V. has arranged the section with care, giving 26 lines
(463–88) to portents, and a further 26 to the civil strife which follows
(489–514). The number 26, curiously, figures prominently in the
numerical ordering at the beginning of Book 2 (2.1–135n.). The section
begins abruptly, in mid-line at 463, and it is accordingly not strictly
speaking a separate section; it is thereby tied closely to the technical
material which precedes.

463–5   The transition from *prognostica* to civil war is almost impercep-
tible; we expect just another *exemplum* (*etiam*, 464, 466), but soon find
ourselves in a very different setting.

464–88   The list of portents is one of the most extensive in ancient
literature, the effect chilling. V. may have found the seed for this passage
in Ap. Rhod. *Arg.* 4.1278–89, where war, storm and threatening por-
tents are linked in a simile describing the shipwrecked Argonauts'
confusion. As in V., statues sweat and eclipse occurs, but the most
compelling similarity is the connection of portents with war and storm;
cf. 480, 481–3nn.

464–5   caecos instare tumultus | saepe monet: Ovid's altera-
tions are such as to identify his model: *magnosque instare tumultus | fibra
monet*, *M.* 15.794–5; elsewhere they amount to 'correction' (476–7, 480,
490–1nn.).

tumultus | ... tumescere: V. perhaps intends a *figura etymologica*.

tumescere: V. otherwise uses the verb only of the sea, when it swells
at the coming of a storm (1.357; 2.479) – again storm and civil strife are
implicitly linked (463–514n.). First attested in V., it is not a comforting
verb, being used, for instance, of the swelling of sores or disease, and cf.
Hor. *Epd.* 16.52 *nec intumescit alta uiperis humus.* Cf. 2.324 *tument* and n.

466–8   The personification of the sun reaches its most intense in
these lines. The list of portents opens and closes (487–8) with meteo-
rological phenomena.

**466   ille etiam exstincto miseratus [sc. est] Caesare
Romam:** V. clearly does not suggest that *signa* could have prevented
these events (the utility of signs is no longer the topic): '*after* the
assassination of Caesar, the sun showed its pity for Rome ...' This
is, perhaps incidentally, in keeping with the facts, since the eclipse

referred to occurred in November of 44 B.C., months after the death of Julius.

miseratus: the form otherwise appears once in the poem, when the other Caesar, Octavian, is invoked and asked to pity the lot of the farmer (41).

467 obscura nitidum: an effective contrast.

ferrugine: literally 'iron-rust', here 'violet gloom'; the *impia saecula* of the next line are the children of the iron age (see n.), and the word may well be chosen in anticipation (there is a similar reference in *ferrum* at 143–4; see n.).

468 impiaque aeternam timuerunt saecula noctem: a power-ful golden line, serving as a clausula, as does that at 497 (117n.). This Catullan device (222n.) may be intended to recall the closing of Cat. 64 (397–408), where familial and civil strife also characterize the debased modern age. That V. has the age of iron specifically in mind is guaran-teed by clear reminiscence of the end of Hor. *Epd.* 16: *Iuppiter illa piae secreuit litora genti,* | *ut inquinauit aere tempus aureum,* | *aere, dehinc ferro durauit saecula, quorum* | *piis secunda uate me datur fuga,* 63–6 (cf. too *impia ... aetas,* 9). *saecula* is used with the same reference to the metallic ages at *E.* 4.5; *A.* 1.291; 8.325; it perhaps has similar implications, carried over from the present line, at 500 *euerso ... saeclo.*

469 tempore quamquam illo: a dramatic opening, stronger than *tum;* cf. 3.245 (the climax of love's destruction) and 531 (the plague): *tempore non alio.*

quamquam: = *tamen;* the sun was not alone in giving signs: 'and yet the earth too and the sea ... '

470 Lines of four words are very rare in V.; in fact, of the six instances in the *Georgics* three (3.550; 4.111, 336) are caused by Greek proper names. Here the effect is heavy and powerful, at 27, solemn – there with similar syntax (dependent genitives replacing adjectives); cf. too 502.

obscenaeque ... importunaeque: the adjectives seem to mean much the same thing: 'accursed', 'ill-omened'.

471 signa dabant: cf. 438–40, 463nn.

471–3 The 'furnaces' (*fornacibus*) of Mt Aetna are the subject of a compelling vignette at *A.* 3.570–87, where V. reworked much of the language of these lines. Cf. too the simile of 4.170–5 (see n.), which is itself employed, no longer as a simile, in the *Aeneid*, at 8.449–53. V.

seems to have in mind Lucr. 6.681–93. According to Servius (*ad* 472), Livy reported that a particularly violent eruption of Aetna occurred before the death of Caesar, and the prodigy-lists of Julius Obsequens, based on the epitomes of Livy, state that eruptions occurred in 135, 126 and 122 B.C. – not, however, in 44.

471 quotiens: only here in the poem; it is the first and most dramatic of a number of references to the frequency and pervasiveness of the portents: 476 *uulgo*, 483–5 *nec ... cessauit*, 487 *non alias ... plura*, 488 *nec ... totiens*.

Cyclopum: cf. *A.* 8.440 *Aetnaei Cyclopes*; they are situated near Aetna at *A.* 3.569, and serve as blacksmiths to the mountain's furnaces.

efferuere: an improvement on Lucretius' *efflet*, 6.682. Cf. 455–6n.

472 uidimus: cf. 478; for the use of *uideo* in such contexts, see 316–18n. (*quotiens* at 471 corresponds to *saepe* in the examples cited there). Cf. Horace's adaptation (501–2n.): *uidimus flauum Tiberim ... ire deiectum monumenta regis*, *Odes* 1.2.13–15 (see Nisbet–Hubbard on 13).

ruptis fornacibus Aetnam: cf. Lucr. 6.682 *uastis fornacibus Aetnae*; *A.* 3.580 *ruptis ... caminis*; see also 4.263 *clausis ... fornacibus*.

473 flammarumque globos liquefactaque uoluere saxa: a vivid line which well compresses its Lucretian model: *hic ubi percaluit calefecitque omnia circum | saxa furens, qua contingit, terramque, et ab ollis | excussit calidum flammis uelocibus ignem, | tollit se ac rectis ita faucibus eicit alte*, 6.686–9; cf. *A.* 3.574–6 *globos flammarum ... liquefactaque saxa*.

474–5 toto ... caelo: the preposition *in* is regularly omitted when the noun is modified by *totus*; cf. 511; 3.367.

Germania ... | audiit: Germany was adjacent to the area of Caesar's operations. The real point, however, is that Germany's awareness of Rome's civil strife will result in her moving against Rome – precisely what happens: *hinc mouet Euphrates, illinc Germania bellum*, 509.

476–7 uox ... | ingens: *uulgo* conveys *fides* (it was not just a single report), whereas Ovid is pointedly sceptical: *cantusque feruntur | auditi sanctis et uerba minantia lucis*, *M.* 15.792–3 (480, 490–1nn.). V.'s language is very close to that of Livy, who describes a number of portents following Tullus Hostilius' defeat of the Sabines: *uisi etiam audire uocem ingentem ex summi cacuminis luco*, 1.31.3. Cf. the omens confronting Dido at *A.* 4.460–1: *hinc exaudiri uoces et uerba uocantis | uisa uiri*.

The effect of the spondaic word *ingens*, at the beginning of the line and followed by a sense-break, is particularly heavy.

477 simulacra modis pallentia miris: with a characteristic change of setting, a direct quotation of Lucr. 1.123. The phrase *modis . . . miris* is applied to the *bugonia* at 4.309 (see n.).

478 uisa: see 472 and n.

obscurum noctis: for the adj. as noun, with a dependent gen., cf. 4.159 *saepta domorum.*

478–9 pecudesque locutae | (infandum!): as with *ingens* at 477 (see n.) the position of *infandum* contributes to the effect of horror. The artful juxtaposition of the virtual opposites, *locutae | (infandum!*)', 'they spoke (unspeakable!)', has attracted no attention from commentators.

479 terraeque dehiscunt: presumably referring to earthquakes; not so at 3.432 *terraeque ardore dehiscunt* (the only other use of the verb in the poem), where the reference is to drought, which brings about an equally ominous situation – the emergence of the deadly snake.

480 inlacrimat templis: although the sweating of statues is a fairly common portent, V. may have a specific source in mind: ἢ ὅταν αὐτόματα ξόανα ῥέηι ἱδρώοντα | αἵματι, 'or when of their own accord the images sweat and run with blood', Ap. Rhod. *Arg.* 4.1284–5 (464–88n.). The wording *inlacrimat templis* ('weeps in temples') is very unusual. With *templis* the preposition *in* must be supplied; this is easy enough, though the omission of *in* generally occurs only where certain adjectives modify the noun (e.g. *totus*, cf. 474 and n.) or where there is a locative sense residing in the verb (e.g. *stare, manere*, etc.) – which is hardly the case with *inlacrimare*. Perhaps *templis* is equivalent to *domi*. But what is unusual here is the use of the compound *inlacrimare* followed by an ambiguous form like *templis*, which *because* of the compound we are initially tempted to take as dative: 'weep over temples' – obvious nonsense. Voss's emendation to *lacrimat* is probably unjustified, but it is worth noting that Ovid also normalized V.'s expression: *mille locis lacrimauit ebur, M.* 15.792; so did Seneca: *fleuit in templis ebur, Thyest.* 702.

481–3 See 325–6n.; the introduction of a flood ties this passage to the storm scene and the flood of those lines. As at 480 (see n.) the source may well be Apollonius, who had a storm preceding sweating statues: ἠέ τιν' ὄμβρον | ἄσπετον, ὅστε βοῶν κατὰ μυρία ἔκλυσεν ἔργα, 'or some mighty storm, which deluges the countless works of oxen', *Arg.* 4.1282–3.

proluit: in the same position as *diluit* at 326.

fluuiorum rex Eridanus: the Po, included in the catalogue of rivers at 4.372–3. Servius (*ad loc.*) refers to Lucan's apparent elaboration of V.'s title, *fluuiorum rex*, at 2.416–20.

fluuiorum: scanned as a molossus; the *i* is consonantal.

camposque per omnis | cum stabulis armenta tulit: a pointed reference to the ultimate futility of observing *signa*; at 355 (see n.) the farmer observed the signs so as to know when to stable his herds: *agricolae propius stabulis armenta tenerent*. This flood swept away herds, stables and all. V. used the image again, in a simile describing the rampage of Pyrrhus and the Greeks through Priam's palace: *spumeus amnis . . . camposque per omnis | cum stabulis armenta trahit, A.* 2.496–9. The plague of *Georgics* 3 has much the same effect (3.471–3).

483–6 A tricolon with three infinitives (*apparere, manare, resonare*) dependent on *nec . . . cessauit*: 'and at that same time there was no respite to the appearance of threatening filaments, etc.'

483 nec tempore eodem: parallel to *non alias* at 487 (see n.); cf. 3.531, introducing the final series of horrors resulting from the plague: *tempore non alio . . .*

484 Haruspicy, consisting chiefly in the examination of the entrails of animals, was probably the most 'official' form of divination. Again there is a parallel from the plague of Book 3, where disease is so far advanced that the very *art* fails (3.490–1).

485–6 et altae | per noctem resonare lupis ululantibus urbes: the sound of *lupis ululantibus* contributes to the sense, and is reinforced by *resonare* (2.328n.). Ovid found dogs more plausible than wolves: *inque foro circumque domos et templa deorum | nocturnos ululasse canes . . . ferunt, M.* 15.796–8.

487–8 The final portents are meteorological, corresponding to those which opened the passage (466–7).

487 non alias: a favoured means of giving temporal or other emphasis, picked up from 483 (see n.); cf. 2.336 *non alios*, 380 *non aliam ob culpam*; 3.245, 531 *tempore non alio*.

489–514 The subject shifts from portents to civil war, this section, like the one which precedes, receiving a total of 26 lines (463–514n.).

489 paribus . . . telis: the adjective is used of the arms of Caesar and Pompey at *A.* 6.826 *paribus . . . armis*; cf. also Lucan 1.6 *pares aquilas*. On the other hand, Antony is barely treated as a Roman in this respect, and Augustus was doubtless delighted with the description at *A.* 8.685 *hinc ope barbarica uariisque Antonius armis.*

concurrere: another reminiscence of the storm: *omnia uentorum concurrere proelia uidi,* 318; the verb otherwise appears in the *Georgics* only at 4.78 (*concurritur*), describing the clash of the bees.

490–1   iterum ... bis: the first time was at the battle of Pharsalus in 48 B.C. The geography is seriously inexact (Philippi cannot easily have 'seen' the engagement at Pharsalus, and Emathia and Haemus are nowhere near that place), but the image, with Philippi personified as a witness, is a powerful one, and, as Page notes, 'it was a remarkable fact that two such battles ... should have taken place so soon after one another both in the same Roman province of Macedonia, and this fact so struck the Roman poets that they not unfrequently speak of the two battles as occurring in the same place' (cf. Ov. *M.* 15.824 *Emathiique iterum madefient caede Philippi*). *iterum* qualifies *uidere* rather than *concurrere*.

491   nec fuit indignum superis: the tone of slight reproach is picked up at 500–1 *saltem ... ne prohibete*.

sanguine nostro: repeated at 501. Cf. Hor. *Odes* 2.1.29–31 *quis non Latino sanguine pinguior | campus sepulcris impia proelia | testatur?*; and cf. *pinguescere campos* in the next line.

492   Haemi ... campos: given the force of *pinguescere* (see n. following) V. surely intends a gloss – 'plains of blood' (cf. Gr. αἷμα).

pinguescere: see 8n. on *pinguis*. The verb *pinguescere*, which occurs only here in V., is grimly ironic: the soil is rich (and the adjective is shortly used, six times, of the farmer's soil: 2.92, 139, 184, 203, 248, 274), but rich with the blood of civil war; for the same type of irony see 495n. The word also effects admirably the transition to the vignette of the farmer at 493–7. Plutarch claims (*Marius* 21) that after Marius' battle against the Ambrones the people of Massilia enclosed their vineyards with the dead bodies, and the following year produced a bumper harvest! He also attributes to Archilochus the claim that the fields are 'fattened' (πιαίνεσθαι = *pinguescere*) by this process.

**493–7   A very vivid picture of the farmer of the future coming upon the weapons and bones of the fallen soldiers. The lines relate the passage to the theme of the poem (the relationship reaches a climax at 508; see n.), and are characterized by a complex temporal presentation: in the future (*tempus ueniet*) the bodies of men contemporary with V. will seem huge (*grandiaque ... ossa*, 497). This is in keeping with the view that man is in constant decline, physically as morally, and it also imparts to the civil war a heroic atmosphere; cf. Hom. *Il.* 1.271–2 and *A.* 12.899–900. For the motif cf. also Herod. 1.68.

**494   The line is repeated, with *dimouit* for *molitus*, at 2.513 (see n.).

495   scabra robigine: as with *pinguescere* at 492, V. uses the words in more than one sense. Here he is describing the rust on the weapons; in Book 2 he uses similar language in the treatment of soil types: *nec scabie et salsa laedit robigine ferrum*, 220.

496   grauibus rastris galeas ... inanis: the weapons of the farmer and the soldier, each modified by an adjective, are carefully juxtaposed, as at 508 *curuae rigidum falces ... ensem*.

497   grandiaque: see 493–7n.

mirabitur: the event is a θαῦμα, 'marvel'; cf. 2.82; 4.309, 554–5nn.

498–514   A prayer that Octavian be permitted to rescue a world in chaos is followed by V.'s dwelling on the desperate state of the country-side and of things in general. The transition from deities (498–9) to Octavian (500–4) is parallel to the progression at the beginning of the book (1–42 and n.), and taken together the two passages form a frame (see 503–5n.).

498   di patrii Indigetes et Romule Vestaque mater 'ancestral gods, heroes of the land, both you, Romulus, and you, mother Vesta'; a general address is followed by specific representatives – the order is reversed – with Romulus standing as an *Indiges*, 'hero of the land', Vesta as a truly ancestral deity who, along with the Lares and Penates, was considered by V. to have been brought by Aeneas from Troy (*A.* 2.296). That the first three words of the line refer to two groups is clear from Ovid's imitation at *M.* 15.861–2 *di ... Aeneae comites ... dique Indigites*.

499   quae ... seruas: strictly modifying Vesta alone, though given his association with the Palatine (not to mention the adjective, *Romana*), Romulus is also intended; cf. Liv. 1.6.4 *Palatium Romulus, Remus Auentinum ad inaugurandum templa capiunt*.

Tuscum: the source of the Tiber, and much of its course, is in Etruria; so winds (e.g. *Africus*, the South Wind) are often designated by the place of their origin.

500   hunc ... iuuenem: Octavian is so called at *E.* 1.42 *illum ... iuuenem*.

saltem: since Julius has been killed the gods are 'at least' to allow Octavian to set things right.

euerso ... saeclo: cf. 468 *impia ... saecula*, and n.

501   ne prohibete: the strong break at the weak caesura of the second foot is extremely unusual (otherwise in the poem only at 2.144, and even there the break is not as strong); the effect is to stress the important opening word (*satis*) of the sentence that follows.

501–2 Horace specifically recalled the lines at the opening of *Odes*
1.2: *iam satis terris niuis atque dirae* | *grandinis misit pater*, 1–2 (see 491n.); the
thought, however, seems to be traditional, since he had said much the
same thing at *Epd*. 7.3–4 *parumne campis atque Neptuno super* | *fusum est
Latini sanguinis . . . ?*. Cf. Acc. *inc.* 657–9 Ribb., also treating the notion of
inherited guilt (that of the house of Atreus), which V. may well have had
in mind: *quinam Tantalidarum internecioni modus* | *paretur? aut quaenam
umquam ob mortem Myrtili* | *poenis luendis dabitur satias supplici?*.

iam pridem: repeated at 503.

sanguine nostro: cf. 491n.

Laomedonteae ... periuria Troiae: on the four-word line cf.
470n. The notion that civil war was visited on Rome as a part of the
inherited guilt or sin going back to the very beginnings of her history is
traditional, but varies greatly in its details. Laomedon's can be seen as
the 'primal sin': king of Troy and father of Priam, he is held to have
cheated Apollo and Poseidon of their payment after they helped to build
the walls of Troy. The adjective *Laomedonteus* is first attested in Latin
here, and seems to be Callimachean (*Aet.* 1, fr. 21.4 Pf.). Other instances
of guilt to be expiated by civil war are Paris' 'cheating' of Hera and
Athena, and his violation (through the seduction of Helen) of the laws of
hospitality (Hor. *Odes* 3.3.23–6); possibly Aeneas' desertion of Dido,
resulting in the Punic, rather than the civil, wars (*A.* 4.622–9); the
murder of Rhea Silvia, or Ilia, mother of Romulus and Remus (Hor.
Odes 1.2.13–20); and, of course, the actual fratricide, which is played out
by the metaphorical fratricide of civil war, the death of Remus: *acerba
fata Romanos agunt* | *scelusque fraternae necis*, | *ut immerentis fluxit in terram Remi*
| *sacer nepotibus cruor*, Hor. *Epd.* 7.17–20; *Odes* 3.3.30–3; on V.'s am-
bivalence towards Romulus see 2.533n.

503–5 'For long now has heaven begrudged us your presence,
Caesar, complaining that you care for triumphs among mortals [which
you are compelled to do], inasmuch as right and wrong are inverted
among them [i.e. among mortals].' *ubi* is a virtual relative, with *hominum*
as its antecedent. The anticipation of Octavian's immortality, with the
added feature of the gods' impatience for its coming about, is recapitu-
lated from 24–5 *tuque adeo, . . . incertum est*. The wish that this event be
delayed as late as possible is repeated by Horace (*serus in caelum redeas
diuque* | *laetus intersis populo Quirini*, | *neue te nostris uitiis iniquum* | *ocior aura* |
tollat, Odes 1.2.45–9) and Ovid (*tarda sit illa dies et nostro serior aeuo . . .*,
M. 15.868).

503   iam pridem: repeated from 501.

504   hominum ... curare triumphos: Horace alludes to V.'s wording and sentiment: *hic magnos potius triumphos, | hic ames dici pater atque princeps, Odes* 1.2.49–50. As 505 makes clear, the somewhat strange phrase *curare triumphos* has to mean 'have a concern for [military action which will set the world right and result in] triumphs'.

505   fas uersum atque nefas: perhaps an allusion to the same context at the end of Cat. 64: *omnia fanda nefanda malo permixta furore | iustificam nobis mentem auertere deorum*, 405–6; *uersum* means 'inverted', not 'overturned'.

505–8   A return to the theme of agriculture, with the countryside in reversion as a result of civil strife (493–7n.).

506   tam multae scelerum facies: so Aeneas, on seeing Tartarus and the punishments meted out by Tisiphone, asks the Sibyl: *quae scelerum facies?, A.* 6.560.

506–7   non ullus aratro | dignus honos 'the plough has not its due honour'; *aratro* is dative. This reverses 168, a line which introduced the section on the plough: *si te digna manet diuini gloria ruris*.

507   squalent abductis arua colonis: it is hard to improve on the note of Page (ad loc.): 'These four words are a model of Virgilian finish. *squalent* means first that the fields being untilled are ragged and full of weeds, but *squaleo, squalor, squalidus* are continually used of *mourning*, and so the fields are also represented as mourning for the husbandmen who have been carried off to the wars: again, *squalent* presents an artistic contrast with *colonis*, for *colonus* suggests *colo* and *cultus* "elegance", "neatness".'

508   et curuae rigidum falces conflantur in ensem: almost a golden line, and the equal of one in the careful ordering of noun and adjective: as at 496 (see n.) – with the addition of chiastic order – the agricultural (*curuae ... falces*) and the military (*rigidum ... ensem*) are juxtaposed and set in contrast. The sentiment of the line is topical (Lucr. 5.1293–6; *A.* 7.635–6; Ov. *Fast.* 1.697–700), but its effect here is no less powerful for that reason.

509   hinc ... illinc: cf. 3.257n.

Euphrates: the Assyrian river occurs three times in V.'s poetry, in progressively submissive light: here it stirs up war on Rome, at 4.561 Octavian brings war to its banks, and at *A.* 8.726 it appears captive on the shield of Aeneas, *mollior undis*. Each of these instances is in the sixth line from the end of its respective book, and that is deliberate, for it is where Virgil found it in *Hymn* 2 of Callimachus, Ἀσσυρίου ποταμοῖο μέγας ῥόος, 'the great flow of the Assyrian river', 108; see Scodel and Thomas (1984).

Germania: cf. 474–5n.

510 uicinae ruptis inter se legibus urbes: word-order reflects sense, as *uicinae* and *urbes* are placed at the beginning and end of the line, and the mediating phrase *inter se* is surrounded by the telling combination *ruptis ... legibus.*

511 saeuit: here Mars rages in a world gone mad with civil strife, at 3.551–2 Tisiphone does likewise (*saeuit ... Tisiphone*) in a world collapsing before the catastrophe of plague, as does the snake, precursor of plague, at 3.434 (*saeuit agris*). Cf. *A.* 8.700 *saeuit medio in certamine Mauors,* where the context is the same as this, the battle of Actium.

toto ... orbe: cf. *toto ... caelo,* 474–5 and n.

512–14   The book ends on a pessimistic note, with a striking simile, that of the chariot and charioteer out of control; it is parallel to the earlier simile, also in three lines, of the rower who, if he relaxes his efforts, is swept downstream (201–3 and n.). V. seems indebted to Hor. *Sat.* 1.1.114–16 (512, 514nn.), and himself drew on the language of these lines in presenting chariot-races at 3.103–12 and *A.* 5.144–7. Cf. 2.541–2n. for similarities to the end of Book 2.

512 ut cum carceribus sese effudere quadrigae: the opening words are perhaps indebted to Hor. *Sat.* 1.1.114 *ut, cum carceribus missos rapit ungula currus;* at 3.104 V. refers to the present line, and perhaps to Horace as well: *ruuntque effusi carcere currus.*

513 addunt in spatia: 'speed on lap after lap'; the MSS offer *spatia, spatio, se in spatia* and *se in spatio,* but the present reading is confirmed by Servius, by Quint. 8.3.78, and, beyond doubt, by Sil. 16.376 *in spatia addebant.* Commentators point to phrases such as *in annos* ('year after year') and *in dies* ('day after day'), assuming an ellipse of *gradum* (*addere gradum* = 'to increase speed'), or, perhaps better, an intransitive use of *addere,* 'to speed up'; some suggest ellipse of *se,* or supply it from 512, but this seems less satisfactory. No solution is entirely satisfying; the oddity may be due to V.'s striving to create a parallel with 2.541, where *spatiis* also occurs, also in the penultimate line of the book.

frustra: all efforts fail; see 192n.

514 fertur equis auriga: also perhaps looks to Horace (*instat equis auriga, Sat.* 1.1.115); reworked at *A.* 1.476, of the doomed Troilus: *fertur equis curruque haeret resupinus inani.*

The coincidence of accent and ictus in all feet but the second is extremely unusual for V. and creates an emphatic rhythm which perhaps reflects the course of the chariot along the track.

Georgics 2

1-135   These lines, technical in nature and leading up to the first 'digression' of the book, the *laudes Italiae* (136-76), are produced with careful attention to numerical order: technical paragraphs of 26 lines (9-34, 47-72, 83-108, 109-135 (129 is interpolated; see n.)) alternate with sections of eight (1-8), 12 (35-46) and ten (73-82) lines respectively. On the number 26 in V.'s structural arrangements see 1.463-514n. Cf. 3.49-94, 384-93.

1-8   The proem

At the outset of the two central books specific and appropriate deities are invoked, Bacchus in these lines, Pales, Apollo and the haunts of Pan at 3.1-2; see n. for the close connection between the beginnings of these, and of all four, books (also 1.1, 5; 2.1, 2; 4.1-2nn.).

   1   Hactenus aruorum cultus et sidera caeli: *hactenus* is recalled in the same position at the beginning of Book 4 (*protinus*) – the two words do not otherwise occur in the poem, *aruorum cultu(s)* recurs in the final summary (4.559), and *sidera* recalls *sidere* in the same position in 1.1; see 9n. *cecini* must be supplied from *canam* in the next line (Forbiger); it might also be supplied from *canere incipiam* at 1.5 (1-8n.).

   2   nunc te, Bacche, canam: cf. 388 *et te, Bacche, uocant*; the words are recalled at 3.1 *te quoque, magna Pales, . . . canemus*; on these uses of *cano* see 1.5n.

   te ... tecum: frequent use of the second person pronoun or adjective (cf. *tuis*, 4; *tibi*, 5), with the repetition of the invocation (*huc, pater o Lenaee*, 4, 7), are typical hymnic features. On the former cf. 388 *te ... tibique*; and Horace's hymn, also to Bacchus, at *Odes* 2.19: *tu ... tu ... tu ... tu ... te*, 17-29; also throughout the prayer to Venus at the beginning of Lucr. 1.

   Bacche: prominently placed (with the title Liber) in the company of Ceres in the prayer of Book 1 (1.7 and n.), he is also treated at 380-96 of the present book.

   2-3   siluestria ... | uirgulta: trees other than the vine and the olive are treated generally at 9-135, then more exclusively at 426-54.

3 prolem tarde crescentis oliuae: cf. Varro, *R.R.* 1.41 *olea in crescendo tarda*. The impression is that the olive will be treated equivalently to the vine (although the omission of Minerva is rather curious); in fact it is given a mere six lines (420–5; see n. and 1.18–19n.).

4 huc, pater o Lenaee: repeated at 7 (see 2n.); the epithet for Bacchus is used only here and at 529 *te libans, Lenaee* (see n.; cf., however, 3.509–10 *latices* ... | *Lenaeos*).

omnia plena: at *E.* 3.60 (*ab Ioue principium Musae: Iouis omnia plena*) V. adapted the opening of Aratus' *Phaenomena*: Ἐκ Διὸς ἀρχώμεσθα ... μεσταὶ δὲ Διὸς πᾶσαι μὲν ἀγυιαί, 'let us begin from Zeus ... full of Zeus are all the streets ...', 1–2. The words *omnia plena* in 4 look to *E.* 3.60, but also, perhaps, directly to Aratus' μεσταί ... πᾶσαι, since, like that reference, the present one comes in a proem.

5 grauidus autumno: an odd ending, with 3.276 the only instance in the poem of a spondaic line which is not in some way indebted to Greek, and which does not in fact end with a *spondeiazon* (1.221n.); the final syllable of *grauidus* is lengthened in ictus (cf. 1.138n.)

6 plenis ... labris 'in full vats'; the repetition of *plena* (4) is casual, as often in Latin poetry; *labrum*, 'vat', is a prose word, here used technically.

7 huc, pater o Lenaee: see 4n.

7–8 ueni ... coturnis: Bacchus is invoked, and invited to participate in the pressing of the new wine. The image is clearly metaphorical, with wine-pressing, and V.'s involvement in it (*mecum*), standing for the poetry of Book 2. There is perhaps a further, more profound, metaphorical reference in the lines, to generic preference. Bacchus' (or Dionysus') traditional involvement with poetry is specific – he is the god of drama, particularly tragedy; hence V. refers to his buskins (*coturnis*), the footwear of the tragic actor. But for the Augustan poets he came to occupy a new position, as favourable to the new poetry; cf. Horace's reference to contemporary poets, himself included, as *cliens Bacchi, Epist.* 2.2.78. Programmatically, V.'s lines may be taken to mean 'Remove the buskins [of tragedy], Bacchus, and join me in soaking your naked legs in the new must [of Virgilian poetry].' Subsequent writers consistently associate the wearing of *coturni* with the writing of tragedy: cf. Ov. *Am.* 2.18.15; 3.1.63–4; Martial 8.3.13; 13.94.2–3. For *musto ... nouo* as a reference to poetry cf. Lucr. 1.927–8 *iuuat integros accedere fontis | atque haurire*; Prop. 3.3.5 *paruaque tam magnis admoram fontibus ora*; that V.'s liquid is wine, rather than water from a spring, follows from the theme of *Georgics* 2.

9–34   Spontaneous and natural reproduction and propagation by man

The two divisions occupy 13 lines each (9–21, 22-34); see 1–135n. These two subsections are answered by 47–82 (see n.), with 9–21 developed by 47–60, 22–34 by 61–72. V.'s didactic model here, and in much of the book, is Theophr. *H.P.* 2, which treats the propagation of trees.

The distinction between spontaneity and cultivation, in mythical and in georgic terms, has already played an important part in the poem (see 1.21–3n.), and continues to do so, particularly in Book 2.

9–21   Three types of natural growth: spontaneous (10–13), from the seed put out by the mother tree (14–16) and from the root of the tree (17–19). The model is Theophr. *H.P.* 2.1.1, which lists seven methods, the first three being precisely these: αἱ γενέσεις ... ἢ αὐτόμαται ἢ ἀπὸ σπέρματος ἢ ἀπὸ ῥίζης, 'they originate either spontaneously, or from seed, or from root'. Theophrastus then notes that the methods from seed and from root may be classed as spontaneous, which is the botanical truth; the ancient tradition, however, seems to have firmly believed in a purely spontaneous type of generation, and Anaxagoras and others believed that the seeds of plants are contained in the air, and are germinated through contact with water or soil (Theophr. *H.P.* 3.1.4; Varro, *R.R.* 1.40.1).

9   Principio: the proems of Books 2 and 4 begin with *hactenus* and *protinus* (1n.); the technical material of both books begins with *principio* (here and at 4.8), a word not otherwise used in the poem.

natura: cf. Theophrastus' adjective φυσικός, 'produced by nature', *H.P.* 2.1.1, but for V. the importance of the word is much greater than this implies: it is repeated, to provide a frame to the passage, at 20, and later, at 49, in a position parallel to this (47–82n.). At 20 it is in contrast to *usus* at the beginning of the section on propagation effected by man (22); nor are the two terms merely set beside each other, rather they are very soon to be in conflict (see 32–4, 69–72, 80–2nn.), for much of V.'s concern in Book 2, as throughout the poem, is to observe and comment upon the struggle of the world of *usus*, which in mythical terms is the

world of Jupiter (1.4n. and 1.133), against the natural world, that of
Saturn (10–11n.).

At the end of the technical part of the book (420–57) V. returns to the
contrast (and conflict; 420–5n.) between natural growth and propaga-
tion by man, thus providing a frame for the whole book.

10   aliae: so the next subsection begins *sunt alii* [*modi*], 22.

10–11   nullis hominum cogentibus ipsae | sponte sua: as at 47
(*sponte sua*, see n.) the language strongly recalls that applied to golden-
age spontaneity (1.127n.), just as at 22 (*usus*), 52 (*artis*) and 61 (*labor*) the
terms are representative of the opposite age, that of Jupiter (9, 48nn.).
The theme is resumed at the end of the book (420–5, 458–540 nn.). The
periphrasis *nullis hominum* is perhaps caused by the fact that *hominibus*
cannot be used in the hexameter.

11–12   camposque ... tenent: vivid imagery invigorates the
purely technical material of Theophrastus.

12–13   The *siler*, broom, poplar and willow are all perceived, falsely
of course, as being generated spontaneously. The exact meaning of *siler*
is unknown; we hear from Pliny (*N.H.* 16.77) that it likes to be near
water, and thus Sargeaunt (1920) and most of the commentators,
without any explicit ancient evidence, suggest some sort of willow (of
which Italy boasted many varieties). Abbe (1965) argues (149–51) that
a member of the Umbelliferae (Carrot family) is more likely.

genistae | ... salicta: see 434n.

glauca: also of willows at 4.182.

14   posito ... de semine 'from the fallen seed'; at first sight this
looks as if it means the opposite (referring to man's involvement), like
the parallel phrase at 57 *seminibus iactis* (47–82n.); but man comes on the
scene only with the word *usus* (22). The two phrases are reworked later
in the book, there referring strictly to man's planting: 317 *semine iacto*,
354 *seminibus positis* (in these two instances *semina* are 'sets' rather than
'seeds').

14–16   Chestnut and oak grow from the fallen seed. *quercus* (or *robor*)
is the English, or Pedunculate, Oak (*Quercus robur*), *aesculus* (not to be
confused with the modern genus *Aesculus* – Buckeye, or Horse-chestnut)
the Durmast Oak (*Quercus petraea*). In fact the latter is a related species
of the former, and they are very similar (both belonging to the white oak
group). The *ilex*, the Holm Oak (*Quercus ilex*), is distinct in appearance,
and is an evergreen.

15 nemorumque ... frondet: the reference is to the oak-trees of Dodona, the oracle of Zeus, as is clear from the words completing line 16 (1.8n.); through the connected and implicit reference to acorns, the food of pre-agricultural man, V. may intend to suggest the golden age (10–11n.).

16 habitae Grais oracula: *Grais* is dative of agent (487n.). V.'s words seem almost to express *diffidentia*: 'oaks, treated as oracles by the Greeks'. For the slight note of polemic cf. 1.38 *quamuis Elysios miretur Graecia campos* (see n. and 3.9on.).

17–19 Cherry, elm and bay send out new growth from the root of the mother tree.

17 pullulat 'sends out new shoots'; the verb is formed on the diminutive of *pullus, pullulus*, lit. 'chick', 'young child'; it is particularly appropriate here given the image of motherhood at 19 (see n.).

18 ut 'as with', 'e.g.'.

Parnasia laurus: the adjective (which conjures up the Apollo of Augustan poetry) is not merely ornamental; the only other use of *Parnasius* in V. (who uses it first in Latin) is in a highly programmatic setting at *E.* 6.29 *nec tantum Phoebo gaudet Parnasia rupes*.

19 The line, complemented by 55 (*nunc altae frondes et rami matris opacant*; see 47–82n.), represents the first instance of personification in *Georgics* 2 – a constant feature throughout the rest of the poem. Plants are presented through the image of a familial bond (esp. that between mother and child), threatened by the will of the efficient man operating under the principles of *labor* (23, 80–2, 268nn.).

parua sub ingenti: a pleasing and vivid contrast.

20 natura: cf. 9n.

22–34 Thirteen lines on the spontaneous and natural forms of generation are followed by another thirteen (9–34n.) on propagation effected by man, namely the planting of suckers, of stems, layers, cuttings, growing from a piece of trunk, and grafting and budding. See 47–72n. on the parallel reiteration of these methods.

22 'there are other methods, which actual experience has in the course of things discovered for herself'. The exact sense of *uia* is somewhat difficult (locative?), but the meaning is clear enough. On the cultural implications of *usus* see 9, 10–11nn. There is a telling contrast with 20.

23 This line establishes the forceful and military nature of arboriculture, an association which pervades the book, surfacing particularly in some details of the *laudes Italiae* (145–8, 161–4, 170–2nn.), in the description of wood-clearing at 207–11, in the military simile at 279–83, at 367–70, and in the attack on Bacchus and wine at 454–7. Military associations were already implicit in this activity (White (1970) 263–6); it is typical of V. that he should have made the association explicit and sustained. His choice of language (*tenero abscindens de corpore matrum*) also serves to break down all barriers between the human and the plant world; for which cf. also 19, 268, 279–83, 362–70nn.

plantas 'suckers', also referred to as *stolones*, in Theophrastus παρασπάς, 'a piece torn off', *H.P.* 2.1.1; Pliny notes *auolsique arboribus stolones uixere* (*N.H.* 17.66), and talks in terms reminiscent of the present line (*e matris … corpore*, 17.67).

24–5 The second method involves the planting of stems, or stocks (*stirpes*; *sudes* and *uallos* merely repeat the term), with the bottom either split in the shape of a cross (*quadrifidasque*) or sharpened (*acuto robore*), to promote rooting.

obruit: Ovid perhaps recalled V. when describing the advent of agriculture at the close of the golden age: *semina tum primum longis Cerealia sulcis | obruta sunt, M.* 1.123–4.

26–7 'Layering' consists of bending over the top (so as to form an *arcus*) or some part of the parent tree, and burying it until it forms its own root system.

exspectant: the personification continues, as the plant is presented as 'waiting for' this process and for the shoots (*plantaria*) which result; contrast 420–1, of the 'uncultivated' olive: *neque illae | procuruam exspectant falcem.*

uiua: unlike the suckers (*plantas*) of 24, these continue their life with the parent plant, but in their own (*sua*) soil.

28–9 Cuttings may even be taken from the the top of the tree, and returned (*referens*) to the earth.

nil radicis egent: not 'need no root', but rather 'need not come from, be associated with, the root area'.

30–1 Theophrastus includes this method: 'or from wood cut up [cf. *sectis*] into small pieces', *H.P.* 2.1.1; also 2.1.4 of the olive, as here.

mirabile dictu: suggests a θαῦμα, 'miracle' and looks in addition to the miraculous graft that follows (32–4); see n. and cf. *miratastque*, 82 and n.

31 truditur: see 335n.

32–4 The topic of grafting, infused with the language of personification, provides a climax to the paragraph, as do 69–72 and 80–2 (47–82n.). Two difficult questions present themselves: are these grafts possible, and if not, did Virgil believe them to be possible? The science of graft compatibility has made little advance since V.'s time: cultivars of the same species may reject a graft (as frequently occurs with the Red Maple, *Acer rubrum*), while successful unions may occur from one genus to another (for instance pear and hawthorn), but one fact (and it is virtually the only fact in this matter) seems certain: for a successful union the stock and scion must be within the same family. 'Between unrelated woody perennials it is doubtful if a definitely compatible union has ever been established' (Garner (1958) 36). It is fairly clear from Varro, *R.R.* 1.40.5–6 that V. was aware of this. Thus the graft proposed at 33 (apple onto pear) is possible (both Rosaceae), while cornel onto plum (34) is impossible (Cornaceae onto Rosaceae), as are the unions of walnut (Juglandaceae) and arbutus (Ericaceae) at 69, plane (Platanaceae) and apple (Rosaceae) at 70, pear (Rosaceae) and elm (Ulmaceae) at 71–2; at 71 chestnut and beech (both Fagaceae) is at least theoretically possible. Of the six grafts four are not possible, and the other two, in that they are not of the same genus, are at least unlikely, and of the normal type of graft (between species within the same genus) V. says nothing. He did realize the impossibility of his choices, for he places such grafts in the area of the θαῦμα ('marvel', 'miracle') when, at *E.* 8.52–3, in a series of *adynata*, he writes: *nunc et ouis ultro fugiat lupus, aurea durae* | *mala ferant quercus, narcisso floreat alnus*, etc. The discussion of impracticable or impossible grafts constitutes the first of a number of deliberate falsehoods in *Georgics* 2 (45–6n.), chiefly in the *laudes Italiae* and in the praise of rustic life at the end of the book; the ultimate effect of these falsehoods is to pose certain questions concerning the 'success' which is generally perceived in this book (see Introduction, pp. 20–1). At the same time, by positing these grafts, V. stresses the transformation of the natural tree at the hands of man and under the application of *labor* (see 33, 80–2, 82nn.).

32 saepe … uidemus: on the combination see 1.316–18n.; the device, whose main function is to impart *fides*, is employed at a moment when *diffidentia* is most likely to be provoked (32–4; 3.274nn.).

33 mutatamque: the nature of the pear tree is transformed; a hint of disruption, which at 82 (*non sua poma*; see n.) becomes explicit and open. See also 268n.

insita: cf. 50 *inserat*, 69 *inseritur*, 73 *inserere*; see 302n.

mala: here and at 70 apples, at 127 the citron (*Malus medica* or *persica*).

34 prunis lapidosa rubescere corna: since the cornel (a form of cherry) is redder than the plum, better 'stony cornels blushing red on plum [trees]' than 'stony cornel trees blushing with plums'; besides, *lapidosa* hardly fits *corna* in the sense of 'cornel trees'. Still, this is somewhat odd in that plums are superior to cornels as fruit, and the graft might be expected to go the other way. *rubescere* is answered by *incanuit* in a parallel context at 71.

35–46   Exhortation of the farmer and enlistment of the support of Maecenas

V. passes from his didactic addressees (*agricolae*) to his patron (Maecenas), delivering, for the first time in the poem, lines of a programmatic nature; the delaying of the invocation until the 'narrative' is under way may owe something to Hellenistic poetry (Thomas (1985) 65).

35 Quare agite: an opening favoured by V., who uses this exhortatory imperative in the same position four times after *quare* (thrice with a following *o*), twice after *ergo* and once after *quin*, these being the only occurrences.

proprios generatim discite cultus 'learn the cultivation proper to each according to *genus*'; with pointed irony, in that the previous line contains a (deliberate) error concerning *genus* – the grafting of cornel onto plum (see 32–4n., and for parallel irony 45–6n.).

36 fructusque feros mollite colendo: the exhortation, with its appealing antithesis (*feros mollite*), is a conflation of Theophr. *H.P.* 2.2.9 (τὸ ἄγριον ἐξημεροῦται, 'the wild becomes cultivated') and Lucr. 5.1368–9 *fructusque feros mansuescere terra | cernebant indulgendo blandeque colendo*; for the thought cf. 49–52, and 239–40 (and n.) *nec mansuescit arando*.

37 neu segnes iaceant terrae: cf. 1.72, where temporary *segnities* (that of fallow land) was encouraged: *segnem patiere situ durescere campum*.

37–8 iuuat … Taburnum: the locale of the vine is Thracian – the range Ismaros, or Ismara, is noted for its wine (Maronean) as early as Hom. *Od* 9.196–8, and is associated with Orpheus at *E.* 6.30; the olive, on the other hand, is situated in Italy, on the Samnian mountain Taburnus, first mentioned here, recurring at *A.* 12.715, and thereafter only at Grat. 509. Cf. 219 *uiridi se gramine uestit*.

39 tuque: V. passes from the farmers to Maecenas, as he did at the beginning of the poem from the gods to Octavian (*tuque*, 1.24).

ades: see 1.18n.

inceptumque: so, at the outset of the poem, *hinc canere incipiam*, 1.5.

decurre laborem: *decurre* begins the nautical metaphor, which continues until 45; it is modelled on Greek κατατρέχω, καταπλέω, 'run, sail in to the shore' (representing the end of the *labor*). *laborem* is an internal accusative, analogous to *cursum* (*currere*). Cf. 4.116 *extremo . . . iam sub fine laborum*; and see 41n.

40 o decus, o famae merito pars maxima nostrae: cf. the addresses to Maecenas at Hor. *Odes* 1.1.2 (*o et praesidium et dulce decus meum*) and Prop. 2.1.74 (*et uitae et morti gloria iusta meae*); both doubtless look to the present line.

41–5 The oddness and complexity of these important programmatic lines have not been sufficiently appreciated. V. first speaks of the poem as a large-scale, even epic, project: *pelagoque uolans da uela patenti* (see Wimmel (1960) 227–33 on the open sea as a metaphor for epic poetry). At 42–4 he seems to have second thoughts, and by 44 a more Callimachean characterization of the poem has been achieved (42–4n.). (Cf. Introduction, pp. 1–3.)

41 Maecenas: cf. 1.2n. on the careful placement of Maecenas' name in the *Georgics*.

pelagoque uolans da uela patenti: the metaphor recurs as V. draws near to the close of the poem: *ni . . . uela traham et terris festinem aduertere proram*, 4.116–17 (cf. 39n.).

42–4 non . . . uox: at Hom. *Il.* 2.488–90 the poet invokes the Muses, without whose aid 'I could not tell of the multitude [of the ships], nor could I name them, not if I had ten tongues, and ten mouths, a voice which could not break, and within me a heart of bronze.' The image appealed to Ennius: *non si, lingua loqui saperet quibus, ora decem sint,* | *innumerum, ferro cor sit pectusque reuinctum*, *Ann.* 469–70 Skutsch; the apodosis is not cited, but was clearly along the lines of [*non*] *dicere possim*. That is certainly how V. himself reworked the image at *A.* 6.625–7 *non,* | *mihi si linguae centum sint oraque centum,* | *ferrea uox, omnis scelerum comprendere formas,* | *omnia poenarum percurrere nomina possim*; cf. too *E.* 8.63 *non omnia possumus omnes*. What is different and striking about the lines in *Georgics* 2, though unremarked by commentators, is that the potentiality of the apodosis in Homer, presumably Ennius, and in the *Aeneid* ('I *could* not enumerate, etc.'), is here a matter of volition or preference ('I do not *wish* to cover everything'); V. has effectively converted a Homeric commonplace into a piece of Callimachean poetics (41–5n.).

43   centum ... centum: V. preserves the anaphora of the Homeric model (δέκα ... δέκα), but for greater effect changes the number from 10 to 100.

44   ferrea uox: at *Il.* 2.490 the voice is described as 'not to be broken', the heart as 'made of bronze'. Ennius, who seems not to have represented the Homeric voice, did update the Homeric heart (42–4n.). V. has conflated his two models.

44–5   ades et primi lege litoris oram; | in manibus terrae: the Callimachean position is now restored, the open sea of 41 (*pelagoque ... patenti*) having been replaced by the more acceptable waters close to the shore (41–5, 42–4nn.). In Prop. 3.3 Apollo, who looks just like the Apollo of the preface to Callimachus' *Aetia* (fr. 1.21–30 Pf.), ends his advice to the poet: *alter remus aquas alter tibi radat harenas, | tutus eris: medio maxima turba mari est*, 23–4.

in manibus 'close at hand'; cf. Ap. Rhod. *Arg.* 1.1112–13 πᾶσα περαίη | Θρηικίης ἐνὶ χερσὶν ἑαῖς προυφαίνετ' ἰδέσθαι, 'and the whole coast of Thrace appeared to their view close at hand'.

45–6   non hic te carmine ficto | ... tenebo: poets are not always bound to reality or truth; so the Muses of Hesiod: ἴδμεν ψεύδεα πολλὰ λέγειν ἐτύμοισιν ὁμοῖα, | ἴδμεν δ' εὖτ' ἐθέλωμεν ἀληθέα γηρύσασθαι, 'We know how to tell many plausible falsehoods, but we know, when we wish, how to utter the truth', *Theog.* 27–8. Cf. Horace's adaptation: *ficta uoluptatis causa sint proxima ueris*, *A.P.* 338. V.'s *non hic* implies that distortion is for him a possibility. Why the disclaimer here in the programmatic invocation of *Georgics* 2 – in the invocation of a book which 25 lines later presents three unequivocally fictitious grafts (69–72), which presents praises of Italy which distort reality, and in places amount to no praises at all (136–76 and n.), and which ends (458–540) with a description of the joys of rustic life whose details are completely at variance with the agricultural realities of the poem? The very claim is itself a piece of ironical fiction, like *generatim* at 35 (see n.), with which it frames the invocation.

non ... per ambages et longa exorsa 'nor through digressions and long preludes'; this book contains three passages which have been characterized by critics as 'digressions', and there is only one other book in V.'s corpus (*Georgics* 3) which is still involved in its prelude as late as line 46.

47–82   Spontaneous and natural reproduction, and propagation by man:
recapitulation and development

The theme of 9–34 is resumed, again to receive 26 lines (1–135n.), with careful repetition designed to point to the parallelism, and with inversion of the way in which the two types of propagation are carried out: 9–21 enumerated the types of spontaneous or naturally propagated trees, while 22–34 listed the arboricultural methods. The present lines investigate the application of arboriculture to *spontaneous and natural* growth (47–60) and enumerate the types of trees most commonly propagated by man. This inversion is attended by a similar transference within each of the two categories: under natural reproduction, at 53–6 growth from the root of another tree (= 17–19) now precedes growth from a seed put out by the parent tree (57–60 = 14–16); in the earlier passage, moreover, each sub-category received three lines – now each receives four. The same reversal of order occurs in the treatment of arboricultural methods: at 63 growth from parts of the trunk (= 30–1), at 63–4 from layers (= 26–7), at 64 from stems (= 24–5), at 65–8 from suckers (= 23–4). Only grafting disrupts the neatness of this reversal, in both passages being purposely placed in the final, climactic position (69–72 = 32–4), and receiving its own recapitulation at 73–82 (see n., also at 32–4, 69–72). As often, it is the material of a predominantly technical nature that is most artfully presented.

   47   Sponte sua quae se tollunt in luminis oras: the first words recall 11 (*sponte sua*). The line is in part an amalgam of Lucretian language: *sponte sua nequeant liquidas existere in auras*, 5.212 (from a passage which influenced V. at 1.197–9; see n.); *nec sine te quicquam dias in luminis oras | exoritur*, 1.22 – on this Page aptly cites Munro: '*luminis oras*, a favourite phrase by which he [Lucretius] seems to denote the line or border which divides light from darkness, being from nonbeing'. The phrase occurs seven more times in Lucretius, at 5.781 with *tollere*, as here.

   48   infecunda quidem, sed laeta et fortia: important terms for the poem; spontaneous and natural growth, while not productive of fruit, is strong (see 1.1n. on *laetus*, 446n. on *fecundus*) and hardy. This is

almost the language of primitivism, with spontaneous trees charac-
terized as products of a golden, or Saturnian, age, to be tamed by the *ars*
of the new, agricultural age (49–51 and 10–11n.).

49   quippe solo natura subest 'for a natural power is present in
their soil'; explaining *laeta et fortia*, while *tamen* looks back to *infecunda*:
'although infertile, they can nevertheless be trained...'

50   inserat: cf. 33n.

scrobibus ... subactis 'well-worked trenches'; *scrobis* is a technical
word, rare in poetry, and used by V. only here and at 2.235, 260, 288
(all in this inflection).

mutata 'transplanted', as at 268 (*mutatam ... matrem*, referring to the
new soil into which the transplanted tree is set), not (as at 33) 'when
grafted' (Page). Transplanting away from the shade of the mother tree
clearly produces a change in character at 53–6.

51   exuerint siluestrem animum: here, and in the following line
(*in quascumque uoces artis*), the language suits anthropology as much as
arboriculture: trees, like man at the end of the Saturnian age, shed their
spontaneous and natural attributes and become part of the world of
cultus and the *artes* (see 1.145), the world of Jupiter (9, 10–11, 48nn.); for
V.'s ambivalent attitude to this development cf. 1.145–6n. When used
in this sense, *exuo* elsewhere regularly has an animate subject (*ThLL* v.
2.2114–15), and Ovid characterized Numa's cultural improvements
with the words *exuitur feritas*, *Fast.* 3.281.

52   uoces: the reading *uoles* has somewhat better support (it is read
by the Medicean, the only ancient MS to preserve these lines) but *uoces*,
in Servius and the ninth-century MSS, sits much more comfortably with
sequentur, and continues the personification (51n.); *uoles* looks like a
trivialization. For the combination of *uoco* and *sequor* cf. *A.* 5.22–3
superat quoniam Fortuna, sequamur, | *quoque uocat uertamus iter*, and 9.21–2
sequor omina tanta, | *quisquis in arma uoces*; cf. too *E.* 3.49 *ueniam quocumque
uocaris.*

53   sterilis: cf. 48 *infecunda* and see 440n.

54   hoc faciat 'would do likewise'; i.e. would abandon its wild
nature and become productive, under the guidance of *cultus.*

uacuos si sit digesta per agros so at 266–7, also treating tran-
splanting, *locum ... quo mox digesta feratur.*

55   nunc: νῦν δέ, 'as it is'; i.e. if man does not interfere. Picked up by
iam, 57.

rami matris opacant: cf. 19 (and n.).

56 uruntque 'blight'; the effect here is the opposite of *uro* in its common sense, for the mother tree deprives the sapling of light and heat. Cf. *frigus adurat*, 1.93 (and n.).

57 seminibus iactis 'from seeds put out [by the mother tree]'; cf. 14 *posito . . . de semine*, and n.

58 tarda: the opposite of the tree which receives *cultus*: *haud tarda*, 52.

seris factura nepotibus umbram: so the oak (*aesculus*) at 290–7 outlasts many generations (*multosque nepotes*, 294), providing the same service: *media ipsa ingentem sustinet umbram*.

59 degenerant: picked up by *turpis*, 60. The verb is used by V. only here and at 1.198, where decline occurs if *uis humana*, also the theme of 61–2 (see n.), is not applied.

sucos oblita priores: the personification continues (cf. 80–2). The accusative with *obliuiscor* is not uncommon (*OLD* s.v.).

61–2   The couplet applies both to spontaneous and natural growth (which has preceded) and to man's methods (which follow), and it contains thought central to the book and to the poem. The choice is between leaving *natura* to itself, with resulting degeneration (*pomaque degenerant*, 59), and obeying with force and vigour the imperatives of *labor* (*omnibus est labor impendendus*), which may result in success, but which involves a spiritual loss associated with the transformation and distortion of *natura*. The theme of grafting is a paradigm for this distortion (80–2n.), which is exemplified on a different level in the *laudes Italiae* (136–76), the climax of the first movement of this book.

Gerundives recur in tricola only five times in V., and four of the five instances are in *Georgics* 2 (365–6, 399–400, 418–19, also 1.178–9; see nn.). The obvious effect of this device is to suggest force, strengthened in the present instance by the unremitting nature of the verbs (*impendendus, cogendae, domandae*) and by the heavy union of spondees and elisions in 62; see Thomas (1982a) 50–1.

scilicet 'of a surety' (Page). The more ironical sense, 'to be sure', 'it is true', would require some sort of qualification, which is not forthcoming; *sed* at 63 contrasts natural and artificial methods.

labor impendendus: cf. 3.74 *impende laborem*; 3.124 *impendunt curas*.

multa mercede 'at the cost of great effort'; cf. Liv. 8.39.11 *expiandum id bellum magna mercede luendumque esse*.

domandae: the gerund of the same verb is used of taming young cattle at 3.164, and colts at 3.206.

63–72   On the responsion of these lines to 23–34, for the most part in reverse order, see 47–72n.

64   respondent: personification, as at 61–2; see 80–2n.

Paphiae ... myrtus: cf. 1.28n.

65   edurae 'very hard'; few now print *et durae*, which has better MS support, while *edurae* is supported by 4.145 *eduramque pirum*.

65–8   nascuntur ... nascitur: sc. *plantis*. The old punctuation has been retained; most editors place a period after *coryli*, and take *nascuntur* as 'spring from seeds'. Though the oak and ash do not easily grow from slips, there seems to have been some room for debate (περὶ δὲ δρυὸς ἀμφισβητοῦσιν, 'on the oak people are divided', Theophr. *H.P.* 2.2.3), so that V. should perhaps not be pressed on the point. Besides, he has already demonstrated his ability to ignore the realities of plant propagation (32–4n.). It seems less satisfactory to take *nascuntur* as beginning a new category (growth from seeds), since that belongs in the previous section (47–60; cf. 57–60), and since neither in Theophrastus nor in the corresponding lines of *Georgics* 2 (23–34; cf. 47–72n.) is such growth included as an instance of arboricultural propagation; it is strictly regarded as a *natural* type. Nor need *nascuntur* and *nascitur* be tied closely to their cognate, *natura*: cf. 85 *nascuntur oliuae* (olives are not generally grown by natural means); at 111 *nascuntur* merely = 'grow'.

66   Herculeaeque arbos umbrosa coronae: the poplar, as at *E.* 7.61 *populus Alcidae gratissima*. The scholia to Theocr. 2.121 claim that Hercules made himself a crown from the tree's foliage after bringing Cerberus up from Hades; Pausanias, on the other hand (5.14.2), merely observes that Hercules brought the white poplar to Greece, having found it on the banks of the river Acheron in Thesprotis.

67   ardua palma: the adjective specifies the long-stemmed date palm; Sargeaunt (1920) notes that the palm was imported into Sicily (*palmosa Selinus, A.* 3.705) and southern Italy. On the palm cf. 3.12n.

68   casus abies uisura marinos: the personification in *uisura* is strongly felt. The fir, along with pine and cedar, is mentioned as a wood suitable for shipbuilding by Theophrastus (*H.P.* 5.7.1–3), and in this connection becomes in Latin the subject of a ζήτημα ('topic of debate'). At *Med.* 4 Euripides referred to the *Argo* as made of pine (πεύκη), but Ennius translated this with *abiegnae ... trabes (Scen.* 247 V.). Catullus responded with *pinus* (64.1), but V., though not involving himself in this particular debate, has ships built of pine (1.256; 2.443; *E.* 4.38), as well as of fir – though apart from here only in the *Aeneid* (5.663; 8.91); in the second of these examples *abies = nauis*; cf. Thomas (1982c) 161.

69–72 Five of the six grafts are impossible, as V. doubtless knew (32–4, 45–6nn.).

69 A hypermetric line, on which see 1.295–6n.; the use of a dactylic word in the final position of such lines seems odd, but also occurs at 3.449 (*sulpur(a)*); in both places there exist variants designed to cure the problem (here *horrens*, there *sulpura uiua*) – rightly rejected by most editors.

inseritur: cf. 33n.

71 castaneas fagus: Scaliger's emendation for *castaneae fagos* of the MSS preserves the logical progression of 69–72. V. speaks of the grafting of fertile, fruit-producing trees onto sterile or wild trees: walnut onto arbutus, apple onto plane, etc. It makes less sense to have a beech grafted onto a chestnut tree, since the fruit of the sweet chestnut is the more sensible object of such a union. Nor is it easy to take *fagos* as 'beech-nuts', the word for the nut being *fagum*. The second syllable of *fagus* must be treated as long, but that poses no problem (1.138n.).

incanuit albo: a colourful pleonasm.

73–82 Grafting and its partner inoculation receive parallel and expanded treatment, designed to lead to the arresting clausula at 80–2.

73 Nec modus ... simplex: *simplex* = 'one', 'the same': 'nor is the method of grafting and of budding the same'. Cf. 3.482 *nec uia mortis erat simplex*.

inserere ... imponere: infinitives standing for gerunds in the genitive, *inserendi ... imponendi*, as at 1.213 *tempus ... tegere et ... incumbere*, and 3.60 *aetas ... pati*.

74 gemmae 'buds', the *oculi* of 73 and *germen* of 76.

trudunt: see 335n.

76 The strong break before the third foot creates an unusual rhythm.

aliena ex arbore: a bud is implanted 'from a foreign tree'; so, when grafting occurs, the tree which receives the graft will marvel at 'fruit not its own' (*non sua poma*, 82 and n.).

77 docent: The personification continues (82n.); teaching and learning in the *Georgics* are activities alien to the natural world and linked with the age of Jupiter (1.147–8n.).

78   enodes 'knotless'; with such trees grafting, a more radical and violent method than budding, must be applied.

78–80   resecantur ... alte | finditur ... immittuntur: the verbs all express force against the tree.

79–80   feraces | plantae 'slips from a fruitful tree'; cf. 4.114–15.

80–2   The lines capture the essence of the book, and ultimately of the poem. Through man's forceful intervention the world of nature, after Saturn subject to degeneration, is transformed and made 'productive'; in the process it loses its original identity, and can only stand, personified in the extreme, marvelling at its strange new leaves and fruits which are not its own (82 and n., 268n.). This moment represents the *artes* of *labor* at the pinnacle of their success: technology is triumphant. Those who associate successful technology with success will feel comfortable; others may feel ambivalent (cf. Introduction, pp. 19–21; also Ross (1987) 108–9).

81   ramis felicibus 'with [now] fruitful branches'; cf. *feraces*, 79. *felix*, like *laetus* (1.1n.) often holds its primary sense 'fertile', 'fruitful' in the *Georgics* (cf. 1.54, 345; 2.188; 4.329).

82   miratastque nouas frondes et non sua poma: modern commentatores ignore the *nature* of this personification. Servius, on the other hand, was aware of the potential force of the verb *miror*; his notice is short but apt: *ingens phantasia*, 'a remarkable apparition'. The tree is surprised at *frondes* and *poma* which are new, strange (often the implication of *nouus*; cf. 3.370; 4.316nn.) and no longer its own (80–2n.). The use of *miror* is like that of *admiror* at Cat. 64.15, where the Nereids are amazed (*mirantur*) at the *Argo*, the first ship to sail the seas; or cf. the Tiber's reaction to the first ships (those of Aeneas) to sail its waters: *mirantur et undae,* | *miratur nemus insuetum, A.* 8.91–2. Even closer is [Virg.] *Ciris* 81–2 where Scylla marvels at her own metamorphosis: *heu quotiens mirata nouos expalluit artus* | *ipsa suos*.

miratastque: Servius and the MSS record *miratastque, miraturque, mirata estque, miratasque, mirataque*; Wagner added *mirata usque*. But *miratastque* could easily have generated the other forms, and sits best with *exiit*.

83–108   The great variety of the earth's trees, particularly vines

Again in a section of 26 lines (1–135n.) V. treats the theme of the variety of trees; there follow 26 on the variety of lands (109–35). There is a heightening of poetic language, with a great concentration of proper names, apostrophe to two of the wines (95–6, 101–2), and the elegant literary figure which serves as a culmination at 103–8.

83–8   Larger trees, olives and fruit-trees are treated in one large period, in purely paratactic style, as attested by the eleven conjunctions. It is as if V. were eager to move on to the subject of the vine, which occupies him most here and throughout the book.

83   Praeterea: see 1.204n.

genus haud unum: the general proposition is stated at the outset, as in the next section: *nec uero terrae ferre omnes omnia possunt,* 109.

85   pingues ... oliuae: cf. 425 *pinguem ... oliuam* (in the same metrical position).

unam in faciem 'with one appearance', 'of one type'; cf. 131 *faciemque simillima lauro.*

86   orchades ... radii ... pausia: three types of olive, the first oval-shaped, from Greek ὀρχάδες, also ὄρχεις (root meaning 'testicles'), the second elongated, from *radius,* 'shuttle', the third (var. *posia, posea*) a type which was picked early, and hence was bitter (*amara ... baca*). Cato lists eight types, including these three (*Agr.* 6.1); V. is not concerned to be exhaustive.

There is hiatus at the main caesura, before the second *et.*

87   pomaque et Alcinoi siluae 'so too with orchard-fruit such as that of Alcinous'; *et* is epexegetic. The gardens of Alcinous (Hom. *Od.* 7.112–32) are proverbial and miraculous, their fruits growing in abundance throughout the year. This is the first hint of the θαύματα ('marvels') to come in the next section (109–35), and particularly in the *laudes Italiae* (136–76).

87–8   nec surculus idem ... 'for the cutting is not the same for ...'; *uariatio* for *genus haud unum* ...

88   Three types of pear balance the three of olive at 86; Cato lists five, only the *uolema* coinciding with V.'s but he is selective: *item alia genera quam plurima serito aut inserito, Agr.* 7.3–4. Pliny is more complete, giving over 30 varieties (*N.H.* 15.53–6); he considers Crustumian, Falernian and Syrian to be the best (*gratissima*).

grauibusque: perhaps a 'gloss' on *uolemis,* 'handfuls': *quod uolam complent magnitudine, hoc est mediam manum,* Isid. *orig.* 17.7.67; so too Serv. *ad loc.* Serv. Auct. claims that it is derived from a Gaulish word meaning large, and this may be nearer to the truth, if not to V.'s intent;

see Whatmough (1931) 143–4, who connects it to Oscan *ualaimo-* ('*optimus*') in a discussion of the change of Indo-European *o* to *a*.

89–102 V.'s enthusiasm increases as he proceeds with an extremely selective catalogue of vines. Columella, who quotes the feigned despair of *G*. 2.104–6, lists only a selection of 60 types (3.2), and Pliny merely states that there are 185 types, or double that figure, *si species uero aestimentur*, *N.H.* 14.150. In Conington's day '1,400 [had] been collected in the garden of the Luxembourg, a number supposed to be not more than half of those cultivated in France alone' (on 103). As Page notes: 'If anyone will take a nurseryman's catalogue of grapes, pears, apples, or the like, and try to put it into verse, he will begin to be able to grasp the extraordinary skill which Virgil exhibits in this passage.' That comment, modified, holds for much of the poem. V. is coining a type of catalogue poetry, of which a more conventional, but more complex, instance may be found at 4.333–86 (see n.).

89–90 V. begins by distinguishing Italian vines (*arboribus . . . nostris*) from Greek (*quam . . . carpit . . . Lesbos*), but returns to specifically Italian varieties at 95–6.

90 quam Methymnaeo carpit de palmite Lesbos: rather an odd way of putting it; Methymna is a town on the island of Lesbos.

91–2 An artful couplet with anaphora (*sunt . . . sunt*) reinforced by the elaboration of the second line (*hae . . . illae*), and with the two epithets of that line contrasted (*pinguibus . . . leuioribus*).

Mareotides: an Egyptian variety, the wine of which Horace fancied deranged the mind of Cleopatra at Actium: *mentemque lymphatam Mareotico*, *Odes* 1.37.14. V.'s form (Μαρεῶτις) is the first attestation of the third declension for the vine (or the wine); it is elsewhere the form for the lake itself (var. Μάρεια). The Greek form for the wine is normally Horace's *Mareoticus* (Μαρεωτικός), or the second declension noun Μαρεώτης; perhaps V. confused Μαρεῶτις and Μαρεώτης, but, given the proximity of the lake to Alexandria, it is also possible that he found the form in a favoured source, now lost.

93 passo psithia utilior 'the psithia, better for raisin-wine'; cf. 4.269 *psithia passos de uite racemos* (i.e. raisins). The meaning of the Greek word *psithia*, once treated as a proper name, is not known.

tenuisque 'subtle' (Page); as Servius noted, *tenuis* can hardly mean 'light', given the elaboration of 94; he suggests *penetrabilis, quae cito descendit in uenas*.

94 temptatura pedes olim uincturaque linguam: taken, according to the Berne scholia, from Calvus: *lingua uino temptantur et pedes*, p. 87 Morel. The use of *olim* and the future participles is generally taken to mean 'which will, in the future, after it has been made into wine'; but V. perhaps implies 'which is sure to, in the future, if enough is imbibed'.

95–6 quo te carmine dicam, | Rhaetica? nec cellis ideo contende Falernis: the previous line referred to Calvus, these to his fellow neoteric Catullus, and to the Elder Cato. On 95 Servius reports: *hanc [sc. Rhaeticam] uuam Cato praecipue laudat* (a view, it seems, shared by Augustus (Suet. *Aug.* 77 *Augustum Rhaetica maxime delectatum*)). Catullus, exhibiting an absence of pride in his native Verona (the grape was grown just to the north, at the foot of the Rhaetian Alps) did not agree: Servius continues, *contra Catullus (fr. 5) eam uituperat et dicit nulli rei esse aptam, miraturque cur eam laudauerit Cato*. V. seems to find a middle road, accommodating both predecessors, as he begins with an apostrophe which seeks terms in which to praise the wine – implying that it is to be praised – but in 96 sets definite limits on the praise: it is not to vie with Falernian, that most famous of Italian wines.

nec ... ideo 'but not on that account'; i.e. 'even so' ('though you are to be praised, the praise is not to equal that for Falernian').

97 firmissima 'full-bodied'; a bit of oenologists' jargon? (cf. Pliny at 100n.).

98 Tmolius adsurgit quibus et rex ipse Phanaeus: wines from Lydia and Chios, the latter a king at that, rise in respect before the Amminean wine of Campania. The superiority of Italian over Greek will recur in a more profound context at 3.19–20 (see n.)

Tmolius: the use of the adjective is an extreme Graecism; in Greek, the masculine noun οἶνος ('wine') is regularly in ellipse with the adjective (e.g. Τμώλιος). Though V. has been using the feminine *uitis*, οἶνος must be understood here. An ellipse of *mons* (Tmolus is a mountain) is unlikely, for it is the wine, not the place, that pays homage.

rex: sc. *uinorum*.

99 argitisque minor: some wines were classified *maior* and *minor*; this is a white wine, whence, according to Isid. 17.5.23, its name (from ἀργός, 'shining', 'white').

cui non certauerit ulla: the competitive language continues (cf. 96 *nec ... contende;* 98 *adsurgit*), with the superior wine in each case an Italian, specifically Campanian, variety (98n.) – preparation for the *laudes Italiae* (136–76)? The perfect subjunctive is parallel to that at 102 (*transierim*), sometimes called the 'subjunctive of polite assertion': 'nor would any vie ...'; 'I would not pass you over'.

100 '[match] either in abundance of stream or in lasting through so many years'; the infinitives may be complementary (since *certo* implies potentiality and is therefore analogous to *possum*), or extensions of the usual construction after *certo* 'strive to (do something)'.

Pliny modified V.'s enthusiasm somewhat: *e diuerso arceraca Vergilio argitis dicta ultro solum laetius facit, ipsa contra imbres et senectam fortissima, uino quidem uix annua ac uilitatis cibariae sed ubertate praecipua, N.H.* 14.35.

101 mensis ... secundis 'dessert course'; *dis et mensis* is a syllepsis.

102 transierim: cf. 99n.

tumidis, bumaste, racemis: with *tumidis* ('swelling') V. provides an elegant gloss on the etymology of *bumastus*, lit. 'with huge breasts' (βου- a prefix indicating large size, from βοῦς, 'ox'; μαστός, 'breast'). Pliny made the image specific: *tument uero mammarum modo bumasti, N.H.* 14.15; Servius was even more graphic: *uua in mammae bouis similitudinem, ad loc.*

bumaste: best seen as introducing a new vine, with the *ThLL* (s.v. *bumastus*) and other editors, *uua* being understood with *Rhodia*. Williams seems to take *Rhodia ... bumaste* together (*bumastus* can be feminine): '*bumastus* was a large-sized grape from Rhodes'. With this reading the *et* of 102 rather awkwardly connects *accepta* with *tumidis ... racemis. bumastus* is not elsewhere connected with Rhodes.

103–8 The section ends on a literary note as V. affects despair at the prospect of enumerating all the varieties of vines (89–102n.). His immediate model, particularly in 105–8, is Cat. 7.3–6 *quam magnus numerus Libyssae harenae | lasarpiciferis iacet Cyrenis | oraculum Iouis inter aestuosi | et Batti ueteris sacrum sepulcrum.* Catullus mentioned only the sands of the desert and at 7 the stars, but V., by including the waves of the sea, has conflated Catullus with Ap. Rhod. *Arg.* 4.214–15 'as many as the waves of the stormy sea when they are whipped into crests by the wind'; or with Theocr. 16.60–1 'as great a task is it to number the waves on the beach when the wind along with the grey sea rolls them to the shore'; cf. Gow's note on the motif.

105–8 The proper names provide colour and give the lines structure: the Libyan desert (103–8n.) and Ionian sea provide the outer frames, with each of the two central lines occupied by the West and the East wind.

109–35   The varied products of the earth's lands

The variety of species is replaced by a section on the varied products of the world, also in 26 lines (1–135n.), 129 being interpolated. V. draws heavily on Theophrastus, now from *H.P.* 4, which treats trees by region, and which, since 83, has replaced *H.P.* 2 as V.'s chief model. Varro has a similar treatment (*R.R.* 1.6–7), but there is nothing to suggest that V. drew directly from him. The ethnographical emphasis serves to lead up to the *laudes Italiae* (136–76 and n.), but the passage also develops a theme important for the *Georgics* as a whole (109n.).

109   Nec uero terrae ferre omnes omnia possunt: not the case before Jupiter brought the golden age to an end: *omnis feret omnia tellus*, *E.* 4.39; *ipsaque tellus | omnia liberius nullo poscente ferebat*, 1.127–8 (see n.). It is a central premise of the *Georgics*, as of agricultural reality, that productivity is restricted by region; cf. 1.51–3 (and 1.53n.). V.'s wording is indebted to Lucretius, who denies that life can spring from nothingness: *si de nilo fierent ... ferre omnes omnia possent*, 1.159–66 (cf. 149n.).

110–13   V. begins with a general catalogue of trees preferring certain *types* of land. At 114 the scope becomes more international, as he treats the products of different *lands*.

111   nascuntur 'grow'; cf. 65–8n.

112   litora myrtetis laetissima: cf. 4.124 *amantis litora myrtos*, and see 1.28n.

apertos 'open [to the sun]'; i.e. a southerly exposure, while the yew in 113 prefers a northern slope. See 188 and 298n. on the dispute in antiquity concerning the ideal exposure for the vine.

113   amat: cf. 3.315 *amantis ardua dumos*; 4.124 *amantis litora myrtos*; so we speak of a plant's 'liking' sun, shade, sandy soil, etc.

taxi: see 257 and n.

114–35   Exotic lands and their products are treated, with an emphasis on θαύματα ('marvels'). Theophr. *H.P.* 4.2–11, V.'s model, treats in succession the trees, shrubs and herbs of Egypt, Libya, Asia, etc., and V., as in his treatment of vines (89–102 and n.), is extremely selective – once again, instruction is not the primary goal. The places he chooses recur in reverse order at 136–9 (136–42n.), thus providing an elegant transition to the praises of Italy, with which they and their produce are contrasted.

114 extremis: a transferred epithet: the ends of the earth are conquered by cultivators. Six lines from the end of the *laudes Italiae*, as this is six from the beginning of a section complementary to the *laudes Italiae* (136–42n.), *extremis* recurs in the same position, now referring to the *real* conquest of the ends of the earth by Octavian.

115 Eoasque: see 1.221n. on the quantity of the first syllable.

pictosque Gelonos 'tattooed Geloni'; a touch of ethnographical colour, paralleled by 168 *Volscosque uerutos* (on such epithets in ethnographies, see Thomas (1982a) 94). Herodotus (5.6) mentions tattooing as a Thracian practice; the Geloni were Scythians.

116 diuisae arboribus patriae 'trees have their allotted homelands'. The style results from V.'s imitation of Theophr. *H.P.* 4.1.1 'for wild varieties, no less than cultivated ones, have their own positions'. The assignation of *patriae* to trees (perhaps developed from Theophrastus' word οἰκεῖος, 'own'; lit. 'of the same household'), creates a personification already observed elsewhere (32–4n.); the word is similarly used of horses (3.121) and bees (4.155).

116–17 The same pair (India and the Sabaeans) served to exemplify the world's variety at 1.57; there they produced ivory (*ebur*) and frankincense (*tus*) respectively, here ebony (*hebenum*) and sprays of frankincense (*turea uirga*).

sola India nigrum | fert hebenum: V. is again close to his model: 'ebony is peculiar to this country [India]', Theophr. *H.P.* 4.4.6. Pliny discusses the wood at *N.H.* 12.17–20, and corrects the claim that it is exclusively Indian, citing Herodotus' (3.97) ascription of it to Ethiopia.

solis est turea uirga Sabaeis: the Sabaeans inhabited the southwest of the Arabian peninsula. Theophr. *H.P.* 9.4 treats their methods of collecting myrrh and frankincense. Ovid has Myrrha end her flight in the land of the Sabaeans, and there turn into a myrrh-tree (*M.* 10.476–502).

118–25 The style is highly rhetorical; V. employs a virtual *praeteritio*, presenting his ethnographical excursus in an extended tricolon (*quid ... referam, ... quid ..., aut ...*), and ending with a gnomic tag (125) worthy of Tacitus (and very much a feature of ethnographical writing).

118–19 odorato ... sudantia ligno | balsamaque 'balsam dripping from its fragrant wood [i.e. bark]'. Theophrastus deals with the collection of the gum at *H.P.* 9.6; he situates the tree in Syria.

-que: otiose: 'balsam and acanthus-berry'; cf. *A.* 5.467 *dixitque et proelia uoce diremit.*

bacas semper frondentis acanthi: this is the acacia (called acanthus because it is spiny), not the acanthus of the *Eclogues* and 4.123. V. intends the Egyptian variety, treated at Theophr. *H.P.* 4.2.8. He is wrong to give it a berry (*bacas*): 'its fruit is in a pod' (ὁ δὲ καρπὸς ἔλλοβος). Since V. pairs the acacia with the balsam-tree, and the acacia does produce a gum, somewhat like myrrh (*H.P.* 4.4.12; 9.1.2), Martyn suggests that *bacas* = 'drops of gum', a sense not otherwise attested, though the word is used to refer to rounded objects such as olives, pearls, links of a chain, etc.

120   molli … lana: the cotton-plant was put by Theophrastus in India and in Arabia (specifically Bahrain), *H.P.* 4.4.8; 4.7.7, 8. V. has already dealt with Arabia; hence *Aethiopum*. The Greeks did not have a word for it, merely referring to it, as does V., as 'the wool-bearing tree'. Pliny (*N.H.* 12.38, 39; 19.14) calls it *gossypinum* or *gossypion*, words of obscure origin, not otherwise attested.

121 'and how the Chinese comb fine fleeces from leaves'. Pliny also thought silk grew on trees (*N.H.* 6.54); Aristotle knew better (*H.A.* 551b13–17).

tenuia: scanned as a dactyl (the *u* is treated as consonantal).

122–35 V. focuses on two trees, which appear consecutively in Theophrastus, but in reverse order (*H.P.* 4.4.2–4); the banyan tree of India (not named but clearly described: 122, 123–4nn.) and the citron of Media.

122   quos … lucos: Theophrastus frequently in *H.P.* 4.2–11 omits the name of the tree or shrub, merely giving, as here, its unusual characteristics: e.g. 4.4.5 'and there is another tree which is of great size ….' Theophrastus may not have known this tree's name (the jack-fruit), whereas V.'s suppression is designed as an allusive reference to the tradition which he imitates, for the banyan *was* in fact named by Theophrastus (122–35).

Oceano propior: i.e. at the ends of the earth, as the next line makes clear.

gerit 'produces', as at 70.

123–4   The size is presented as a marvel (θαῦμα). V. has altered and added colour to his source, Theophr. *H.P.* 4.4.4, where the banyan tree is described as forming a tent-like area beneath it (in which men actually live), casting its shade two furlongs, having a trunk up to sixty paces across, and a leaf the size of a shield.

aëra uincere summum | arboris: no arrows can 'surpass the air at the top of the tree'; this should mean 'clear the breadth' – banyans spread profusely.

125   illa quidem: cf. 3.217n.

pharetris: arrows lead inevitably to thoughts of the Parthians (cf. 3.31; 4.313–14), as Easterners somewhat freely associated with India. The relevance of the line has been questioned, and interpolation suggested, but ethnographical observation frequently culminates in a gnomic tag of a contemporary and moral nature. So Lucan on the timber of North Africa: *tantum Maurusia genti | robora diuitiae, quarum non nouerat usum, | sed citri contenta comis uiuebat et umbra. | in nemus ignotum nostrae uenere secures, | extremoque epulas mensasque petimus ab orbe*, 9.426–30; see Thomas (1982a) 110–11.

126–35   In his treatment of the citron V. comes extremely close to Theophrastus, and at the same time enlivens the technical material through original contributions (cf. 128, 134–5).

126   tristis 'sour', 'tart'; cf. 246–77 *ora | tristia temptantum sensu torquebit amaro*; 1.75 *tristisque lupini*.

tardumque 'lingering'.

127   felicis mali 'health-giving citron'; V. takes the tree and most of its attributes directly from Theophrastus: 'the apple called "Median" or "Persian" [the citron]', *H.P.* 4.4.2.

praesentius 'more efficacious'; rendering Theophrastus' χρήσιμον, 'useful' (*H.P.* 4.4.2).

128   pocula si quando saeuae infecere nouercae: Theophrastus, who mentions that it works as an emetic, merely says 'it is useful when someone has drunk deadly poison', *H.P.* 4.4.2. As in 125 and 134–5 (see nn.), V. has added colour, and, by including a reference to contemporary morality, given the description a strong ethnographical flavour. The maligning of stepmothers is a favoured motif of Latin poetry (cf. 3.282–3; also Cat. 64.402; *E.* 3.33).

129   The line, not present in the Medicean, has been imported from 3.283; it creates an excessive separation between *quo non praesentius ullum* and the rest of the predicate in 130, and disrupts Virgil's careful numerical arrangement (1–135n.).

130   membris agit atra uenena: Virgilian, or Augustan, sensibility causes suppression of the details: 'when administered with wine it upsets the stomach and brings up the poison', Theophr. *H.P.* 4.4.2; for similar restraint, cf. 3.250–1n.

atra: cf. 1.129n.

131 ipsa ingens arbos faciemque simillima lauro: from Theophr. *H.P.* 4.4.2: 'this tree has a leaf resembling and almost identical with that of the andrachne'. But the bay is not the andrachne. V. and Athenaeus both read from corrupt texts of Theophrastus, for the best MSS of Athen. 3.83d, a citation of the above passage of *H.P.* 4.4.2, have δάφνης (= *laurus*) for ἀνδράχλης (*Arbutus andrachne*). It is true that the leaves of the bay and the andrachne are similar in appearance. It is quite likely that V. had not seen the citron-tree; Pliny (*N.H.* 12.15–16) states that although imported in his day from Persia and Media and used as potted plants, they consistently refused to grow.

faciemque: accusative of respect; a Graecism in a line translating a Greek source – which did not, however, contain this feature (see 1.281–2n., on *Pelio*).

133 erat: the indicative in the apodosis of a present contrary-to-fact conditional conveys emphasis: 'if its scent were not different, it would *be* a bay'.

folia haud ullis labentia uentis: the detail is implied by Theophrastus: 'it bears its fruit in every season', *H.P.* 4.4.3.

134 ad prima 'particularly'; apparently a unique variant of *in primis*.

tenax: Theophrastus discusses the blossom, but says nothing explicit of its clinging powers (but cf. 133n.).

134–35 As at 128 (see n.) V. concludes on a personal note: Theophr. *H.P.* 4.4.3 mentions its freshening powers ('it improves the breath'), but V., immediately before his ethnographically based treatment of Italy, presents it in a typically ethnographical style: 'the Medes use it to freshen their breaths and malodorous mouths, and to cure asthma in the old'.

136–76   The 'Praises' of Italy

These lines, along with the praise of rustic life at the end of the book (458–542), are the best-known of the poem. In the study and the classroom they tend to be read in isolation from the rest of the poem, and

that in part accounts for the inadequate interpretation they have re-
ceived: the passage must be considered within the fabric of the poem of
which it is a part.

Praise of one's native land is a traditional theme, going back at least
to Sophocles' *laudes Atticae* at *O.C.* 668–719. Praises of Italy were pro-
duced before V. by Cato (*ap.* Solin. 2.2) and Varro (*R.R.* 1.2.3–6;
Ant. Rer. Hum. 11), and perhaps by Polybius and Posidonius (Thomas
(1982a) 39), after them by Propertius (3.22), Strabo (6.4.1), Vitruvius
(6.1.10–11), Dionysius of Halicarnassus (*Ant. Rom.* 1.36–7), Pliny
(*N.H.* 3.39–42; 37.201–2) and Aelian (*V.H.* 9.16); in other words, the
theme was, or at some point became, a rhetorical set piece, as Servius
noted: *iam incipit laus Italiae quam exsequitur secundum praecepta rhetorica: nam
dicit eam et habere omnia bona et carere malis uniuersis* (on 136). But the very
fact that the theme is rhetorical in nature should invite caution: this is
not a poet accustomed to reproducing rhetorical topoi for use in the
classroom. V. presents obvious fictions, demonstrably in conflict with
the reality of Italy as it exists in the 'technical' sections of the poem (148,
150, 151–4nn.), and characterizes Italy with detail which is hardly
laudatory, and which is pointedly in conflict with the final designation
of the country as *Saturnia tellus* (145–8, 155–7, 161–4, 165–6, 169–
72nn.) – itself a deliberate falsehood, both here and at the end of the
book (458–74, 532–40nn.; also 1.118–46n.).

The description is presented in the format of an ethnographical study
(cf. 109–35n.), as V. depicts an environment which will find parallels
and contrasts with the descriptions of Libya and Scythia at 3.339–83,
and with the treatment of the old man of Tarentum at 4.125–48 (see nn.
and passim in the present lines).

Offering distortions of reality, and depicting civilized man imposing
his will on a natural, innocent or unwarlike world, the *laudes Italiae* are
no excursus or digression, but rather a demonstration, on a different and
more poetical level, of the only way in which the ethics of *labor* can
'succeed' (23, 33, 61–2, 80–2, 207–11, 279–83, 362–70, 454–7nn.). On
the passage, and on its relationship to the *Georgics* as a whole, see
Thomas (1982a) 36–51; Ross (1987) 116–28.

The first part (136–54) is generally concerned with natural features
such as climate, flora and fauna, etc., while the second (155–72) treats
man's works in Italy.

136–42   Italy is introduced through a contrast: no foreign land, in

spite of its θαύματα ('marvels'; see 138n.), can compare with it; the same
technique is found at Soph. *O.C.* 694-701 (136-76n.). In the process V.
effects a neat transition from the previous section, for the lands he
mentions here are mirrored by those at 114-35: Media was the last
treated (126-35), the Ganges takes us to India at 122-5, the Hermus (in
Lydia) is not represented, Bactria borders on China (121), the repeti-
tion of India looks to 116-17, while Panchaia (*turiferis ... harenis*) is a
mythical island east of Arabia (*solis est turea uirga Sabaeis*, 117).

136-9 For the style cf. 3.252-3n.

136 Sed neque ...: cf. the opening words of the parallel ethno-
graphical description of Scythia: *at non ...* (136-76n.).

ditissima terra: better taken, with recent editors, as appositive to
siluae; some print *Medorum, siluae ditissima, terra*, 'the land of the Medes,
rich in woodland'; and evidently Manilius so read the words: *et molles
Arabas, siluarum ditia regna*, 4.754.

137 auro turbidus Hermus: traditionally it is the Pactolus, also
a Lydian river, which is 'muddied with gold-dust': *Pactolusque inrigat
auro, A.* 10.142. *turbidus* occurs twice in the *Georgics*, both times of rivers
– here and, also in the second line of its section, in the description of
Scythia 3.350 (see 139n.); cf. too 4.126 *qua niger umectat flauentia culta
Galaesus* (136-76, 139nn.). At 165-6 the rivers of Italy are said to flow
with metals, including gold: *auro plurima fluxit*.

138 laudibus Italiae certent: hence the traditional title of the
section, *laudes Italiae*, though in 138 *Italiae* is dat. with *certent*, *laudibus* abl.
of respect. Propertius is clearly referring to this line at 3.22.17 *omnia
Romanae cedent miracula terrae*.

139 totaque turiferis Panchaia pinguis harenis: the allitera-
tion (*t t P p h*) is noteworthy, particularly since it is recalled at 3.350,
where the final word is the same: *turbidus et torquens flauentis Hister harenas
(t t f H h)*; the ethnographical connections are constantly stressed
(136-76, 137nn.).

Pānchāïă: four syllables, while at 4.379 the adjective *Pānchaēïs* is
trisyllabic.

140-4 haec loca non ... nec ...; sed ...: in the treatment of
produce, one of the ethnographical categories (136-76n.), V. again
links the present passage, this time stylistically, with the account of
Scythia (*illic* [*non*] *... neque ... aut ... aut ...; sed ...*, 3.352-5), and with
the description of the old man of Tarentum (*nec fertilis illa ... nec ... nec*

.... *hic* ... *tamen*, 4.128–33); in each case denial is followed by asser-
tion of the real situation, with the three divisions of agronomy treated
in each passage (143–4n.). The style seems to be a feature of ethno-
graphical description, particularly of Utopian locations; so at Hom. *Od.*
9.119–24, the description of the island off the coast from the land of the
Cyclopes: οὐ μὲν γάρ ... οὐδέ ... οὔτ' ... οὔτ' ..., ἀλλ' ..., 'for neither is
there any ... nor ... nor ... nor ..., but [there is ...]' – the details
conspire to make it a golden-age world.

The claim that Italy contains no miraculous (i.e. false) features (*haec
loca non* ...) may be disingenuous, like the claim at 45–6 *non hic te carmine
ficto* ... *tenebo* (see n.).

140 tauri spirantes naribus ignem: the bulls tamed by Jason, as
is clear from 141 and from Ap. Rhod. *Arg.* 3.1292 [ταύροι] πυρὸς σέλας
ἀμπνείοντες, '[bulls] breathing flaming fire'. For the wording V. is
perhaps indebted to Lucretius, though his context and animals are
different: *equi spirantes naribus ignem*, 5.30.

141 inuertere: cf. 1.65n.

satis immanis dentibus hydri 'for the sowing of the huge dragon's
teeth'; *satis* would more correctly be *serendis*, and Page prefers to take it
as ablative absolute: 'when the dragon's teeth were sown'; but that
rather makes the sowing precede the ploughing.

142 nec galeis densisque uirum seges horruit hastis: cf.
1.314n. on the union of military and agricultural in this line, particu-
larly through the verb, *horruit*. *densis* is to be taken ἀπὸ κοινοῦ.

143–4 Crops, wine and olives, and livestock, the three categories of
agronomy, the subjects of Books 1, 2 and 3, are all represented in
abundance (*grauidae* ... *impleuere* ... *laeta*). In Scythia the opposite
obtains (3.352–3), and the old man of Tarentum has land unfit for such
activity (4.128–9); see 136–76.

These three divisions, usually mentioned in a single couplet, recur
elsewhere in the poem (1.443–4; 2.221–3, 516–17; 4.329–31, 559–60);
the function varies from instance to instance (see nn.); but they serve as
a group to reinforce the sense that *Georgics* 4 is a separable book, that
with the bees and the song of Proteus V. has moved to a different plane
(see 4.559–60n.; Introduction, pp. 21–4).

grauidae 'teeming', like *laeta* in the next line (1.1n.); the word
implies pregnancy or fullness; cf. 150; 3.139, 155, 275, 317.

Bacchi Massicus umor: at 3.526–7 (*Massica Bacchi | munera*) a
mark of luxury.

tenent: also at 3.352, although in a different sense (see preceding n.).

144 For the same hiatus preceding *armentaque*, cf. 3.155.

145–8 Ethnographical convention calls only for the details of 143–4, but mention of *armenta* leads to an elaboration: here is the war-horse, here the herds of bulls to be used in military triumph. These four lines, which depart from the tradition in which V. is writing, and which stress the military use of animals to a degree not represented in the treatment of livestock in Book 3 (the war-horse is mentioned at 83–94, while sacrificial animals receive four words, *aut aris seruare sacros*, 160), create the first serious disjunction between the details of the *laudes Italiae* and the final designation of it as *Saturnia tellus* – war does not exist in the age of Saturn (Hes. *W.D.* 189–93; Ov. *M.* 1.98–100); see 136–76, 155–7, 161–4, 165–6, 169–72nn.

145 hinc bellator equus: at *A.* 3.539–42, after the Trojans catch their first glimpse of Italy, Anchises delivers a virtual prophecy: *bellum, o terra hospita, portas: | bello armantur equi, bellum haec armenta minantur. | sed tamen idem olim curru succedere sueti | quadripedes et frena iugo concordia ferre: | spes et pacis.* In the Italy of the present lines the role of the horse is purely military.

campo sese arduus infert: used of Turnus at *A.* 9.53, perhaps an echo of this passage.

146–7 'hence come bulls, the snowy herd and noblest of victims'; best seen as hendiadys, rather than 'snowy flocks [i.e. sheep] and bulls'. Cf. Propertius 2.19.25–6 *qua formosa suo Clitumnus flumina luco | integit, et niueos abluit unda boues*; thereafter the white bulls of the Clitumnus become a topos. Servius claims that Pliny thought they became white by drinking from the Clitumnus (in fact Plin. *N.H.* 2.230 places the phenomenon around Falerii, some 50 miles south of the Umbrian river), while V.'s implication is that this is brought about by their swimming in it. White bulls were used in triumphal sacrifices (148).

Clitumne: the vocative, here affectionate in tone, is also used of Lakes Como (*Lari*, 159) and Garda (*Benace*, 160); and above of the wines, Rhaetic (96) and Rhodian and *bumastus* (102). Given that rivers are also river-gods, the degree of personification is not as great here.

maxima taurus | uictima: for the surrounding of an appositive noun or phrase by the adjective and noun to which it is apposed, see 2.385; 4.168; 246; *E.* 1.57; cf. Tarrant (1976) 321.

147 tuo perfusi flumine sacro: this use of the possessive adjective together with a descriptive epithet is a feature of archaic poetry

(Conington): Enn. *Ann.* 26 Skutsch *teque, pater Tiberine, tuo cum flumine sancto*; also Lucr. 1.38 *tuo recubantem corpore sancto*; *A.* 8.72 *tuque, o Thybri tuo genitor cum flumine sancto* (adapted directly from Ennius); in the *Georgics*, 2.219 *suo semper uiridi se gramine uestit.*

149 A lie in terms of the realities of Italy within and outside the *Georgics*: it is a premise of the poem, as of the real world, that the normal cycle of seasons operates in Italy. Lucretius claimed that things do not grow from nothing: *quod si de nilo fierent, subito exorerentur | incerto spatio atque alienis partibus anni,* 1.180–1; Conington's words are, by accident, apt: 'Virg. may have had the expression of Lucr. in mind when he said that Italy really enjoyed that which Lucr. gives as a derangement of nature' (see 45–6, 136–76nn.).

hic uer adsiduum 'here spring is incessant', not merely 'spring is long', as is clear from Ovid's understanding of the words: *uer erat aeternum*, *M.* 1.107 (336–42n.). Servius expressed some surprise: *uerna temperies; nam uer adsiduum esse non potest* (ad loc.). This is not mere quibbling; what is expected here is indeed some reference to *temperies*, a concept which is of vital importance to V., but one which he never mentions by name (1.237–8n.). The words also prepare us for the *laus ueris* later in the book (323–45), behind which lies the vital assumption that spring operates *along with* the other seasons.

Horace imitated and 'corrected' V.'s line while drawing from him in other ways (Thomas (1982a) 26–7) at *Odes* 2.6.17–18 [*Tarentum*] *uer ubi longum tepidasque praebet | Iuppiter brumas.*

150 bis grauidae pecudes, bis pomis utilis arbos: more lies, or as good as. In the technical tradition there are claims of double productivity for isolated trees (see Varro, *R.R.* 1.7.6, and cf. 4.119 *biferique rosaria Paesti*), but this is very different from the claim that *Italy* so operates. Varro speaks of sows bearing twice a year (*R.R.* 2.4.14 *bis parit in anno*), but they presumably do so everywhere (Varro has just spoken of sows in Gaul, Spain and Arcadia), and for V. *pecudes* implies larger animals as well (2.340; 3.243, 368). These claims are parallel with those concerning grafting at 32–4 and 69–72 (see nn.).

For the anaphora of *bis* (a fitting word so to be used) cf. 410–11; 1.48; *A.* 6.134–5; also *E.* 3.30 *bis ... binos*; *A.* 4.231 *bis ... duo*. All but one of these instances are agricultural in nature (323n.).

151–4 No tigers, lions, aconite or large snakes. The first two details are true, though many other lands are so blessed. The purpose is to

justify the subsequent claim that Italy is a Saturnian land, since in the
golden age these features are either absent or harmless; but if these
claims are demonstrably false, so is the conclusion to which they lead
(136–76n.).

151   absunt: in negative contrast with *hinc … hinc … hic* (145–9);
cf. 471 *non absunt*; 4.13–24 *absint … ; adsint …* .

151–2   saeua leonum | semina: cf., with the same enjambment,
Lucr. 3.741–2 *triste leonum | seminium*. In the golden age of *E.* 4.22 lions
are not absent, just harmless: *nec magnos metuent armenta leones. semina =*
'races', 'breeds'; cf. Cic. *Phil.* 4.13 *Romani generis et seminis*.

152   nec … legentis: 'and there is no aconite to deceive wretched
gatherers'. Dioscorides (4.78) and Servius attempted to exonerate V.
from the falsehood he clearly intended (136–76n.) by emphasizing
fallunt ('it is there, but nobody mistakes it for an edible plant') – the
word is used to create a parallel with *E.* 4.24–5: when the golden age
arrives, *fallax herba ueneni | occidet*. Sargeaunt (1920) resorted to botanical
niceties, in this case no more satisfactory: V. means the pale yellow
monkshood (*Aconitum anthora* – the identification is rejected by Abbe
(1965) 191–3), which grew only in the mountains of Liguria.

fallunt: cf. 467n.

**153–4   One can only save V. from the even more obvious lie of these
lines (again intentional) by laying great stress upon *tanto*: there are
snakes in Italy but they are not as large. But *tanto* here = *magno*, a snake
is a snake, size has nothing to do with venom or danger, and *no* snake is
to exist in the golden age (*occidet et serpens, E.* 4.24 – there preceding, here
following, the reference to aconite; cf. too 3.544–5n.), which is why V.
here excludes them. This exclusion is in harmony with the claim of 173
(*Saturnia tellus*), but at odds with the reality of Italy, and of the Italy of
the rest of the poem (cf. 214–16; 3.414–39).

V. artfully begins the sentence with the verb (*nec rapit*) and ends it
with the subject (*anguis*).

**155–7   The cities of Italy. The picture of the Italian hill-cities, with
rivers gliding by below, is indeed attractive, but it needs to be viewed in
cultural terms, and in terms of the poem as a whole, not merely as a
vignette. These towns belong to the age of Jupiter and toil (hence the
designation *operumque laborem*), and their construction is a product of
exertion, possibly even of force (the most common implication of *manu*)
– see 161–4n. Most importantly, V. presents them in a special way, as

walled: *oppida . . . fluminaque antiquos subterlabentia muros*. The detail again belies the claim at 173 (*salue . . . Saturnia tellus*), for V. well knew when walls were first put around towns: at *E.* 4.31–3, as the golden age returns, he notes that there will be some evil resistance to the blessed time: *pauca tamen suberunt priscae uestigia fraudis,* | *. . . quae cingere muris* | *oppida . . . iubeant*. Ovid is emphatic about the cultural status of walls in the golden age: *nondum praecipites cingebant oppida fossae, M.* 1.97 (*praecipites* perhaps referring pointedly to the present passage; cf. *praeruptis,* 156).

fluminaque ... subterlabentia: some editors treat *subter* as an actual preposition and print *subter labentia*. There is, perhaps, support for that in Lucr. 2.362 *fluminaque . . . labentia* (both in the same position as in the present line), but cf. *E.* 10.4 *cum fluctus subterlabere Sicanos* (so printed by all editors).

158 supra ... infra: the Adriatic and the Tyrrhenian, or Tuscan, seas; the line is repeated, with *teneant* for *memorem* at *A.* 8.149.

an ... memorem: highly rhetorical, creating a virtual *praeteritio* (= *non memoro*) (see 4.147–8n); the words are repeated at 161.

159 te, Lari ... teque, | **... Benace:** cf. 146–7n.

160 marino 'worthy of the ocean' (taken with *fluctibus* and *fremitu*). The lake, situated about 20 miles north of V.'s native Mantua, is the largest in the country.

161–4 As at 145–8 (see n.) factual and neutral description (at 143–4 of produce, at 158–60 of bodies of water) is followed by four lines of elaboration, which create a troubling and far from harmonious image (see too 169–72n.). Harbours form a traditional part of ethnographies (Strabo referred to Italy's 'large and impressive harbours', λιμένας μεγάλους ... καὶ θαυμαστούς, 6.4.1), but V.'s selection is odd: he has chosen two, the Lucrine and the Avernus, neither of which was originally a harbour, but which were transformed by the works of man. The Lucrine, a lake on the Campanian coast, had its breakwater strengthened by Agrippa in 37 B.C., and at the same time a channel was cut through to Lake Avernus, situated inland. Traditionally critics see the choice as a glorification of the engineering feats of Agrippa, and indirectly of Octavian (Serv. Auct. says the work was started by Julius; hence *Iulia ... unda,* 163), but the lines are not reassuring in the context of the poem as a whole. One of the themes of this book is man's use of force against nature, and his alteration of a natural state by means of that force:

it is stated here on a somewhat different, but complementary and consistent, level (32–4, 80–2n.). V.'s language (161–2n.) supports the sense of a violent act against nature, and Serv. Auct. knew of a report that when the Lucrine and Avernus were joined, various troubling prodigies occurred (including the sweating of a statue; see 1.480n.), necessitating pontifical expiation.

161 an memorem: cf. 158n.

161–2 Lucrinoque addita claustra | atque indignatum magnis stridoribus aequor: the wording and the personification suggest violence and reaction against violence. The imposing of barriers (*claustra*) on a natural force, particularly on water, was at best a hazardous undertaking in antiquity; Serv. Auct. connected the word *indignatum* directly with the prodigies which followed the linking of the two lakes (161–4n.). Nor is the word reassuring elsewhere in V.; it is used in the unsettling final line of the *Aeneid* (*uitaque cum gemitu fugit indignata sub umbras*, 12.952), and, perhaps more relevantly, of the Araxes river, captive on the shield of Aeneas, but objecting to the bridge placed over it: *pontem indignatus Araxes* (*A.* 8.728). On this Servius noted *hic fluuius Armeniae quem pontibus nisus est Xerxes conscendere*. Xerxes, the yoker of the Hellespont and paradigm of violence against nature, was never near the river, but he naturally came to the mind of Servius. Nor were Alexander or Octavian connected with the river (at least, not with the Armenian one; cf. *RE* s.v. *Araxes*), but Serv. Auct. has them building and strengthening the bridge; some tradition seems to have connected them with Xerxes (170–2n.).

163 The sound of the line (with *on/un* occurring four times) perhaps suggests the booming of the waves; cf. Cat. 11.3–4 *litus ut longe resonante Eoa | tunditur unda*.

164 Tyrrhenusque fretis immittitur aestus Auernis: not a golden line, but as effective as one, and like most of V.'s golden lines, here serving as a clausula (cf. 1.117n.); the pattern (A–n–V–N–a), with chiasmus of noun and adjective, and here with proper names framing the line, is very mannered.

165–6 In the ethnographical tradition mineral wealth is associated with agricultural products (Ogilvie and Richmond (1967) 164). V., however, relates it to the effects of man upon his environment, with two conclusions implicit. The claim that silver, bronze and gold exist in abundance carries with it the suggestion that the morality of the in-

habitants is corrupt, as is clear from Horace, *Odes* 3.24.47–50, a poem
dealing with the superiority of primitive races over the modern Italian:
*uel nos in mare proximum | gemmas et lapides, aurum et inutile, | summi materiem
mali, | mittamus, scelerum si bene paenitet.* Tacitus, in his ethnography of
Germany, was to state: *argentum et aurum propitiine an irati dii negauerint
dubito, Germ.* 5.3. And abundance of bronze can only suggest warfare,
hardly an art of the Saturnian age, but the theme of the very next lines,
particularly of 169–72 (on this see Lucretius' discussion of mining at
5.1241–80, with the stated purpose at 1266 *ut sibi tela parent*). Ovid may
be reacting against Virgil (155–7n.) when he situates the discovery of
mining in general and of gold (and iron) in particular in the debased
bronze and iron ages: *sed itum est in uiscera terrae, | quasque recondiderat
Stygiisque admouerat umbris, | effodiuntur opes, irritamenta malorum. | iamque
nocens ferrum ferroque nocentius aurum | prodierat, M.* 1.138–42. Of com-
mentators only Forbiger seems to have felt uneasiness about this couplet,
but he overcomes it by stressing *ostendit*: Italy only *displays* her mineral
wealth, it is not actually *used* (he cites senatorial restrictions on the use
of precious metals; V., however, does not, though Pliny does, *N.H.*
37.202). In the same way critics stress *fallunt* at 152 and *tanto* at 153 (152,
153–4nn.), ultimately making Rome's greatest poet an inept exponent
of his language (see too 169–72n. on the treatment of *imbellem*).

haec eadem: sc. *tellus*; so *haec* at 167.

plurima: adverbial, 'in abundance'; cf. 183, and 1.187n.

167   genus acre uirum: cf. 3.382 *gens effrena uirum* (136–76n.); at
A. 9.603 the Italian warrior Numanus Remulus characterizes his race as
durum a stirpe genus. The phrase *genus acre* is otherwise used by V. only of
wolves (3.264).

168   adsuetumque malo: cf. of the contented farmer at 472 *ex-
iguoque adsueta iuuentus,* and the Italians at *A.* 9.607 *paruoque adsueta
iuuentus* (see 167n.).

Volscosque uerutos: the epithet ('equipped with the *ueru,* "short
dart"') is ethnographical in tone (cf. 115 *pictosque Gelonos*).

169–72 V. again departs from the ethnographical tradition, in
which individuals are not treated; they figure in no other version of the
laudes Italiae. As at 145–8 and 161–4, he elaborates (here on the subject
of inhabitants), with four lines of detail calculated to conflict with the
claim at 173 (*salue ... Saturnia tellus*): the Decii, C. Marius, Furius
Camillus (the plural for these last two is a poeticism) and the Scipios are

all military figures (on Octavian see 170–2n.), and are all mentioned in the prophecy of Anchises at *A.* 6.824–5, 842–3 – with the exception of Marius, about whom the critics seem content to note 'the conqueror of Jugurtha' or 'defeated the Teutones and the Cimbri'; he has other, stronger, associations as the man who did his best to tear apart the Roman republic, who, with others *tumultum ex tumultu, bellum ex bello serunt,* Sall. *Hist.* 1.77.7M. What sort of *Saturnia tellus* is this?

170   Scipiadas duros bello: their name in its usual form (*Scipiones*) will not go into the hexameter, but that problem had long been solved by Lucilius, and by Lucretius: *Scipiadas, belli fulmen,* 3.1034 – where it is nom. sing., here acc. pl. At *A.* 6.842–3 V. combines the present reference (to both Scipios) with Lucretius' diction: *geminos, duo fulmina belli* |, *Scipiadas.*

With the words *duros bello,* the ethnographically positive attribute, *duritia* (normally a moral, as much as a military, designation) becomes specific.

170–2   'and you, greatest Caesar, who now victorious on the furthest shores of Asia turn away the unwarlike Indian from the hills of Rome'. This is the natural way to take the lines; whatever unnatural sense is forced upon them, V. must have been aware that this meaning was the most natural. Serv. Auct. (*ad* 172) was the first to react: *ceterum quid grande, si imbellem auertis?* Servius had already provided an escape, taking *imbellem* proleptically: *id est auertendo reddis imbellem* – hardly the natural sense. Moreover, on ethnographical grounds, such a reading of *imbellem* is virtually ruled out; easterners are in this tradition portrayed as *by nature* unwarlike: *fertilis ager eoque abundans omnium copia rerum est regio, et imbelles, quod plerumque in uberi agro euenit, barbari sunt,* Liv. 29.25.12. The other solution, to take *imbellem* = 'without war', i.e. through diplomatic activity, is barely worth mentioning.

The natural meaning is intended, and with this meaning the final detail of the *laudes Italiae* conveys on a political level precisely the theme that has been sustained, and will continue to be, on the agricultural level: 'success' is bought at the cost of forceful subjugation (23, 80–2nn.).

extremis ... in oris: reinforces the sense of the gratuitous conveyed by *imbellem*; see too 114n.

173   salue ... Saturnia tellus: as a climax V. presents Italy as a Saturnian land. Two crucial facts belie the greeting. First, for the world

of the *Georgics*, this is an impossibility; the ethics of *labor*, which concern
V. throughout the poem (both before and after the *laudes Italiae*), are
visited on man precisely because the golden age has *ended* – the realities
of agricultural activity in the *Georgics* are totally antithetical to the
idealized status of the golden or Saturnian age (1.118–46, 145–6nn.).
The claim, then, is at variance with the rest of the poem. Secondly, it
conflicts with the very details of the description in the preceding lines
(136–76n.).

174 magna [parens] uirum: cf. *A.* 6.784 [*Roma*] *felix prole uirum.*

174–5 tibi ... | ingredior 'for thee I embark on a subject and
craft of great glory'. The Medicean has *artis* (an easier reading), but *res*
and *ars* are a pair: the theme and the craft involved in expounding it, the
subject matter and the style, are praiseworthy.

175 ingredior sanctos ausus recludere fontis: the wording is
perhaps indebted to Lucr. 1.927–8 *iuuat integros accedere fontis atque haurire*
(also about the poet's own poetry), though with *recludere* V.'s image is
distinct. Propertius had his eye on this line: *primus ego ingredior puro de
fonte sacerdos | Itala per Graios orgia ferre choros*, 3.1.3–4; see 3.11n.

176 Ascraeumque cano Romana per oppida carmen: the
clausula is elegantly ordered, in the manner of a golden line (1.117n.),
and with balancing references to the Greek tradition (*Ascraeum ...
carmen* = Hesiodic) and to the Roman application (*Romana per oppida*).
Such juxtaposition, reflecting the dual traditions of Augustan poetry,
was favoured by Horace; e.g. *Odes* 2.16.38 *spiritum Graiae tenuem Camenae*
(McDermott (1977) 364–6).

The adjective *Ascraeum* refers primarily to Hesiod (cf. *E.* 6.70 *Ascraeo
... seni*). His influence, however, has by now receded somewhat, and
there is a secondary, and ultimately more important, reference, to him as
the model favoured over Homer by V.'s Alexandrian models, chiefly
Callimachus and Aratus. The epithet Ἀσκραῖος (*Ascraeus*), applied to
Hesiod, first appears in the Hellenistic period, in Nicander (*Ther.* 11)
and in Greek epigram, and given Callimachus' interest in Hesiod, he
may well have used it first; if so, the double allusion here will have been
clearer. Propertius' use of *Ascraeus* (*nondum etiam Ascraeos norunt mea
carmina fontis, | sed modo Permessi flumine lauit Amor*, 2.10.25–6) constitutes
a clear reference to Callimachus; cf. 3.11n. and Wimmel (1960) 235–8;
Ross (1975) 119–20. In the complex and allusive *laudes Italiae* a subtle
reference to Callimachus is fully in place here, at its very end.

cano: cf. 1.5n.

177–225 *Different types of soil and suitability of each for olives, vines,*
crops and livestock

A return to technical material, the importance of soil-types. The topic,
obviously important, had been treated by Theophrastus (*C.P.* 2.4),
Cato (*Agr.* 6) and Varro (*R.R.* 1.7.5–10, 1.9); and White (1970) 86–109
provides a good discussion, particularly in his Appendix (97–102) on
terms used to describe different soils (180n.). V.'s treatment is distin-
guished by picturesque vignettes (186–8, 193–4, 205–6), by mention of
specific Italian areas (197–9, 224–5), and by a brief digression which
takes the reader away from the immediate technical subject to issues
central to the larger poetic concerns of the poem (207–11n.).

177 Nunc: used again at 226 to begin the next section; cf. Lucr.
2.184 (also the beginning of a new section): *nunc locus est ...*

aruorum ingeniis: the slight personification, even of soils, is con-
sistent with V.'s general stance. The words perhaps look back to the
beginning of the treatment of trees: *arboribus ... natura*, 9 (and see 178n.).
V. uses a great variety of words for 'soil', avoiding repetition of the
common word *solum* (cf. Cat. 64, where 'ship' is represented by *pinus*,
puppis, *currus*, but not by *nauis*): *arua*, 177; *terra*, 179, 203; *humus*, 184;
campus, 185; *solum*, 204; *ager*, 215.

178 quis color [cuique]: cf. 256 *et quis cui color* (see n.) and 3.102
et quis cuique dolor uicto.

et quae sit rebus natura ferendis 'and what its [the soil's] native
power is for growing things'; cf. 9 *arboribus uaria est natura creandis*.

179 difficiles: in the same metrical position as, and opposite in
sense to, *et facilem* at 223; the words provide a frame to the passage,
occurring three lines from the beginning and end respectively. Cf.
1–135, 184–94, 190–2, 238; 1.43–70nn.

maligni: the exact sense, as of *difficiles*, is elaborated in the next line.
Cf. Pliny on the soil in the garden of his villa: *morus et ficus ... quarum
arborum illa uel maxime ferax terra est, malignior ceteris, Ep.* 2.17.15.

180 tenuis ... argilla: not 'lean clay' (as opposed to other clays),
but rather 'lean clayey soil'. *tenuis* is the opposite of *pinguis* ('rich'), an
important word in the *Georgics* (1.8n.), and is used of soil at 184 (see n.).
It is not, however, the word generally opposed to *pinguis* in the agri-
cultural writers (otherwise used only by Pliny (*N.H.* 18.123); so White
(1970) 102); that word was *macer*, which does not appear in the *Georgics*,
but was used once by V., correctly opposed to *pinguis* and in an agri-

cultural sense, at *E.* 3.100 *heu heu, quam pingui macer est mihi taurus in eruo.* The Callimachean V. prefers to use *tenuis* as the opposite of *pinguis* (1.433n.), though there is perhaps a paradox here, in that in this context *tenuis* is bad, *pinguis* good.

181 Palladia … silua uiuacis oliuae: the olive was the tree of Pallas Athena; cf. 1.18–19 *oleaeque Minerua | inuentrix.*

gaudent: cf. 4.120n.

182 indicio est 'is an indication [of such soil]'; *indicio* is dat. used for predicative nom.

oleaster: the wild olive is emblematic of the wild and uncultivated; it springs up freely (*plurimus*; 165–6n.), and strews the ground with wild (*siluestribus*) berries. On the dangers of introducing grafts onto the wild olive, and the threat which it poses to cultivated trees, see 303–14 and n.

184–94 quae… | quique … quique…, | hic … hic … | hic …, qualem … : for the syntax and thought cf. 217–25 – V. again provides a frame for the entire section (179n.): *quae … et … et … quaeque … , illa … illa … illam … . talem …* The change in gender is a result of V.'s use of a variety of words for 'soil' (177n.).

184 pinguis: rich soil is ideal for the vine (as for crops; cf. 203), as its opposite, lean soil (180n.), was suited to the olive; here, as elsewhere, V. contrasts the two trees, and especially their products (420–5, 454–7; 3.123–4nn.); on the word throughout the poem see 1.8n.

dulcique uligine laeta: taste is also used to detect a bitter or brackish soil at 246–7, where *amaro* is the opposite of *dulci.*

185 fertilis: in contrast to *difficiles* and *maligni* at 179.

ubere: cf. 234, 275nn.

186 qualem: relative and correlative pronouns are used throughout the section to introduce examples of the various soil-types: 192 *qualem,* 198 *qualem,* 224 *talem.*

187 despicere: V. depicts observation from a neighbouring hill down onto the valley floor.

188 felicemque … limum 'fertile silt'; the very opposite of *tenuis … argilla,* 180.

editus Austro 'elevated from the south', i.e. facing the south; cf. Livy 2.50.10 *duxit uia in editum leniter collem.* Cf. 112–13 *denique apertos | Bacchus amat collis,* and see 298n. on the ideal exposure for the vine.

189 inuisam … aratris: the personification continues, here of the plough, to which the root system of the fern is a great hindrance.

190–2   hic tibi ... hic ... | hic: cf. 221–2 *illa tibi* ... | *illa ... illam*
and 184–94n. The anaphora here is for emphasis (the vine is the subject
of each unit), while at 221–2 the subjects change (vine, olive and
livestock, and crops).

praeualidas: used by V. only here and at 253, where it conveys a
sense of excess (252–3n.).

191   uuae: best seen as an objective gen., the verbal force of *fertilis*
(from *fero*) still being felt; cf. Sall. *B.J.* 17.5 (*ager frugum fertilis, bonus
pecori, arbori infecundus*), where *fertilis* is the only adjective with a verbal
base – hence the datives with *bonus* and *fecundus*; see 222n. Williams calls
it a gen. of respect (analogous to *diues opum*, 468, etc.).

192–4 Some see these lines as an instance of the close relationship
between agriculture and religion (cf. 1.335–50n.); they are, however,
merely descriptive of sacrifice, almost an aside.

192   qualem: cf. 186n.

pateris ... et auro 'in bowls of gold' (lit. 'from bowls and gold');
hendiadys (cf. 1.346n.).

193   inflauit ... aras: a highly colourful and somewhat puzzling
line, which looks as if it should have a specific and personal reference.
The commentators refer to Cat. 39.11 *obesus Etruscus*, and Page imagines
that 'we may assume that these sleek Etruscan performers on the pipe
were well-known figures at sacrifices'; that, however, is probably prefer-
able to Servius' gloss on *pinguis*: *uictimarum scilicet carnibus*; see 396n.

194   reddimus: *reddo* is used of the due rendering of obligation,
debt, etc. (see *OLD* s.v. sect. 9), the compound implying that sacrifice is
performed in return for the favour of the gods.

195   sin armenta magis studium uitulosque tueri: cf. 3.179, of
training horses, *sin ad bella magis studium*; also 1.21 *studium quibus arua tueri.*

196   urentis culta capellas: see 1.93n. on *uro*, which V. uses
broadly for 'blasting', 'withering', etc.; also 376–96 on the sacrifice of
the goat to Bacchus in retribution for the damage it does to the vine; cf.
378–9 *durique uenenum dentis.*

197   Tarenti: the area around Tarentum in southern Italy was
famous for the quality of its sheep, and particularly for their protective
jackets: Varro, *R.R.* 2.2.18 ... *ouibus pellitis, quae propter lanae bonitatem, ut
sunt Tarentinae et Atticae, pellibus integuntur, ne lana inquinetur*; also Plin.
N.H. 8.189. But for both V. and Horace the place assumed a different
importance. Horace named it as an alternative to Tibur as the seat of his
old age and final resting-place, in terms which may recall the present

line: *unde si Parcae prohibent iniquae,* | *dulce pellitis ouibus Galaesi* | *flumen et regnata petam Laconi* | *rura Phalantho, Odes* 2.6.9–12 (for the protasis cf. 195 *sin armenta* . . .); and V. himself presents Tarentum as the ideal locale at 4.125–48, a passage to which Horace was later to respond; see n. and Thomas (1982a) 13–15, 56–60.

petito: see 408–13n. on V.'s use of the archaic and legal form of the imperative in didactic prescriptions.

198–9   et qualem infelix amisit Mantua campum | pascentem niueos herboso flumine cycnos: the pathos of *amisit* takes the reader back to V.'s native town in the *Eclogues* and to the indications that his fellow townsmen lost their land as a result of Octavian's settling soldiers there (*nam Mantuanorum fuerat communis expulsio,* Serv. *ad E.* 1.12). In this respect and in the mention of swans on the Mincius (cf. also 3.15) the lines specifically recall *E.* 9.27–9 '*Vare, tuum nomen, superet modo Mantua nobis,* | *Mantua uae miserae nimium uicina Cremonae,* | *cantantes sublime ferent ad sidera cycni.*' The couplet is also curiously reminiscent of *E.* 6.46–54, where the words *infelix* and *niueus* occur twice (46–7, 52–3), in the same metrical position as here, and where V.'s Calvan model (*herbis pasceris amaris,* p. 85 Morel) recalls the words *pascentem niueos herboso* | *flumine.*

198   A near-golden line.

200–2   The lines are artfully composed, with the first occupied by two parallel units (*non . . . non*), and the next two devoted to a correlative sentence (*quantum . . . tantum*), with the diction contrasted from clause to clause: *longis/exigua, carpent/reponet, diebus/nocte.* The futures are idiomatic: 'you will find that . . . '

200   deerunt: scanned as a spondee.

201–2   quantum . . . reponet 'the cool dew restores in the brief night as much [sc. grass] as the herds graze through the lengthy days'. The thought is similar at Hor. *Odes* 4.5.17–18 *bos . . . rura perambulat* | *nutrit rura Ceres,* where *perambulat* = *pascitur* (Shackleton Bailey (1982) 137–8). Cf. the picture of early summer at 3.324–6.

203   nigra: cf. 255 *promptum est oculis praediscere nigram.*

fere 'for the most part', with *optima frumentis,* 205.

presso . . . sub uomere: with *impulso uomere* (211) forms a frame to the present subsection (203–11: best soil for crops).

204   et cui putre solum 'and with a friable soil', the most desirable type, particularly for crops; cf. 262–3 *optima putri* | *arua solo.*

205–6   V. evokes a colourful image to demonstrate the fertility of this type of land; the tone is very much like that at 1.273–5, the picture of the donkey-driver who trades his product in a nearby town.

205   non ullo ex aequore cernes: cf. 1.487n.

207–11   A resumption of the theme of the violence directed by agricultural man against the natural world (23n.). V. does not merely describe the act, necessary in the world of *labor*, of clearing a grove (a hazardous operation in religious terms; cf. Cato's prescriptions at *Agr.* 139); he presents the process from the viewpoint of the birds whose ancestral home is overturned (*euertit*) by the ploughman's act of anger (*iratus ... arator*). Nowhere in V. does *ira* find favour; Page attempts justification: '"angry", because as a "Ploughman" he cannot bear to see such good ground "idle" (*ignaua*) and unproductive'. The image recurs at 4.511–15, where in a simile Orpheus becomes equivalent to the bird whose young have been destroyed, again by the violence of a plough-man (*durus arator*); see n. and Introduction, pp. 23–4.

207   iratus ... arator: V. regularly used vivid adjectives to charac-terize his ploughmen: *robustus ... arator*, *E.* 4.41; *tristis arator*, 3.517 and n.; *durus arator*, 4.512; also *robustus ... fossor*, 2.264.

The near jingle, reinforced by the placing of the adjective and noun at main caesura and line-end respectively, is uncharacteristic; does V. intend some sort of gloss?

208   euertit: not a mild word: *postquam res Asiae Priamique euertere gentem | immeritam uisum superis, A.* 3.1 2; *Priami regnorum euersor Achilles*, 12.545; cf. 210n.

ignaua: from the viewpoint of the *arator*, representative of the age of Jupiter; and from a cultural aspect the reference is close in sense to 1.124 *nec [Iuppiter] torpere graui passus sua regna ueterno* (see n.). To the native inhabitant things look different.

209   antiquasque domos auium: cf. Lucr. 1.18 *frondiferasque domos auium.* V.'s adjective carries the pathetic implication that the old gives way to the new; this notion was to be developed in the account of the end of Troy: *A.* 2.363 *urbs antiqua ruit multos dominata per annos* (cf. *multos ignaua per annos* at 208); and Aeneas describes his own house in Troy, soon to fall with the city, as *antiquas ... domos, A.* 2.635 (he uses the phrase nowhere else). See 210n.

210   eruit: strong implications of violence (cf. 208 *euertit*) are rein-forced by the placement and the diaeresis (1.109n.). V. uses this form of the verb, in the same position and with the same effect, at *A.* 2.611–12, where Neptune aids in the destruction of Troy: *fundamenta quatit totamque a sedibus urbem | eruit*; see 209n.

210–11   illae altum nidis petiere relictis, | at rudis enituit impulso uomere campus: this captures the dilemma of Book 2, and of the poem as a whole: cultural progress imposes loss and suffering on nature; to ignore the latter ('*enituit* suggests beauty and order in contrast with what was previously wild and rugged' (**Page**)) is to simplify and distort the poem. An age which has seen that 'order' and 'beauty' are not necessary partners may read V. with a keener eye.

rudis: with *enituit* creates a cultural image: the 'rough' field acquires polish.

enituit: cf. Plin. *N.H.* 17.37 *post uomerem nitescens*; at 1.46 the soil has the same effect on the plough: *sulco attritus splendescere uomer*. For the 'lengthening' of the final syllable of *enituit*, see 1.138n.

212   nam … '[I have focused on these soils] for hungry gravel of hilly country is inferior'.

ieiuna: the word looks metaphorical, but was in fact already in the technical tradition: *in mediocri autem terra … quo propius accedit ut non sit macra, quam ut sit ieiuna …*, Varro, *R.R.* 1.9.6; also Colum. 3.5.1.

213   uix humilis apibus casias … ministrat: so the bee-keeper is advised, *haec circum casiae uirides … floreat*, 4.30–2; cf. 466n. on *casia*, 'cinnamon'.

roremque: i.e. *rorem marinum*, 'rosemary'. This is the only sure instance of the abbreviation: see Renehan (1981) 471–2, but also Shackleton Bailey (1983) 301.

214–16   V. spends three lines on the snakes which make their home in tufa and chalky soil, contradicting the claim at 153–4 that Italy was free from snakes (see n.), and presenting a somewhat ominous image which is fully developed at 3.414–39.

214   nigris … chelydris: dat. of agent, with a perfect passive (*exesa*).

The *chelydrus* reappears at 3.414–39, and is extremely venomous according to Nicander (*Ther.* 411–37), to whom V. is there indebted (see n.).

215–16   negant … alios aeque … praebere: the style of personification of the soil, with the note of pride in its superiority (a dubious one), is very similar to that of Cat. 4.1–4 *phaselus ille … | ait fuisse nauium* *celerrimus,* | *neque ullius natantis impetum trabis* | *nequisse praeterire.* Cf. 234 *negabunt* [*harenae*].

216 An unusually symmetrical line: a–v–n *et* a–v–n; cf. 3.208.

dulcem ... cibum: cf. 4.17 *dulcem ... escam; cibus,* used by V. only here, is avoided in Augustan poetry: Propertius does not have it, Tibullus used it only once, Horace confined it to the *Epodes* and *Satires;* Ovid, however, used it 56 times (s.v. *ThLL* III.1038.81–3).

curuas ... latebras: cf. 3.544–5 and n.

217–25: cf. 184–94n.

217–18 No adjective is used for the soil, but V. is thinking of the dry, porous type, the opposite of saturated, marshy soil (*uliginosus*) which neither absorbs nor releases its moisture.

217 fumosque uolucres 'curling mists'.

218 bibit umorem: cf. the description of drainage at 1.113–14 *umorem bibula deducit harena.*

cum uult 'just as easily'; the verbs of this sentence (*exhalat, bibit, remittit, se uestit, laedit*) all sustain the personification of the soil (177n.).

219 suo 'native'.

uiridi se gramine uestit: cf. 38 *olea magnum uestire Taburnum.*

220 nec scabie et salsa laedit robigine ferrum: though *ferrum* here refers to the plough, the line perhaps recalls the rusting of weapons after the battle of Philippi: *exesa inueniet [agricola] scabra robigine pila,* 1.495 and n. Pliny responded with some pique: *ferroque omnis [terra] robiginem obducit, N.H.* 17.27; cf. 227–37n.

221–3 Another reference to the activities of Books 1–3 (143–4n.)

221–2 illa tibi ... | illa ... illam: cf. 190–2n.

222 oleae: there is a strong case for reading the objective gen. of *olea,* the word regularly used by V. for 'olive'. Although *oleo,* which has better MS support, and might rank as *lectio difficilior,* is acceptable, it is noteworthy that V. otherwise uses *oleum* only when clearly thinking of the end-product – taken to town by the donkey-driver at 1.273, used as fuel at 1.392 and *A.* 6.254, and as body-oil for wrestlers and rowers at *A.* 3.281 and 5.135. The phrase *ferax oleae* also finds support from *fertilis uuae* at 191, in a context to which this is parallel (190–2, 191nn.); and from the fact that *ferax* with the dat. or abl. (the occurrences are all ambiguous: either case is possible) otherwise occurs only twice in Statius, once in ps.-Quintilian, and once, *uariationis causa,* in Ovid (*terra ferax Cereris multoque feracior uuis, Am.* 2.16.7), whereas examples of the gen. are frequent, and include Ov. *M.* 7.470 *ferax Peparethos oliuae*; indeed, with the special exception of *Am.* 2.16.7, some of V.'s most careful readers, Ovid, Columella and Pliny the Elder, all use the gen. For *oleo* commentators cite Sall. *B.J.* 17.5 *arbori infecundus* (in which case *oleo* is to be seen as a dat., against *ThLL* VI.489.11 (abl.)); the very sentence in which those words appear begins *ager frugum fertilis*. If *oleae* is correct, *oleo* may well be due to the influence of *facilem pecori* in the next line.

223   facilem pecori 'well-disposed to livestock'; cf. 4.129 *nec commoda Baccho* (where the context is the same). The bold use of *facilis*, not quite parallel to 4.272 *facilis quaerentibus herba*, is perhaps motivated by V.'s desire to provide a connection with *difficiles* at 179 (see n.).

224–5   The section ends with references to four places in Italy (parallel to 197–9 on Tarentum and Mantua), in the same metrical position and of the same shape from line to line: *Capua/Clanius* (although the last syllable of Capua suffers elision); *Vesaeuo/Acerris*. Capua and Acerrae are towns, Clanius is a river, and *Vesaeuo . . . iugo* the mountain (*Vesaeuo* may be seen as an adjectival use of the noun, or perhaps as appositional).

224   talem ... arat Capua: cf. 198 *qualem . . . amisit Mantua*, and 186n.

225   ora: the report of Gellius (6.20) that V. changed *Nola* to *ora* following a dispute over water-rights with that town is certainly odd, but probably deserves little credence; mention of a fifth town would disrupt the careful symmetry of the other four places (224–5n.).

uacuis: so Juvenal was to refer to the depopulation of towns in Latium (*uacuis Vlubris*, 10.102) and Campania (*uacuis Cumis*, 3.2); given that V. is here treating areas with rich soil, he is probably not thinking specifically of the very real desolation which occurred, particularly in Latium, as a result of soil exhaustion (White (1970) 71–2).

226–58   On testing soil-types

The topic is handled before V. only briefly by Varro (*R.R.* 1.9), who mainly judges the soil from the plants it supports; cf. White (1970) 91–4. V.'s lines are severely didactic in appearance and have been held to be rather dull. The details, however, are of interest in that V. is at pains to stress man's contact with the soil as he tests it: at 227–37, there is the 'hole' method, at 238–47 the test by taste, at 248–50 by touch, and at

255–8 by sight. Along the way he specifically mentions the eyes (*oculis*, 230, 255), feet (*pedibus*, 232), mouth (*ora*, 246), hands (*manibus*, 249) and fingers (*digitos*, 250) – the focus, then, is ultimately not simply didactic. In addition the apostrophe at 252–3 contains a theme of great importance to the poem (see n.).

226 nunc: cf. 177n.

quo quamque modo possis cognoscere dicam: a typical didactic opening; cf. 1.351 *haec ut certis possemus discere signis* (see n.), 393–4 *nec minus … certis poteris cognoscere signis*; 4.253 *quod iam non dubiis poteris cognoscere signis*. For *quo … modo* cf. 4.284n.

227–37 V.'s precise version of the 'recipe' style, prevalent in the tradition and best exemplified by Cato (*Agr.* 108–14, passim): the author begins with the protasis of a conditional, as here (best translated 'To test soil texture', 'To season olives', etc.), and proceeds with imperatives (the details of the recipe), or, as here, with their equivalents (230–2n.): e.g. Cato, *Agr.* 112.1 *uinum Coum si uoles facere, aquam … marinam sumito … in dolium fundito … nolito implere*, etc. The style is precisely that of the modern manual or cook-book.

The method of digging a hole and determining the nature of the soil by its capacity to fill the hole again is first found here; Pliny is clearly 'correcting' V. when he states *scrobes quidem regesta in eosdem nulla [terra] complet, ut densa atque rara ad hunc modum deprehendi possit, N.H.* 16.27.

227–9 V. provides an elegant accumulation of doublets while treating the two opposing textures, light (*rara*) and compacted (*densa*) – in the technical writings *solutus* and *densus* or *spissus* (used at 236); Colum. 2.9.3, 7; Pliny, *N.H.* 17.27; 18.79 (Pliny also opposes *densus* and *rarus*, while virtually quoting V.'s lines; cf. 227–37n.): the two types are mentioned twice (*rara … densa* / *densa magis … rarissima*), as are the two types of produce they each favour (*altera frumentis … altera Baccho* / *Cereri … Lyaeo*); on this last pairing see 1.7–9 and n.

227 rara sit an …: i.e. *utrum rara sit an …*

228–9 Only crops and trees (vines) are mentioned, not livestock (cf. 143–4n.); the ancient tradition tended to view animal husbandry as separate from agriculture proper (though cf. 233 *pecorique et uitibus*); cf. Varro, *R.R.* 2 *Praef.* 5 *alia, inquam, ratio ac scientia coloni, alia pastoris.* Cf. the similar parenthesis at 239–40.

229 magis: goes with *densa*, the two balancing *rarissima quaeque*, not with *Cereri*, which is answered by *Lyaeo*.

230–2   capies … iubebis … repones … aequabis: futures for imperatives, as often in didactic poetry (1.71–2n.).

230   ante … oculis 'first look around and pick out a place'; cf. 254 *promptum est oculis praediscere nigram*; this 'framing' repetition is character-istic (179n.).

iubebis: a reference (unique in the poem) to the existence of a bailiff or labourer, significantly in a passage with an intense didactic tone; in Cato such practicalities abound (e.g. *Agr.* 2, 5, 10, 11), but V.'s concerns generally differ.

232   harenas: i.e. *solum*; an unusual usage.

234   uber: 'the richness of the soil', as at 185 (*fertilis ubere campus*) and 275 (*in denso non segnior ubere campus*; see n.).

posse negabunt: cf. 215 *negant* and 215–16n.; also *E.* 3.24 (*reddere posse negabat*), where the reflexive subject of *posse* is also omitted, since, as here, ambiguity cannot arise.

236   spissus: cf. 227–9n.

237   ualidis … iuuencis: strong oxen will be needed to break up compacted soil, especially in the first ploughing (*proscinde*). The verb is otherwise used by V., also of the first ploughing, only at 1.97 *proscisso … aequore*, a line which also contains his only other use of *terga* (236) = 'ridge of soil'. He may intend a reference to Lucr. 5.209 *terram pressis pro-scindere aratris*. The simple form *scindere* is used in the same sense at 399; 1.50; 3.160.

238–47   Bitter or brackish soil, which appears in the agricultural writings only in passing at Colum. 3.11.9 and Plin. *N.H.* 17.33, is good for nothing (cf. 239–40n. and 243 *ager ille malus*). V. presents its bitter taste as the opposite of that of rich (*pinguis*) soil (246–7n.). Columella also described the taste test (2.2.20), but V.'s account is the most complete, and again stresses the relationship and contact between man and the soil (226–58n.).

238   salsa autem tellus: already referred to negatively at 220.

quae perhibetur amara: cf. 246–7n. This is the first attestation of the adjective to describe soil, but it can be assumed from *perhibetur* and from its presence in Pliny and Columella that it was the standard word – its absence from Cato and Varro is doubtless a result of their lack of interest in such soil.

V. again provides a frame for this subsection, by placing forms of *amarus*, the key word, at the end of the first and last (247) line; see 179n.

239–40   frugibus ... arando, | ... Baccho ... aut pomis: such land is worthless for crops and trees, very much like the plot of the old man of Tarentum at 4.128–9 (see n.); on the omission of livestock cf. 228–9n.

frugibus infelix: so Sallust described the soil of Libya as *frugum fertilis, B.J.* 17.5.

nec mansuescit arando: such land is beyond the control of *labor*, and, although strictly soil and not plants is the subject, the words constitute a defiance of the general prescription of *Georgics 2: fructusque feros mollite colendo*, 36; in both places V.'s wording is influenced by Lucr. 5.1368–9 (36n.).

240 'nor does it preserve for the vine its lineage, for fruit-trees their names'; i.e. good strains yield inferior fruit, which does not live up to the name. The use of *genus* and *nomina* creates a special personification, placing these trees in the sphere of the aristocracy. V. had already explored such metaphor (*Aminneae uites ... | Tmolius adsurgit quibus et rex ipse Phanaeus*, 97–8), and the personification is not new with him; cf. Cato *Agr.* 25 *ne uinum nomen perdat.*

241   specimen: with the exceptions of *agmen* and *certamen*, compound nouns in -*men* are used sparingly by V., and often under the influence of his poetic tradition; *specimen* otherwise occurs only at *A.* 12.164, and may be indebted to Lucr. 5.1361 (*at specimen sationis*), the opening of a passage which has just influenced V. (239–40n.); see 352–3n. for a more subtle use of such nouns.

241–2   qualos | colaque: best taken as hendiadys; both terms refer to wicker baskets. Alternatively -*que* may be disjunctive (= *ue*).

242   fumosis ... tectis: where wooden or wicker equipment is seasoned and stored: *et suspensa focis explorat robora fumus*, 1.175.

243   ager ille malus: the judgement is almost a moral one: 'that worthless soil'; cf. 256 *sceleratum ...frigus* (also of soil).

dulcesque: see 246–7n.; the sweet spring-water will be soured (*tristia ... amaro*) by such soil.

244   ad plenum calcentur 'they should be filled to the brim and pressed down'.

245   scilicet 'you will see'.

grandes ... guttae: cf. *A.* 11.90 *it lacrimans guttisque umectat grandibus ora*; the combination seems rather elevated for this context, perhaps to atone for the mundaneness of the theme.

246-7   The results of the test. Such soil is in contrast to the rich soil of
184. Some later MSS have *amaror* (known also to Gellius and Servius),
which some editors have printed, comparing Lucr. 4.224 and 6.934
(*tangit amaror*); but *amaro* gives a more elegant line (otherwise *sensu* seems
rather isolated), provides a neater frame with *amara* (238 and n.) and
contrast with *dulcique* (184), and also finds support in Lucretius (*centauri
foedo pertorquent ora sapore*, 2.401).

Page well notes the accommodation of sound and sense at 247, 'the
alliterative *t*-sounds, especially if *temptantum* be pronounced strongly,
mark the feelings of a person who has tasted something which he desires
to spit out'.

248   pinguis: cf. 184n.

hoc denique pacto: strongly technical and didactic, this being the
only instance of *hoc* (*eo, eodem, alio*, etc.) *pacto* in the Virgilian corpus; it
was favoured by Lucretius; e.g. 1.980; 3.110. *denique* goes closely with
hoc: 'in this way alone'.

249-50   'when worked [lit. 'tossed'] in the hands it never breaks up,
but just like pitch, by being held it becomes sticky to the fingers'. The
test of touch follows that of taste (226-58n.).

habendo: used much like *tegendo* at 3.454.

251-2   umida ... laetior: the abundance here is not desirable, for
when the foliage (*herbas*) grows too tall and too rapidly (*maiores, iusto |
laetior*) – an indication of a high nitrogen level in the soil – the fruit or
produce is robbed of its nutriment (252-3n.).

252-3   a, ... aristis: the theme of the preceding sentence, fear of
excessive luxuriance, is repeated on a higher poetic level, with anxiety
imparted by the use of 'neoteric' exclamatory *a* (the only other instance
in the poem is at 4.526, appropriately in an intensely neoteric context;
see n.), and by the intrusion of the didactic narrator (*ne sit mihi*); very
similar are 1.456-7 *non illa quisquam me nocte ... moneat* and 3.435-6 *ne
mihi tum ... libeat*; see nn. The theme of excessive fertility is brought up at
1.111-12, where grazing down corrected the situation, and at 3.135-7,
in a powerful and suggestive metaphor; see 1.111; 3.135-7nn. on other
implications of excessive growth, which, like any excess, V. regards as
dangerous in and of itself.

254-5   quae grauis est ... | quaeque leuis: V. deals in opposites,
as at 227-9 (*rara/densa*); see n.

255-7   The treatment of dark and cold soils is carefully presented:
the beginning (*promptum est*) is the reverse of the end (*difficile est*), the

whole begins and ends after the second-foot ictus (of 255 and 257), giving a total, in feet, of two lines exactly (spread over three), and the parallel phrases *praediscere nigram* and *exquirere frigus* are of the same shape and occupy the same metrical positions.

255 praediscere: see 1.51n.

nigram: see 203n.

256 et quis cui color: *cui* is variously taken as = *cuique* ('what colour each soil has'); as = *alicui* ('what colour any soil has'); or as an interrogative ('which soil has what colour'). The first of these is not now much favoured, and the usage does not seem to recur before Tacitus (*ut quis ex longinquo reuenerat, miracula narrabant, Ann.* 2.24.4; also 2.26.1; 4.23.2), but is probably correct, and finds support from the homophonous words at 3.102 *et quis cuique dolor uicto*; if that phrase occurred to V. first, *cui* in the present line might be seen as a sort of apocope, parallel to the omission of the prefix when a compound verb is repeated: e.g. Prop. 1.1.19–25 *deductae ... ducere* (on which see Clausen (1955) 49–51; Ross (1975) 65–6). This option is also supported by 1.51–3 *praediscere* (cf. 255) ... *et quid quaeque ferat regio et quid quaeque recuset*, and, closer at hand 2.177–8 *quae robora cuique | quis* [sc. *cuique*] *color*.

sceleratum ... frigus: cf. 243, 252–3nn.; such references help to elevate above the realm of mere 'didactic'. *sceleratus* otherwise occurs only in the *Aeneid*, and always carries with it the sense of flawed morality – again personification.

257 taxique nocentes: yews (whose seeds and foliage are toxic to animals) are to be avoided by bees at 4.47 (*neu propius tectis taxum sine*) and *E.* 9.30 (*sic tua Cyrneas fugiant examina taxos*); when we meet them next in *Georgics* 2 they are *nocentes* in a different way (*Ituraeos taxi torquentur in arcus*, 448). The only other occurrence of the yew in V. is in the same context: *Aquilonem et frigora taxi [amant]*, 113.

258 pandunt uestigia [sc. frigoris]: like the yew (113), ivy generally prefers a colder northerly exposure, and so it may be seen as 'revealing traces of cold'.

259–87   *Preparation of the soil of the vineyard and transplantation of the cuttings*

As in the previous two sections the didactic material is enlivened by personification – of a special variety (268n.) – and by elevated language, in the form of a thematically important simile at 279–83 (see n.).

259   His animaduersis: the phrase recurs only at 3.123 (V. uses no other form of this prosaic verb – though cf. *A.* 2.712 *animis aduertite uestris*), where also it is transitional at the beginning of a new paragraph.

259–61   ante ... | excoquere et ... concidere ... | ante ... ostendere: the three infinitives form a tricolon, and the repetition of *ante* in asyndeton isolates and emphasizes *ostendere* and the third clause of the tricolon. This, together with the diction (*magnos ... concidere montis*; *supinatas Aquiloni ostendere glaebas*), creates an elevated effect. Lucretius wrote of giants *qui ... possent | ... magnos manibus diuellere montis*, 1.200–1.
The soil is to be exposed to sun (*excoquere*) and cold (*Aquiloni ostendere*), as at 1.48 *bis quae solem, bis frigora sensit.*

ostendere: the normal word for 'exposing' to the elements: *ager soli ostentus erit*, Cato, *Agr.* 6.2, 4; *qui locus optimus uino sit et ostentus soli*, Varro, *R.R.* 1.25 (a virtual citation of Cato, *Agr.* 6.4); cf. Hes. *W.D.* 612 δεῖξαι δ' ἠελίωι 'expose [grapes] to the sun'.

262–3   optima putri | arua solo: *putri ... solo* is presumably an instrumental ablative: it is by means of a friable soil that fields are superior. Cf. 203–5 *terra | ... cui putre solum ... | optima frumentis.* There is ellipsis of *est* in both passages, as at 2.319 (*optima uinetis satio, cum ...*), which is superficially similar.

263   id: i.e. that the soil be friable.

263–4   uenti ... pruinae | ... fossor: tricolon abundans, with natural forces and man sharing the same verb (*curant*), resulting in a virtual syllepsis. Wind had the same effect on the soil at 1.44 *Zephyro putris se glaeba resoluit.*

264   labefacta mouens ... iugera: 'loosens and stirs the fields'; this preliminary digging was known as *pastinatio.*

robustus ... fossor: cf. *E.* 4.41 *robustus ... arator*; on such epithets see 207n. This is the first attestation of *fossor* in its neutral, agricultural sense (and V. uses it only here), but that it was the correct term is clear from Cat. 22.9–11 (the only occurrence before the present one), where it appears as a synonym for 'country-bumpkin', *bellus ille et urbanus | Suffenus unus caprimulgus aut fossor | rursus uidetur.* It looks to *infodias* at 262.

265   'men whose watchful eye nothing escapes'; lit. 'men whom no watchfulness has escaped'.

266–7   The soil is to be the same (*locum similem*) both where the young vines are first readied for their supporting trees (*ubi ... seges*) and where they will eventually be permanently transplanted (*et quo ... feratur*).

267   digesta feratur: almost hysteron-proteron, = *feratur et dige-ratur*, 'carried and planted out'.

268   mutatam ... matrem: the personification continues (*matrem* here = *terram natiuam*), with the implication that arboriculture may lead to the separation of natural mother and child, much as at 23 *hic plantas tenero abscindens de corpore matrum*; see n. This is coupled with another important theme, the notion that such activity transforms (*mutatam*) the natural status of the plant, as earlier: *mutatamque insita mala | ferre pirum*, 33–4 and 33n. (these being the only two occurrences of the form *mutatam* in V.). Cf. too *mutata*, 50 and n.

ignorent: the relationship between vine and soil is much like that between the parent tree and the alien species grafted onto it at 82; see 80–2n.

semina: cf. 301–2n.

269–72   Cato, who treats transplanting in some detail (*Agr.* 28), does not mention this practice, and Pliny clearly did not consider it valid, since before a virtual citation of V.'s lines he remarked *non omisisset idem* [Cato] *si attineret* (*N.H.* 17.83), recording also that some in fact did the opposite, changing the direction of the plant (*permutantes in contrarium*, 17.84) – presumably to harden it. Columella (5.6.20) endorses the practice. V.'s source is Theophr. *C.P.* 3.5.2; his main aim seems to be to stress the fragility of the young plant (272, 301–2, 362–70nn.).

270   quo quaeque modo: the cadence appealed to V.; cf. (in the same position) 226 *quo quamque modo*; *A.* 3.459; 6 892 *quo quemque modo*.

270–1   qua ... axi: the two clauses are appositive to *quo quaeque modo steterit*: 'that they may restore the position in which each stood – the part with which it bore the heat of the south, and the back which it turned to the pole'.

steterit, tulerit and *obuerterit* are subjunctives in indirect question (*quo, qua* and *quae* being interrogative pronominal adjectives).

272   adeo ... est: an important note is struck, that of the initial fragility of the plant; cf. 343 *nec res hunc tenerae possent perferre laborem*; 363 *parcendum teneris*. See 269–72n.

The words have an epigrammatic effect (imparted by *adeo*), giving the rationale of what has preceded; cf. 3.112 *tantus amor laudum, tantae est uictoria curae*; 4.205 *tantus amor florum et generandi gloria mellis*.

273–4   collibus an plano melius sit ... | quaere: cf. 227 *rara sit an supra morem si densa requires*.

274   pinguis agros ... campi 'fields in [lit. 'of'] a rich plain'; *campi* responds to *plano* (273), while *collibus* in the same line is resumed by *collisque* at 276.

275   densa sere 'plant closely'; the adjective has just been used of soil (227–37), but here refers to the closeness of the plants; it may be adverbial, or, perhaps better, modifies *semina*, which is easily supplied from the root of *sere*.

in denso ... Bacchus 'in land closely planted Bacchus is far from sluggish in fruitfulness'. *uber* refers to productivity, as at 175, and goes closely with *segnior*. Some connect *ubere* with *in denso*, but that would most readily mean 'in a compacted soil' (as at 227, 229, and cf. 234 *rarum uber* – the opposite of *densum uber*), and it weakens the repetition from *densa* at the beginning of the line.

276   supinos 'gently sloping'.

277   indulge ordinibus 'give the rows room'; the method is given in what follows. In fact, as Theophrastus noted (*C.P.* 3.7.2), vines in hilly areas need *smaller* intervals, since their roots and foliage are less developed.

277–8 'no less [than when you planted close], when the trees have been planted, let every pathway make a perfect right angle (*in unguem ... quadret*) with its intersected cross-path (*secto ... limite*)'. This describes the *quincunx*, mentioned by Cicero (*Sen.* 59) and Varro (*R.R.* 1.7.2); the name refers to the fact that the pattern may be viewed as a series of juxtaposed and overlapping groups of five:

V. however is thinking, not of the pattern of the trees, but of the spaces which it creates – the pathways (*uia* and *limite*) which cross each other at right angles, with each tree surrounded by a square of pathway:

nec setius: cf. 3.367 *non setius*.

in unguem 'to a nicety'; the nail is passed over a join in masonry, as a check of the perfection of the work: *lapis ad unguem coaequatus*, Apul. *Flor.* 23; cf. Hor. *Sat.* 1.5.32–3 *ad unguem* | *factus homo*; *A.P.* 292–4 *carmen reprehendite quod ... | praesectum decies non castigauit ad unguem.*

279–83   The picture of the *quincunx* leads into a simile, which is far more than a mere imitation of Lucr. 2.323–32. While those lines provided V. with a model, he reproduces little of Lucretius' language (281–2n.), and in fact inverts the very essence of the simile. For Lucretius an army on the march (*cursu*, 2.323) exemplified the disorderly wandering of sheep on a distant hillside (*lanigerae reptant pecudes quo quam-⟨que⟩ uocantes | inuitant herbae*, 2.318–19); V. applies the simile to an orderly army, not on the move (*campo stetit agmen aperto*, 280) nor yet engaged in battle (*necdum horrida miscent | proelia*, 282–3), to exemplify the orderly appearance of the *quincunx*. Moreover the matter of the simile takes over from the reality exemplified, particularly in 282–3. By the time the reader reaches those lines, the sense is no longer of a neat row of trees, but rather of an actual impending battle-scene; the impression is surely calculated, and contributes to the portrayal throughout the book of arboriculture as warfare between man and nature (23n.).

279–80   'as often [occurs] when in mighty warfare the legion has formed open order by deploying its cohorts ...'; *longa* is predicative. The simile has no main verb (it must be supplied from the sense of *quadret*, 278). The verbs in 279–83 are all with *cum* (279), though some take *miscent* and *errat* with *ut*; that, however, would require *nondum* at 282, non-connective *necdum* being rare and late.

280   stetit agmen: a careful pairing: the army on the move (*agmen*) has come to a halt (*stetit*); cf. 3.347–8 *uiam ... carpit, et ... stat in agmine.*

281–2   late ... tellus 'far and wide the whole land ripples with gleaming bronze'. The image looks ultimately to Hom. *Il.* 19.362–3 'and all the earth was sparkling (γέλασσε, lit. 'laughed') about them under the gleam of bronze'. V. has changed the Homeric metaphor of the earth's 'laughing', or 'sparkling', replacing it with one equally original (s.v. *fluctuo, ThLL* VI.942.43–7), and conflating the Homeric lines with the overall Lucretian model: *totaque circum | aere renidescit tellus*, 2.325–6 (279–83n.). At the same time the idea of 'sparkling' contained in the Homeric γελάω is kept (*renidenti*), but is transferred from the earth to the bronze.

283   dubius ... Mars: perhaps suggested by the formulaic meto-

nymy *dubio Marte* ('with an uncertain outcome to the war'), for which cf.
Vell. 2.55.3; also *A*. 11.899; 12.497 *Marte secundo*; 12.1 *aduerso Marte*.
Such formulas, however, normally refer to the outcome of the battle;
V.'s wording creates a more specific image of the war-god roaming
among the battle-lines, as yet unsure where he will grant his favour. Cf.
1.511 *saeuit toto Mars impius orbe*.

284   paribus numeris ... uiarum 'with equal measurements of
paths'; some take *uiarum* with *omnia* ('all the paths').

285   non animum modo uti pascat prospectus inanem: the
end is not merely aesthetic; space is required to allow equal nutriment to
the trees, and to give their branches room to grow, as V. proceeds to
relate (286–7).

V. was to rework the line in the moving scene in *A*. 1, where Aeneas
stands before the scenes of the Trojan war depicted on Dido's temple:
animum pictura pascit inani, 464. That line supports the interpretation of
inanem as a transferred epithet, in sense going with *prospectus* rather than
with *animum*.

287   in uacuum poterunt se extendere rami: cf. 296 and
296–7n.

in uacuum 'into free air'; the neuter of *uacuus*, used as a substantive,
seems to be first attested here, and is not otherwise found in V. Cf. 364
per purum, of the young vine-shoot.

> *288–97   At what depth to plant the vine; the roots and crown of the oak*

The didactic material occupies only two lines (288–9), and is somewhat
confused. V. refers to two methods of planting, in holes (*scrobes*), and in
furrows (*sulci*), as if they were the same – which is far from true (White
(1970) 236–7). He may have had no written account to follow (the
extant treatments occur only in subsequent writers). What occupied V.
was the picture of the oak (introduced ostensibly in its capacity as a
support-tree for the vine; 291–7n.). The oak is seen as occupying a
position between the sky and the Underworld (cf. 291–2n.), a polari-
zation which will concern V. in the great song of Proteus (4.453–527).

288   Forsitan ... quae sint ... quaeras: the same opening style,
which creates a close relationship between narrator and audience,
occurs at *A*. 2.506 *forsitan et Priami fuerint quae fata requiras*.

fastigia: normally refers to height, here (and perhaps only here) to depth; comparable to *altus*, which has the same range ('high' or 'deep'), and which appears at 290. At Luc. 4.295–6 (*puteusque cauati | montis ad inrigui premitur fastigia campi*) the word refers not simply to depth but to the level of the water. See 354–5n.

289   uitem committere sulco: cf. 1.223 *sulcis committas semina*.

290   arbos: not just 'a tree' (which would include the vine), but '*the* tree', i.e. 'the support-tree'.

291–7   Pliny (*N.H.* 17.201) claims that the Transpadanes used the oak (*quercus*) as a support-tree. He places it last in a list of seven trees so used in this region, and given the shade provided by the oak (cf. *ingentem ... umbram*, 297), it will not have been popular in this capacity. But V. was motivated chiefly by literary tradition, for he recalls the simile at Hom. *Il.* 12.132–4 'they stood like oaks which lift up their crowns in the mountains, and day upon day resist the wind and rain, perpetually gripping the ground with mighty roots'. He adapts fairly closely, choosing the same tree, stressing the size of its root-system, its resistance to wind and rain, and its longevity. He later restored the lines to their Homeric context, that of simile, when in the *Aeneid* he portrayed the resistance of Aeneas to the entreaties of Anna (4.441–6); see 291–2n.

291–2   quantum ... Tartara: the parallel syntax, with contrasting diction (*uertice/radice*; *auras aetherias/Tartara*) places the oak between the upper and lower worlds (288–97n.). In fact, the root-system of the oak, though spreading, is not particularly deep; V.'s concern is to create a vivid image. The lines are repeated at *A.* 4.445–6 (291–7n.).

293   flabra: a Lucretian word, extremely rare in classical Latin in spite of its usefulness as a metrical variant for *uenti*: it is found twice in the *Georgics* (here and at 3.199; see n.), once in Propertius (2.27.12), and otherwise once in Petronius and occasionally in subsequent Latin. V. recalls Lucretius again at 294–5 (see n. and cf. 281–2n.).

294   conuellunt: the violent sense of the word is reinforced by its shape and position: molossus with a strong break at the main caesura of the second foot (cf. 1.478–9n.).

294–5   'it remains unshaken and by enduring outlives many generations, many ages of men, as it sees them roll by [lit. 'rolling them by']'. The thought is bold, as 'the tree is said to *do* that which it *sees done*' (Page). The expression is adapted from Lucr. 1.202 *multaque uiuendo uitalia uincere saecula*; also 3.948 *uiuendo uincere saecula*. For *uoluens* cf. 402 *uoluitur annus*; V. extends the concept of time or the seasons 'rolling' events by: *casus uoluit uarios* | *semper nobis metuenda dies*, [Sen.] *Oct.* 927–8. The longevity of the tree was suggested in similar terms at 58.

296–7 bracchia ... umbram: the personification is intense, as the tree almost takes on the appearance of an Atlas, *aetherios umero qui sustinet orbis, A.* 8.137.

tendens: some editors prefer *pandens*, supported by the Vaticanus and the Berne scholia; this avoids the repetition of *tendit* from 292. Though there is support for *pandens* at *A.* 6.282–3 (*in medio ramos annosaque bracchia pandit* | *ulmus opaca*), the repetition has a purpose: the tree 'stretches' its roots down to Tartarus, 'stretches' its branches out wide. And cf. 3.332–3 *quercus* | ... *tendat ramos*.

298–314 Prohibitions

The didactic prohibitions introduce the main theme of the lines, the fire in the trees (303–14n.). This pattern, of didactic opening succeeded by material of a higher poetical status, is repeated from the preceding section (288–97n.), and continues in the next.

298–302 Neue ... neue ... neue ... neu ... neue: in a series of prohibitions, particularly in poetry, *neue/neu* may replace initial *ne*; cf. 4.47–8 *neu ... neue ... neu*. When dealing with a group of only two prohibitions V. uses *ne ... neue/neu*: 1.80; 3.435–6; *A.* 2.606–7; 6.832–3; 7.96–7, 202; 9.114–15; 12.72. The effect of a series such as in the present lines (unparalleled in V.) is intensely didactic, though its origin is legal or sacral: *ne sumptuosa respersio* ... ⟨*ne murrata potio*⟩ ... *ne longae coronae* ... *ne acerrae, Tab.* 10.6.

298 At 112–13 and 188 V. recommended a southerly exposure for the vine, and the same may be assumed here. The subject *de situ uitearum* seems to have been a ζήτημα ('topic of debate'): Columella (3.12.5) noted [*caeli*] *cuius regionem quam spectare debeant uineae uetus est dissensio*, reporting that various technical writers, all prior to V. (Saserna, Tremelius Scrofa, Mago and Democritus), among them favoured all four points of the compass; he also observed that the ideal exposure depends largely on prevailing climate. On V.'s involvement in such debates cf. 3.147–8n.

299 neue inter uitis corylum sere: cf. Plin. *N.H.* 17.240 *odit* [*uitis*] *et corylum.* The hazel has a large root-system which will deprive the vines of nutrients. A sense of this danger seems to have been sublimated into cult practice (396n.).

299-300 'and do not lop off the shoot at the top of the vine, or break off cuttings from the tree-top'; as in the next precept V. stresses the fragility of the vine, for at 28–9 he recommended cuttings from the top. Theophrastus (*C.P.* 3.5.3) preferred cuttings from the lower part, but not for the vine! Columella is emphatic about the desirability of taking them from the top (3.10.2–3), while Pliny (*N.H.* 17.105) quotes these lines of V. and seems to agree with them.

defringe: a strong word, not merely = 'take a cutting', as is clear from Varro, *R.R.* 1.40.4 *deplantes potius quam defringas*; at Cic. *Caec.* 60 the word, in a similar context, implies violence and vandalism: *uinces profecto ... non fuisse armatos eos qui praetereuntes ramum defringerent arboris.*

301 (tantus amor terrae): sc. 'that cuttings from the part closest to the earth do best'. Cf. 3.112 *tantus amor laudum* (of the racehorse); 4.205 *tantus amor florum* (of the bees); this is one of the many instances of V.'s bringing his subjects – trees, animals and bees (men) – into a close relationship.

301-2 neu ferro laede retunso | semina: this situation will change when the fragility of the vine passes: *... tum stringe comas, tum bracchia tonde | (ante reformidant ferrum)*, 368–9.

semina = *plantae*, or young plants, as at 268, 317, 354.

302 neue oleae siluestris insere truncos: some take this 'and do not plant wild olive-trunks [among vines – as supports]', on the grounds that the alternative, 'do not graft wild olive-trunks [with olive]', introduces discussion of the olive where V. has been exclusively concerned with the vine. This second reading is surely correct. *insero* in this book (33, 50, 69, 73) means 'graft', and to take it as = *intersero* is all but impossible. When Palladius writes *sed ut oleastro inseras, contra illud, quod ex oliueto insito et casu incenso renascitur oleaster infelix, sic prouidendum est* (*Agr.* 5.2), there is no reason to assume he is parroting this reading of 302.

The presence of the olive in a discussion of vines is necessitated by literary motives: V. ends the first half of the book, which resumes with the praises of spring (315–45), just as he had the first half of Book 1, with catastrophe, with the forces of nature – in Book 1 the great storm (311–34), here a firestorm – resurgent and destructive of the work of man (136–76, 303–14nn.). The olive, rather than the vine, is subject to destruction because the latter is to represent the 'successful' object of *labor*; its deficiencies are more complex (454–7n.).

303-14 The forces of nature return, here in the form of fire, as destructive as its opposite, the cold and wet of the storm in Book 1 (*agmen* *aquarum ... imbribus atris*, 322–3). At 310 an actual storm joins the destruction, bringing the lines even closer to 1.311–34. The storm simile at 3.196–201, occurring just before the introduction of the topic of *amor*, is also a part of this fabric (and cf. 3.470–1). As throughout the poem, an imbalance of the elements heralds failure, be it through storms, the power of *amor*, or the plague. The result is the sterility which attends the failure of *labor* in the age of Jupiter: *infelix superat foliis oleaster amaris* (314); cf. 1.154 *infelix lolium et steriles dominantur auenae*; see too 440n.

303   nam: not purely explanatory (though it also has that function here), but as often, like *namque*, marking the opening of an aetion or episode; cf. 4.125, 287.

saepe: so began the storm of Book 1: *saepe ego ...*, 316; see 1.316–18n. An occurrence such as this will hardly happen 'often', but it suits V.'s purpose to suggest that it does (303–14n.).

incautis ... pastoribus: *incautus* occurs three times in the *Georgics*: here, at 3.469, where the shepherd must kill the diseased sheep before it infects the entire flock (*incautum ... uulgus*), and at 4.488 where Orpheus, on the point of success, forgets his instructions and glances back (*incautum ... amantem*; see n.). The present instance is close to 4.488, for in both catastrophe results from an emotional or human failure, from a lapse of prudence – and there is no room for such a lapse in the world of *labor* (1.199–203n.).

304–11   The lines take the fire from its initial point beneath the bark (*sub cortice*, 304), up into the foliage (*frondesque ... in altas*, 305), to the branches (*per ramos*, 307), and to the top (*perque alta cacumina*, 307), where it is met by a storm from above (*tempestas a uertice siluis | incubuit*, 310–11).

304–5   furtim ... comprendit: the fire lurks beneath the bark before breaking out, much as the diseases of love (also a 'fire') and plague in Book 3 first take hold from within; cf. 3.271 *continuoque auidis ubi subdita flamma medullis*. So with Dido at *A.* 4.66–7 *est mollis flamma medullas | interea et tacitum uiuit sub pectore uulnus.*

306   ingentem ... sonitum: the noise of the fire is parallel to that of the storm at 1.324, 327; cf. 3.199–200.

307   uictor ... regnat: a colourful expression for the destructive force of the fire.

308–9   ruit ... nubem: suggests something larger than a mere fire among the olives; for the wording cf. the eruption of Aetna at *A.* 3.572–4.

ruit: cf. 1.324n. for the use of this verb in related contexts; here it is transitive.

310   praesertim: in V. only here and at 1.115, here under the influence of Lucr. 2.32 *praesertim cum tempestas*.

tempestas: a storm is introduced, partly to intensify the conflagration, but also to strengthen the parallel with the storm of Book 1 (302, 303–14nn.)

a uertice '"from the zenith", κατ' ἄκρης, coming sheer down' (Page); so at *A.* 1.114 *ingens a uertice pontus*.

311   incubuit 'has swooped down upon'; *incubui* is the perfect of both *incubo* and *incumbo*, and though the two were confused even in antiquity (*ThLL* VII.1071.51–3), the latter, which implies greater activity than *incubo*, is intended. The same form, in the same emphatic position, is used of the storm at 3.197 (303–14n.). V. may have had in mind Lucr. 6.1143 (*mortifer aestus* ...) | *incubuit*, from a context which occupies him in the second half of Book 3.

glomeratque: of the wind's gathering the flames into a mass, as at 1.323–4 of the clouds' effect on the storm: *et foedam glomerant tempestatem imbribus atris | collectae ex alto nubes*. The use of *glomero* here seems the more natural; possibly 1.323–4 were composed subsequently as V. revised with concern for the larger fabric of the poem. The verb is also used at *A.* 3.577, of the eruption of Aetna (cf. 308–9n.).

ferens 'favouring' (the spreading of the fire).

312   hoc ubi: *subaudis 'contigerit'* (Servius).

312–13   non ... terra 'they [the engrafted olives] get no strength from the stock [the wild olive] and when cut away [where burnt] cannot come back and resume their former vigour from the earth's depths'. *-que* of *caesaeque* is disjunctive. Those who see 302 as referring to the planting of vines among wild olives (see n.) take the vines as the subject of *ualent*.

314   infelix superat foliis oleaster amaris: a crucial line; after nature's assault on man's works only the wild olive, useless and barren, remains (303–14n.). As Cato noted, *'felices' arbores ... quae fructum ferunt, 'infelices' quae non ferunt, ex* Fest. p. 81.26 Lindsay.

This same tree figures at the end of the *Aeneid* as the tree sacred to Faunus (*sacer Fauno foliis oleaster amaris, A.* 12.766), who, entreated by Turnus, holds onto the spear of Aeneas. Given the status of the Trojans as 'civilizers' or representatives of the age of Jupiter, it may be noteworthy that V. puts this tree, described with the same words, 'on the side of' the Latins.

infelix ... amaris: paired at 239–47, in the description of worthless, brackish soil (*ager ille malus*, 243).

superat 'survives', 'wins out', exactly as at 1.154, where the arts of *labor* also fail, and barren plants prevail (*dominantur*); see 303–14n.

315–45   When to plough and plant the vine; the praises of spring

The pattern of the two previous sections is repeated: a didactic section on the best times for ploughing and sowing (315–22, spring or autumn) leads into a more colourful or 'poetical' passage praising the fecundity and beneficence of spring (323–45n.).

315–16   Nec tibi tam prudens quisquam persuadeat auctor |
... mouere: i.e. *nec quisquam auctor tam prudens uideatur ut tibi persuadeat ut ... moueas.* The infinitive is metrically useful, and is less prosaic than a jussive noun clause; cf. 1.456–7 (parallel in other ways) *non illa quisquam me nocte per altum | ire neque a terra moneat conuellere funem*; also 4.264–5.

nec: ostensibly a return to the list of prohibitions of 298–302 (*neue ... neue ...*, etc.).

prudens: only here in V., as only once in Lucretius (3.762), whose influence is evident throughout this passage.

Borea ... spirante: cf. 3.356 *semper spirantes frigora Cauri*.

317   rura gelu tum claudit hiems: spring does the opposite: [*Zephyri*] *... laxant arua sinus*, 331, and 330–1n.

semine iacto: cf. 14, 301–2nn.

318   concretam: there is no need to read *concretum* (with the Medicean); the root is frozen along with the soil, and therefore does not take.

adfigere: i.e. *se adfigere*.

319   optima uinetis satio: see 262–3 *optima putri | arua solo*, and n.

**319–22   The four seasons are mentioned in four lines; cf. 4.134–8n. Summer and winter, unsuitable times, appear in negative terms: *nondum hiemem ...; praeterit aestas.* See 330–9n.

319–20   cum ... | candida uenit auis longis inuisa colubris: the manner of reference in 320 (the stork is not named, but must be identified from its habit of preying on young snakes; see Plin. *N.H.* 10.62; Juv. 14.74–5) is in essence Alexandrian (1.14–15n.). Cf. Callim. *Hecale*, fr. 271 Pf. (spoken by another bird?) σὺν δ' ἡμῖν ὁ πελαργὸς ἀμορβεύεσκεν ἀλοίτης, 'and the avenging stork was our travelling-companion' (where ἀλοίτης might refer to its killing of snakes).

rubenti 'blushing [with flowers]'.

321   autumni sub frigora: late autumn, just before (*sub*) it turns cold; cf. *usque sub extremum brumae intractabilis imbrem*, 1.211, and n.

rapidus Sol: cf. 1.92 *rapidiue potentia solis*.

323–45   The praises of spring come between the 'praises' of Italy (136–76 and n.) and the praises of 'rustic' life (458–540 and n.). Though the present passage seems more straightforward, the status of spring is ambivalent throughout the *Georgics*: the unseasonable spring storms of Book 1 (*cum ruit imbriferum uer*, 313), the palpably false assignation of eternal spring to Italy at 2.149 (*hic uer adsiduum*), and the fact that at 3.272 (see n.) spring is a particularly dangerous time (since it is then that the *furor* of sexual passion is at its peak), all of these must be considered in judging the status of these praises; see also 325–35n. At 325 the connection between spring and sexuality or reproduction is developed, a theme already treated by Lucretius (1.250–64; 2.992–1022; 5.783–820) and (in different ways) by Horace (*Odes* 1.4) and the poet of the *Peruigilium Veneris*.

323–4   uer ... uer ... | uere: a tricolon abundans, with anaphora of the key word, serves as an emphatic opening; see 1.289–90 and n. Cf. 338 *uer ... uer.*

323   uer adeo frondi nemorum, uer utile siluis: the shape and diction resemble 150 (*bis grauidae pecudes, bis pomis utilis arbos*) and 442 (*dant alios aliae fetus, dant utile lignum*); in each there is anaphora of a monosyllable, a form of *utilis* occupying the fifth foot (the positive degree of the adjective occurs nowhere else in V., *utilior* once, at 2.93), and each line ends with a related word (*arbos*; *siluis*; *lignum*).

adeo: see 1.24n.

324   This powerful line leads into the personification of the fertilizing union between rain and earth as a sexual union between Aether and Terra (325–35 and n.).

tument: like *tumesco*, the verb signifies teeming activity, occurring out of sight; see 1.464–5n.

genitalia semina 'seeds, which bring about reproduction'; cf. Lucr. 5.851–2; 1.58, 167 *genitalia corpora*. The adjective occurs in V. only here and in a related context at 3.136; see 3.135–7n.

325–35   V. describes the process of fertilization as an act of intercourse (*in gremium ... descendit*) between heaven (*pater ... Aether*) and the earth (*coniugis ... laetae*). In this he elaborates on Lucr. 1.250–3, particularly on the first two lines: *postremo pereunt imbres, ubi eos pater aether | in gremium matris terrai praecipitauit*; also 2.992–8. The notion already figured in the agricultural tradition earlier in the first century, as is clear from Columella's quotation (2.1.2) of Tremelius Scrofa: *credidit* [sc. Tremelius] *parentem omnium terram, sicut muliebrem sexum aetate anili iam confectam, progenerandis esse fetibus inhabilem*; such an attitude towards the topic of soil-exhaustion seems to come from Theophr. *C.P.* 4.4.10. At *Sen.* 51 Cicero gives a quite remarkable description, packed with metaphorical nuance, of the earth's reproductive powers: *quae* [*terra*] *cum gremio mollito ac subacto sparsum semen excepit, primum id occaecatum cohibet ... deinde tepefactum uapore et compressu suo diffundit et elicit herbescentem ex eo uiriditatem ...* By Tertullian's time the theme had become a thorough topos: *quis enim non caelum et terram matrem ac patrem uenerationis et honoris gratia appellet?, Apol.* 10.

V.'s introduction of the theme of sexual union – the major component of the *laus ueris* – and his implication of the animal world, as figurative language becomes explicit (*et Venerem certis repetunt armenta diebus*, 329), will assume a special significance when the reader arrives at Book 3 and looks back; cf. 3.99, 135–7, 272nn.

325–6 A development not only of Lucr. 1.250–3, but also of E. 7.60 *Iuppiter et laeto descendet plurimus imbri* (cf. *fecundis imbribus, descendit*), where, however, the sexual metaphor is not apparent.

326 laetae 'fertile', as often (1.1n.), though the other sense may also be present.

326–7 'and mingling his might with her mighty body nurtures all growth'. Cf. Anchises' description of the effects of *mens* upon the cosmos at *A.* 6.726–7.

magnus alit magno: cf. 1.190 *magnaque cum magno*; Conington points to the Homeric phrase μέγας μεγαλωστί, 'great in [his] greatness' (*Il.* 16.776, *passim*), which may be at the root of the Virgilian repetition.

alit: repeated in its adjectival form at 330 *almus*; see 1.7n.

commixtus: *commisceo* is one of the 'polite' verbs for joining in sexual union (Adams (1982) 180–1).

328 auia tum resonant auibus: the words surrounding *resonant* (*auia ... auibus*) draw attention to its meaning (the difference in quantity is immaterial), as at 3.338 *alcyonen resonant, acalanthida*, and *E.* 2.13 *ardenti resonant arbusta*. Less perfect instances of such play with *resonare* occur at 1.358 (see n.) and *A.* 3.432 *Scyllam et caeruleis canibus resonantia saxa*.

329 Almost imperceptibly, and only for one line, the focus moves from plant reproduction and metaphor to the explicit language of animal reproduction (325–35n.).

Venerem ... repetunt 'again seek sexual union'; this is frequently the force of *Venus* (3.64, 137, 210).

330–9 As all four seasons were named in 319–22 (see n.), so here all four principal winds figure.

330 **parturit:** only used by V., as here, in a transferred sense; cf. *E.* 3.56 *nunc omnis parturit arbos.*

almus: see 326–7n. (on *alit*).

330–1 **Zephyrique tepentibus auris | laxant arua sinus:** cf. Ov. *M.* 1.107–8 *placidique tepentibus auris | mulcebant Zephyri*; cf. 336–42n.

In a brilliant image the warm west winds are presented as assisting in the birth, and are at the same time opposite in their effect (*laxant*) to the winter of 317 (*claudit*). Cf. 1.44 *Zephyro putris se glaeba resoluit.*

331 **superat** 'abounds'; not quite as at 314 (see n.).

332–3 **inque ... | credere:** the personification is extreme, as the young shoots emerge in the spring much like the herd at 3.322–3 and the bees at 4.51–2. For the conflation of the animal and the plant world see 325–35, 350, 361, 362–3, 369–70, 372nn.

gramina: *germina* (in some later MSS and read by Celsus, according to Serv. Auct.) is at first attractive, but *gramina* is strongly supported by Hor. *Odes* 4.7.1 (*diffugere niues, redeunt iam gramina campis*), and *germina* would somewhat anticipate 335 *trudit gemmas.* V. refers to all plants, not specifically the vine, to which he returns at 333–5.

credere: so the bees at 4.192 [*nec*] *credunt caelo aduentantibus Euris.*

333 **nec metuit surgentis pampinus Austros:** again personification; normally it is man who fears the coming of adverse weather: 1.335 *hoc metuens caeli mensis et sidera serua*; 2.419 *et iam maturis metuendus Iuppiter uuis*; at 4.37 the bees are wary of extremes of heat and cold: *utraque uis apibus pariter metuenda.* See 491–2; 1.335; 4.239nn. on *metus.*

334 But such storms do occur (*uel cum ruit imbriferum uer*, 1.313), and should be feared (*hoc metuens*, 1.335).

335 The vivid description of the appearance of bud and leaf is again from the viewpoint of the plant (*trudit; explicat*).

trudit gemmas: cf. 31 *truditur e sicco radix oleagina ligno*; 74 *se medio trudunt de cortice gemmae*; cf. too 1.310n.

336–42 V. postulates that the beginning of the earth must have been characterized by spring-like conditions; it is partly from here that Ovid may have made the connection (apparently original to him), between the golden age and continuous spring: *uer erat aeternum*, *M.* 1.107; cf. 148n. V.'s picture is suggested by Lucr. 5.780–820, where the primal earth is described as enjoying temperate conditions.

336–7   non alios ... dies: cf. 1.487n.

prima crescentis origine mundi: cf. Lucr. 5.780 *nunc redeo ad mundi nouitatem*.

338   crediderim: cf. 99n.

uer ... uer: the anaphora resumes that of 323–4 (see n.).

340   lucem ... hausere 'drank in the light'; the expression is clear enough, but is virtually unique, though parallel to e.g. *A.* 10.898–9 *ut auras | suspiciens hausit caelum mentemque recepit*.

341   terrea: for this reading cf. Lucr. 5.925–6 *at genus humanum multo fuit illud in aruis | durius, ut decuit, tellus quod dura creasset*, and 5.1411 *siluestre genus ... terrigenarum*; which, however, do not rule out *ferrea* (found in most MSS), since the concept of early men as in some way *terrigenae* is in any case contained in V.'s *duris caput extulit aruis*. Cf. also 1.61–3 *quo tempore primum | Deucalion uacuum lapides iactauit in orbem, | unde homines nati, durum genus*; but V. cannot here be thinking of the *second* creation by Deucalion, which was certainly not when beasts were put in the woods and stars in the sky (342); cf. Ov. *M.* 1.69–75. *ferrea* would refer to the time following the golden age when man first had to deal with the problem of the seasons, and with their effect on agricultural activity. For this reading cf. *A.* 9.609 (*omne aeuum ferro teritur*), a reference to the hardy lifestyle of the Latins before the arrival of the Trojans. V. tends to conflate and renovate standard accounts of cultural change (1.61, 118–46nn.), and the choice of reading here must remain uncertain.

caput extulit aruis: a rather odd reminiscence (perhaps) of Hor. *Epd.* 2.17–18 *pomis caput | Autumnus agris extulit*. Cf. *A.* 1.127.

**342   For Ovid this occurs before the first creation of man: *astra tenent caeleste solum formaeque deorum | ... terra feras cepit*, *M.* 1.73–5; see 341–2n.

**343–5   Balance and alternation among the seasons are required if men are to survive in the age of *labor*. This is as close as V. comes to mentioning the vital notion of *temperies*; see 1.237–8n.

343   nec res hunc tenerae possent perferre laborem: a pastiche of Lucretian language (*res teneras*, 1.179; *non ... poterit perferre* *dolorem*, 3.990; *hunc possint ferre laborem*, 5.1214) reworked, as often, into a new context. The combination *perferre laborem/labores* is used in the *Aeneid* of human endurance (5.617, 769; 6.437; 12.177).

The phrase *hunc . . . laborem* is deliberately vague, referring to the trial not only from heat and cold, but from all the toil and threats which assail the young plant in the age of Jupiter. The assigning of *labor* to plants is pointed; cf. 1.145–6n.

344   A hypermetric line (1.295–6n.).

345   caeli indulgentia: cf. the characterization of the temperate zones at 1.238 *munere concessae diuum*.

346–53   Manuring, drainage and protection for the young plants

Jermyn (1952) examines the debt of the passage to Theophr. *C.P.* 3.4.3 and 3.6.1–2 (see also 350–2n.) His contention that it was hastily composed and intrudes in the progression from spring (315–45) to the words *seminibus positis* (354) does not convince: manuring and the assurance of proper drainage naturally precede hoeing and other cultivation (354–70).

346   Quod superest 'next' (Kenney (1971) 123). Lucretius has the transitional phrase 19 times, always in this position, and in half of the instances at the beginning of a new paragraph, as here. It occurs once again in the *Georgics*, with the same function, at 4.51. *superest* is repeated at the beginning of the next section (354), which, like this one, also occupies eight lines.

premes 'plant', as at 4.131, perhaps with the idea of firming down the soil.

347   sparge fimo pingui: cf. 1.80 *ne saturare fimo pingui pudeat sola*.

multa memor occule terra: this seems to mean that the slip should be well buried, and is perhaps a misunderstanding of Theophr. *C.P.* 3.6.1 which states that the *manure* should be buried before the slip is put in the trench (to prevent burning of the roots, as any vegetable gardener knows).

The present text concurs with Wilkinson (1969) 250 in having a period after *terra*. Otherwise drainage (348) becomes an alternative to manuring.

348   aut ... aut 'either ... or'.

lapidem bibulum: not 'sandstone', as Servius thought, but a layer of stones to produce a porous effect (like the shells: *squalentis ... conchas*); cf. 1.114 *bibula ... harena*, and n.

Columella claims (3.15.4) that V. is here following Mago, who recommended placing a few stones in the bottom of the trench; but the detail is in Theophrastus (*C.P.* 3.4.3; so Jermyn (1952) 9–10).

349-50   inter ... | halitus: cf. the effect spontaneously produced by the good soil of 217–23; for the language cf. 217–18.

350   animos tollent sata: personification again, and of the sort (cf. 332–3n.) that approximates plant to animal, for at 3.207 V. describes colts before they are broken with the words *ingentis tollent animos*; the vines will be 'broken' at 369–70 (see n.).

350-2 'and before now some have been found who press down on top with a rock and with the weight of a large jar', to protect the roots against denudation by rain or drying out in the summer heat (352–3), but the advice is oddly phrased so as to suggest a weight bearing down heavily on the plant. It is standard modern gardening practice to use stones or tiles to shade the roots of some plants, esp. clematis. It is not necessary to suppose with Jermyn (1952) that V. has misunderstood Theophr. *C.P.* 3.5.4–5, which recommends placing a potsherd (ὄστρακον, i.e. *testa*) on top of a *decapitated* plant in order to protect the cut from the elements. The violent language (*urgerent*) may be motivated by the same reasons as at 368–70.

352-3   hoc ... arua: there are two levels of reference. V. is clearly drawing from Cat. 68.62 *cum grauis exustos aestus hiulcat agros*, though he chose not to reproduce the apparently over-audacious verb *hiulco* (which does not otherwise occur until ps.-Augustine). He also noted *leuamen* in the previous line of Cat. 68, a word which seems to have been coined by Catullus, and is certainly first attested in him, as *munimen* (352) is first attested in V. For V.'s restricted use of nouns in *-men* see 241n.

The heat associated with the Dog Star's (Sirius') rising (mid-July) and subsequent visibility is proverbial; e.g. Hor. *Odes* 1.17.17–18 *hic in reducta ualle Caniculae | uitabis aestus*; Tib. 1.7.21 *arentes cum findit* [taken from V.?] *Sirius agros*.

hiulca: proleptic; they gape after they have been split open. Cf. 3.432 *dehiscunt*.

354–61   Cultivate with hoe or plough, and prepare support-stakes

The choice between hoe and plough was based on the amount of room between the rows: *tum deinde relicto spatio, prout cuique mos est uineas colendi uel aratro uel bidente, sequentem ordinem instituunt*, Colum. 3.13.3.

354   Seminibus positis: cf. 14, 301–2nn.

superest: cf. 346n.

354–5   diducere terram | ... ad capita 'break up the soil up to the roots', i.e. keep the soil loose around the young vines (cf. what follows), not 'heap up soil to the plants' – the misunderstanding that doubtless bred the variant *deducere* (in the Medicean and elsewhere).

capita 'roots', as at Cato, *Agr.* 33.3 *circum capita addito stercus, paleas, uinaceas*; modern horticulture thinks in the same way of both the root and the upper growth point (both called apical meristems), and the notion is in Aristotle: 'the "head" is the name for the top of the plant as well as for the root', *De Long. et Breu. Vitae* 6.467b2. Less easy is *A.* 6.360 *capita aspera montis*, where the meaning is also 'roots' (of the mountain); see Norden *ad loc.* and 4.319n. for the same range of the word applied to parts of rivers. Cf. also 288n. on *fastigium*.

355   duros ... bidentis: cf. 399–400 *glaebaque uersis | aeternum frangenda bidentibus*, and see 356n.

356   aut: if there is room; see 354–61n.

presso ... uomere: cf. 1.45 *depresso ... aratro*, and Lucr. 5.209 *terram pressis proscindere aratris* – where in the previous line *ualido ... bidenti* occurs in the same position as V.'s *duros ... bidentis* in 355.

358–61   See White (1970) 232–6 for the different methods of growing supported vines. V.'s technical expertise is perhaps in question here: though in the first three lines he is dealing with staked vines (specifically the *uitis iugata*), at 362 he seems to be thinking of the *uitis arbustiua*, the tree-supported vine, which is obviously distinct. Viticultural reality is sacrificed to poetical form: we are taken from flimsy supports (358 and n.), through stronger stakes (359n.), to the strongest of all, the *arbustum*. Williams follows Page in seeing the stakes and props as 'supports to lead the vines to the trees up which they finally climb', but though he cites Varro, *R.R.* 1.8.2, there is no evidence there or in the lengthy discussions of Columella (5.6) and Pliny (*N.H.* 17.199–214) that *uitis arbustiua* and *iugata* were ever so combined – the stem of the *arbustiua* was merely tied to that of the support tree, and when the vine reached the branches of the tree it proceeded to spread out, as it does at 361 (see n.).

358   tum: sc. *superest*.

calamos ... hastilia: Columella (4.12) recommends reeds (*harundines*) and canes (*hastilia*) as stakes (*pedamenta*), to which cross-bars (*iuga*) are tied, thus producing the *uitis iugata*, but if V. is really thinking about exact reality (358–61n.), he probably intends these for the cross-bars, as the reed (*harundo*) was for Varro (*R.R.* 1.8), since 359 seems to refer to the *pedamenta*.

359   fraxineasque ... sudes furcasque ualentis: as *pedamenta* (358n.), as seems clear from *ualentis*. They would be forked at the top to cradle the cross-bars (*iuga*).

360   contemnere uentos: recurs at *A*. 3.77, also in personification.

361   adsuescant: subjunctive in a relative clause of purpose.

In the same way bullocks will 'become accustomed to' the servitude of the yoke: *ubi libera colla | seruitio adsuerint*, 3.167–8 (332–3n.).

summasque sequi tabulata per ulmos 'and to run in tiers through the upper parts of the elms'. The *arbustum* is pruned and trained into 'storeys', with at least three feet between branches so that the grapes hanging from the upper branch will not touch the lower one; cf. Colum. 5.6.11 *cum deinde adolescere incipient [arbores], falce formandae, et tabulata instituenda sunt*. See too Plin. *N.H.* 17.208 and 358–61n.

ulmos: used as supports at 221 and 1.2; 4.144; see nn. Along with the black poplar and ash, the elm was the most commonly used *arbustum*.

362–70   Restraint and freedom with the pruning-knife

These transitional lines are of great importance to the book. In the preceding section the stress has been on the fragility of the young plant, and on the need for restraint and tenderness (299–300, 301–2nn.), but as the vine grows stronger, the attitude changes and the call for severe action through pruning re-establishes the notion of viticulture as warfare against the natural tendencies of the tree (23n.). That the vine in fact will not survive successfully without such pruning is convenient for V.'s poetic purposes: the dilemma of the age of Jupiter is that success can come only at the cost of a violent meeting between man and nature (136–76, 207–11nn.). And it is chiefly in the *language* he chooses that V. stresses this violence (368, 369–70, 397–419nn.).

As in the lines immediately preceding (358–61n.) there is here a tripartite movement from weakness to strength (*prima ... aetas*, 362; *se laetus ad auras | palmes agit*, 363–4; *ubi iam ualidis ... stirpibus*, 367), to which three responding levels of force are applied (*parcendum ... uncis | carpendae manibus frondes interque legendae | ... tum stringe comas, tum bracchia tonde*, etc.). The development of the horse at 3.187–208 follows the same pattern (see n.): *primo*, 187; *tribus exactis ubi quarta accesserit aetas*, 190; *tum demum*, 205. Cf. 332–3, 362–3nn.

362–3   dum ... adolescit ... aetas, | parcendum teneris: the personification is extreme here and throughout the section as V. speaks in terms applicable to the upbringing of children. As elsewhere (332–3n.) the language looks to the presentation of the animal world in Book 3; e.g. 3.163–5. Cf. the famous 'education' speech of Aeneas to Ascanius: *mox cum matura adoleuerit aetas*, *A*. 12.438; also Lucr. 3.447–9 (which refers to children) *nam uelut infirmo pueri teneroque uagantur | corpore, ... | inde ubi robustis adoleuit uiribus aetas.*

362   To all intents and purposes a golden line (1.117n.).

teneris: see 23n.

363–4   dum ... habenis: developed from Lucr. 5.786–7 *arboribus- que datumst uariis exinde per auras | crescendi magnum immissis certamen habenis.*

laxis ... immissus habenis: a variation of *immissis ... habenis*, which seems to be the more regular expression: so Lucretius (cf. preceding n.) and *A*. 5.662 *furit immissis Volcanus habenis*; and cf. 6.1.

per purum: cf. 287 *in uacuum*, of the tree's branches.

365–6   acie nondum falcis temptanda [sc. aetas], sed ... | carpendae ... interque legendae: in this middle stage (362–70n.) the force is to be limited. On tricola of gerundives in this book see 61–2, 397–419nn.

uncis | ... manibus 'with bent fingers'; i.e. with the nails of the thumb and (e.g.) forefinger.

interque legendae: tmesis of *interlego* ('to thin out') occurs only here and at Pallad. 3.25.16.

367   inde ubi: also at 3.327 and five times in the *Aeneid*; seven times in Lucretius, including 3.449, which V. has just adapted (362–3n.).

368–70   A powerful tricolon abundans (interrupted by the paren- thesis at 369), with anaphora of *tum* driving home the urgency, and with the four forceful imperatives (one in each of the first two cola, two in the climactic third) stressing the need for violent action.

368 tum stringe comas, tum bracchia tonde: the combination of imperatives and personification creates a compelling and ultimately disturbing image – V. does not otherwise use *comae* of the foliage of trees in the *Georgics*, although he does refer to the narcissus as *comantem* (4.122) and some part of the hyacinth as *comam* (4.137; see n.), but flower-heads are somewhat different (362–70n.).

369 (ante reformidant ferrum): so at 301–2 *neu ferro laede retunso | semina*, and 365 *acie nondum falcis.*

This is the first attestation of the verb *reformido* ('shrink back in fear') with an insentient subject – if it is legitimate so to regard the vine here.

369–70 tum denique ... fluentis: the language of 368 continues, but with *dura | exerce imperia* it becomes more specifically military, as at 1.99 *exercetque frequens tellurem atque imperat aruis* (see n.). The words also have a political dimension, carrying the implication that nature's luxuriance is an act of revolt against the tenets of *labor* (362–70n.). Cf. 3.206–7 on young colts.

compesce: a strong verb, otherwise used only once by V., also in the imperative, and with *ferrum* (cf. 369), when he recommends the slaughter of diseased sheep at 3.468 *continuo culpam ferro compesce* – a measure which fails to prevent nature's onslaught.

371–96   The threat posed by heat and cold, cattle and goats; the latter are therefore sacrificed to Bacchus at his rural festivals. The origins of Greek drama and Roman poetry

371 Texendae ... tenendum: the prescriptive gerundives continue (61–2, 397–419nn.) as the plant and animal worlds now for the first time come into contact (372n.), with the latter presenting a threat to the young vine. The same animals will threaten the bee's flowers and pastures at 4.10–12.

On *saepes* see 436n.

372 dum frons tenera imprudensque laborum: coming immediately after *pecus omne tenendum*, this at first glance looks curiously as if it might refer to cattle: *frons (frontis) tenera* is a standard attribute of young cattle or goats ([Ov.] *Hal.* 3 *uitulus ... | qui nondum gerit in tenera iam cornua fronte*; Colum. 3.2.4 *tenerae frontes iuuencorum*), and *imprudens laborum* could easily refer to animals (3.182 *primus equi labor est ...*; also 3.189 *inscius aeui*). However, the reference must be to young foliage (*frons, frondis* – this nom. sing. occurs in V. only here). The momentary confusion may be intentional – another, somewhat different, instance of V.'s deliberate mingling of the plant and the animal kingdoms (332–3n.).

373   cui: referring to *frons*, and object of *inludunt*.

indignas 'cruel'; an extension of the passive sense, 'undeserved'. Servius quotes Ennius (*indignas turres*, *Op. inc.* 13 Skutsch); the only parallel with a context given by *ThLL* (s.v. VII. 1.192.47) is [Virg.] *Cir.* 247, which is no parallel at all. The boldness of V.'s application creates personification: the winter is cruel to the young plant, which is undeserving of such hardship.

solemque potentem: cf. 1.92 *rapidiue potentia solis*.

374   uri: the wild ox, or aurochs, now extinct, may have frequented Gaul, but certainly not V.'s Italy: ?Caes. *B.G.* 6.28 *tertium est genus eorum qui uri appellantur. hi sunt magnitudine paulo infra elephantos, specie et colore et figura tauri. magna uis eorum est et magna uelocitas; neque homini neque ferae, quam conspexerunt, parcunt*; Pliny (*N.H.* 8.38) situates them in Germany. Here and at 3.532 V. was thinking of the buffalo (*bubalus*), domesticated in Italy, and Pliny may have him in mind when he writes with some scorn of the confusion of the two: *uros, quibus imperitum uulgus bubalorum nomen imponit*.

sequaces 'persistent', 'pestering'; cf. *adsidue* in the same line.

375   inludunt: so of the assault on the threshing-floor at 1.181 *tum uariae inludunt pestes*; and cf. this same threat to the bees at 4.10–11 *neque oues haedique petulci | floribus insultent* (371n.)

pascuntur: there is ellipsis of the object, *quam* or *qua*, easily supplied from *cui* (373).

auidae: ἀπὸ κοινοῦ with *oues* and *iuuencae*.

376–9   Stress upon the destructive damage of animals introduces the retributive sacrifice of the goat at 380–96 – the main focus of the passage.

376–8   frigora ... aestas: an elaboration of 373, with each element occupying a single line, and with the key words at the beginning and end.

The verb of the main clause is to be supplied from the relative clause (*nocuere*, 378).

376   concreta: cf. 318 *concretam (radicem)*.

377   grauis incumbens: cf. 1.163n. for an adjective with adverbial force qualifying a present participle.

scopulis arentibus: cf. 522n.

378 illi: dative object of *nocuere* (referring back to *frons*), not nom. plur. with *greges*. Its position (like that of *illae* at 435) is unusual.

378–9 A perfect tricolon abundans, with each member the subject of *nocuere*.

durique uenenum | dentis: V. is now thinking specifically of the goat, the subject of 380–96; cf. 196 *urentis culta capellas*. Varro speaks of the poisonous powers of goats, and relates this to their sacrifice at *R.R.* 1.2.18–19. Goats will eat not only the foliage of a tree, but also its bark, thus creating a break in the cambium if done in a complete ring around the trunk (called 'girdling'), and killing it as surely as an axe does. Observation of the phenomenon doubtless gave rise to the view that the goat's bite was 'poisonous'.

379 admorso: it is hard to decide between *admorso* 'the scar impressed on the gnawed stem', and *admorsu* 'the scar impressed with a bite on the stem'. Both have good MS support, but the expression with *admorso* seems somewhat more poetical. The Palatinus has *admorsum*, which Ribbeck accepted as *ad morsum*. *stirps* is more often feminine than masculine: this could explain the change from *admorso* to *admorsu*.

380–96 The description of the festival and sacrifice to Bacchus is developed from an account by Varro (*R.R.* 1.2.19–20), who mentions the sacrifice of the goat to Dionysus on the Athenian Acropolis, where apart from this annual ritual goats were not allowed on account of their poisonous effects on the olive, which originated on the Acropolis. V. has grafted these events onto an Italian context, the festival Compitalia, at which, however, it seems there was no goat-sacrifice – a fact which will have caused him little concern. His main interest is to present the figure of Bacchus, the tutelary deity of the book (1–8, 2nn.), and to make connections between him and the origins of Greek drama and Roman poetry (380–3, 382, 386nn.). In addition, the inhabitants of these early times anticipate the 'happy rustic' at the end of the book (383, 388nn.).

380–3 V. seems to be subtly involving himself in the question, already much debated by his time, and as yet unresolved in ours, of the origin of Greek drama. At 380–1 he links the sacrifice of the *caper*, 'he-goat' (Gr. τράγος) with dramatic festivals; the association of the word 'tragedy' with Dionysus and the 'goat-song' (τράγων ᾠδή), whatever that means, and whether or not the association is valid, is clearly much older than the Parian Marble (soon after 263 B.C.), where it first appears. His position is conveyed implicitly through the gloss in *caper*.

At 382-3 he speaks of dramatic prizes being established by the Athenians (*Thesidae*) around the villages and crossroads. Here, through the gloss contained in *pagus* (Gr. κώμη, 'village'), V. alludes to the theory, wrong but in Aristotle (*Poet.* 1448a36), that the word 'comedy' derives from itinerant players who left the city and performed 'around the villages' (κατὰ κώμας; see too 382n. The hidden poetics of these lines perhaps lends support to the view expressed at 7–8n. that the Bacchus of this book is very much a literary figure. Cf. Pickard-Cambridge (1962) 112–24, 132.

380 non aliam ob culpam: cf. 1.487n. for this as an opening device. It is in fact a poetic restatement of Varro's *sic factum ut* ... (*R.R.* 1.2.19; above, 378–9n.).

381 caeditur: the position is emphatic, as at 415; so also at 1.173.

382 ingeniis: normally taken 'for genius' or 'for works of genius', but given the subject (dramatic poetry, and archaic at that) V. possibly intends a suggestion of literary talent lacking *ars* (technical skill, the desirable quality for neoteric and Augustan poets; cf. Ov. *Trist.* 2.424 *Ennius ingenio maximus, arte rudis*). At 386 (see n.) early Roman poetry is characterized by artistic shortcomings: *uersibus incomptis*.

pagos et compita: apart from the gloss mentioned at 380–3n. V. also intends a reference to the Paganalia and Compitalia, the two rustic festivals which will be the *Italian* settings at 385–96.

383 inter pocula laeti: cf. the early Italians at 388 *per carmina laeta*. So the rustic at 528 *socii cratera coronant* (388n.), and the Scythian at 3.379–80, who substitutes ?beer, but enjoys it as much: *pocula laeti* | *fermento atque acidis imitantur uitea sorbis*.

384 unctos saluere per utres 'danced on greased goat-skins'; the Greeks called this sport ἀσκωλιασμός (Poll. 9.21).

385 Ausonii, Troia gens missa, coloni: this seems to be the first extant occurrence of *Ausonia/Ausones/Ausonius*, which appears some 40 times in the *Aeneid* (and otherwise not in V.). It is perhaps noteworthy that this first instance is misapplied, for strictly they are the primitive inhabitants of Campania, later of Italy in general, and in the *Aeneid* are definitely not identified with the Trojans. But V. is here concerned to establish a transition from Greek (*Thesidae*, 383) to Italian. The words *Troia gens missa* foreshadow the *Aeneid*.

For this enclosing of an appositional noun or, in this case noun phrase, between the adjective and noun to which it is apposed, see 146–7n.

386–90 As if to compensate for mention of the rustic and unpolished verse of archaic Italy, V. composes in these five lines two golden lines (387, 390), and two which in the balance they show, though they differ from each other, are the artistic equivalent of golden lines (386, 389; cf. 531n.); such a concentration is unparalleled in his verse, indeed usually avoided (1.117n.). Moreover the centrally placed 388 elegantly begins with *et te* and ends with *tibique*; see too 391n.

386 uersibus incomptis ludunt risuque soluto: *ludunt* looks back to the Greek *ludi* (381), and implies a context of festivals for early Italian poetry (380–3n.). With this and with the words *uersibus incomptis* V. intends *uersus Fescennini*, abusive amoebean exercises popularly held to have influenced the beginnings of Roman drama, and rooted in the countryside. Horace has a more elaborate picture of this stage of Roman poetry at *Epist.* 2.1.139–46, where he specifies the type (*Fescennina ... licentia*), and refers to the 'poets' as *agricolae prisci* (so V.'s *coloni*). In *uersibus incomptis* there is also a reference to technical inelegance, specifically that of the Saturnian verse, to which Horace refers a few lines later in his account: *sic horridus ille | defluxit numerus Saturnius* (at the importation of the Greek hexameter), 157–8 (see 380–96n.).

387 oraque 'masks', lit. 'faces', like the Greek πρόσωπα.

corticibus: curved from the shape of the tree, bark provides an ideal mask.

388 et te, Bacche, uocant: the rustic at the end of the book does the same: *te libans, Lenaee, uocat*, 529 (see n. and 380–96n.). Cf. too *nunc te, Bacche, canam*, 2; *huc, pater o Lenaee*, 4, 7.

uocant: cf. 1.42n.

te ... tibique: for the anaphora in such contexts see 2n.

389 oscilla 'small faces', 'masks'; cf. *ora*, 387. These effigies seem to have been hung on trees to assure fertility (390–2).

mollia: referring to the material from which the effigies were made (wool or wax), but perhaps = 'genial', 'beneficent', which is certainly possible, and which finds support from the wording of 392; see n.; and Servius thought it meant *pensilia*, Serv. Auct., *mobilia* – both interpretations describing the action of the things on the tree.

390 omnis largo pubescit uinea fetu: so of the fruit-tree at 429 *nec minus interea fetu nemus omne grauescit*; these two verbs, *pubesco* and *grauesco*, which in the present contexts mean much the same, appear only here in V., except for one other instance of *pubesco* at *A.* 3.491.

391 The regular order of noun and adjective is striking (386–90n.); *complentur* is emphatic: 'they teem'.

392 'and to whatever quarter the god has made his venerable head revolve'; *circum* ... *egit* is a tmesis, and the image is on one level a very literal one: the 'head' of the god is that depicted on the *oscilla* of 389, which turn in the breeze, and favour whatever land they face.

393 Therefore prayers and sacrifice are to be carried out in order to secure the propitious attention of Bacchus. As at 1.335–50 (see n.) there is no attempt to link religious observance with the actual *practice* of the farmer, or to show how it affects the realities of scientific agricultural endeavour. These two worlds, the one of piety and the other of knowledge, soon become prominent, but not as compatible options (475–94n.); see 395n.

394 lancesque: for the *exta* (396), as at 194 *lancibus ... exta*.

395 A return to the theme of 380–1, the sacrifice of the goat to Bacchus. These words are recalled at 3.486 *saepe in honore deum medio stans hostia ad aram*, at a sacrifice which, like all religious activity, fails spectacularly to stave off the plague; see 3.455–6, 486–93nn.

396 Not a golden line, but the chiastic word-order is as artful: A–n–V–N–a; so too at 531 (see n.), which like the present instance forms a fitting clausula (1.117n).

pinguiaque ... exta: cf. 193 (and n.); *exta* occurs at the end of 194.

colurnis: the adjectival form of *corylus* (a contraction of **corylinus*). Servius is doubtless right in stating that hazel spits were used because the roots of that tree, like the goat, were a threat to the vine; cf. 299 (and n.).

*397–419   Further precepts for the vine-dresser: hoeing, pruning and
other toil is unending*

The lines are carefully arranged to stress the formidable nature of *labor*, and the resultant need for force: the passage begins (398–401) and ends (418–19) with tricola of gerundives (61–2n.), and all but one of the six gerundives imply force and toil – the sixth, *metuendus* (419) suggests, at the end of the passage, that even when the work is done, the danger is not over (see n.). Within this frame six imperatives (balancing the six gerundives) carry forward the theme of unremitting toil – and incidentally the key word, *labor* (1.145–6n.), occurs three times (397, 401, 412). The toil involved with the vine, and the ethical connotations of the word *labor*, are stressed in order to set up a contrast with what follows – the purported effortlessness of growing olives (420–5n.).

397   ille labor ... alter 'that other task', i.e. the care of the grown vine (*curandis uitibus*), as opposed to all that has preceded, namely the transplanting, training, protection, eventual pruning, etc. of the young plant.

398   cui numquam exhausti satis est 'on which there is never enough effort expended'; *exhausti* is the partitive genitive (with *satis*) of the neuter of the participle, here used as a noun = 'effort expended'. Cf. 3.348 *ante exspectatum*.

398–401   Virtually every word in this sentence conveys a sense of unending toil, to be carried out with relentless force: the whole area must be worked (*omne ... solum*; *omne ... nemus*), and continuously (*quotannis* | *terque quaterque*; *aeternum*); and the three gerundives (61–2, 397–419nn.) drive the point home.

As above (cf. 354–61n.), cultivation may be by plough (*solum scindendum*) or hoe (*uersis ... bidentibus*).

398   quotannis: cf. the similar context at 1.198–9 ... *ni uis humana quotannis* | *maxima quaeque manu legeret*; see 1.197–9n.

399   terque quaterque: otherwise used three times in the *Aeneid*, at moments of high emotion: 1.94; 4.589; 12.155.

scindendum: cf. 237n.

399–400   glaebaque uersis | ... frangenda bidentibus: cf. 1.94 *rastris glaebas qui frangit inertis*; 3.161 *fractis ... glaebis*; see also 355 *duros iactare bidentis*.

aeternum: adverbial.

401   fronde: abl. of separation: 'relieved of its foliage'; presumably refers to the radical pruning of both vine and *arbustum*.

401–2   In a brilliant and vivid image, reminiscent of that at 199–203, V. depicts the cyclical nature of *labor* (*actus in orbem*), which returns on the same path along with a personified year (*in se per sua uestigia*). The sense is not that toil in general 'comes back', but that the toil of *each season* returns with each part of the year – as is clear from what follows at 403–7 (the toil of winter).

uoluitur annus: cf. 295 *uoluens ... saecula*, and 294–5n.

403–5   ac iam olim ... iam tum ...: the sequence conveys a sense of the urgency of new *labor*, even when the growing season is over. Cf. 3.303–4 *cum ... olim* | *iam*.

403   seras posuit cum uinea frondes: again the vine is mildly personified. For similar expression, and the same use of *pono* (= *depono*), cf. *A.* 12.209 [*sceptrum*] *posuitque comas et bracchia ferro*.

404   frigidus et siluis Aquilo decussit honorem: Servius notes: *Varronis hic uersus est*; there is no reason to doubt the ascription to Varro of Atax, whose poetry V. elsewhere adapted very closely (1.374–87, 397nn.), at times unchanged (1.377n.). In Book 1 V. had good reason to adapt closely the text of Varro, but it is hard to see his motive here (though see 406n.). Cf. Hor. *Epd.* 11.5–6 *hic tertius December … siluis honorem decutit.*

405   iam tum acer: the elision of the monosyllable resembles that at 1.360 *iam sibi tum a curuis* (see n.).

405–6   acer … | rusticus: cf. 3.346 (and n.) *acer Romanus.*

curas uenientem extendit in annum: by pruning in early winter (407) he shows his concern about the next growing season.

406   curuo Saturni dente: the periphrasis for the pruning-hook is not purely ornamental, for the associations of the word in Greek (δρέπανον/δρεπάνη) seem to have been a topic of lively debate (a ζήτημα) in Alexandria. Apollonius, in discussing the island of Corcyra (called Drepane, because it is roughly sickle-shaped), gives two aetiologies: it is so named because beneath the island is buried the sickle with which Cronus (Saturn) castrated his father; or, alternatively, it is named after the reaping-hook of Demeter, who stayed on the island and taught the Titans agriculture (*Arg.* 4.982–92). Callimachus was involved in the debate, we know not for sure on what side (*Aet.* 1, fr. 14 Pf.), and at *Aet.* 2, fr. 43.68–71 seems to have extended it to include the Sicilian town of Zancle (Messana), ζάγκλον being the Sicilian word for 'sickle' (δρέπανον) – Callimachus opts for the sickle of Cronus, and no mention is made of Demeter. Perhaps Varro of Atax, whom V. has just quoted (404n.), revived the debate; whether he did or not, *Saturni* is perhaps to be seen as a statement of affiliation.

relictam: the best sense seems to be that the vine is left alone after the vintage, and pruned after it has lost its leaves.

407   The act of pruning is pursued with vigour (*persequitur*), much like the irrigation (*insequitur*) at 1.104–5 (see n.).

attondens: V. otherwise uses the verb only of the grazing goats at *E.* 10.7.

fingitque putando 'and prunes it into shape'; cf. Apollo's taming of the Sibyl's frenzy at *A.* 6.80 *fingitque premendo*, and even the she-wolf's attentions to Romulus and Remus: *corpora fingere lingua, A.* 8.634.

408–13   The strongly didactic series of imperatives in *-to* looks back to the beginning of the technical tradition, as can best be seen from

Cato, *Agr.* 151.1–2, which quotes or paraphrases Minius Percennius of Nola, and may well represent the first individual agricultural writings (on this see Speranza (1974) 12–13): *eum locum stercorato primum bene stercore caprino aut ouillo, tum uortito bipalio, terram cum stercore bene permisceto, depurgato ab herba graminibusque, bene terram conminuito*. By V.'s time the style is definitely archaic: Varro avoids it, preferring *oportet*, the passive periphrastic, or a jussive subjunctive; at *R.R.* 1.2.25 there is clearly amusement at the *style*, as well as the content (inappropriate for a work on agriculture) of Saserna: *cum subrisisset Scrofa, quod non ignorabat libros* [*Sasernae*] . . . *coepit: scribit* [*Saserna*] *cimices quem ad modum interfici oporteat his uerbis: 'cucumerem anguinum condito in aquam eamque infundito quo uoles, nulli accedent; uel fel bubulum cum aceto mixtum, unguito lectum'*.

On the function of these imperatives within the whole section, see 397–419n. And see 412–13n. on *laudato . . . colito*, which has a different ethos.

408–10 primus . . . primus . . . primus . . . postremus: a tricolon with anaphora of the key word, *primus* (1.289–90), is balanced by a terse command, with *postremus* creating an apparent contrast. Cf. on a less artful level Cato, *Agr.* 5.5 *primus cubitu surgat, postremus cubitum eat.* Early action is enjoined at 3.64 (*mitte in Venerem pecuaria primus*), and, in a somewhat different way, is associated with the success of the old man of Tarentum: *primus . . . primus*, 4.134, 140; see 4.134n.

Anaphora continues in the following lines: *bis . . . bis*, 410–11; *iam . . . iam . . . iam*, 416–17.

408–9 Early digging is in fact crucial, not so incinerating pruned branches, nor bringing in the vine-poles (though if left out for the winter they will rot); V. is concerned with the overall didactic effect of the lines, with the sense of urgency they impart, and with recalling the precepts of Cato and the tradition: *opera omnia mature conficias face. nam res rustica sic est, si unam rem sero feceris, omnia opera sero facies*, *Agr.* 5.7.

410 postremus metito: clearly the one act to be postponed as long as possible (408–10n.).

410–12 The twice-yearly tasks of *pampinatio* ('vine-trimming') and *runcatio* ('weeding'), conveyed in the words *durus uterque labor*, are implied by what necessitates them – the growth of foliage and weeds.

bis . . . bis: see 150n.

umbra, | . . . herbae: excessive shade and weeds were also paired as a threat to crops at 1.120–1, 155–7.

segetem 'the vineyard'; i.e. 'the ground'.

durus uterque labor: cf. 3.118 *aequus uterque labor*. The words and the theme recall 1.145–6 *labor omnia uicit | improbus et duris urgens in rebus egestas*.

412–13 laudato ingentia rura, | exiguum colito: sc. because there is so much toil involved. Though syntactically identical, the commands are distinct from those that preceded (408–10), which were pieces of specific advice concerning the vine. The sentiment is a clever reversal and correction of Hes. *W.D.* 643 νῆ᾽ ὀλίγην αἰνεῖν, μεγάληι δ᾽ ἐνὶ φορτία θέσθαι, 'praise a small ship, but put your cargo in a big one' (cf. 1.111n.). Servius claims that Cato had written the same in the agricultural precepts directed to his son, but the words are probably not Cato's: Columella quotes the lines (3.1.8) without mentioning him, and it is possible that Servius was misled by the fact that the whole sequence from 408–13 *sounds* so much like Cato that the association could easily have been made. Cf. 468n.

V.'s words can be read metaphorically. Horace prayed for a small farm (*modus agri non ita magnus, Sat.* 2.6.1), and a Callimachean *ingenium* to match it: *pingue pecus domino facias et cetera praeter | ingenium,* 14–15; see Shackleton Bailey (1982) 37 n. 9.

413–15 Broom (*rusti*), reeds (*harundo*) and willow (*salicti*) – each at the end of its line – were used to tie the vines, and for the many other jobs now done with twine or even wire. Cato (*Agr.* 1.7) lists the planting of an osier-bed (*salictum*) third in a rated series of nine uses for a farm of 100 *iugera*, and states (11.1) that a vineyard of the same size should employ one willow-worker (*salictarius*).

415 caeditur: cf. 381n.

incultique: it requires no cultivation, but care (*cura*) is still needed in gathering the shoots of the willow.

416–19 In two distinct couplets V. presents two distinct sequences of the device tricolon abundans, the first defined by repeated *iam* (408–10n.), the second by the gerundive in each colon; this immediate recurrence of the device is unusual in the poem (also at 514–17), and is in keeping with the careful structural arrangement of the present section (397–419, 408–10nn.).

416–17 In a neat sequence the year closes: vines are bound, pruning finishes, and the vine-dresser sings of the completion of his task.

416 falcem arbusta reponunt 'the vineyards lay aside the pruning-knife'; i.e. *sinunt reponi*, 'no longer need them'; cf. of the olives 420 *neque illae | procuruam exspectant falcem*.

417 So at 1.293 the farmer's wife sings as she works, like the pruner at *E.* 1.56 *hinc alta sub rupe canet frondator ad auras*.

antes 'rows'; the word is a virtual hapax legomenon, with one real exception: according to Philargyrius, Cato in the *De Re Militari* applied it to 'files [of cavalry]': *pedites quattuor agminibus, equites duobus antibus ducas*, p. 81.16 Jord. The military sense seems prior; V. has transferred the word to a viticultural context, in keeping with the military language he employs elsewhere (23, 279–83nn.). He will shortly stress the associations of the olive with peace (420–5n.). Outside the grammarians the word otherwise occurs only at Colum. 10.376, of rows in a garden, in his only book written in verse, conceived as 'filling in the gaps' of the *Georgics* (4.147–8n.).

418–19 On the gerundives, see 61–2, 397–419nn.; together with those at 399–400 they form a frame to the passage.

418 sollicitanda ... tellus puluisque mouendus: in sense, as in syntax, parallel to 399–400 *solum scindendum glaebaque ... frangenda*.

sollicitanda: used of the cultural equivalent to agriculture, seafaring, at 503 *sollicitant alii remis freta caeca* (see n.); also 4.262 *mare sollicitum*.

tamen: in spite of appearances (417), *labor* remains (as always in the age of Jupiter). The same word, with the same force, is used at 1.118, where, in spite of correct irrigation, drainage, etc. a threat still remains from birds, weeds and shade, and at 1.198, where, in spite of careful seed-selection, decline may set in (*degenerare tamen*); see 1.197–9n.

419 maturis ... uuis: given the personification at 416 and throughout, this is best taken as dat. of agent 'must be feared by the ripe grapes', rather than an indirect object: '[the vine-dresser] must be afraid of rains for the sake of his grapes'.

metuendus Iuppiter: for Jupiter Pluuius, and a virtual metonymy for *imber*, although it is noteworthy that, at the end of a passage stressing the realities of ceaseless *labor* in the age of Jupiter, V. should use the name without qualification; at 1.418 he is described as *Iuppiter uuidus Austris*. See 1.1–42n. on the position of Jupiter in the poem.

On *metus/metuo*, see 333, 491–2; 1.335nn. (there a parallel context, the fear of unseasonable storms), and notably 33 [*uere*] *nec metuit surgentis pampinus Auster*; for the gerundive cf. 4.37 *utraque uis [frigus et calor] apibus pariter metuenda. metus* of a related type will soon figure in an important way (491).

420–5   The olive

To quote White (1970) 226: ' "By contrast, olives need no cultivation."
Virgil's brief dismissal is not supported by the agronomists.' The olive
may not require as much work as the vine (but see 420n.), yet that
hardly justifies, from the technical point of view, the fact that the vine
occupies 150 lines, while the olive receives a mere six. In the prayer at
the beginning of Book 1, Minerva was dismissed with three words
(*oleaeque Minerua* | *inuentrix* (1.18–19n.), and she was not even mentioned
in the proem to Book 2, devoted entirely to Bacchus – though the olive
itself was introduced with a prominence which led the reader to expect
more than the present treatment: *et prolem tarde crescentis oliuae*, 3 and n.
V.'s preoccupation with the vine at the expense of the olive (and other
trees, which are treated together in the next section) must have a
literary, rather than a technical, motivation. The success of *labor* in Book
2 is virtually synonymous with successful viticulture, while the olive is
(falsely) removed from the area of *labor* – that is the import of the words
non ulla . . . cultura at 420; V., against the facts, presents the growing of
olives as an effortless enterprise, placing them in a category with uncul-
tivated trees (426n.), whereas in reality it is, like the vine, a highly
cultivated tree. The 'success' of viticulture, moreover, has been consis-
tently depicted as resulting from a kind of warfare between man and the
vine (362–70, 369–70, 407nn.). As in production, so in result, the vine
and the olive are contrasted: the olive represents peace: *hoc pinguem et
placitam Paci nutritor oliuam*, 425, while the vine, with which V. has not yet
finished, will receive a surprising final treatment in the last 'technical'
lines of the poem (454–7) – a *uituperatio* for its instigation (through wine)
of violence and madness (see n.); see Introduction pp. 19–20.

     The theme of 420–57 is the contrast between spontaneous and cul-
tivated (the very theme of the beginning; see 9–34 and 9n.); in that
458–542 are separate from the technical body of the book, the present
lines form a frame with the opening theme.

     420   Contra 'in contrast [to the vine]'; the word, which appears
otherwise in the poem only at 4.440, establishes at the outset the
contrasted requirements, and ultimately (420–5n.) the contrasted na-
tures, of the vine and the olive.

     non ulla . . . cultura: the olive-tree needs manuring, some pruning,
ploughing between rows, fencing in, sometimes grafting, and great care
with propagation and in the early years before transplanting – in other

words, though the care is not as intensive, in all but training and pruning it needs the same *type* of care as the vine. For an oliveyard of 240 *iugera* Cato (*Agr.* 11) states that 13 persons (in various capacities) are needed; that is fewer than the 16 required for a vineyard of 100 *iugera*, but it does not justify V.'s words, or the brevity of his treatment – nor indeed does the relative importance of the product. Indeed, as Columella records, *cultura* of the olive was even accorded the status of a proverb: *nam ueteris prouerbii meminisse conuenit 'eum qui aret oliuetum, rogare fructum; qui stercoret, exorare; qui caedat, cogere'*, 5.9.15.

420–1   neque illae | procuruam exspectant falcem: as for the vine, so for the olive, personification continues; cf. 416 *falcem arbusta reponunt.* The statement is false, though the olive is pruned less frequently than the vine (420–5, 420nn.).

[neque ... exspectant] rastrosque tenacis: false: *sed id* [sc. *oliuetum*] *minime bis anno arari debet: et bidentibus alte circumfodiri*, Colum. 5.9.12 (420–5, 420nn.).

422   I.e. once they have matured. Pruning and ploughing (420–1 and n.) are in fact needed throughout. And what of the early years, which in the case of the vine were V.'s major concern (288–370)?

423–4   ipsa satis tellus ... | sufficit umorem: commentators are divided on *satis:* 'provides moisture for the plants' or 'provides sufficient moisture' (the Loeb has it both ways: 'yields moisture enough for the plants'). The former is supported by 435–6 *illae* [*salices et genistae*] ... *pastoribus umbram | sufficiunt saepemque satis*, but there the *sata* are crops, and though V. uses the word of the young vine (350), it is perhaps doubtful whether he would use it of mature olive-trees. In support of the adverb is 1.127–8 *ipsaque tellus | omnia liberius nullo poscente ferebat*, in a similar context; see 420–5n. This also gives a development from *satis* to *grauidas*: 'when hoed and ploughed it yields sufficient moisture and teeming fruits' (see n. below).

cum dente ... fruges: this cannot mean that the olive only needs the ground to be slightly opened to receive moisture, somewhat more to produce fruit, which is hardly a valid contrast. The two must be taken together: 'provides moisture and fruit when opened with the hoe and the plough'. In any case this seems a reversal of 420, and certainly amounts to *cultura*, in spite of the claim that the digging need not be deep – which in any case is not correct: *bidentibus alte circumfodiri* (see 420–1n.).

425　hoc: either 'therefore' (because it gives plentiful fruit), or 'thus' (with ploughing and hoeing); the former seems preferable.

placitam Paci ... oliuam: see 420–5n.

nutritor: the deponent of *nutrio* (1.187n.) seems to occur only here, and is cited along with that of *bello* (*A.* 11.660) by Priscian (*Inst.* 8.26) as a Virgilian oddity.

The verb *nutrio* is otherwise absent from the *Georgics*, which is perhaps significant: it implies a concern with the object's well-being, not merely with its productivity, and is reserved for a special relationship, that between man and a plant which exists in the age of Jupiter, but which is not subject to *labor* or *cultura*.

426–57　Other trees; the uituperatio uitis

In briefly treating trees other than the vine and olive, V. expands on the theme of the last six lines (420–5n.): all these trees are removed from the sphere of *labor*, as they come to exhibit features of the Saturnian age (426, 428, 430, 433, 438–9, 440nn.) – appropriately, since the section will be followed by the praises of the happy 'rustic', who himself resembles man before the rule of Jupiter (458–540n.). V. ends the section with a return to the vine (the tree of *labor*); see 454–7n.; Introduction, pp. 19–20.

426　quoque: fruit-trees (*poma*) and the other trees of this passage (*nec minus ... nemus omne*, 429) are linked closely with the olive, and separated likewise from the vine (420–5n.); indeed many editors treat 420–57 as one section.

ut primum truncos sensere ualentis: for the personification and wording cf. 1.136, where rivers feel the first ships: *tunc alnos primum fluuii sensere cauatas.*

427　ad sidera: so the young vine-shoot, before it is subject to cultivation, *se laetus ad auras | palmes agit*, 363–4; and the spontaneous trees of 47 *se tollunt in luminis oras.*

428　ui propria ... opisque haud indiga nostrae: the language of spontaneity, and ultimately of the Saturnian age; cf. 10–11 (and n.); 426–57n. The line is adapted from Lucr. 2.650, which describes the self-sufficiency of Epicurean divinity: *ipsa suis pollens opibus, nil indiga nostri*; that the borrowing is direct and unmistakable is clear from the fact that *indigus* is found first in Lucretius, there and at 5.223, in V. only here, and except for once in Ovid not again until silver Latin.

429   nec minus: cf. 426n.

fetu nemus omne grauescit: cf. 390 (and n.) *omnis largo pubescit uinea fetu.*

nemus omne: i.e. *arbores omnes,* which, of course, the hexameter poet cannot use (cf. 1.55n.).

430   sanguineisque inculta rubent auiaria bacis: a clear reminiscence of the spontaneous vines of the golden age of *E.* 4.29 *incultisque rubens pendebit sentibus uua.*

431   tondentur cytisi: i.e. 'cytisus may be used for grazing'. This fodder-shrub (*Medicago arborea*) is recommended for a high milk-yield at 3.394, but otherwise belongs to the *Eclogues* (1.78; 2.64; 9.31; 10.30), where, particularly in its flowering stage, it is popular with goats.

432   pascunturque ignes: on the *taedae* of 431; the compression is the same as with *tondentur.*

[433]   The line, omitted by the Medicean and probably not known to Servius, should be treated as interpolated. In its apparent favour the diction, in isolation, is Virgilian: cf. 2.61 *est labor impendendus;* 3.74 *impende laborem;* 3.124 *impendunt curas;* 4.241-2 *at suffire ... | quis dubitet?;* but interpolators are often good imitators. A double rhetorical question is hard to parallel in V. – Geymonat perhaps acknowledges this by beginning a new paragraph at 434. But the chief objection is that the thought has no place whatever in the sequence begun at 420 and continuing through to 457 and beyond. After treating the vine, paradigm of plants which call for the expending of toil and care, V. turns to the olive, which he falsely claims needs no *cultura,* but which is abundant and ethically superior (*placitam Paci,* 425), and then to other trees which are outside the domain of *labor,* but nevertheless supply man with all he needs (426-53). Within this sequence there is no place for an 'indignant outburst' (Page) in support of the type of tree which is the object of man's care and toil (if nature on her own can produce such trees) – and the line is virtually contradicted by 438-9 (see n.). It seems likely that an early reader of V. noted what the poet was necessarily implying about the vine and the status of *labor* (454-7n.), was puzzled, and attempted to alter the train of thought by producing an eminently Virgilian line which has no place in the text.

434   quid maiora sequar? 'why pursue larger themes (when the lowly [*humilesque* elaborates on *maiora*] willow and broom satisfy such simple needs)?'

salices ... genistae: the two trees are among those spontaneously generated (12–13).

435   aut illae pecori frondem aut pastoribus umbram | sufficiunt: cf. 489. So the trees of Horace's Sabine farm: *Epist.* 1.16.9–10 [*quid*] *si quercus et ilex | multa fruge pecus multa dominum iuuet umbra?*; cf. 4.145–6n. On the affinities of Horace's farm with the golden age, and with the *Georgics*, see Thomas (1982a) 13–15.

illae: oddly positioned, like *illi* at 378.

436   saepemque satis: cf. 371 *texendae saepes*; 1.270 *segeti praetendere saepem*.

satis: cf. 423–4n.

pabula melli: i.e. *pabula apibus*; in the previous line V. is thinking of those who will use the trees (*pecori ... pastoribus*), in this line of the ends to which they may be used (*satis ... melli*).

437–8   iuuat ... iuuat: not only is natural growth possible, but it is also pleasing.

437   undantem buxo ... Cytorum: the Paphlagonian town is mentioned in the *Iliad* (2.853) and at Ap. Rhod. *Arg.* 2.942, where it seems to have become a mountain (ὑλήεντα Κύτωρον, 'woody Cytorus'), also the context of V. and his obvious source, Cat. 4.13 *Cytore buxifer*. Strabo speaks of the abundance of box-trees (12.544–5), and 'boxwood to Cytorus' seems to have been one of the many ancient equivalents of 'coals to Newcastle' (Eustath. on *Il.* 1.20).

The phrase *undantem buxo* is an alternative, perhaps unique, for *fluctuo* + abl., for which see 281–2 *fluctuat ... | aere ... tellus.* Cf. also 3.28 (and n.) *undantem*.

438   Naryciaeque: first here in Latin and very rare in Greek, of the colony in Bruttium in southern Italy, named after the mother-city in Opuntian Locri. Columella also associates the place with pitch-pine (10.386), but he may merely be mimicking V. Pliny (*N.H.* 14.126–7) is dismissive of V.'s claim, believing it to refer to actual pitch; he too, however, states that good pitch-pines were produced in Bruttium (Wilkinson (1969) 273).

438–9   arua ... | non rastris, hominum non ulli obnoxia curae: a line which does not sit well with 433 (see n.). The language is that of the Saturnian age (426–57n.); cf. 10–11, 428 *ui propria ... opisque haud indiga nostrae.* Dismissal of the need for implements (*non rastris ... obnoxia*) recalls the golden age of *E.* 4.40 *non rastros patietur humus, non uinea* *falcem*; cf. also Ovid's own golden age: *ipsa quoque immunis rastroque intacta nec ullis | saucia uomeribus per se dabat omnia tellus, M.* 1.101–2.

440   ipsae: i.e. *sponte sua* (1.127–8n.); cf. 10–11 *ipsae | sponte sua ueniunt*, and see 426–57n.

steriles 'not bearing fruit [but still useful for their wood]'; the word is consistently used of trees or plants growing outside the bounds of man's control; *sterilitas* occurs when *labor* fails, and to that extent is what the purely natural world produces after the Saturnian age: *infelix lolium et steriles dominantur auenae,* 1.154 (and n.). Cf. 53, 70 (where *cultus* compels such trees to serve the ends of *labor*). V.'s attitude to this natural type of growth is ambiguous, both here and at 47–8 *sponte sua quae se tollunt in luminis oras, | infecunda quidem, sed laeta et fortia surgunt* (47, 446nn.).

441   animosi: surely intended as a gloss on *Euri*, being perceived as formed on either *animus* or *anima* (Cic. *Tusc.* 1.19), one meaning of the latter being 'wind'; it is rarely used to modify a wind (strictly speaking otherwise only at Ov. *Am.* 1.6.51 *animoso ... uento*), and here for the first time. V. may even have in mind the Greek cognate ἄνεμος ('wind'; cf. ἀνεμώδης, etc. 'windy'), a connection specified at Lact. *Op.* 17.2.

442–53 V. enumerates the uses to which uncultivated trees may be put, and though such trees are in nature outside the activity of *labor* it is significant that the actual uses are situated in the age of Jupiter: for shipbuilding, for houses, wagon-wheels, keels and weapons, and to house bees. Taken with 454–7 (see n.), the implication is that *usus* may be derived, and is better derived, from the *uncultivated*.

Theophr. *H.P.* 5 treats the various uses of timber.

442 Cf. 323n.

443   pinus ... cedrumque cupressosque: the accusatives are in apposition to *lignum* (442): 'different trees [*siluae*, 440] give different products [*fetus*], give useful timber – pine for ships, cedar and cypress for houses'.

The line is hypermetric (1.295–6n.).

444   hinc ... hinc: the type of wood is not specified.

radios ... tympana: two different types of wheel are referred to, spoked and solid respectively.

444–5   triuere ... posuere: gnomic perfects: 'have often shaped with the lathe ... have often fashioned keels for boats'.

445   agricolae: better taken as the subject of *triuere* (rather than

gen. dependent on *plaustris*); a change of subject must then be assumed
for the rest of the line, but the alternative ('they shape with the lathe
wheels for the farmer's wagon') seems rather cryptic.

446 fecundae: V. plays on the word with some pointed irony, for in
that the willow, elm, myrtle and cornel produce no valuable fruit
(though the myrtle-berry was used for medicinal purposes, and the fruit
of the cornel was an inferior food – neither product is mentioned by V.),
they are to be regarded, like naturally growing trees in general, as
infecundae (48, 440nn.); however, in the products they do yield (wicker,
leaves for fodder, spear-shafts), they are in a sense *fecundae*.

447–8 I.e. *myrtus et bona bello cornus fecundae sunt ualidis hastilibus.*
Myrtles and cornels appear together at *A.* 3.22–3, where they are
modified by the phrase *densis hastilibus.*

448 Ituraeos: hardly a 'purely ornamental epithet' (Page). The
people are mentioned in the same context by Cicero (*cur homines omnium
gentium maxime barbaros Ituraeos cum sagittis deducis in forum?, Phil.* 2.112;
also 2.19) and also by Strabo (16.729, 760), but V. may have found the
epithet in an earlier source – possibly Hellenistic, given the area (N. E.
Palestine). Cf. Luc. 7.230 *Ituraeis ... sagittis.* Servius identifies these
people with the Parthians, and V. may even intend such an identifi-
cation (125n.).

taxi: see 257n.

449–52 nec ... non ... nec non ... nec non: such lack of *uariatio* in
the use of connectives is unusual in V.

449 tiliae leues: cf. 1.173 *tilia ... leuis*, and 1.173–4n.; also 451 *leuis
... alnus.*
As is clear from the words *torno rasile* ('lathe-polished'), *leuis* is here
proleptic: the linden, like the box, becomes smooth *after* it has been
worked on the lathe.

450 formam accipiunt: so at 1.170 the elm is trained (while
growing) to the shape for which it will be used: *curui formam accipit ulmus
aratri.* There, as here, the wording implies a 'civilizing' of a wild, or
natural, force.

ferroque cauantur acuto: though the linden and box were used for
small products, such as tools, boxes, etc. rather than for shipbuilding,
that will be the next topic (451–2n.), and these words recall 1.136 *tunc
alnos primum fluuii sensere cauatas*; cf. also 1.262 *cauat arbore lintres*, where,
however, *lintres* = 'wine-vats' (see n.).

451–2   nec ... Pado: the alder also figured at 1.136, where sailing
began with the age of Jupiter; the activity which most exemplifies that
age is here pursued with trees which grow naturally and need no
arboricultural *labor* (442–53n.).

torrentem undam ... innatat: this use of the accusative with
innatare = 'swim in, on, or through', rather than dative or ablative (as at
A. 8.691), or *per* + acc. is unique – the accusative should imply 'swim
into [a hole, opening, etc.]', as at Cic. *N.D.* 2.123 *cum pisciculi parui in
concham hiantem innatauerunt.* V. uses *innare* in the same way at 3.142 and
A. 6.134, a usage which otherwise occurs once in Silius (4.363), and
subsequently very rarely. They are best seen as extensions, with the
compound merely intensifying, of the transitive use of *natare* (as at 3.260
natat caeca ... freta), but they are nevertheless audacious (cf. 1.480;
4.565nn.).

missa Pado: cf. 3.447 [*aries*] *missusque secundo defluit amni.*
The reference to the Po is curiously specific in this context, but
balances and contrasts with *Ituraeos* at 448.

452–3   V. refers to two types of hives, one (man-made) of bark
(*corticibusque cauis*), the other established by the bees themselves in a
rotting holm-oak (*uitiosaeque ilicis aluo*); cf. 4.33, 43–4. The second,
existing without man's help, recalls the natural beehives of the golden
age (*et durae quercus sudabunt roscida mella, E.* 4.30), terminated by Jupiter
when he imposed *labor*: *mellaque decussit foliis*, 1.131.

aluo: the 'belly' or 'hollow' of the tree; it is also the word for 'beehive',
and here doubtless alludes to that sense. In Book 4 V. never uses the
word (*aluaria* appears once, at 4.34), using instead *tecta, aula*, etc., which
serve to approximate the bees to men (4.8n.).

454–7   V. returns to the vine, only to deliver an invective (*uituperatio
uitis*, Servius *ad* 458): the vine, and man's propagation, control and cul-
tivation of it, achieved through the application of *labor*, and frequently
depicted as a kind of warfare against its natural tendencies, have
been the subject of most of the book; here in the finale of the 'technical'
part of the book (the peroration of 458–542 functions on a different,
although obviously closely related, level), V. openly disparages the very
product which is the fruit of this toil, and affirms as simply as he can the
'ethical' superiority of the natural and spontaneous order (420–25n.;
Introduction p. 20). The lines are a clear embarrassment to critics
who would simply see the book as an affirmation of the tenets of *labor*.

Peerlkamp and Forbiger, but no subsequent editor, ejected all four lines, Page does not address the question, Conington imagines that V. loses control ('Virg. sets out to show that the wild trees have their merits as well as the vine, and at last is carried away into showing that they are better than the vine'), Williams states that 'the final lines are playful', while Otis (1963) 168 refers to 455–7 as 'the splendid conclusion', somehow deriving from the lines the reading 'when so much has been given, how can man so greatly abuse it?' But as Wilkinson (1969) 184, whose assessment is honest ('[the lines seem] an odd and unsatisfactory conclusion to Book 2'), points out, 'Virgil has phrased it as a disparagement of *Baccheia dona*, not of men, unequivocally'. Even Servius knew of a remedy: *alii legunt 'et quae'* (for *aeque*). Cf. 170–2n. for very similar attempts, at an equally important point in the poem, to avoid having the text say what it must.

Pliny provides a superb commentary on the lines; having devoted an entire book to the subject of the vine, he launches into his own *uituperatio*, a passage which, like V.'s lines, calls into question the expenditure of so much *labor* (*N.H.* 14.137).

454   Baccheia: the first instance of this form, a transliteration of the (unattested) Greek form, Βακχήϊος; it otherwise appears in Latin only at Auson. *Mos.* 153, and in a fourth-century inscription (the normal forms, *Baccheus, Bacchius, Bacchicus* will not go into this line). V. may have taken it from a specific source, since lost.

455   Bacchus et ad culpam causas dedit 'Bacchus has even provided grounds for blame'. Forbiger found fault with this use of *ad*, and used this as evidence of the spurious nature of 454–7 (see n.), but the use of the preposition to mean 'so as to produce' is paralleled by such phrases as *ad perniciem* (Cic. *Cat.* 2.11; 4.15).

455–7 The famous battle between the Centaurs and Lapiths, occasioned by excessive drinking at the wedding of Pirithous and Hippodamia, is used as a paradigm for the damage perpetrated by wine, as it was by Homer, *Od.* 21.295–304. The encounter was popular in art (it was depicted both on the Parthenon and on the temple of Zeus at Olympia), and it received a full-scale treatment, with Homeric detail, from Ovid, at *M.* 12.210–535. The Lapiths figure at 3.115, Chiron – the centaur who taught Achilles – at 3.550.

455–6   furentis | ... leto domuit 'drove them mad and vanquished them in death'. Wine has the same effect at 3.509–14, where it is tried as a medicine for the plague-ridden horses (cf. the Centaurs in the present passage), seeming to provide relief, but in reality bringing death with renewed madness; see 3.509–10n.

456 Rhoecumque: the case for *Rhoecum*, the *lectio difficilior*, is considerably strengthened by the Centaurs of Callim. *H.* 3.222 οὐδὲ μὲν 'Υλαῖόν [in the same position as V.'s *Hylaeum* at 457] τε καὶ ἄφρονα 'Ροῖκον ἔολπα, 'nor do I think that Hylaeus and Rhoecus ...' These two Centaurs were killed by Atalanta, after they insulted her, but it is in the Alexandrian manner to situate them in a different story, as V. has done. *Rhoetum* has stronger MS support than *Rhoecum*, was read by Serv. Auct., is paralleled by Ovid (*M.* 12.271, 285), and has the apparent support of *A.* 9.344–5 (457n.); and Rhoetus is a giant at Hor. *Odes* 2.19.23.

457 magno ... cratere: there is a significant reminiscence of the phrase at *A.* 9.346, where Rhoetus (456n.) tries unsuccessfully to escape Euryalus by hiding behind a large bowl, *magnum ... cratere* (in the same position). The raid of Nisus and Euryalus is facilitated by the drunkenness of the Latins.

458–540   The praises of 'rustic' life; the poet's preferences

The lines are perhaps the most famous of the poem, and both in the classroom and elsewhere are often excerpted (along with the *laudes Italiae*; see 136–76n.) – indeed they represent for many readers the poem itself (for the influence of the passage, see Wilkinson (1969) 294, 296–8). However, the details of this section must be tested against those of the rest of the poem, of which it is only a part.

Praise of the country over the city holds a natural appeal, particularly in sophisticated and troubled cultures, and is well represented in the early Augustan period by Hor. *Epd.* 2 and *Sat.* 2.6. And the theme becomes a rhetorical topos: *theses autem quae sumuntur ex rerum comparatione (ut 'rusticane uita an urbana potior' ...) mire sunt ad exercitationem dicendi speciosae atque uberes*, Quint. 2.4.24. But it is wrong to think of 458–540 as a rhetorical exercise (though they had that status for the likes of Quintilian); the appropriate questions are rather: 'what is the nature of the praise, and what is its end in the poem?'

The country of these lines, and the farmer's involvement with it, constitute a deliberate invocation of the Saturnian or golden age (459–60, 471–2, 473–4, 500–1, 501–2, 503, 520, 524–5, 536–8,

539–40nn.); this depiction has little to do with the farmer who has struggled and failed with *labor* and the dominion of Jupiter (1.311–50, 463–514nn.), or with the farmer who has successfully combated nature, only to have the fruits of his toil morally denigrated in favour of the products of the natural, spontaneous world (420–5, 426–57, 454–7nn.). This farmer belongs to neither group, nor to any cultural level except that of Saturn, whose beneficence is no longer a feature of the real world (1.118–46 and n.) and functions nowhere else in the poem – with one grim exception (3.537–45n.). At the same time the agricultural details of these lines are deliberately at odds with those existing in the 'technical' portions of the poem (467, 516–17nn.). In short, the praises of rustic existence are, in terms of the rest of the poem, as much a fiction as were the praises of Italy (136–76n.). The positive depiction of this existence has individual applications, which are explored in the poetic manifesto at 475–94 (see n.), but it plays no part in resolving the tensions surrounding the issue of how man functions in the age of *labor*.

The bibliography on these lines is daunting, but the analyses of Klingner (1931) and (1963) 119–35, especially his investigations of thematic parallels between 458–74 and 495–540, are particularly useful.

458–74 The farmer's existence is praised in terms which set it in the Saturnian age (458–540n.). At 495–540 V. resumes the theme, picking up these lines (see n.). [Virg.] *Cul.* 58–97 (*o bona pastoris . . .*) is a fairly obvious imitation of V.'s praise.

458–9 O fortunatos nimium, sua si bona norint, | agricolas: the use of *o* with the accusative of exclamation occurs only here in V., and gives an effect of great excitement; the avoidance of the vocative perhaps has the additional effect of separating these *agricolae* from the didactic addressees of 36. Cf. *A.* 11.252–3 *o fortunatae gentes, Saturnia regna, | antiqui Ausonii*, recalling the present opening, as well as the designation *Saturnia tellus* in the *laudes Italiae* (173); cf. 458–540, 459–6onn.

fortunatos nimium: cf. 493 *fortunatus et ille*; *nimium* almost makes *fortunatos* a superlative; cf. *A.* 4.657 *felix, heu nimium felix, si . . .*

si . . . norint: syncope for *nouerint*, normally taken as fut. perf. It could as easily be perf. subj. in a future less vivid conditional: 'if they should ever come to realize . . .'

459–60   quibus ... tellus: i.e. they enjoy the spontaneous be-
neficence of the Saturnian age – a sense guaranteed by every word in
the two lines; cf. 1.127–8 *ipsaque tellus | omnia liberius nullo poscente ferebat*;
E. 4.23 *ipsa [tellus] tibi blandos fundet cunabula flores* (following Geymonat);
Ov. *M.* 1.101–2 *ipsa quoque immunis rastroque intacta nec ullis | saucia
uomeribus per se dabat omnia tellus*; for the wording see 1.127–8; 2.10–11nn.
Such language does not suit the *agricola* of the *Georgics* (458–540,
500–1nn.).

The lines form a frame with 473–4, which also situate the farmer in
the golden age (see n.), through reference to *Iustitia* (cf. 460 *iustissima*);
this is the primary purpose of the superlative, to underscore the Saturnian
features of this land, though V. may also have known of Philemon fr. 105
Kock δικαιότατον πρᾶγμ' ἐστὶν ἀνθρώποις ἀγρός, 'land is a very just thing
for men.'

fundit ... facilem uictum: a pointed contradiction of 1.121–2 *pater
ipse colendi | haud facilem esse uiam uoluit*.

461–6   Stock topics to exemplify urban degeneracy: dependence on
patronage and extravagance in furnishings, clothing and food. See
Griffin (1976) for these motifs. V.'s debt to Lucretius' attack on luxury
(2.20–36) is clear (469–71n.). The positive attributes at 467–74 pro-
vide a contrast.

461–2   So the happy farmer of Hor. *Epd.* 2.7–8 *forumque uitat et
superba ciuium | potentiorum limina.*

si non ... : the protasis is easily supplied: 'What if no great house ... ';
if the connection is slightly obscure, that is because V. is here recalling
Lucretius: *si non aurea sunt iuuenum simulacra per aedes ...* , 2.24.

foribus ... superbis: with *alta*.

totis uomit aedibus 'spews out from the whole palace'. Ennius
wrote *et Tiberis flumen* [cf. V.'s *aquam*] ⟨*flauom*⟩ *uomit in mare salsum* (*Ann.*
453 Skutsch), a line modified at *A.* 7.30–2 *Tiberinus ... | uerticibus rapidis
et multa flauus harena | in mare prorumpit*. The late word *uomitoria* (entrance-
ways in the theatre) is close in sense to V.'s use: *uomitoria ... unde homines
glomeratim ingredientes in sedilia se fundunt*, Macrob. *Sat.* 6.4.3.

463   inhiant: the verb is not flattering: 'stand with mouth gaping
open at', like the observers of Camilla's finery at *A.* 7.813–14 *turbaque ...
attonitis inhians animis*; and cf. Hor. *Sat.* 1.1.70–1 for a context close to
this: *congestis undique saccis | indormis inhians*. At 508 *plausus hiantem* has the
same force (495–540, 508–10nn.).

464   inlusasque auro uestis 'garments tricked with gold'; strands of gold are woven in. The variant *inclusasque* may be an attempt to simplify the expression; or perhaps it arose from Lucr. 4.1126–7, which refers to the setting of emeralds in gold: *grandes uiridi cum luce zmaragdi | auro includuntur*.

Ephyreiaque aera 'Corinthian bronzes'; V., perhaps following Callimachus and Apollonius, prefers the old name for Corinth, like the two Alexandrians avoiding the common name altogether (4.343n.).

465   A golden line (1.117n.).

alba neque Assyrio fucatur lana ueneno: dyes were a particular mark of luxury; the theme is resumed at 506 *Sarrano dormiat ostro* (495–540, 506–7nn.); also 4.334–5 *uellera ... hyali saturo fucata colore*. The use of *uenenum* for dye may be pejorative in this context; cf. Hor. *Epist.* 2.1.207 *lana Tarentino uiolas imitata ueneno* (466n.). The curious self-dyeing sheep of V.'s golden age (*E.* 4.42–5) may also be invoked (the opening *nec uarios ...* occurs only at 463 and *E.* 4.42).

466   casia: not the shrub of 213, 4.30 and *E.* 2.49, but *Laurus cinnamomum*, an eastern plant, and here specifically its bark which was imported as a perfume; *usus oliui* therefore refers to the use of olive oil as an unguent.

corrumpitur: a strong word, with the same effect as *ueneno* in the preceding line; it is otherwise used in the poem only of the effect of the plague on lakes: *corrupitque lacus*, 3.481; also of plague at *A.* 3.138 *corrupto caeli tractu*.

467–74   The positive possessions of the rustic, balancing what he lacks (461–6); they are at odds with the realities of the farmer's existence (458–540, 467, 468, 469–71nn.).

467   at: provides a strong contrast with what has preceded ('and yet ...'). The repetition at 468 and 469 gives the effect of a list.

secura quies: what of Jupiter's very first act, at 1.123 *curis acuens mortalia corda*? *curae* are constant for the real farmer, particularly in Book 3 (3.123–4n.). The absence of care, on the other hand, (*se-curus*) is otherwise found only once in the poem, at 3.376, where the Scythians *secura ... otia agunt*, a people who live outside the bounds of agricultural activity (349–83n.); cf. also 3.530 (of the idealized life of the ox), and Lucr. 3.939 *securam ... quietem*.

nescia fallere uita: the words have a moral dimension, in contrast to the corruption of urban life, but there is also a suggestion that nature knows no deceit, the same claim which was made (falsely) in those other 'praises': *nec miseros fallunt aconita legentis*, 152 (and n.). This again is a mark of the golden age: *fallax herba ueneni | occidet*, E. 4.24–5. And in reality the absence of deceit is not absolute, but is conditional upon the correct pursuit of *labor*; cf. 1.424–6.

468 diues opum uariarum: so of the old man of Tarentum, and the fruits of his vegetable garden: *regum aequabat opes animis*, 4.132 and n. *opum* is gen. of respect.

latis otia fundis: the commentators reject the possibility of a reference to *latifundia*, once again accusing V. of a carelessness which seems to occur predominantly at such important junctures (170–2, 454–7nn.). Why on earth did he use the noun *fundi* (the only occurrence in his corpus) with the adjective *lati* if he did not intend precisely that connotation? – and the connotation is already current in V.'s period, as is clear from Varro, *R.R.* 1.16.4 *quam partem lati fundi diuites domesticae copiae mandare solent.* This rustic is again distinct from the real farmer of the *Georgics*; cf. 412–13 *laudato ingentia rura, | exiguum colito* (see n.).

469 speluncae: it is only the non-agricultural Scythians, with their affinities to the golden age (467n.), who are otherwise so associated: *ipsi in defossis specubus secura sub alta | otia agunt terra*, 3.376–7.

uiuique lacus: 'natural, opposed to artificial reservoirs' (Conington); such artificially produced bodies of water provided one of the climactic focuses of the *laudes Italiae* (161–4n.).

469–71 et ... absunt: these details belong to the fiction of pastoral, not the reality of the agricultural *Georgics*. The words *frigida tempe*, though the noun came to be used merely for 'valleys', look to the scenery of Greece, real mooing is not otherwise encouraging in the *Georgics* (*mugitus* occurs twice elsewhere: when the cattle are afflicted by the gadfly at 3.150 *furit mugitibus aether*, and at 3.554–5, when they are taken off by plague: *crebris mugitibus amnes | ... sonant*), and as for sleeping outside, it is mentioned at 1.341–2 (see n.), but the Italian who knows about snakes will generally avoid it (cf. 3.435–6).

The last detail is developed from Lucr. 2.29–30, where it is also contrasted with more luxurious activities: *cum tamen inter se prostrati in gramine molli | propter aquae riuum sub ramis arboris altae ...* (461–6n.).

absunt: otherwise in the poem only at 151, in the *laudes Italiae* (see n.).

471–2 illic ... iuuentus: the picture of youths hunting and the diction of 472 have to do with aristocratic primitivism, not everyday agriculture; they are revitalized at *A.* 9.605–7, where the Latin Numanus Remulus contrasts the primitivism of his race with the decadence of the Trojans.

473   sacra deum sanctique patres: religion and piety function only at such peaceful moments in the poem; elsewhere, where *labor* is in effect, they are of little avail (1.335–50; 3.455–6, 486–93nn.).

sacra deum: the combination otherwise occurs only at 4.521, where it provides the setting for the σπαραγμός ('tearing apart') of Orpheus. Here it provides a neat transition to the next section, where V. characterizes himself as the bearer of the *sacra* [*Musarum*], 476.

473–4   extrema ... fecit: another invocation of the Saturnian age, as at 538. V. refers to Arat. *Phaen.* 96–136 (as at 537; see n.), on the sign Virgo, also known as Astraea (Ov. *M.* 1.149–50 *uirgo caede madentis | ultima caelestum terras Astraea reliquit*) and Justice ('and men called her Justice', *Phaen.* 105), the title chosen by V. (but cf. *E.* 4.6 *iam redit et Virgo*). She was the last immortal to leave the earth, at the advent of the age of bronze: 'and then Justice came to despise that race of men, and she flew up to heaven', *Phaen.* 133–4. V. doubtless also intends a reference to Cat. 64: *sed postquam tellus scelere est imbuta nefando | iustitiamque omnes cupida de mente fugarunt ...*, 397–8; *quare nec talis dignantur* [*dei*] *uisere coetus*, 407.

Iustitia: cf. *iustissima*, 460, and 459–60n.

475–94   *The poet's options*

The lines are carefully fashioned to express preference and alternative, with a subsequent recapitulation of the options. V. begins (475–82) with the hope that he may understand the workings of the universe. If his intellect is not equal to this goal, then let the countryside be enough for him (483–9). The first option is then recapitulated with the beatitude of 490–2 (*felix qui potuit rerum cognoscere causas ...*), while the alternative is answered by 493–4 (*fortunatus et ille deos qui nouit agrestis ...*). The passage as a whole is best understood as applying to Virgil and his career. The topics of 477–82 are peripherally agricultural, and many of them were covered in the second half of Book 1; and in that the *Georgics* may be seen as a poem which attempts to understand the workings of nature, these lines, along with 490–2, appear to express a wish for the success of the poem. The alternative (483–9, 493–4) is contentment with a pastoral world, the world represented by the *Eclogues*. Incidentally, if these lines are seen as discussing the *Eclogues* and *Georgics*, a significant structural pattern emerges: at the end of the first half of the poem, V. refers to his present and past projects, while at the beginning of the second half (3.1–48n.) his concern is with present and future (the *Aeneid*) poems – the whole corpus extends across the middle of the middle work.

The traditional view of these lines has been to see Lucretius as the figure behind the 'scientific' option, and some even identify him closely with the *qui* of 490. While Lucretius may be representative of such poetry, V. at 491–3 is dealing with his *own* poetic ambitions, and with his place in the tradition of poets such as Aratus and Lucretius, a point obscured by strict and exclusive identification with Lucretius. Nor do lines 493–4 have much to do with Virgilian poetry outside the *Eclogues*. And finally, dictional or even thematic reference to Lucretius does not require an identification with Lucretius himself; it is typical of Virgilian imitation that he creates a new, individual situation through reference to a predecessor. On the case against assigning a central position to Lucretius see Ross (1975) 29–31.

475   Me uero 'but as for me', shifting the focus from the *agricolae* of the preceding lines and indicating that what follows primarily refers to V.'s own poetry.

dulces ante omnia: i.e. *dulcissimae*; cf. *E.* 2.62 *nobis placeant ante omnia siluae*. The hexameter excludes superlatives in the nominative feminine plural.

475–6   Musae, | quarum sacra fero: cf. 473n. V. presents himself as a priest of the Muses, as do Horace (*Musarum sacerdos, Odes* 3.1.3) and Propertius (*sacerdos*, 3.1.3) – there seems to be some allusion at work among these poets.

ingenti percussus amore: cf. 3.285 (and n.) *capti ... amore*; *A.* 9.197–8 *obstipuit magno laudum percussus amore | Euryalus*; the impulse may come from Lucr. 1.922–3 *sed acri | percussit thyrso laudis spes magna meum cor*.

477–82   Though there is reminiscence of Lucretius in these lines, the themes are not exclusively Lucretian. As is clear from *E.* 6.31–40 (Song of Silenus) and *A.* 1.742–6 (Song of Iopas; see 478, 481–2nn.), V. was active in reshaping the Song of Orpheus at Ap. Rhod. *Arg.* 1.496–511

(477n.). His themes, like those of these other songs, are scientific, treating the workings of the cosmos in a general way, and should not be associated with any philosophical school.

477 caelique uias et sidera: in effect a hendiadys: 'the paths of the stars in the sky'; cf. Ap. Rhod. *Arg.* 1.500 'the stars and the moon and the paths of the sun'; for the sun and moon, see 478. Knowledge such as this has been vital to the *Georgics* since the first line: *quo sidere terram | uertere* (475–94n.); cf. too 1.335 *caeli mensis et sidera serua.*

478 'the various failings [eclipses] of the sun and toils [phases] of the moon'. The line is modelled on Lucr. 5.751 *solis item quoque defectus lunaeque latebras* – Virgil does not otherwise use *defectus* – but the theme is as Virgilian as it is Lucretian: the workings of the sun and moon were the theme of 1.351–464, and the historical eclipse of the sun was the climax of that movement (1.466–8). At *A.* 1.742 V. remodelled the line for the Song of Iopas: *hic canit errantem lunam solisque labores* (477–82n.).

479 unde tremor terris: earthquakes are treated by Lucretius at 6.577–600.

479–80 qua ... residant: given the language (*obicibus ruptis*) probably not simply the workings of tides (though implicitly these may be included), but exceptional tidal activity, associated with earthquakes (*unde tremor terris*). Thuc. 3.89 describes an earthquake and resulting tidal wave on Euboea.

maria alta tumescant 'the seas swell high'; *alta* is adverbial or proleptic; there may be a reference to a line from Hor. *Epd.* 16 (*neque intumescit alta uiperis humus*, 52), a poem V. knew well.

obicibus: the first syllable of *obex* is long (except at Sil. 4.24), because it originates from *ob (j) icio.*

481–2 Repeated without change at *A.* 1.745–6, as the final topic of the Song of Iopas (477–82n.). The subject (the varying length of night and day) was treated at Lucr. 5.680–704, but it is also tangential to material in the *Georgics* (1.247–51; cf. following n.).

Oceano properent se tingere: cf. 1.246; *A.* 11.913–14 *gurgite Phoebus Hibero | tingat equos.*

tardis ... noctibus: Servius explains '*tarde uenientibus, id est aestiuis*', but it is better to understand *hibernis* or *tarde exeuntibus*, giving a better balance between *soles* (= *dies*) and *noctibus*: 'why the winter days end so quickly, or what makes the [winter] nights last so long'. Cf. also Lucr. 5.699–700 *propterea noctes hiberno tempore longae | cessant.*

483–4   sin ... sanguis 'but if the cold blood surrounding my heart hinders my capacity for reaching these realms of nature'; that is, if the intellect is unequal to the goal. The theory is taken, perhaps with a degree of irony, from Empedocles, for whom 'the blood surrounding man's heart is "intellect"', αἷμα γὰρ ἀνθρώποις περικάρδιόν ἐστι νόημα, Emped. fr. 105 Diels–Kranz; cf. Cic. *Tusc. Disp.* 1.19 *Empedocles animum esse censet cordi suffusum sanguinem.* It became something of a caricature, to judge from Horace's play with it: *deus immortalis haberi | dum cupit Empedocles, ardentem frigidus Aetnam | insiluit, A.P.* 464–6; Horace, like V., has added the elements of heat and cold, appropriate to poetic intellect.

The failure of intellect is best understood as connected with the *Georgics*; V.'s hope is for understanding of the natural world with which he is presently occupied. This seems clear from what follows (485–9): as an alternative he will settle for the streams and woods of the countryside, specifying locales in Laconia, Thessaly and Thrace. These lines hardly constitute reference to the *Georgics*, as some would wish; they rather suggest pastoral, and look specifically to the *Eclogues* (475–94n.).

483   sin: Greek εἰ δὲ μή, introducing the alternative to the preferred wish of 475–7.

has ... naturae ... partis: the demonstrative indicates in part the lines preceding, in part perhaps 'these realms of nature' of the *Georgics* themselves (483–4n.).

485–6   The individual's contentment with the idyllic countryside (much like that of Horace at *Sat.* 2.6.1–3) has little application to the *Georgics*, outside the peroration of 458–540.

The structure is elegant, with *rura* and *amnes* the subjects of *placeant*, *flumina* and *siluas* the objects of *amem*.

486   inglorius: emphatically placed. The adjective is more easily applied to the *Eclogues* than to the *Georgics*, from which V. did expect *gloria*; cf. 4.6–7.

486–9   o ubi campi | ...! o qui me ... | sistat ...!: the tone is emotional and personal, and very close, as is the subject, to that of Hor. *Sat.* 2.6.60–65 *o rus, quando ego te aspiciam? ... o quando faba Pythagorae cognata ...? o noctes cenaeque deum!.* Cf. too [Virg.] *Culex* 94 *o pecudes, o Panes et o gratissima Tempe ...*, from a passage indebted to these lines (458–74n.).

The place-names conjure up an idyllic image, with little association with the *Georgics* (*Taygeti* occurs at 3.44, because that book treats

hunting-dogs, for which Laconia was famous; see 3.405): Spercheus is a
river in Thessaly, Taygetus a mountain in Laconia, and Haemus a
mountain-range in Thrace. In 487 mention of the maenads perhaps
suggests, through Bacchus, the theme of poetic inspiration; cf. Hor. *Odes*
2.19.

487   uirginibus ... Lacaenis: dat. of agent with the perfect pas-
sive, *bacchata* ('traversed in their revels by', Page).

488   Taygeta: scanned *Tāўgĕt(ă)*; cf. 3.44.

488–9   o qui me ... | sistat: i.e. *o utinam aliquis me sistat.*

489   ingenti ramorum protegat umbra: see 435n.

490   felix qui potuit rerum cognoscere causas: the line resumes
the movement of 475–82, as V. delivers a beatitude on the man who
understands the workings of the universe – his own ambition in the
Georgics (475–94, 483–4nn.). It is 'understanding' of nature that is the
goal throughout the *Georgics*: *ni refugis tenuisque piget cognoscere curas,*
1.177; *certis poteris cognoscere signis,* 1.394; *quo quamque modo possis cognoscere*
dicam, 2.226; *non dubiis poteris cognoscere signis,* 4.253 (these examples, with
that at 490, account for all instances of the infinitive in the *Georgics*, and
for half of all the instances in V.). The language is also redolent of
Lucretius (*naturam ... cognoscere rerum,* 3.1072), and he is one of those who
is thus blessed in V.'s eyes; but to make the line a specific reference to
Lucretius (indeed the closest verbal parallel is in Aristot. *P.A.* 2.645a5
τοῖς δυναμένοις τὰς αἰτίας γνωρίζειν, 'those able to understand causes'), or
even to Lucretius and his Greek masters, is to obliterate the careful
structure of 475–94, and to misjudge the nature of Virgilian imitation
(491–2n.). And if *qui* here is specifically referred to Lucretius, then *ille* at
493 must indicate an equally specific individual; and though the details
of that line and 494 fit the *Eclogues,* they are hardly a plausible charac-
terization of the aims of the *Georgics,* which 490–2 fit perfectly (491–2,
493–4nn.).

potuit: as with *subiecit,* the aspect is ambiguous, referring to those
who in the past have been capable of this (Lucretius, Epicurus, etc.), as
well as to those who are capable (V. himself, *Musis adiuuantibus*).

491–2   atque ... auari: on a literal level, this is the end almost
achieved by Orpheus at 4.467–84. As Ross (1975) 23–7, 66, 93–6 has
shown, Orpheus is for V. the figure who understands and controls
nature, the representative of 'scientific' poetry. To the extent that
Orpheus in many ways represents man in the world of *labor,* exercising

his control over nature (4.453–527, 511–15nn.), the present lines have
wide application within the *Georgics*. On another level the triumph
described in these lines applies directly to V. himself, for he will shortly
claim an indirect triumph over the infernal elements, as *Inuidia* against
his art is rendered ineffective and banished to the Underworld (3.37–9,
where *metus* also figures and *non exsuperabile* means much the same as
inexorabile). The overcoming of *metus* is one of the aims of man in the age
of Jupiter (333n., Thomas (1982a) 79–80) – an aim which will fail at the
end of Book 3 (cf. 3.552n.).

That these lines, like 490, are reminiscent of Lucretius (*religio pedibus
subiecta*, 1.78; *et metus ille foras praeceps Acheruntis agendus*, 3.37), does not
require an exclusive equation of their subject with the person of Lucre-
tius (see Introduction, pp. 3–4).

493–4   fortunatus et ille ...: as *felix qui ...* looks to the scientific
understanding of 477–82, so this resumes the alternative of pastoral
contentment at 485–9, and to that extent, as in the linguistic difference
between *felix* ('blessed') and *fortunatus* ('happy') the present option is a
compromise (*sin has ne possim ...*, 483–4). But it is a compromise within
V.'s own aspirations, which are presented, as are his achievements at
4.563–6, with self-deprecation; the alternative of 493–4 will be his lot if
his present ambition of *rerum cognoscere causas*, the aim of the *Georgics*, is
unsuccessful. Most commentators, who see only the present lines as
referring to V., are compelled to see acquaintance with and adoration of
rustic deities and woodland nymphs as a legitimate representation of the
aims and content of the *Georgics*. Pan, Silvanus, and the Dryads appear
in the prayer at 1.11, 17 and 20, but are otherwise deities of the *Eclogues*,
not the *Georgics* – Silvanus, after all, is the god of *untilled* land.

495–540   The praise of rustic life is resumed, preceded by and
opposed to an elaboration of the evils of urban life. The transition is
smooth, as the passage appears at first to be merely an appendage to
493–5: *fortunatus et ille ... illum non populi fasces*. V. hereby chooses as
his rustic representative a figure who is more pastoral than georgic
(493–4n.), a choice consonant with the fact that the existence of the
rustic in these praises has little in common with that of the real farmer of
the poem (458–540, 459–60, 469–71nn.).

The section is carefully constructed to balance and expand on the
same theme at 458–74: in both, urban vignettes precede rustic, and
the details respond (496, 500–1, 506–7, 508–10, 532–40, 537nn.).

495–9 illum non ... non ... et ... aut ... non ... -que ... neque ... aut ... aut ...: the style is highly rhetorical, and recalls that of 461–6 (*si non ... nec ... -que ... -que ... neque ... nec*): V. communicates the evils of civic life negatively, by stressing the rustic's lack of participation in such activities. This method was favoured by Horace: *Epd.* 2.5–8, 49–55; *Odes* 3.24.9–20 and especially 3.3.1–6 *iustum et tenacem propositi uirum* | *non ciuium ardor praua iubentium,* | *non uultus instantis tyranni* | *mente quatit solida neque Auster,* | *dux inquieti turbidus Hadriae,* | *nec fulminantis magna manus Iouis.*

495–8 Rhetorical also is the juxtaposition of two tricola, the first abundans (*fasces/purpura/discordia*), the second decrescens (*Dacus/res/ regna*), with the two units separated by *aut*, and all going with the verb *flexit*.

495 populi fasces: cf. Lucretius' characterization of Sisyphus: *qui petere a populo fasces ... imbibit,* 3.996–7.

496–502 flexit ... doluit ... inuidit ... tulere ... carpsit ... uidit: habitual perfects; these conditions have always pertained in the country.

496 infidos agitans discordia fratres: a conventional paradigm for civil war; cf. Lucr. 3.70–2 *sanguine ciuili rem conflant ...* | *crudeles gaudent in tristi funere fratris*; Cat. 64.399 *perfudere manus fraterno sanguine fratres.* Some see the words merely as a reference to fraternal rivalry, but the diction seems to require a more specific sense; see 510 (and n.), which with this line helps to frame the depiction of 495–512.

discordia: recalls *discordibus,* in the same position at 459, both in the second line of their sections.

497 coniurato ... Histro: V. uses the verb only here, at 1.280 (of the Giants' assault on Olympus), and at *A.* 8.5 (of the actions of Turnus). The figure of a foreign river in conspiracy against Rome occurs at 1.509 *hinc mouet Euphrates,* and is ultimately answered by the depiction of conquered rivers (the Euphrates, Rhine and Araxes) on the shield of Aeneas (*A.* 8.726–8).

498 res Romanae perituraque regna: had V. wished to avoid the reader's connecting *peritura* with *res Romanae* (as well as with *regna* [*externa*]), he could have done so (170–2, 454–7nn.).

498–9 neque ille | aut doluit miserans inopem aut inuidit habenti: but the 'real' farmer, when his work fails, does precisely this (see 1.158–9); and pity for the farmer was the ostensible motivation for the poem: *ignarosque uiae mecum miseratus agrestis* | *ingredere,* 1.41–2. Here, as is clear from 500–1 (see n.), the figure described belongs in the golden age: *[post regnum Saturni] amor successit habendi*, *A*. 8.327, and cf. 4.177 (and n.), where the bees, those other children of *labor*, are characterized as motivated by acquisitiveness: *amor urget habendi*.

500–1 quos … carpsit: an appealing reference to golden-age existence, though in terms outside the realities of agriculture in the *Georgics*; cf. 458–540, 459–60, 1.127–8nn.

501–2 nec ferrea iura … uidit: laws do not exist in the golden age: *poena metusque aberant, nec uerba minantia fixo | aere legebantur*, Ov. *M*. 1.91–2. It is noteworthy that V. uses the adjective *ferreus*, for laws were written on bronze: the cultural sense of the word is here active; cf. *in ferrum*, 504 (1.143–4n.).

insanumque forum: so Allius, frequenter of the forum, on the joys of life in the country: *forumque uitat*, Hor. *Epd*. 2.7.

populi tabularia 'record-offices'. The public records were normally kept in temples; the phrase here has the same contemptuous force as our use of 'the bureaucracy' to designate any uncooperative or regulation-bound government agency.

503–12 The style becomes that of the priamel (a series of options, activities, etc., generally culminating in that preferred by the poet or speaker), as V. presents the (rejected) preferences of various people (*alii … hic … alius … hic … hunc*), which lead up to, and are contrasted with, the desired alternative, emphatically positioned (*agricola*, 513). The style, and the details, are similar to those of Hor. *Odes* 1.1 (where *me* at 29 is the precise equivalent of V.'s *agricola*); on the device, with a reference to this instance, see Race (1982) 120. The *alii* of the priamel are not normally to be specifically identified, and it is unlikely that V., as some would have it, is here thinking of actual figures (Marius, Crassus, Pompey, etc.).

503 sollicitant alii remis freta caeca: i.e. traders. The words suggest the folly of sailing, an activity discovered only after the golden age (1.136–8); cf. Hor. *Odes* 1.3.21–4 *nequiquam deus abscidit | prudens Oceano dissociabili | terras, si tamen impiae | non tangenda rates transiliunt uada*.

sollicitant: the verb has recently been used of the cultural equivalent of seafaring, agricultural activity: *sollicitanda tamen tellus*, 418 (see n., and 1.50n. on V.'s consistent linking of agriculture and seafaring). This further separates the rustic of 458–540 from the real *agricola* of the poem.

freta caeca: cf. 3.260 *nocte natat caeca serus freta* (where, of course, *caeca* modifies *nocte*); *A*. 1.536 *in uada caeca*.

503–4 ruuntque | in ferrum: the words denote an eagerness for war; but see too 501–2n.

504 penetrant: the verb suggests the unseemly obsequiousness of the courtier; cf. Hor. *Epd*. 2.7–8 *forumque uitat et superba ciuium | potentiorum limina* (501–2n.). Some see a reference to the sacking of palaces (cf. *A*. 2.484 *apparent Priami et ueterum penetralia regum*, as Pyrrhus makes his way into the inner recesses of the palace), but that topic comes in the next line.

505 petit excidiis urbem: a more poetical expression for *fert excidium urbi*.

506–7 Although the two lines are syntactically distinct, V. fashions them to mirror each other (*Sarrano dormiat ostro | defossoqu(e) incubat auro*), and the thought and diction of the two (as Macrobius noted, *Sat*. 6.1.40) clearly expand on a line from the *De Morte* of Varius Rufus: *incubet ut Tyriis atque ex solido bibat auro*, p. 100 Morel; cf. also Hor. *Sat*. 1.70–2 *congestis undique saccis | indormis inhians* – cf. *hiantem* at 508; also, for 507 (especially *defossoque . . . auro*), *Sat*. 1.1.41–2 *quid iuuat immensum te argenti pondus et auri | furtim defossa timidum deponere terra?*

gemma . . . ostro: instrumental ablatives, a somewhat bold alteration of the more 'correct' formations of Varius (see preceding n.): *incubet . . . Tyriis . . . ex . . . bibat auro* (though *ostro* could be a locative).

Sarrano . . . ostro 'Tyrian purple'; balances *Assyrio . . . ueneno* at 465 (495–540n.); cf. 3.17 *Tyrio . . . ostro*, 307; *A*. 4.262. V.'s *Sarrano* is a true translation of Varius' *Tyriis*, *Sarra* being the old Latin version of the city's Hebrew name (*Tsor*); Servius claims the name comes from a fish, called *sar* (the purple dye does come from the shellfish *murex*). Like *Tyrius*, *Sarranus* comes to be used for 'purple' (Juv. 10.38; Sil. 15.205).

incubat: cf. *A*. 6.610, where a place is reserved in the Underworld for those who 'brood over' (*incubuere*) their wealth; see 311n. for *incumbo/incubo*.

508–10 With *stupet, attonitus* and *hiantem* (cf. 463 *inhiant* and n.), V. conveys the absurdity of the novice's admiration for political or oratorical prowess (*hic . . . rostris*), and of the seasoned politician's pleasure at the applause of the crowd (*hunc . . . corripuit* 'this man stands gaping as he is transported by the applause of people and senators which redoubles along the rows of the theatre'). Cf. the reaction of the *turba matrum* to the

appearance of Camilla at *A.* 7.814 *attonitis inhians animis.* Horace's
priamel (503-12n.) has a similar detail: *hunc [iuvat], si mobilium turba
Quiritium | certat tergeminis tollere honoribus.*

enim: the first attested use of *enim* to emphasize the word it follows
(*geminatus*); see *ThLL* v.2.572.63. Cf. 3.70; *A.* 10.873-4 *hic Aenean ...
uocauit. | Aeneas agnouit enim laetusque precatur.*

510   gaudent perfusi sanguine fratrum: forms a frame with 496
(see n.).

perfusi: the participle, expressing cause, after a verb of emotion
(*gaudent*) is a Graecism (e.g. ἥδομαι + part., 'take pleasure in doing
something').

511-12   Exile forms the climax of the depiction of political life. The
lines are recalled when the bull of Book 3, bested in the fight for the herd,
is forced into exile (3.224-5, 228); the effect of those lines, in which
the present couplet helps, is to create a strong personification. Horace
adapted 511-12 in criticizing the voluntary exile of trading and busi-
ness which men choose over *otium*: *quid terras alio calentis | sole mutamus?*,
Odes 2.16.18-19.

512   For the word-order see 386-90, 531; 1.117nn.

513-40   The farmer, in contrast, lives the ideal life. The passage
begins on a plausible note – at least ploughing occurs, and there is
initially an absence of language suggesting golden-age spontaneity
(unlike 459-60, 500-1). But stress is soon placed on the unstinting
beneficence of nature and the ample *otium* of the *agricola*, elements not
greatly in evidence in the body of the *Georgics* (527n.), and the finale of
the passage (532-40) states what has been implied since 458, that this
existence is in essence Saturnian (458-540n.).

513   agricola ...: the farmer, emphatically placed at the beginning
of the line and the passage, provides the climax and contrast of the
priamel (503-12n.).

The line recalls 1.494, where the farmer is also contrasted, there with
the soldier whose weapons he will come upon years after the battle
(1.493-7n.).

514   hinc anni labor: *hinc* of the MSS (also Servius) seems prefer-
able to *hic*, a correction in the ninth-century Gudianus printed by
Mynors and Geymonat, following Markland (*ad* Stat. *Silu.* 1.2.144), on
the basis of 3.288 *hic labor, hinc laudem fortes sperate coloni.* Two arguments
support *hinc*: it gives a typical tricolon, with anaphora of the key adverb

(1.289–90n.): cf. 1.266–7 *nunc ... nunc ... nunc*; 2.368–9 *tum ... tum ...
tum* (after 3.288 there is no repetition of *hinc*); perhaps more importantly,
it provides more vivid sense: 'the farmer ploughs: this is the source of
(*hinc*) his toil, the source of sustenance for nation and family, the source
of sustenance for his animals'.

515 armenta boum meritosque iuuencos: see 3.525–6 for the
fate of the 'deserving bullocks', there dying of plague; cf. 3.525n.

516 nec requies, quin: i.e. *sine mora*; the words *nec requies* begin
Lucr. 6.1177, but the sense is different. Cf. 3.110n.

516–17 pomis ... fetu pecorum ... Cerealis mergite culmi:
the mode of reference to the three products expands in precision as the
tricolon proceeds; see 143–4n.

mergite 'sheaf [of corn]'; *merges* appears only here and in Avienus,
and possibly at Plin. *N.H.* 18.296 – unless it is to be emended to *mergas*
('reaping-board'), which is in fact what Pliny means.

516–18 exuberet ... uincat: the cornucopia delivers effortlessly,
merely on ploughing the ground (513); cf. 458–540, 513–40nn.

horrea uincat: cf. 1.49 *ruperunt horrea messes*.

519 uenit hiems: teritur ...: more vivid than *cum uenit hiems*,
teritur ... Not quite the same as simple asyndeton, since the first clause is
really subordinate to the second; it seems colloquial: cf. Hor. *Sat.* 1.3.49
parcius hic uiuit: frugi dicatur.

520 Again V. suggests features of the golden age: the animals, it is
implied, return well-fed and of their own accord (see *E.* 4.21 *ipsae lacte
domum referent distenta capellae*), and the acorn and the leaves or fruit of the
arbutus have a distinct cultural association; they failed at the end of the
Saturnian age, when Ceres introduced agriculture (1.148–9). That
they were actually used as fodder does not diminish this impact of the
line (458–540n.).

521 uarios ... fetus: cf. 468 *opum uariarum*.

ponit: better taken as 'serves up' (cf. *A.* 1.706 *pocula ponunt*), rather
than 'lets fall' (i.e. *deponit*, as at 403).

522 As often (540 and 1.117n.), a golden line marks the end of a
movement; the next sentence ends similarly (526n.), and the con-
centration of such lines in this passage may owe something to its rhetor-
ical nature (see also 512, 531nn.).

apricis ... saxis: the vineyards are terraced on sunny rocks –
sometimes too sunny (cf. 377).

523–40 The focus shifts to the 'farmer' himself; nine lines describe his blissful leisure (523–31), with a further nine (532–40) – the finale of the book – unequivocally identifying this figure with the inhabitant of the golden age.

523 dulces pendent circum oscula nati 'his sweet children hang upon his kisses'; *pendent* is here used both = 'hang in embrace' (*ubi complexu Aeneae colloque pependit, A.* 1.715), and, more figuratively, 'hang on the lips [i.e. words] of' (*pendetque iterum narrantis ab ore, A.* 4.79). V. has adapted Lucr. 3.895–6, on the joys of which the deceased are deprived: *nec dulces occurrent oscula nati | praeripere* (524n.).

524 casta pudicitiam seruat domus: for *casta domus* cf. Cat. 64.384 *domos inuisere castas*; Hor. *Odes* 4.5.21 *nullis polluitur casta domus stupris*; for the thought cf. *Epd.* 2.39–40 *quodsi pudica mulier in partem iuuet | domum atque dulcis liberos.* Here, however, *domus* is equivalent to 'wife', for which there is no precise parallel. V. seems to have adapted and compressed Lucr. 3.894–5 (523n.): *iam iam non domus accipiet te laeta nec uxor | optima.* The word *uxor* (and not only the word?) did not appeal to V. (he preferred the less specific *coniunx*), the only instance being technical, in the context of a wedding hymn: *Mopse, nouas incide faces: tibi ducitur uxor, E.* 8.29; cf. Cat. 61.184–5 *iam licet uenias, marite: uxor in thalamo tibi est.*

524–5 ubera uaccae | lactea demittunt: suggesting a willingness again associated with the golden age: *E.* 4.21–2 (520n.); Hor. *Epd.* 16.49–50 *illic iniussae ueniunt ad mulctra capellae, | refertque tenta grex amicus ubera* (458–54on.).

525 in gramine laeto: here the arena for the sport of kids (*haedi*), at 3.494 the scene of death for the young cattle; see 515n.

526 The period ends with a rhythmic line, not quite golden, but artfully ordered in the same way (522n.).

527 ipse dies agitat festos: *dies festi* were the subject of 1.268–75. There the demands of *labor* are not relaxed on sacred days: irrigation, fencing, snaring, burning brambles, sheep-dipping and trading are all enjoined (see n.). This leisurely vignette, then, is in direct conflict with details elsewhere (458–54on.).

fususque per herbam: cf. 3.436 (and n.) *iacuisse per herbas.*

528 Thought by some to be a mistranslation of the Homeric line κοῦροι μὲν κρατῆρας ἐπεστέψαντο ποτοῖο, 'the young men filled the bowls with wine', *Il.* 1.470; *Od.* 1.148; if so, it was doubtless deliberate, for at *A.*

3.525–6, V. renders both senses of ἐπιστέφομαι – 'to fill' and 'to crown or wreathe' (*tum pater Anchises magnum cratera corona | induit impleuitque mero*). Evidently he was aware of the scholiastic debate on the word subsequently reported by Eustathius and Scholia ABT on *Il.* 1.470, and by Athenaeus (1.13d–e; 15.674f). Cf. too *A.* 1.724 *crateras magnos statuunt et uina coronant*. That the bowls were really 'crowned' is clear from Tib. 2.5.98 *coronatus stabit et ipse calix* and Stat. *Silu.* 3.1.76 *festasque dapes redimitaque uina*.

529   te libans, Lenaee, uocat: cf. 388 *et te, Bacche, uocant* (also in the context of a festival; see n.); the words also help to form a frame to the entire book, looking back to the invocations of Bacchus in the prologue: *nunc te, Bacche, canam*, 2; *huc, pater o Lenaee*, 4, 7; V. confirms the connection by using the address *Lenaee* only at 4, 7 and 529 of *Georgics* 2, and nowhere else in the corpus.

pecorisque magistris: cf. *E.* 2.33 *ouiumque magistros*, a periphrasis for *pastores*, whereas the *magister pecoris* (as opposed to the *armentarius*; 3.344; cf. 3.344–6n.) was the *chief* herdsman, equivalent to the *uilicus*: *quocirca principes qui utrique rei praeponuntur uocabulis quoque sunt diuersi, quod unus uocatur 'uilicus', alter 'magister pecoris'*, Varro, *R.R.* 1.2.14.

530   certamina ponit: attractively ambiguous; the primary sense (*in ulmo*) is 'sets up targets for their rivalry', but the sense 'establishes contests' is also present, cf. *A.* 5.66 *prima citae Teucris ponam certamina classis*.

531   The subsection ends with a line which, although not strictly golden, is just as artful – perhaps more so in its chiastic arrangement (N–a–V–A–n); the same pattern at 389, 396, 512; 4.24, which also serve as clausulae; see 522; 1.117nn.

agresti ... palaestra: so the inhabitants of the Elysian Fields: *pars in gramineis exercent membra palaestris*, *A.* 6.642.

praedura: the adjective, intensified by *prae-*, conjures up the idealized notion of *duritia*, assigned to primitive and ethically superior peoples: cf. *gensque uirum truncis et duro robore nata*, *A.* 8.315; *durum a stirpe genus*, *A.* 9.603. Thus the word anticipates *Sabini* in the next line (532–40n.).

532–40   The rustic life of the peroration is equated first to that of the Sabines, then to that of early Rome, and finally to the Saturnian existence, the ending parallel to that at 473–4 (495–540n.).

532   ueteres ... Sabini: this hardiness suggests a moral superiority to contemporary Romans: cf. Hor. *Epd.* 2.39–41 *quodsi pudica mulier in partem iuuet | domum atque dulcis liberos, | Sabina qualis.*

533 hanc Remus et frater: a somewhat surprising reference, particularly in the substitution of *frater* for Romulus. V. has twice mentioned fraternal discord and fratricide as features of urban life (*infidos agitans discordia fratres*, 496; *gaudent perfusi sanguine fratrum*, 510), and it is very odd that he should choose to stress the relationship, paradigmatic of civil strife (*acerba fata Romanos agunt | scelusque fraternae necis*, Hor. *Epd.* 7.17–18), here. *A.* 1.292–3 (*cana Fides et Vesta, Remo cum fratre Quirinus | iura dabunt*) is parallel in diction, but does not really help to explain the present instance, since it is part of Jupiter's pronouncement specifically granting *absolution* from the guilt incurred by the fratricide (535n.).

534 scilicet: cf. 1.281–2 *ter sunt conati imponere Pelio Ossam | scilicet,* where the word is in the same position, qualifying, as here, what precedes and not, as some hold, what follows.

rerum ... pulcherrima 'the fairest city on earth' (Page); Horace's *dulcissime rerum* (*Sat.* 1.9.4) and and Ovid's *pulcherrime rerum* (*M.* 8.49) show that V.'s *pulcherrima* modifies [*urbs*], not [*res*].

535 'and as one city surrounded her seven hills with a wall'; cf. *A.* 6.783 (in Anchises' prophecy): *septemque una sibi muro circumdabit arces.* Mention of Rome's wall sits rather uneasily with the approximation to the golden age which follows; cf. *E.* 4.31–3 *pauca tamen suberunt priscae uestigia fraudis | ... quae cingere muris | oppida ... iubeant.*

536–8 This clearly states that the existence of the rustic is the same as that provided by Saturn in the golden age (*aureus ... Saturnus*), before the rule of Jupiter (*ante ... sceptrum Dictaei regis*). That agrees with the characterization of the farmer throughout the passage (458–540n.), but is completely at odds with the cultural situation established at 1.121–49, as with the agricultural realities which stem therefrom.

536 Dictaei regis: Jupiter was reared on Mt Dicte in Crete; cf. 4.152 *Dictaeo caeli regem pauere sub antro* (and see 4.149–50n.). The epithet *Dictaeus* is exclusively Hellenistic, and V. almost certainly took it from Callimachus: πῶς καί μιν, Δικταῖον ἀείσομεν ἠὲ Λυκαῖον; how shall we sing of him, as Dictaean or Lycaean?', *H.* 1.4; cf. at 46 of the same hymn the Dictaean Meliae (Δικταῖαι Μελίαι), who nurtured the young god. Cf. 4.152n.

537 'before an impious race feasted on slaughtered bullocks';

adapted from Aratus, for whom this characterized the worst race, that of Bronze: 'they were the first to feed on the flesh of ploughing-oxen', *Phaen.* 132. The next line in Aratus describes the consequent departure of Justice (Δίκη) from the earth, and by this reference to the motivation for her departure, V. creates a close parallel to the statement at 473–4 (see n.) – both sections end, or almost end, with a close adaptation of consecutive lines of Aratus (495–540n.).

impia ... gens: cf. Hor. *Epd.* 16.63–6 on the Blessed Isles, reserved for those not implicated in the debasement of the ages: *piae ... genti*.

538 aureus ... Saturnus: a conflation of the golden and Saturnian ages (culturally identical anyway; cf. *A.* 8.324 *aurea quae perhibent illo sub rege* [sc. *Saturno*] *fuere* | *saecula*).

The identification of rustic life as Saturnian is not original with V.; Varro reports: *nec sine causa terram eandem appellabant* [*maiores nostri*] *matrem et Cererem, et qui eam colerent, piam et utilem agere uitam credebant atque eos solos reliquos esse ex stirpe Saturni regis, R.R.* 3.1.4–5. But whereas for Varro this is anecdotal, for V. it is part of a developed theme which creates and is intended to create contradictions with the body of the poem (458–540n.).

539–40 Cf. Ovid's characterization of the golden age at *M.* 1.98–9: *non tuba derecti, non aeris cornua flexi,* | *non galeae, non ensis erat* – the same sequence precisely. V. holds this detail to the very end in order to refer the reader to the end of the previous book, and with it the realities of the situation: *et curuae rigidum falces conflantur in ensem,* 1.508 – these are the only two occurrences of *ensis* outside the *Aeneid*.

540 A golden line ends the peroration (522, 1.117nn.).

impositos ... incudibus: varied at 4.173 *impositis incudibus*.

541–2 Like 4 this book ends with a personal statement, while the other two books, whose conclusions are more dramatic, end with narrative. The image of this couplet, completion of a journey by chariot, looks to the subject of the book to follow, and at the same time is linked to the final image of Book 1 – the simile of the horse and chariot out of control; a form of *equus* occurs in the last line of each, of *spatium* in the penultimate.

V.'s image may owe something to Lucr. 6.92–4 *tu mihi supremae praescripta ad candida calcis* | *currenti spatium praemonstra, callida Musa* | *Calliope*; but it goes back to Pindar (*O.* 9.80–3; *P.* 10.65). V. perhaps had in mind the beginning of Varro's treatment of horses at *R.R.*

2.71 *Lucienus: ego quoque adueniens aperiam carceres, inquit, et equos emittere incipiam.*

541   This is at best ambiguous (and the ambiguity is resolved only with *equum* in the next line), since *aequor* refers as easily to the sea, particularly in the company of *immensum*: *immensa per aequora, A.* 6.355; cf. also *G.* 1.29 *immensi ... maris*; 3.541 *maris immensi.* V. elsewhere (4.116–17) speaks of his task as a sea-journey. Cf. 1.50 and n.

542   equum fumantia soluere colla: cf. Callim. *H.* 5.9–10 (of Athena after the battle with the Giants): ὑφ' ἅρματος αὐχένας ἵππων | λυσαμένα, 'releasing the horses' necks from the chariot'. See also 3.111n.

fumantia: cf. 3.515 (of the dying bull) *fumans.*

BIBLIOGRAPHY

The list includes only those works cited in the Introduction or Commentary. These are generally cited in order to resolve textual or interpretative issues, and the list is therefore selective in the extreme. For a full bibliography of scholarship on the *Georgics* from 1875 to 1975 see W. Suerbaum in H. Temporini and W. Haase, edd., *Aufstieg und Niedergang der römischen Welt* II 31.1 (Berlin and New York 1980) 395–499; for works since 1975 see the bibliographies published in each issue of *Vergilius*.

1 Abbreviations

K–S R. Kühner and C. Stegman, *Ausführliche Grammatik der lateinischen Sprache*, Zweiter Teil (Hanover 1971)
LS C. T. Lewis and C. Short, *A Latin dictionary* (Oxford 1879)
OLD P. G. W. Glare, ed., *Oxford Latin dictionary* (Oxford 1982)
PGL *Papiri greci e latini* (Florence 1912–)
SH H. Lloyd-Jones and P. Parsons, edd., *Supplementum Hellenisticum* (Berlin 1983)
ThLL *Thesaurus linguae latinae* (Leipzig 1900–)

2 Editions, commentaries, etc.

Büchner K. Büchner, rev. edn of Morel (Leipzig 1982)
Conington J. Conington and H. Nettleship, rev. F. Haverfield, *The works of Virgil, with a commentary* I, 5th edn (London 1898)
Forbiger A. Forbiger, ed. with comm., *P. Vergili Maronis Opera* I, 4th edn (Leipzig 1872)
Geymonat M. Geymonat, *P. Vergili Maronis opera* (Paravia 1973)
Gow A. S. F. Gow, ed. with trans. and comm., *Theocritus*, 2 vols. (Cambridge 1952)
Gow and A. S. F. Gow and A. F. Scholfield, ed. with trans. and
  Scholfield notes, *Nicander. The poems and poetical fragments* (Cambridge 1953)
Malcovati H. Malcovati, *Oratorum Romanorum fragmenta liberae rei publicae* I (Paravia 1953)

265

Martyn   J. Martyn. *Publii Virgilii Maronis Georgicorum libri quatuor*,
             5th edn (Oxford 1827)
Morel   W. Morel, *Fragmenta poetarum Latinorum epicorum et ly-
             ricorum praeter Ennium et Lucilium* (Stuttgart 1963)
Mynors   R. A. B. Mynors, *P. Vergili Maronis opera* (Oxford 1980)
Nisbet–   R. G. M. Nisbet and M. Hubbard, *A commentary on
  Hubbard   Horace: Odes Book 1, Book 2* (Oxford 1975, 1978)
Norden   E. Norden, *P. Vergilius Maro, Aeneis Buch VI*, 5th edn
             (Stuttgart 1970)
Page   T. E. Page, ed. with intro. and notes, *P. Vergili Maronis
             Bucolica et Georgica* (London 1898)
Pfeiffer   R. Pfeiffer, ed., *Callimachus*, 2 vols. (Oxford 1965)
Powell   J. U. Powell, ed., *Collectanea Alexandrina* (Oxford 1925)
Richter   W. Richter, ed. with intro. and comm., *P. Vergilii
             Maronis Georgica*, Das Wort der Antike 5 (1957)
Skutsch   O. Skutsch, ed. with intro. and comm., *The Annals of
             Quintus Ennius* (Oxford 1985)
Williams   R. D. Williams, ed. with intro. and notes, *Virgil, The
             Eclogues and Georgics* (New York 1979)

3 Other works

Abbe, E. (1965). *The plants of Virgil's Georgics*. Ithaca.
Adams, J. N. (1982). *The Latin sexual vocabulary*. London.
Aitken, R. (1956). 'Virgil's plough', *J.R.S.* 46:97–106.
Allen, W. S. (1973). *Accent and rhythm. Prosodic features of Latin and Greek: a
    study in theory and reconstruction*. Cambridge.
Altevogt, H. (1952). *Labor improbus. Eine Vergilstudie*. Orbis Antiquus 8.
    Münster.
Anderson, W. B. (1933). 'Gallus and the Fourth *Georgic*', *C.Q.*
    27:36–45.
Axelson, B. (1945). *Unpoetische Wörter. Ein Beitrag zur Kenntnis der lateinis-
    chen Dichtersprache*. Skrifter utgivna av Vetenskaps-societeten i
    Lund 29. Lund.
Bennett, C. E. (1898). 'What was ictus in Latin prosody?', *A.J.P.*
    19:361–83.
Brown, E. (1963). *Numeri Vergilianae. Studies in Eclogues and Georgics*. Coll.
    Latomus 63. Brussels.
Clausen, W. V. (1955). '*Silua coniecturarum*', *A.J.P.* 77:47–62.

(1976). 'Cynthia', *A.J.P.* 97:245–7.

(1982). 'Theocritus and Virgil', in E. J. Kenney and W. V.Clausen, edd., *The age of Augustus* (Cambridge History of Classical Literature II 3). Cambridge.

Coleman, R. (1962). 'Gallus, the *Bucolics*, and the end of the Fourth *Georgic*', *A.J.P.* 83:55–71.

Crabbe, A. M. (1977). '*Ignoscenda quidem* . . . Catullus 64 and the Fourth *Georgic*', *C.Q.* N.S. 27:342–51.

Dahlmann, H. (1954). *Der Bienenstaat in Vergils Georgica*. Akad. der Wissen. und der Lit. Mainz 10. Mainz.

Flintoff. E. (1983). 'The Noric cattle plague', *Q.U.U.C.* 42:85–111.

Frentz, W. (1967). *Mythologisches in Vergils Georgica*. Beitr. zur klass. Philol. 21. Meisenheim.

Garner, R. J. (1958). *The grafter's handbook*. Oxford.

Getty, R. J. (1948). 'Some astronomical cruces in the *Georgics*', *T.A.P.A.* 79:24–45.

Griffin, J. (1976). 'Augustan poetry and the life of luxury', *J.R.S.* 66:87–105.

(1979). 'The Fourth *Georgic*, Virgil and Rome', *G. & R.* 26:61–80.

Hardie, C. (1971). *The Georgics. A transitional poem*. Abingdon-on-Thames, Berkshire.

Harrison, E. L. (1979). 'The Noric plague and Vergil's Third *Georgic*', *P.L.L.S.* 2:1–65.

Hopkinson, N. (1984), ed. *Callimachus, Hymn to Demeter*. Cambridge.

Jacobson, H. (1982). 'Vergil, *Georgics* 3.280–281', *M.H.* 39:217.

(1984). 'Aristaeus, Orpheus, and the *laudes Galli*', *A.J.P.* 105:271–300.

Jahn, P. (1903). 'Eine Prosaquelle Vergils und ihre Umsetzung in Poesie durch den Dichter', *Hermes* 38:244–64.

Jermyn, L. A. S. (1951). 'Weather-signs in Virgil', *G. & R.* 20:46–69.

(1954). *The ostrakon*. Sanderstead, Surrey.

Kenney, E. J. (1971), ed. *Lucretius, De Rerum Natura Book III*. Cambridge.

(1984), ed. *The ploughman's lunch. Moretum. A poem ascribed to Virgil*. Bristol.

(1986). 'Prodelided *est*: a note on orthography', *C.Q.* N.S. 36:542.

Kent, R. G. (1920). 'The alleged conflict of accents in Latin verse', *T.A.P.A.* 51:19–29.

Knight, W. F. J. (1939). *Accentual symmetry in Vergil*. Oxford.

Koenen, L. (1976). 'Egyptian influence in Tibullus', *I.C.S.* 1:127–59.

Klingner, F. (1931). 'Über das Lob des Landlebens in Virgils Georgica', *Hermes* 66:159–89.

(1963). *Virgils Georgica.* Zurich.

Leach, E. W. (1977). '*Sedes apibus*: from the *Georgics* to the *Aeneid*', *Vergilius* 23:2–16.

Lyne, R. O. A. M. (1978), ed. *Ciris. A poem attributed to Vergil.* Cambridge.

McDermott, E. (1977). '*Horatius callidus*', *A.J.P.* 98:363–80.

Mackail, J. W. (1912). 'Virgil's use of the word *ingens*', *C.R.* 26:251–4.

McKay, A. J. (1972). 'Virgil's glorification of Italy (*Georgics* II 136–174)', in J. R. C. Martyn, ed., *Cicero and Virgil.* Amsterdam.

Merrill, W. A. (1916). 'Parallels and coincidences in Lucretius and Virgil', *U. Calif. Public. in Class. Philol.* 3:135–247.

Miles, G. B. (1980). *Virgil's Georgics. A new interpretation.* Berkeley and Los Angeles.

Mittsdörffer, W. (1938). 'Vergils Georgica und Theophrast', *Philol.* 93:449–75.

Norden, E. (1934). 'Orpheus und Eurydice. Ein nachträgliches Gedenkblatt für Vergil', *Sitzb. preuss. Akad. Wiss.* 22:626–83. Berlin.

Nougaret, L. (1946). 'Les fins d'hexamètre et l'accent', *R.E.L.* 24:261–71.

Ogilvie, R. M. and Richmond, I. (1967), edd. *Cornelii Taciti de uita Agricolae.* Oxford.

Otis, B. (1964). *Virgil. A study in civilized poetry.* Oxford.

Perkell, C. G. (1981). 'On the Corycian farmer of Virgil's Fourth Georgic', *T.A.P.A.* 111:167–77.

Pickard-Cambridge, A. (1962). *Dithyramb, tragedy and comedy*, 2nd edn, rev. T. B. L. Webster. Oxford.

Putnam, M. C. J. (1975). 'Italian Virgil and the idea of Rome', in *Janus. Essays in ancient and modern studies*, 171–99. Ann Arbor.

(1979). *Virgil's poem of the earth. Studies in the Georgics.* Princeton.

Race, W. H. (1982). *The classical priamel from Homer to Boethius. Mnemos.* Supp. 74. Leiden.

Renehan, R. (1981). 'Anthologia Latina 14 Riese', *C.Q.* N.S. 31:471–2.

Ross, D. O. (1969). *Style and tradition in Catullus.* Cambridge, Mass.

(1975). *Backgrounds to Augustan poetry. Gallus, elegy and Rome.* Cambridge.

(1979). 'Ancient logs and old saws (Horace, *Epode* 2.43)', *A.J.P.* 100:241–4.

(1980). '*Non sua poma*. Varro, Virgil and grafting', *I.C.S.* 5:63–71.

(1987). *Virgil's elements. Physics and poetry in the Georgics*. Princeton.

Sargeaunt, J. (1920). *The trees, shrubs and plants of Virgil*. Oxford.

Schechter, S. (1975). 'The "aition" and Virgil's "Georgics"', *T.A.P.A.* 105:347–91.

Schroeder, A. (1921). *De ethnographiae antiquae locis quibusdam communibus obseruationes*. Diss. Halle.

Scodel, R. S. and Thomas, R. F. (1984). 'Virgil and the Euphrates', *A.J.P.* 105:339.

Shackleton Bailey, D. R. (1976). Rev. of L. Håkanson, *Textkritische Studien zu den grösseren pseudoquintilianischen Deklamationen*, in *A.J.P.* 97:73–9.

(1982). *Profile of Horace*. London.

(1983). '*Anth. Lat.* 24.3 (Riese)', *C.Q.* n.s. 33:301.

Speranza, F. (1974). *Scriptorum Romanorum de re rustica reliquiae* 1. Messina.

Stinton, T. C. W. (1976). '"Si credere dignum est": some expressions of disbelief in Euripides and others', *P.C.P.S.* 22:60–89.

Syme, R. (1939). *The Roman revolution*. Oxford.

Tarrant, R. J. (1976), ed. *Seneca, Agamemnon*. Cambridge.

Thomas, G. S. (1961). *The old shrub roses*. London.

Thomas, R. F. (1978). 'Ovid's attempt at tragedy (*Amores* 3.1.63–64)', *A.J.P.* 99:175–8

(1979). 'Theocritus, Calvus and *Eclogue* 6', *C.P.* 74:337–9.

(1982a). *Lands and peoples in Roman poetry. The ethnographical tradition*. Camb. Philol. Soc. Supp. 7. Cambridge.

(1982b). 'Gadflies (Virg. *Geo.* 3.146–148)', *H.S.C.P.* 86:81–5.

(1982c). 'Catullus and the polemics of poetic reference (64.1–18)', *A.J.P.* 103:144–64.

(1983a). 'Virgil's ecphrastic centrepieces', *H.S.C.P.* 87:175–84.

(1983b). 'Callimachus, the *Victoria Berenices* and Roman poetry', *C.Q.* n.s. 33:92–113.

(1985). 'From *recusatio* to commitment. The evolution of the Virgilian programme', *P.L.L.S.* 5 (1986) 61–73.

(1986a). 'Unwanted mice (Arat. *Phaen.* 1140–1)', *H.S.C.P.* 90:91–2.

(1986b). 'Virgil's *Georgics* and the art of reference', *H.S.C.P.* 90:171–98.

Wellesley, K. (1985). 'Virgil, *Georgics* 3.44, emended', *L.C.M.* 10.3:35.

West, D. (1979). 'Two plagues: Virgil, *Georgics* 3.478–566 and Lucretius 6.1090–1286', in D. West and T. Woodman, edd., *Creative imitation and Latin literature*. Cambridge.

Whatmough, J. (1931). 'The *Osi* of Tacitus – Germanic or Illyrian?', *H.S.C.P.* 42:139–55.

White, K. D. (1967). *Agricultural implements of the Roman world*. Cambridge.

(1970). *Roman farming*. London.

Wild, J. P. (1970). *Textile manufacture in the northern Roman provinces*. Cambridge.

Wilkinson, L. P. (1946). *Horace and his lyric poetry*. Cambridge.

(1963). *Golden Latin artistry*. Cambridge.

(1969). *The Georgics of Virgil. A critical survey*. Cambridge.

(1970). 'Pindar and the proem to the Third Georgic', *Festschr. K. Büchner*, 286–90. Wiesbaden.

(1982). 'The *Georgics*', in E. J. Kenney and W. V. Clausen, edd., *The age of Augustus* (Cambridge History of Classical Literature II 3). Cambridge.

Williams, F. (1978), ed. *Callimachus, Hymn to Apollo*. Oxford.

Williams, R. D. (1956). Rev. of Dahlmann (1954) in *C.R.* N.S. 6:170.

Wimmel, W. (1960) *Kallimachos in Rom. Die Nachfolge seines apologetischen Dichtens in der Augusteerzeit*. Hermes Einzelschriften 16. Wiesbaden.

INDEXES

References are to lemmata in the commentary, or page numbers in the Introduction.

271

3 Greek words

For EU product safety concerns, contact us at Calle de José Abascal, 56–1°,
28003 Madrid, Spain or eugpsr@cambridge.org.

www.ingramcontent.com/pod-product-compliance
Ingram Content Group UK Ltd.
Pitfield, Milton Keynes, MK11 3LW, UK
UKHW040615240426
470322UK00010B/138